TWENTY-SEVEN YEARS
IN CANADA WEST

TWENTY-SEVEN YEARS
IN
CANADA WEST

OR

THE EXPERIENCE OF AN EARLY SETTLER

BY SAMUEL STRICKLAND, C.M.

EDITED BY AGNES STRICKLAND

And when those toils rewarding,
  Broad lands at length they'll claim,
They'll call the new possession
  By some familiar name.
          AGNES STRICKLAND.—*Historic Scenes.*

TWO VOLUMES IN ONE

M. G. HURTIG LTD.
Booksellers & Publishers
EDMONTON

INTRODUCTION TO THE
NEW EDITION

WHEN Samuel Strickland (born in 1804?) went to
Canada in 1825, he left behind him in his home at
Reydon Hall, Suffolk, five sisters who would
become known as writers. Agnes, principal author
of *Lives of the Queens of England* (1840–1848) and
Lives of the Queens of Scotland (1850–1859), was
destined to become famous. Eliza would be her
silent partner, but a very active researcher and
collaborator; Jane Margaret would write the
Life of Agnes Strickland. Two sisters would emigrate to Canada in 1832: Catharine Parr (Mrs.
Traill), author of *The Backwoods of Canada* (1836)
and other books, and Susanna (Mrs. Moodie), who
would write poems, novels, and two emigrant
books of her own, *Roughing It in the Bush* (1852)
and *Life in the Clearings* (1853).

Samuel published his one and only book in
1853. By that time he was a colonial veteran of
twenty-seven years' experience, which began in
the bush in Darlington Township (about forty
miles east of Toronto) and continued farther
"back" near Peterborough. In April 1828 he left
what is now eastern Ontario and joined the Canada
Company of John Galt and "Tiger" Dunlop,
which was developing the Huron Tract in south-

western Ontario. As he had done earlier in
Darlington, Samuel successfully took on jobs for
which he had little previous training. After a year
in Guelph he moved to Goderich and became a
near neighbour of the celebrated Dr. Dunlop.
Here he had had the honour "of putting the first
plough into the ground of the Huron Tract."

His record of experiences in the midst of hardships and calamities by fire and water could, in
other hands, have become a romantic tale. But
Samuel's first literary stimulation in Canada was
received in a school characterized by realism with
more than a dash of rough humour or wit—the
school of "Tiger" Dunlop, his frequent companion
in the bush.

This was the Dr. Dunlop of whom William
Maginn wrote in *Fraser's Magazine*: "Meet him
wherever we may, we shall meet a good fellow,
whose various wanderings over the world have
filled him with shrewd good sense, and stored him
with wealth of tale and anecdote beyond that of
any other man now living." The doctor had been
an assistant surgeon on the Niagara frontier in
1814, a road-maker near Penetanguishene, a
journalist in India, a lecturer on jurisprudence at
Edinburgh, a newspaper editor in London, and in
1827 John Galt's "Warden" of the Canada Company's Forests.

"As he [Dunlop] told a story admirably well,"
Strickland recorded in a supreme but characteristic
understatement, "I was delighted to hear him
discuss his peregrinations over a glass of brandy-
punch, of which he was very fond." Many new
stories developed while Samuel was with the

doctor, and he had an incomparable opportunity to be a kind of Boswell near the beginning of Dunlop's Canadian career. Roughly a third of *Twenty-Seven Years in Canada West* is devoted to Samuel's three years in the Huron Tract. Since the pages of this book which describe events of the next twenty years are also full of anecdotes, it may be assumed that Strickland had acquired some of the master's literary habits, if not Dunlop's coarseness or genius.

Samuel left Goderich early in 1831 and returned to the east to sell his lot on the Otonabee and to settle, about twelve miles farther into the bush, in the township of Douro (at Lakefield). Here also he was to have literary persons as his companions, for in 1832 his two sisters, Mrs. Catharine Parr Traill and Mrs. Susanna Moodie, arrived with their husbands to begin pioneer life in the vicinity of Samuel's new home. These two would achieve fame in Canada and abroad—Catharine because of *The Backwoods of Canada* in 1836, and Susanna because of her major contributions in verse and fiction to *The Literary Garland*, a Montreal journal which flourished from 1838 until 1851.

Their flood of emigrant books reached its height in the early 1850s, with Susanna's *Roughing It in the Bush* (1852) and *Life in the Clearings versus the Bush* (1853), Catharine's *Canadian Crusoes* (1852), and Samuel's *Twenty-Seven Years in Canada West* (1853). This would have been an incredible performance if they had been compelled to seek Canadian publishers. It is evident that their invasion of the English market was sponsored by the Old Country branch of the Strickland family. Susanna's and Samuel's books were published by the same firm, that of Richard Bentley in London, England. On the title page of *Roughing It* there was a dedication to Agnes Strickland, and on the title-pages of Catharine's and Samuel's volumes, Agnes was named as editor.

Some of these Canadian manuscripts may have been carried abroad by Samuel, but a passage in Jane Margaret's *Life of Agnes Strickland* makes it clear that *Twenty-Seven Years* was a product of writing during the autumn and winter of 1851–1852 at Reydon Hall in Suffolk, the home of Samuel's three "English" sisters. It may have been the example, or the demands of these scribbling sisters at Reydon Hall which encouraged him to "give [his] colonial experience." Emulation of their research may account for his own display of footnote references to Lyell, Mactaggart, Mac-Gregor, Hind, and even Charlevoix.

A certain amount of resistance must have gone into attempting "a plain, practical manner" while literary women were looking over his shoulder. Even Catharine and Susanna were living presences in England because their books were making the bush not entirely an untouched subject. Catharine was still writing about her backwoods, and Susanna had begun publishing dramatic sketches of her own intense struggles in the wilderness and her escape to the clearings.

With none of these would Samuel have cared to compete, and yet the settings and themes which they had pre-empted were also his stock-in-trade as a literary man. Susanna's attitude, however, left room for another emigrant book about their part of Canada. Her own experience prompted her to warn English gentlemen of very limited means not to take up "their grants of wild land in remote and unfavourable localities, far from churches, schools, and markets," where among other dangers they were easy prey for land speculators. "It was to warn such settlers . . . ," she added, "that my work *Roughing It in the Bush* was written. I gave the experience of the first seven years we passed in the woods, attempting to clear a bush farm, as a warning to others."

Samuel did not deny that gentlemen failed under such circumstances, often through drunkenness, but he, like Catharine, emphasized the possibility of success. The bush, after all, was a man's world where nerves and muscles could be trained and where there were special rewards for those who came with education and social position. It was not his purpose to expose the flood of over-optimistic emigrant literature as Susanna had done, nor to register the frustration of wives who could lose by proxy if their husbands failed to win. His approach was masculine and empirical; "no one," he said, "can give an adequate view of the general life of a colonist, unless he has been one himself."

He knew that he was typical of the educated men of old British families who arrived in the bush "not being overgifted with the good things of this world," as his sister said. His special preparation for his new tasks had been only a slight "practical knowledge of farming, acquired upon [his] mother's estate" and little more than observation of carpentering done at Reydon Hall. In Upper Canada he "experienced all the various gradations of colonial existence, from that of the pioneer in the backwoods and the inhabitant of a shanty, up to the epoch of his career" when he achieved financial competence, comfort, even luxury. In addition, status had come to him in the community which he had helped to build; before 1853 he had become "Commissioner of the Court of Requests" and "Justice of the Peace," as well as a major in the Militia.

During all those years there had been little time for the practice of composition, especially on the scale of two volumes with a total of 655 pages. A reader feels Samuel's uneasy advance into such a wealth of material. Earnest but somewhat old-fashioned adherence to literary conventions is evident in passages of stiff exposition, awkward rhetoric, stock diction, or narrative which lacks immediacy. Before one dismisses his work as chiefly documentary, one ought to remember that he was, so to speak, keeping three balls in the air: autobiography, description of an unfamiliar country, and advice for prospective emigrants. Blame for his getting into this confused situation must be shared with the British travelling journalists and the publishers who were serving the market for this Canadian "genre."

Catharine had produced her masterpiece, *The Backwoods of Canada*, by virtue of her practised hand and her feminine charm. Lacking these, Samuel did share her self-reliance and a keen respect for cultivated readers. Credit must be given him for forthright detail and especially for the acumen with which he tackled the problems of composition. His overall planning stressed methods which may be described as comparison, understatement, anecdote, and parable.

Comparison was a method nicely applicable to his messages. Conditions in Upper Canada as he knew them in the early 1850s were immensely improved; those he had known in the 1820s and 1830s were past. Repeated comparison would serve to keep them in the past, interesting in reminiscence, of course, but almost old enough to be legendary. The uncolloquial tone of some of his writing contributes, perhaps deliberately, to this end. He is at his best in understatement, when he avoids linguistic exercises and gives a true impression of a "plain, practical" man, unaffected by contemporary books of travel. Anecdotes fortunately predominate, and the transitions between them improve in pace and rhythm as the book progresses.

The book as a whole is a parable: the story of his own career makes his point, in the controversy about success or failure of gentlemanly emigrants, by total illustration rather than by argument. In this connection one more thing must be kept very clear: the visit to England during which he wrote *Twenty-Seven Years in Canada West* was only an interlude for the purposes of seeing his mother and sisters and of finding a change of scene for his widowed daughter. While he was there, he met and proposed marriage to Catharine Rackham whom he had known in his youthful days at home. The

irony of fate or fortune which had permitted her
to survive in quiet England while his two Canadian
wives had died on colonial farms is not recognized
in the message of his book.

She agreed to marry Strickland, but not until
she was relieved of responsibility for her ailing
mother. In 1855 he would be in England to claim
her as his bride, and in 1865 both of them would
again visit the Old Country. But Upper Canada
was definitely Samuel's home. His manifest
acceptance of life there, together with Upper
Canada's acceptance of him, is the theme of
Twenty-Seven Years in Canada West. His character,
style, and good humour epitomize his message:
a gentleman could succeed in Canada, and Canada
could make him her own kind of gentleman.

During the years 1853–1855, before Catharine
Rackham came to Canada, Samuel devised practical means of reinforcing that message—an agricultural school for young English gentlemen. For
a description of this unique institution one is
indebted to Charles Richard Weld, who visited
the major's home and wrote about it in *A
Vacation Tour in the United States and Canada*
(1855). Weld found himself surrounded by
many young men wearing a kind of "brigand-
ish" backwoods uniform. These, Strickland
explained, "were his pupils, whom he received into
his house for a term of years, and instructed in
various agricultural pursuits and matters relating
to a settler's life." "A small annual sum" was paid
by each one.

Weld indulged in considerable detail about the
operation of the school in the fresh air of the

country or in a tobacco-filled room: the activities
he saw were chiefly sporting or convivial. Add to
these the suggestions lying in the remark that
Strickland was still "agent to the Canada Land
Company," and one may be sure that some re-
creation of the life of the Huron Tract, of Dunlop
and the other pioneers, had a place in the training
of youths destined for the quite different colonial
world of the 1850s. Colonel Strickland was a
patriarchal figure before he was sixty. He lived
only a little beyond that age, and died early in
1867, a few months before colonialism officially
ended with Confederation.

CARL F. KLINCK

PREFACE

No one can give an adequate view of the general life of a colonist, unless he has been one himself. Unless he has experienced all the various gradations of colonial existence, from that of the pioneer in the backwoods and the inhabitant of a shanty, up to the epoch of his career, when he becomes the owner, by his own exertions, of a comfortable house and well-cleared farm, affording him the comforts and many of the luxuries of civilization, he is hardly competent to write on such a subject. I have myself passed through all these grades. I have had the honour of filling many colonial appointments, such as Commissioner of the Court of Requests, and Justice of the Peace. My commisson in her Majesty's Militia, and my connection with the Canada Company, have also afforded me some opportunities of acquiring additional information. I was in the Company's service during the early settlement of Guelph and also of Goderich,

in the Huron tract.   I am, therefore, as intimately acquainted with those flourishing settlements as with the townships in my own county
of Peterborough.

Upon my return to my native country in
August, on a visit to my venerable mother, I was
advised by my family to give my colonial experience to the world in a plain, practical manner.
I followed the flattering suggestions of relatives
so distinguished for literary attainments, and so
dear to my affections, and " Twenty-seven Years
in Canada West ; or, The Experience of an Early
Settler," is the result of my compliance with
their wishes.

The subject of colonization is, indeed, one of
vital importance, and demands much consideration, for it is the wholesome channel through
which the superfluous population of England and
Ireland passes, from a state of poverty to one of
comfort.   It is true that the independence of the
Canadian settler must be the fruit of his own
labour, for none but the industrious can hope to
obtain that reward.   In fact, idle and indolent
persons will not change their natures by going out
to Canada.   Poverty and discontent will be the
lot of the sluggard in the Bush, as it was in his
native land—nay, deeper poverty; for " he cannot

work, to beg he is ashamed," and if he be surrounded by a family, those nearest and dearest to
him will share in his disappointment and regret.

But let the steady, the industrious, the cheerful man go forth in hope, and turn his talents to
account in a new country, whose resources are not
confined to tillage alone—where the engineer, the
land-surveyor, the navigator, the accountant, the
lawyer, the medical practitioner, the manufacturer, will each find a suitable field for the exercise of his talents ; where, too, the services of
the clergyman are much required, and the pastoral
character is valued and appreciated as it ought
to be.

To the artizan, the hand-loom weaver, and the
peasant, Canada is indeed a true land of Goshen.
In fact, the stream of migration cannot flow too
freely in that direction. However numerous the
emigrants may be, employment can be obtained
for all.

That the industrial classes do become the
richest men cannot be denied, because their ar-
tificial wants are fewer, and their labours greater
than those of the higher ranks. However, the
man of education and refinement will always
keep the balance steady, and will hold offices in
the Colony and responsible situations which his

richer but less learned neighbour can never fill
with ease or propriety.

The Canadian settler possesses vast social advantages over other colonists.   He has no convict
neighbours—no cruel savages, now, to contend
with—no war—no arid soil wherewith to contend.
The land is, generally speaking, of a rich quality,
and the colonist has fire-wood for the labour of
cutting, fish for the catching, game for the pleasant exercise of hunting and shooting in Nature's
own preserves, without the expense of a licence,
or the annoyance of being warned off by a surly
gamekeeper.

The climate of Canada West is healthier and
really pleasanter than that of England or Ireland.
The cold is bracing, and easily mitigated by good
fires and warm clothing; but it is not so really chilling as the damp atmosphere of the mother-country.
Those who have not visited the Canadas are apt
to endow the Upper Province with the severe
climate of the Lower one, whereas that of Western Canada is neither so extremely hot nor so
cold as many districts of the United States.

Emigration to Canada is no longer attended
with the difficulties and disadvantages experienced
by the early settlers, of which such lamentable,
and perhaps exaggerated accounts have frequently

issued from the press. The civilizing efforts of
the Canada Company have covered much of the
wild forest-land with smiling corn-fields and
populous villages. Indeed, the liberal manner
in which the Company have offered their lands
on sale or lease, have greatly conduced to the
prosperity of the Western Province.

If the facts and suggestions contained in the
following pages should prove useful and beneficial
to the emigrant, by smoothing his rough path to
comfort and independence, my object will be
attained, and my first literary effort will not have
been made in vain.

TWENTY-SEVEN YEARS
IN
CANADA WEST

OR

THE EXPERIENCE OF AN EARLY SETTLER

BY SAMUEL STRICKLAND, C.M.

EDITED BY AGNES STRICKLAND

And when those toils rewarding,
  Broad lands at length they'll claim,
They'll call the new possession
  By some familiar name.
          AGNES STRICKLAND.—*Historic Scenes.*

VOLUME 1

TABLE OF CONTENTS

OF THE FIRST VOLUME.

CHAPTER I.

PAGE

Embarkation for Canada.—Voyage out.—Sea-life.—Ice-oergs.—Passage up the St. Lawrence.—Quebec.—Memorials of General Wolfe.—Cathedral.—Hospitality.—Earthquakes. —Nuns.—Montreal.—Progress up the Country.—My Roman Catholic Fellow-traveller. —Attempt at Conversion.—The Township of Whitby.   1

CHAPTER II.

Arrival at Darlington.—Kind Reception.—My Friend's Location.—His Inexperience.—Damage to his Land by Fire.— Great Conflagration at Miramichi.—Forest Fires.—Mighty Conflagration of the 6th of October.—Affecting Story of a Lumber-foreman.— His Presence of Mind, and wonderful Preservation.—The sad Fate of his Companions   .   .   18

CHAPTER III.

Inexperience of my Friend.—Bad State of his Land.—Fall Wheat.— Fencing.— Grasses.— Invitation to a " Bee."— United Labour.—Canadian Sports.—Degeneracy of Bees.   .   31

CHAPTER IV.

My Marriage.—I become a Settler on my own Account— I purchase Land in Otonabee.—Return to Darlington.—My first Attempt at driving a Span.—Active Measures to remedy a Disaster.—Patience of my Father-in-law.—My first Bear-hunt. — Beaver-meadows. — Canadian Thunder-storms.— Fright of a Settler's Family   .   .   .   38

CHAPTER V.

PAGE

Canadian Harvest.—Preparing Timber for Frame-buildings.
—Raising " Bee."—Beauty of the Canadian Autumn.—Visit
to Otonabee.— Rough Conveyance.—Disaccommodation.—
Learned Landlord.—Cobourg.—Otonabee River.—Church of
Gore's Landing.—Effects of persevering Industry .   . 50

CHAPTER VI.

Wood-duck Shooting.—Adventure on Rice Lake.— Irish
Howl.—Arrival at Gore's Landing.—General Howling for
the Defunct.—Dangers of our Journey.—Safe Arrival at Co-
bourg.—Salmon-fishing.—Canoe-building after a bad Fashion.
—Salmon-spearing.— Canadian Fish and Fisheries.—Indian
Summer.—Sleighs and Sleighing.—Domestic Love .   . 66

CHAPTER VII.

Employments of a Man of Education in the Colony.—Yankee
Wedding.—My Commission.—Winter in Canada.—Healthi-
ness of the Canadian Climate.—Search for Land.— Purchase
Wild Land at Douro.—My Flitting.—Put up a Shanty.—
Inexperience in Clearing.—Plan-heaps   .   .   . 81

CHAPTER VIII.

A Logging-Bee.—Lime-burning.— Shingling.— Arrival of
my Brother-in-law.—Birth of my Son.—Sad Journey to Darlington.—Lose my Way.--Am refused a Lift.—My boyish
Anger.—My Wife's Death.—The Funeral.—I leave Darlington   96

CHAPTER IX.

Return to Otonabee.—Benevolence of my Neighbour.—
Serious Accident to a Settler.—His singular Misfortunes.—
Particulars of his Life   106

CHAPTER X.

PAGE

Preparations for my second Marriage.—Dangerous Adventure.—My Wife's nocturnal Visitor.—We prepare for the
Reception of our uninvited Guest.—Bruin's unwelcome Visit
to an Irish Shanty.—Our Bear-hunt.—Major Elliott's Duel
with Bruin.—His Wounds and Victory   .   .   . 121

CHAPTER XI.

Canada the Poor Man's Country.—Disadvantages of Inexperience.—Township of Harvey Settlement.—Pauper Emigration.—Superior Advantages of the Labourer Colonist.—
Temperance and Temperance Societies.— A dry Answer
to watery Arguments. — British and Foreign Temperance
Society   134

CHAPTER XII.

Want of Home-pasturage in Canada.—Danger of being
lost in the Woods.—Plain Directions to the Traveller in the
Bush.—Story of a Settler from Emily.—An old Woman's
Ramble in the Woods.—Adventure of a Trapper.—Fortunate
Meeting with his Partner   146

CHAPTER XIII.

Directions for ascertaining the Quality of Land in the Bush.
—Site of Log-shanty.—Chopping.—Preparation for Spring-
crops.— Method of planting Indian Corn.—Pumpkins and
Potatoes.—Making Pot-ash 162

CHAPTER XIV.

My first Shot at a Buck.—Hunting and Shooting Parties.
—Destructiveness of Wolves.—Loss of my Flocks.—Cowardice of the Wolf.—The Lady and her Pet.—Colonel Crawford's Adventure.—Ingenious Trick of an American Trapper.
—A disagreeable Adventure.—How to poison Wolves.—A
stern Chase   173

CHAPTER XV.

PAGE

Formation of the Canada Company.—Interview with Mr. Galt.—His personal Description and Character.—Guelph.— Dr. Dunlop.—My Medical Services at Guelph.—Dr. Dunlop and the Paisley Bodies.—An eccentric Character.—An unfortunate wife   196

CHAPTER XVI.

Porcupine-catching.—Handsome Behaviour of Mr. Galt.— Owlingale.—Introduction to the Son of the celebrated Indian Chief, Brandt.—Expedition to Wilmot.—Sham Wolves.— Night in a Barn with Dr. Dunlop.—The Doctor and his Snuffbox.—His Bath in the Nith.—Louis XVIII. and his Tabatière.—Camp in the Woods.—Return to Guelph   .   . 215

CHAPTER XVII.

A new Way of keeping a Birthday.—Lost in the Woods. —Kindness of Mr. Galt.—Advice to new Settlers.—Unexpected Retirement of Mr. Galt.—I accompany him to the Landing-place.—Receive orders to leave Guelph for Goderich.—Whirlwinds at Guelph and Douro   .   .   . 233

CHAPTER XVIII.

The Huron tract.—Journal of Dr. Dunlop.—His Hardships. —I leave Guelph for Goderich.—Want of Accommodation.— Curious Supper.—Remarkable Trees.—The Beverly Oak.— Noble Butter-wood Trees.—Goderich.—Fine Wheat Crop. —Purchase a Log-house.—Construction of a Raft   .   . 247

CHAPTER XIX.

My new House at Goderich.—Carpentry an essential Art. —American Energy.—Agreeable Visitors.—My Wife's Disasters.—Hints for Anglers.—The Nine-mile Creek Frolic.— The Tempest.—Our Skipper and his Lemon-punch.—Short Commons.—Camp in the Woods.—Return on Foot.—Ludicrous termination to our Frolic   263

CHAPTER XX.

PAGE

Choice of a Location.—The Company's Lands.—Crown Lands.—Tables published by the Canada Company.—Progressive Improvement of the Huron Tract . . . 281

CHAPTER XXI.

The King proclaimed in the Bush.—Fête and Ball in the Evening.—My Yankee Fellow-traveller.—Awful Storm.—My lonely Journey.—Magical Effect of a Name . . 288

CHAPTER XXII.

Visit of the Passenger-pigeon to the Canadas.—Canadian Blackbirds.—Breeding-places of the Passenger-pigeons. — Squirrels 297

CHAPTER XXIII.

The Rebel, Von Egmond, the first agricultural Settler on the Huron.—Cutting the first Sheaf . . . 305

TWENTY-SEVEN YEARS
IN CANADA WEST.

CHAPTER I.

EMBARKATION FOR CANADA.—VOYAGE OUT.—SEA-LIFE.—ICEBERGS.
—PASSAGE UP THE ST. LAWRENCE.—QUEBEC.—MEMORIALS OF
GENERAL WOLFE.—CATHEDRAL.—HOSPITALITY.—EARTHQUAKES.
—NUNS. — MONTREAL. — PROGRESS UP THE COUNTRY. — MY
ROMAN CATHOLIC FELLOW-TRAVELLER. — ATTEMPT AT CONVER-
SION.—THE TOWNSHIP OF WHITBY.

A PREFERENCE for an active, rather than a professional life, induced me to accept the offer made
by an old friend, of joining him at Darlington, in
Upper Canada, in the year 1825. I therefore took
leave of my family and pleasant home, in Suffolk,
and engaged a passage in the brig "William
M'Gilevray," commanded by William Stoddart, an
experienced American seaman.

On the 28th of March we left the London
Docks, and dropped down the river to Gravesend,
and on the following day put our pilot ashore

off Deal, and reached down as far as the coast of Sussex, where we were becalmed for two days. Here one of our cabin-boys, a German, met with a very serious accident by falling down the after hatchway, and fracturing several of his ribs. On this occasion I officiated as a surgeon, and bled him twice, with excellent effect, for he quickly recovered from the severe injury he had received. Before quitting Suffolk I had learned the art of blood-letting from our own medical attendant. Every person intending to settle in a distant colony ought to acquire this simple branch of surgery : I have often exercised it myself for the benefit of my fellow-creatures when no medical assistance could be procured.

It blew so fresh for two or three days, that we made up for our lost time, and were soon out of sight of Scilly : then I bade a long farewell to old England. I had often been on the sea before, but this was my first long voyage ; every object, therefore, was new to me. I caught some birds in the rigging—they were of a species unknown to me, but very beautiful. Being in want, too, of something to do, I amused myself with cleaning the captain's guns, which I hoped to use for our joint benefit before the end of the voyage.

The 18th and 19th of April were very stormy :

the sea ran mountains high; we had a foot of water in the cabin, and all hands were at the pumps to lessen the growing evil. The gale lasted till the following morning. In the night the aurora borealis was particularly brilliant; but though the storm lulled, the wind was against us. On the 26th of April, I saw a whale, and, boy-like, fired at the huge creature : the shot must have hit him, for he made the water fly in all directions.

To vary the monotony of a sea-life, I sometimes played draughts with the mate, whom I always beat; but he took his defeats in good part, being a very easy-tempered fellow.

I awoke on the 21st of April literally wet to my skin by the deluge of water pouring down the cabin. I dressed myself in great haste and hurried upon deck to learn the cause of this disaster, which I found originated in the coming on of a terrible hurricane, which would not permit us to show a stitch of canvas, and found us continual employment at the pumps; my chest in the cabin shipped a sea which did not improve the appearance of my wardrobe. The following day we had calmer weather, and pursued our course steadily, no longer exposed to the fury of the elements.

On the following day I killed several birds, and

saw two whales and many porpoises. The weather was foggy, but the wind favourable for us.
As we were near the bank of Newfoundland, we
got our fishing tackle-ready, with the hope of
mending our fare with cod ; but the water was
not calm enough for the purpose, and the fish
would not bite. We passed over the Great Bank
without any danger, though the wind was high
and the sea rough.

On the 29th of April we fell in with some
icebergs. A more magnificent and imposing
spectacle cannot be conceived; but it is very
fearful and sufficiently appalling. Suddenly, we
found ourselves close to an immense body of ice,
whose vicinity had been concealed from us by the
denseness of the fog. Our dangerous neighbour
towered in majestic grandeur in the form of a
triple cone rising from a square base, and sur-
passed the tallest cathedral in altitude. The
centre cone being cleft in the middle by the force
of the waves, displayed the phenomenon of a water-
fall, the water rushing into the sea from the height
of thirty feet. If the sun had pierced the va-
poury veil which concealed it from our view, the
refraction of his rays would have given to the ice
the many-coloured tints of the rainbow. We
took care to keep a good look out; but the fog was

thick. We fell in with many other icebergs; but none so beautiful as this.

We doubled Cape Ray, and entered, on the 5th of May, the Gulf of St. Lawrence. The thermometer fell many degrees—a change caused by the vicinity of the ice. On the 5th of May we passed the Bird Rocks, three in number, to windward, so called from the immense number of geese and aquatic birds which resort thither to rear their broods. These rocks rise to the height of four hundred feet, perpendicularly from the sea. The fishermen, nevertheless, contrive to climb them for the sake of the eggs they find there.

The 6th of May found us in the river St. Lawrence, between the westernmost point of Anticosti to the north, and Cape Gaspè to the south, in the middle of the channel, surrounded by ships tacking up the stream, bound for Quebec and Montreal. We had plenty of sea-room, as the river was more than ninety miles in breadth, and it is supposed to be full a hundred at its *embouchure*.

The land was partially covered with snow, which fell throughout the day. On the 8th of May we sailed as far as the Seven Islands. The day was glorious, and the prospect most beautiful. Our vicinity to "the cold and pitiless Labrador," rendered the air chilly, and we could hear the howling of the wolves at night, to me a new and dismal sound. The aurora borealis was particularly splendid, for the air was clear and frosty.

On the 10th of May we stood for the Island of Bic, and took on board a pilot. He was a handsome young man, a French-Canadian, under whose guidance we made the place, but we were becalmed before it for the whole forenoon.

The beauty of the scenery atoned, however, for the delay. Nothing, indeed, could surpass it in my eyes, which had then only been accustomed to the highly-cultivated and richly-wooded tracts in Suffolk and Norfolk, and therefore dwelt with wonder and delight upon the picturesque shores and lofty heights that crowned the noble St. Lawrence.

The wind changing in our favour, carried us swiftly up the stream, which was still thirty-six miles in breadth, though distant 280 miles from the Gulf. We passed Green Island and the Kamouraska Island, and Goose and Crane Islands. These beautiful islets, which stud the broad bosom of the St. Lawrence, are evidently of volcanic origin. That of Kamouraska displays vast masses of granite, which rise in the form of conical hills, one of which attains the height of five hundred feet. The same features are discernible in the

Penguins, and even the strata about Quebec still indicate the same mysterious agency.*

Our progress through the river continually presented the new continent in an attractive point of view. The shores were dotted with farm-houses and adorned with fine gardens and orchards, while lovely islands, covered with lofty trees, rose from the river and delighted the eye. I thought Canada then—and I have never changed my opinion since—the most beautiful country in the world.

On the 13th of May we passed the Island of Orleans, which we no sooner rounded than the Falls of Montmorenci burst upon my sight. I was unprepared for the scene, which I contemplated in silent astonishment. No words written down by the man, at this distance of time, can describe the vivid feelings of the boy. I have since beheld the mighty cataracts of Niagara, so finely described by its Indian name, "The Thunder of Waters;" but I concur in the general opinion, that if those of Niagara are more stupendous, the Falls of Montmorenci are more beautiful and picturesque.

Quebec soon came in view, with its strong fortress crowning the imposing height of Cape Diamond. No one can look upon the old capital of Canada without remembering that the most

* "Encyclopædia of Geography," p. 1304.

gallant British soldier of the age fell in the battle that added the colony to the other dependencies of the English crown.

I remembered, too, with some pleasure, that the paternal dining-room contained a looking-glass— one of the fine old Venetian plates, framed with ebony, which had once formed a part of the General's personal property. It had been for two centuries in his family, but had since become a valued heir-loom in mine. His manly features must often have been reflected on its brilliant surface, and that circumstance, which had formerly endeared it to his aged mother, had made it prized by mine.

We have also a bureau, very complete, but evidently constructed more for use than orna-ment, which might have once contained the papers of this distinguished soldier, while the book-case, to which it was annexed, had probably held his little library. His cruet-stand, which looks as if it had been made in the patriarchal times, is still in use at Reydon Hall.

The reader must pardon this digression, since distinguished worth and valour give an interest even to trivial objects.

Quebec consists of two towns, the Upper and Lower, and is adorned with a cathedral, whose metallic roof glitters in the sun like a vast dia-

mond.   Indeed, the tin-roofs of the churches and
public buildings give this city a splendid look on a
bright sunshiny day, testifying, moreover, to the
dryness of the air.   Captain Stoddart took me all
over this curious city, and kindly introduced me to
one of the partners of a great mercantile house, who
invited us both to dinner.   We regaled ourselves
on smelts, fillet of veal, and old English roast
beef, to which hospitable meal we did ample justice, not forgetting to pledge our absent friends in
bumpers of excellent wine.

The inhabitants of Quebec are very kind to
strangers, and are a fine race of people.   French
is spoken here—not, however, very purely, being
a *patois* as old as the time of Henry IV. of France,
when this part of Canada was first colonized ; but
English is generally understood by the mercantile
classes.

This city is visited, at intervals, with slight
shocks of earthquake.*   Nothing serious has yet
followed this periodical phenomenon.   But will
this visitation be only confined to the mountain
range north of Quebec, where the great earthquake that convulsed a portion of the globe in
1663 has left visible marks of its influence, by
overturning the sand-stone rocks of a tract ex-

* Lyell's " Elements of Geology."

tending over three hundred miles ?* Quebec contains several nunneries, for the French inhabitants
are mostly Roman catholics. The nuns are very
useful to emigrants, who have often been bountifully relieved by these charitable vestals, who
employ themselves in nursing the sick and feeding the hungry.

The inhabitants—or *habitans,* as the French
Canadians are usually termed—are an amiable,
hospitable, simple people, kind in manner, and
generous in disposition. The women are lively
and agreeable, and as fond of dress in Quebec as
in other civilized places. They are pretty in early
youth in the Lower Province, but lose their com-
plexions sooner than the English ladies, owing,
perhaps, to the rigour of the climate.† However,
they possess charms superior to beauty, and seem
to retain the affections of their husbands to the
last hour of their lives.

Short as was my stay in Quebec, I could not
leave without regret the hospitable city where I
had received from strangers such a warm welcome.
I have never visited the Lower Province since;
but my remembrance of its old capital is still as

---

* " Encyclopædia of Geography."

† Mac Taggart's " Three Years' Residence in Canada."

agreeable as it is distinct. The next day our brig was taken in tow by the fine steam-boat, the "Richelieu de Chambly," and with a leading wind and tide in our favour we proceeded at a rapid rate up the river.

I shall not attempt to describe the charming scenery of this most beautiful of all rivers, which has already been so amply described by abler writers. I was delighted with everything I saw ; but nothing occurred worthy of narration.

The next day saw us safely moored in the port of Montreal, just forty-five days from our departure from the London Docks. Montreal is a handsome town, well situated, and must eventually become the most important city in British North America. The river here is very broad. The Lachine rapids commence immediately above the town, which are an impediment to the navigation, now obviated by a canal terminating at the village of Lachine, I believe nine miles distant from Montreal.

I took my passage in a Durham boat, bound for Kingston, which started the next day. We had hard work poling up the rapids. I found I had fallen in with a rough set of customers, and determined in my own mind to leave them as soon as possible, which I happily effected the next

evening when we landed at Les Cèdres. Here the
great Otawá pours its mighty stream into the St.
Lawrence, tinging its green waters with a darker
hue, which can be traced for miles, till it is ultimately lost in the rapids below.

I now determined to walk to Prescot, where I
knew I should be able to take the steam-boat for
Kingston, on Lake Ontario. At the Coteau du
Lac I fell in with a Roman Catholic Irishman,
named Mooney. We travelled in company for
three days, and as I had nothing else to do, I
thought I might as well make an effort to convert
him. However, I signally failed; and only en-
dangered my own head by my zeal.

In the heat of argument and the indiscretion
of youth, I used expressions which the Papist considered insulting to his religion.   He was not one
to put up patiently with this, so he would fire up,
twirl his blackthorn round his head, and say, "By
St. Patrick, you had better not say that again!"
In everything else we agreed well enough ; but I
found, on parting, that all my eloquence had been
entirely thrown away.   Mr. Mooney remained just
as firm a Roman Catholic as ever.   Indeed, it was
the height of presumption in me, a boy in my
twentieth year, to attempt the conversion of such
a strict Romanist as this Irishman.

The weather was excessively fine. The trees were just bursting into leaf. The islands in the St. Lawrence, which are here numerous, wore the brightest hues, and presented a charming contrast to the foaming rapids.

I remained two or three days at Prescot, waiting the arrival of my baggage, which I had left on board the Durham boat. I amused myself during the interval by taking walks in the neighbourhood. The land appeared very sandy, the timber being chiefly hemlock : the situation of the town is good. Steam-navigation commenced at this place, and now that the Welland Canal is completed, it affords an uninterrupted navigation be borne in mind that at the time of which I am to the head of Lakes Huron and Michigan. It must speaking (1825), the great St. Lawrence Canal and the Rideau were not commenced, but since their completion the Durham boats and small steamers have given place to a set of superb boats affording the best accommodation, whereby the passage from Montreal to Toronto can be performed at half the expense, and in one-third of the time.

My baggage having arrived, I left Prescot by boat in the evening for Kingston, at that time the second town both in size and importance in Canada West. It must, on account of its situation as a military and naval post, always be a place of consequence. I fell in there with an old sea-dog, who had commanded a vessel, for many years trading between London and Quebec. He had had the misfortune to lose his vessel, which was wrecked on the rocks at Gaspè, near the mouth of the St. Lawrence. I was glad to find the friends I was going to reside with had come out passengers in his ship, and that the schooner he then commanded was bound for the Big-bay (now called Windsor), in the township of Whitby, within six or seven miles of my friends' residence, and that they would sail in two days at farthest.

On our passage from Prescot to Kingston we passed Brockville, which looked very pretty from the river, and soon afterwards we were threading our way through the intricacies of the Thousand Islands.* Who has not heard of the far-famed Thousand Islands—the Archipelago of the St. Law-

---

* "The Lake of the Thousand Isles. The expression was thought to be a vague exaggeration, till the Isles were officially surveyed, and found to amount to 1692. A sail through them presents one of the most singular and romantic succession of scenes that can be imagined—the Isles are of every size, form, height and aspect; woody, verdant, rocky; naked, smiling, barren ; and they present as numerous a succession of bays, inlets, and channels as occur in all the rest of the continent put together."— "Encyclopædia of Geography," iv. 1321.

rence ? Nothing can exceed the beauty of this spot. The river is here several miles in width, studded with innumerable islands, of every variety of form. The moon shone brightly on this lovely scene : not a ripple stirred the mirror-like bosom of the stream—

" There was not a breath the blue wave to curl."

The reflection of the trees in the water enhanced the natural beauties I have endeavoured to describe.

The next morning, June the 3rd, I embarked on board the schooner "Shamrock," on my way to Darlington. We passed the Duck islands towards evening, and found ourselves fairly launched on the bosom of the Great Ontario. We anchored next day opposite the town of Cobourg, then a small village, without a harbour, now a fine, handsome, well-built town, containing a population of nearly 4,000 inhabitants. A large sum of money has been laid out in the construction of a harbour, which appears to answer very well.

Cobourg is the county-town for the counties of Northumberland and Durham, which comprehend the following townships :—Darlington, Clarke, Hope, Hamilton, Haldimand, Cramache, Murray, Seymour, Percy, Alnwick, South Monaghan, Cavan, Manvers, and Cartwright. The soil of most of these townships is of excellent quality, particularly the fronts of Hamilton, Haldimand, and all Cavan, being generally composed of a deep rich loam.

These townships are well watered by numerous spring creeks, bounded to the north and east by the river Trent, Skugog and Rice Lakes; and to the south, for about sixty miles, by Lake Ontario. The chief towns are Cobourg, Port Hope, and Bournauville. As I shall have occasion in another place to speak more fully respecting these counties, I shall take my readers again on board the " Shamrock."

Our captain having to land some goods at Cobourg, we were detained there all night. He invited a few friends to pass the evening. A jolly set of fellows they were, and they initiated me into the mysteries of brewing whiskey-punch, a beverage I had never before tasted, and which I found very palatable. The song and the joke went round till the small hours warned us to retire.

On Sunday morning, June the 5th, I landed at the Big-bay (Windsor), in Whitby, and after bidding adieu to my fellow-voyagers, commenced my journey to my friends in Darlington on foot.

Whitby, at the time of which I am speaking, was only partially settled, and chiefly by Americans. This township is justly considered one of the best between Toronto and Kingston. At present the township is well settled and well-cultivated. Nearly all the old settlers are gone, and their farms have, for the most part, been purchased by old country farmers and gentlemen, the log-buildings having given place to substantial stone, brick, or frame houses. The village of Oshawa, in this township, now contains upwards of one thousand inhabitants, more than double the number the whole township could boast of when I first set foot on its soil.

CHAPTER II.

ARRIVAL AT DARLINGTON.—KIND RECEPTION.—MY FRIEND'S LOCA-
TION.—HIS INEXPERIENCE.—DAMAGE TO HIS LAND BY FIRE.—
GREAT CONFLAGRATION AT MIRAMACHI. — FOREST FIRES. —
MIGHTY CONFLAGRATION OF THE 6TH OF OCTOBER.—AFFECTING
STORY OF A LUMBER-FOREMAN. — HIS PRESENCE OF MIND, AND
WONDERFUL PRESERVATION. — THE SAD FATE OF HIS COM-
PANIONS.

I WAS now very near to my ark of refuge,
and the buoyant spirit of early youth, with its
joyous anticipations of a radiant future, bore
me exultingly forward.   It might have been said
of me in the beautiful lines of the poet :—

> " He left his home with a bounding heart,
>   For the world was all before him ;
> And he scarcely felt it a pain to part,
>   Such sun-bright hopes came o'er him." *

Two hours' brisk walking brought me to the
long-looked-for end of my journey.   I was received with the greatest kindness and hospitality;
and, in a few days, felt quite at home and comfortable in my new quarters.

* Alaric A. Watts.

After some days' rest, I commenced operations by assisting my friend on the farm and in the store. From my practical knowledge of farming, acquired upon my mother's estate, I was soon installed as manager in that department.

Our farm contained upwards of two hundred acres of cleared land, the largest proportion of which consisted of meadows and pastures, but the soil was light and sandy, and altogether very indifferent. My friend, Colonel B—— had been imposed upon by the Yankee, of whom he had bought it,—and no wonder, when I tell you that my friend had formerly held a situation under Government, and had lived in London all his life.

Only the first three concessions of this township were settled at this time, the remainder of the land being generally in the hands of absentee proprietors. I am happy to say, the absentee-tax has had the effect of throwing vast quantities of these lands into the market.

This township, like Whitby, is now well settled, and though not generally equal in regard to soil, is still considered a good township. Bowmanville is the principal town, containing about twelve hundred inhabitants. In 1825 it only boasted a grist-mill, saw-mill, a store, and half-a-dozen houses. I mention this, merely to show how much the country has improved in a few years. This is not an isolated fact—it applies to nearly all Canada West.

My intention was, to stay with my friends till the ensuing spring, and to get a little insight into Canadian farming, clearing land, &c., that I might have some experience before commencing operations on my own account.

The situation of my friend's house was close to the Toronto road, partly built of logs and frame-work : it had been designed by the former Yankee proprietor, and could certainly boast of no architectural beauties. We lived about a mile and a half from the lake shore, and I took advantage of my vicinity to the water to bathe daily. I found great refreshment in this, for the weather was very hot and dry. The drought lasted for some time, and among its consequences, I may mention the prevalence of extensive fires.* Several broke out in our neighbourhood, and,

* Fires in Canada are of frequent occurrence, and are generally caused by the burning of brush-wood or log-heaps by the settlers. In dry weather, with a brisk wind, the fire is apt to run on the surface of the ground in the bush, where the dry leaves are thickest. In clearing the land a good deal of brush-wood and tops of trees are thrown into the edge of the woods. It follows, as a matter of course, that the greatest danger to be apprehended is the burning the boundary-fences of farms. I have heard it asserted that these fires are sometimes caused by spontaneous combustion, which I consider altogether a fallacy.

at last, the mischief reached our own farm. It destroyed several thousand rails, and spread over forty or fifty acres of meadow land. We ultimately stopped its further progress in the clearing, by ploughing furrows round the fire, and a thunder-shower in the evening completed its extinction. Fire seldom runs in the woods on good land, and where the timber is chiefly deciduous, but on sandy, pine, or hemlock lands, or where evergreens chiefly prevail.

I have seldom known very serious damage by these fires done in Canada West, although occasionally a barn or house falls a sacrifice to the devouring element. Not so, however, in some parts of Nova Scotia and New Brunswick, where extensive conflagrations often devastate the country for miles round. Of such a character was the great fire at Miramichi, which nearly destroyed Fredericton, and was attended not only with an immense loss of property but with the sad loss of many valuable lives. I will presently give in his own forcible and feeling language the history of a lumberer who escaped from destruction after being for some time in imminent peril of his life. He was one of the few persons who had the good fortune of escaping the great conflagration in Miramichi, which broke out in the October after my

arrival, and excited so much general sympathy.
Fifteen of his comrades perished in the flames.

The narrative which I introduce here, anticipating
by a few months the proper order of narration, was
related to me by the man himself with that native
eloquence which often surprises, and always interests us in the uneducated. The class to which he
belongs is one peculiar to America. Rough in
manners, and often only half-civilized, the lumberer, as an individual, resembles little the woodsman of other lands. He is generally a Canadian
Frenchman, or a breed between the Irish and the
native of the Lower Province. However, some
Yankees may be found among these denizens of
the woods and wilds of Canada. The fearful conflagration to which our poor lumberer nearly fell
a victim, has been thus ably described in M'Gregor's "British America." "In October, 1825, about
a hundred and forty miles in extent, and a vast
breadth of the country on the north, and from
sixty to seventy miles on the south side of Miramachi river, became a scene of perhaps the most
dreadful conflagration that has occurred in the
history of the world.

"In Europe we can scarcely form a conception
of the fury and rapidity with which fires rage
through the forests of America during a dry hot

season, at which period the broken underwood, decayed vegetable substances, fallen branches, bark, and withered trees, are as inflammable as the absence of moisture can make them.   To such irresistible food for combustion we must add the auxiliary afforded by the boundless fir-forests, every tree of which in its trunk, bark, branches, and leaves contains vast quantities of inflammable resin.

" When one of these fires is once in motion, or at least when the flames extend over a few miles of the forest, the surrounding air becomes highly rarefied, and the wind consequently increases till it blows a perfect hurricane.   It appears, that the woods had been on both sides of the north-west partially on fire for some days, but not to an alarming extent until the 7th of October, when it came on to blow furiously from the westward, and the inhabitants along the river were suddenly surprised by an extraordinary roaring in the woods, resembling the crashing and detonation of loud and incessant thunder, while at the same instant the atmosphere became thickly darkened with smoke.

" They had scarcely time to ascertain the cause of this awful phenomenon before all the surrounding woods appeared in one vast blaze, the flames ascending from one to two hundred feet above the tops of the loftiest trees; and the fire rolling forward with inconceivable celerity, presented the terribly sublime appearance of an impetuous flaming ocean. In less than an hour, Douglas Town and Newcastle were in a blaze : many of the wretched inhabitants perished in the flames. More than a hundred miles of the Miramichi were laid waste, independent of the north-west branch, the Baltibag, and the Nappen settlements. From one to two hundred persons perished within immediate observation, while thrice that number were miserably burned or wounded, and at least two thousand were left destitute of the means of subsistence, and were thrown for a time on the humanity of the Province of New Brunswick. The number of lives that were lost in the woods could not at the time be ascertained, but it was thought few were left to tell the tale.

" Newcastle presented a fearful scene of ruin and devastation, only fourteen out of two hundred and fifty houses and stores remained standing.

" The court-house, jail, church, and barracks, Messrs. Gilmour, Rankin, and Co.'s, and Messrs. Abrams and Co.'s establishment, with two ships on the stocks, were reduced to ashes.

" The loss of property is incalculable, for the fire, borne upon the wings of a hurricane, rushed on the wretched inhabitants with such inconceivable rapidity that the preservation of their lives could be their only care.

" Several ships were burned on shore, while others were saved from the flames by the exertions of their owners, after being actually on fire.

" At Douglas Town scarcely any kind of property escaped the ravages of the fire, which swept off the surface everything coming in contact with it, leaving but time for the unfortunate inhabitants to fly to the shore ; and there, by means of boats, canoes, rafts of timber, logs, or any article, however ill calculated for the purpose, they endeavoured to escape from the dreadful scene and reach the town of Chatham, numbers of men, women, and children perishing in the attempt.

" In some parts of the country all the cattle were either destroyed or suffering greatly, for the very soil was parched and burnt up, while scarcely any article of provision was rescued from the flames.

" The hurricane raged with such dreadful violence, that large bodies of timber on fire, as well as trees from the forest and parts of the flaming houses and stores, were carried to the rivers with amazing velocity, to such an extent and affecting the water in such a manner, as to occasion large quantities of salmon and other fish to resort to land, hundreds of which were scattered on the shores of the south and west branches.

"Chatham was filled with three hundred miserable sufferers : every hour brought to it the wounded and burned in the most abject state of distress. Great fires raged about the same time in the forests of the River St. John, which destroyed much property and timber, with the governor's house, and about eighty private houses at Fredericton. Fires raged also at the same time in the northern parts of the Province, as far as the Bay de Chaleur.

"It is impossible to tell how many lives were lost, as many of those who were in the woods among the lumbering parties, had no friends nor connections in the country to remark on their non-appearance. Five hundred have been computed as the least number that actually perished in the flames.

"The destruction of bears, foxes, tiger-cats, martens, hares, squirrels, and other wild animals, was very great. These, when surprised by such fires, are said to lose their usual sense of preservation, and becoming, as it were, either giddy or fasci-

nated, often rush into the face of inevitable destruction : even the birds, except these of very
strong wing, seldom escape. Some, particularly
the partridge, become stupified ; and the density
of the smoke, the rapid velocity of the flames, and
the violence of the winds, effectually prevent the
flight of others."

It was from this mighty destruction that the
forecast and admirable presence of mind displayed
by the lumberer, whose pathetic story I am about
to relate, saved him. I could not fail, while rejoicing in his escape, to impute his self-possession
to the compassion of the all-wise Being who had
made him such an instance of His mercy.

"The weather," said he, "had been unusually
dry for the season, and there had been no rain for
upwards of three weeks before this calamity took
place. We had only just completed our shanty, and
had commenced felling timber ready for squaring,
when it occurred. We had heard from our team-
sters, who had brought us out pork and flour, the
day previous, that fires were raging in the woods
some miles to the eastward of us. However, we
paid but little attention to what appeared to us a
common occurrence.

"After supper, one of our men went out of the
shanty, but immediately returned to tell us ' that

a dreadful conflagration was raging within a mile or so of our dwelling.' We immediately rushed out to ascertain the truth of his assertion. I shall never forget," he continued, " the sight presented to our view : as far as the eye could reach we saw a wall of fire higher than the tree-tops, and we heard the mighty sound of the rushing flames mingled with the crashing fall of the timber.

" A single glance convinced us that not a minute was to be lost ; we did not stop even to try and secure our clothing, but made our way as quickly as possible to a small river about two hundred yards from our shanty, and which we knew was our only chance of preservation.

" We reached the stream in safety, where I determined to take my stand. My comrades, however, were of a different opinion : they contended that the fire would not cross the river, which was upwards of thirty yards in width. Unfortunately, no argument of mine could induce them to stay, though I was well aware, and represented to them that such a body of flame would not be stayed a minute by such a barrier.

"My comrades, hoping to reach an old clearance of some acres, about half a mile in advance, in spite of all entreaties crossed the stream, and were soon lost to my view—never more to be seen alive by me.

" I waded down the stream, till I found a place where the water was up to my arm-pits, and the bank of the river rose about six feet over my head. There I took my stand, and awaited the event in breathless anxiety. I had no time to look around me. The few minutes which had elapsed, had greatly added to the terrors of the scene.

" As the wall of fire advanced, fresh trees in succession were enveloped by the flames. A bright glare crimsoned the clouds with a lurid glow, while the air was filled with a terrible noise. The heat now became intense. I looked up once more; the trees above me caught fire at that instant, the next, I was holding my breath a foot beneath the surface of the running stream. Every few seconds I was compelled to raise my head to breathe, which I accomplished with great difficulty. In a few minutes, which seemed ages to me, I was enabled to stand upright, and look around me. What desolation a short half hour had effected! In front, the conflagration was still raging with unabated fury, while in the rear the fire had consumed all the under-brush and limbs of the trees, leaving a forest of blackened poles still blazing fiercely, though not with the intense heat caused by the balsam and pine-brushwood.

"It was several hours before I durst quit my sanctuary to search for my companions, the blackened remains of whom I found not a quarter of a mile from the river.

"Our shanty,* and all that it contained, was utterly consumed. I, however, succeeded in finding in the cellar beneath its ruins, as much provisions uninjured as served to carry me through to the settlements, which I ultimately reached, though not without great difficulty."

---

* A shanty is a building made with logs, higher in the front than the back, making a fall to the roof, which is generally covered with troughs made of pine or bass-wood logs ; the logs are first split fair in the middle, and hollowed out with the axe and adze. A row of these troughs is then laid from the front or upper wall-plate, sloping down to the back plate, the hollowed side uppermost. The covering-troughs is then placed with the hollow reversed, either edge resting in the centre of the under trough. A door in the front and one window complete the building. Such is commonly the first dwelling of the settler. The lumber-shanty differs both in shape and size, being much larger, and the roof sloping both ways, with a raised hearth in the centre of the floor, with an aperture directly above for the escape of the smoke. It has no window. One door at the end, and two tier of bed berths, one above the other, complete the *tout ensemble.* These shanties are generally constructed to accommodate from two to three gangs of lumber men, with shed-room for twelve or fourteen span of oxen or horses—span being the Canadian term for pair.

CHAPTER III

INEXPERIENCE OF MY FRIEND.— BAD STATE OF HIS LAND.—FALL-
WHEAT. — FENCING. — GRASSES. — INVITATION TO A " BEE." —
UNITED LABOUR.—CANADIAN SPORTS.—DEGENERACY OF BEES.

COLONEL B—— was an old and valued friend
of my family, who had held a lucrative situation
under Government for many years.   His retirement from public life, on some disgust, had
eventually led to his settlement in Canada.

Now, his literary tastes and sedentary habits
had ill-fitted him for the rough customs of the
colony.   Besides having scarcely seen a grain of
corn in its progressive state from the blade to its
earing and harvest, he knew nothing of agricultural operations.   Of stock he was equally ignorant, and of the comparative goodness or badness
of soil he was, of course, no judge.   Such a man,
in the choice of a farm, was sure to be shaved by
the shrewd Yankee proprietor, and my poor friend
was shaved accordingly.

I found my friend's farm had been much neglected. His out-door labourers were all from the south of Ireland, and had never before followed farming operations. In consequence of their inexperience, half the clearing was quite overrun with raspberries and Canadian thistles. (The latter weed is far more troublesome to eradicate than any other I know. It is the same as the common corn-thistle, or *Serratula arvensis,* so well known to English agriculturists).

As we intended to prepare a large piece of ground for summer-fallow, it was necessary to get rid of those stumps of the trees, which, according to the practice of chopping them two or three feet from the ground, present a continual obstacle to the advance of the plough. We, however, succeeded in getting clear of them by hitching a logging-chain round the stump near the top, when a sudden jerk from the oxen was generally sufficient to pull it up. For the larger, and those more firmly fixed in the ground, we made use of a lever about twenty feet long, and about eight or nine inches in diameter, one end of which was securely chained to the stump, the oxen being fastened to the other and made to go in a circular direction, a manœuvre which rarely fails of the desired effect. This plan will not answer unless the roots are sufficiently decayed. During dry weather the application of fire produces more effectual results. A few embers shaken from a cedar-torch on the crown of the stump are sufficient for the purpose : some hundreds of these blazing merrily at night have a very pretty effect.

In ten or twelve years the hard woods, such as oak, ash, beech and maple disappear; but the stumps of the evergreens, such as pine, hemlock and cedar, are much more difficult to eradicate.

The land being of a sandy nature, we had but few stones to contend with. When such is the case, we raise them above the surface, by the help of levers. By these means, stones of half a ton weight can be easily lifted from their beds. The larger ones are generally drawn off the fields to make the foundations of fences, and those of a smaller size are used in the construction of French drains.

To succeed well with your summer fallow, it is necessary to have the sod all turned over with the plough by the end of May, or sooner if possible. Shortly afterwards the fallow should be well harrowed ; in July it should be crossed, ploughed and harrowed, and rolled at least twice before the final ploughing or ridging up, which should be completed by the last week in August.

Fall-wheat should be sown between the first

and fifteenth day of September.* The sooner the better, in my opinion, because the plant is stronger and better able to withstand the frost, and is decidedly less liable to rust. Our fallow. having been prepared in this manner, and sown broad-cast with fall-wheat, the next object was to fence in the field securely, which is done in the following way. Trees of a straight growth— and straight also in the grain—are selected and cut into twelve feet lengths, and are then, by the means of a beetle and wedges, split into rails as nearly four inches square as possible. The rails are then laid in a zigzag direction, crossing each other about a foot from the end, making an angle of about six feet. Seven rails in height, crowned by a stake and rider, complete the fence. The best timbers for making rails, are pine, cedar, oak and black and white ash : these kinds of timbers will last about thirty years. Bass-wood is more commonly used for the first fences, because it is to be procured in greater abundance, and splits more easily ; but as it will not last more than ten years, I would not recommend settlers to use it, if the other sorts can readily be obtained.

* "Fall" is the term usually applied to wheat sown in the autumn by the Canadian farmer, and will be used in this sense throughout a work especially written for the service of the inexperienced settler.

In this country, hay-cutting commences about the first or second week in July. Timothy-grass and clover mixed—or timothy alone—are the best for hay, and the most productive. The quantity of seed required for new land is six quarts of grass-seed and two pounds of clover to the acre ; on old cleared farms nearly double this seed is required. Timothy is a solid grass with a bulbous root. If the weather is hot and dry, the hay should be carted the second day after cutting, for there is no danger in carting it at once into your barn, the climate being so dry that it never heats enough to cause spontaneous combustion. We have other sorts of grasses, such as red-top, blue-joint, &c.: these grasses, however, are inferior, and therefore never grown from choice.

Soon after my arrival at Darlington, one of my neighbours residing on the lake-shore invited me to a mowing and cradling "Bee."* As I had never seen anything of the kind, I accepted the invitation. On my arrival at the farm on the appointed day, I found assembled about forty men and boys. A man with a pail of spring water with a wooden cup floating on the surface in one hand, and a bottle of whiskey and glass in

* What the Canadian settlers call a " Bee " is a neighbourly gathering for any industrious purpose—a friendly clubbing of labour, assisted by an abundance of good cheer.

the other, now approached the swarm, every one
helping himself as he pleased. This man is the
most important personage at the "Bee," and is
known by the appellation of the "Grog-bos."
On this occasion his office was anything but a
sinecure. The heat of the weather, I suppose,
had made our party very thirsty. There were
thirty-five bees cutting hay, among whom I was a
rather awkward volunteer, and ten cradlers* employed in cutting rye.

At eleven o'clock, cakes and pailfuls of tea were
served round. At one, we were summoned by the
sound of a tin bugle to dinner, which we found
laid out in the barn. Some long pine-boards
resting on tressels served for a table, which almost groaned with the good things of this earth,
in the shape of roast lamb and green peas, roast
sucking-pig, shoulder of mutton, apple-sauce, and

---

* The cradle is a scythe of larger dimensions than the common
hay-scythe, and is both wider in the blade and longer. A straight
piece of wood, called a standard, thirty inches long, is fixed upright;
near the end of the snaith, or handle, are four fingers made of wood,
the same bend as the scythe, and from six to seven inches apart,
directly above the scythe, and fixed firmly into the standard, from
which wire braces with nuts and screws to adjust the fingers.
These braces are secured to the fingers about eight inches from
the standard. The other end of the wire is then passed through
the snaith and drawn tight by means of a screw-nut. These ma-
chines are very effective, and in the hands of a person who understands their use will cut from two to three acres a-day of either
wheat, oats, barley, or rye.

pies, puddings, and preserves in abundance, with plenty of beer and Canadian whiskey. Our bees proved so industrious, that before six o'clock all Mr. Burke's hay and rye were finished cutting. Supper was then served on the same scale of profusion, with the addition of tea. After supper a variety of games and gymnastics were introduced, various trials of strength, wrestling, running, jumping, putting the stone, throwing the hammer, &c.

About nine o'clock our party broke up, and returned to their respective homes, well pleased with their day's entertainment, leaving their host perfectly satisfied with their voluntary labour. One word about bees and their attendant frolic. I confess I do not like the system. I acknowledge, that in raising a log-house or barn it is absolutely necessary, especially in the Bush, but the general practice is bad. Some people can do nothing without a bee, and as the work has to be returned in the same manner, it causes a continual round of dissipation—if not of something worse. I have known several cases of manslaughter arising out of quarrels produced by intoxication at these every-day gatherings. As population increases, and labour becomes cheaper, of course there will be less occasion for them.

CHAPTER IV.

MY MARRIAGE.—I BECOME A SETTLER ON MY OWN ACCOUNT.—I PUR-
CHASE LAND IN OTONABEE. — RETURN TO DARLINGTON — MY
FIRST ATTEMPT AT DRIVING A SPAN. — ACTIVE MEASURES TO
REMEDY A DISASTER.—PATIENCE OF MY FATHER-IN-LAW.—MY
FIRST BEAR-HUNT. — BEAVER-MEADOWS.—CANADIAN THUNDER-
STORMS.—FRIGHT OF A SETTLER'S FAMILY.

I MUST now say something of myself. During
my domestication under my friend's roof, I became attached to one of his daughters. The
affection was mutual; and our happiness was
completed by the approbation of our friends. We
were married; and it seemed that there was a
goodly prospect of many years of wedded happiness before us.

But it was necessary that I, who was now
a husband, and might become a father, should
become a settler on my own account, and look
about for lands of my own. I examined, therefore, several locations in the neighbourhood; but
one objection or another presented itself, and I declined fixing my settlement at Darlington. Ultimately, I bought two hundred acres of land in the

township of Otonabee, within a mile of the newly laid out town of Peterborough. It was arranged that I should stop at Darlington, and assist my father-in-law, until it was time to commence operations in the spring. This arrangement proved very beneficial to me, as I was able to learn many useful things, and make myself acquainted with the manners and customs of the people with whom I was going to live.

We kept two pair of horses and a yoke of oxen to work the farm. One pair of our horses were French Canadian. Generally speaking, they are rough-looking beasts, with shaggy manes and tails, but strong, active, and stout for their size, which, however, is much less than that of the Upper Canadian horse. I have seen, nevertheless, some very handsome carriage-horses of this breed. Of late years, both the Upper and Lower Canadian breed of horses have been much improved by the importation of stallions.

The working oxen of this country are very docile and easily managed. They are extremely useful in the new settlement ; indeed, I do not know what could be done without them. It is next to an impossibility to plough among the green stumps and roots with horses—the plough being continually checked by roots and stones—

therefore, till these obstacles are removed, which cannot be effectually done for seven or eight years, oxen are indispensably necessary, particularly for logging up new fallows. Yet notwithstanding their usefulness, I do not know a worse treated set of animals than Canadian oxen. Their weight, when fat, varies from seven to eight hundred weight. A yoke and bows, made of birch or soft maple, is the only harness needed; and, in my opinion, for double draught, better, and certainly less troublesome than the collar and traces used in England.

The ox-yoke is made of a piece of wood, four feet in length, and nine inches deep in the centre, to which a staple is fitted, and from which an iron ring depends, about a foot from the middle of the yoke each way, which is hollowed out, so as to fit on the top of the oxen's necks. A hole is bored, two inches in diameter, on each side of the hollow, through which the bow is passed, and fastened on the upper side of the yoke by a wooden pin. The bow is bent in the shape of a horse-shoe, the upper, or narrow ends being passed through the yoke. If the yoke and bows are properly made and fit the cattle, there is no fear of galling the beast. The bows are made of hickory, white or rock elm, in this way. Cut a piece of elm, five feet and a half long, large enough to split into quarters, each of which will dress to two inches in diameter; put them in a steam-box for an hour at least; take them out hot, and bend on a mould made on purpose; tie the two bent-up ends together until dry. Every settler should know how to do these things, and to make his own axe-handles, and many other articles which are constantly required in the bush.

My first attempt at driving oxen was accompanied by an unfortunate accident, which gave me some trouble and mortification. My father-in-law had lent a neighbour a plough, of which we were much in want. I thought it would be a good opportunity for me to try my hand with the oxen, to fetch it home. Now, it happened the cattle were young, and not very well broken, so that I found some difficulty in yoking and attaching them to the cart. However, I succeeded at last, and drove up to the door of Mr. Stephens' house in great style. I found the family just going to dinner, which they courteously invited me to partake with them. I accepted their hospitality, and left the oxen standing before the door.

I discussed my neighbour's good cheer with an excellent appetite, and was in the very act of pledging mine host, when I heard the cattle start off. We left the table with precipitation, but were, alas! too late to stop the refractory oxen, which galloping down a steep hill, on the summit of which the house was built, stumbled in their descent, and fell to the bottom, where we found them struggling, apparently, in the agonies of death. We cut the bows from their necks as soon as possible, but not in time to save the life of poor Spot, the near ox, who was quite dead; and it was for some minutes doubtful if Dandy—the off "critter," as the Yankees would style him—would survive his companion. I killed the dead one over again to make its flesh fit for consumption, and bled the other, which happily saved its life. But, notwithstanding my careful endeavour to make the best of a foolish matter, I felt myself in an awkward predicament. To my worthy father-in-law the loss of an animal worth thirty dollars was, at that time, particularly inconvenient; but his moral justice was high and his temper mild; so he listened meekly to my account of the misfortune, quietly remarking, that it could not be helped, and that no blame attached to me. It is in these worrying affairs of every-day life that we discern the real beauty of the Christian character. My mother-in-law behaved as well, on this trying occasion, as any lady could do who found her larder suddenly stocked with a quantity of lean tough beef—a prospect, indeed, by no means cheering to any member of the household.

On my return home from my first essay in ox-driving, or rather ox-killing, I found Dennis, our Irish servant, waiting for me with the greatest impatience.

" Och, sir," he exclaimed ; " if you had but been with me you might have shot a bear. I was out in the bush searching for the cows, and just as I was crossing the Big creek, near the beaver meadow, I heard a noise from a thicket of cedar bushes close by me, and thinking it might be one of the lost' cows I ran forward to see, when to my astonishment and dismay I came suddenly upon a large bear."

" Well," said I, " what did you do ? "

" Faith, then, sir, to tell you the truth, I did not do much—only took to my heels, and ran home as fast as I could to tell you ; as I thought yer honour might perhaps get a shot at the baste, and, troth ! he warn't in the laste bit of a hurry to get out my way, sure."

" Well, Dennis, only show me the brute, and it shall be a hard case if I do not make the addition of fat bear to eat with the lean beef, with which I have already stocked the larder."

I loaded my gun with ball, and in company with Dennis and his father started for the place where Master Bruin had been seen. I took Neptune with me—a remarkably fine Irish greyhound —one of the most powerfully built dogs of that breed I had ever seen, and well he proved his strength and courage this day, as you shall hear.

After proceeding nearly two miles in an easterly direction close to the edge of the beaver meadow,* Neptune suddenly raised his head and looked round. In the next instant he was dashing along in full chase of Mr. Bruin, who was making the best of his way up a hill on the opposite side of the meadow.

We joined in the chase with the greatest alacrity, but not in time to witness the first set-to

* These meadows are to be found within two or three miles of each other on almost every creek or small stream in Canada West. Those industrious animals, the beavers, build their dams across the creeks in a very ingenious manner, with clay and brush-wood. It is very astonishing what ingenuity they display, and what sagacity, almost amounting to reason, they show in the choice of situation for the erection of these dams. It has been asserted that some years ago, when the French were masters of the country, the Indians cut away the dams, and killed all the beavers they could possibly find, as they did not wish the reservoirs where the beavers bred to fall into the hands of their white brethren. The size of these meadows varies from two or three acres to two or three hundred, and in some few cases is much larger.

between these savage opponents; for while we were gaining the brow of the hill a desperate fight was going on only a few yards from us. Neptune sometimes having the best of it—sometimes Bruin. I found it quite impossible to fire for fear of killing the dog. We then tried to pull him off so as to enable me to shoot the bear. This we found equally difficult, the dog had such fast hold of his throat. He was, indeed, perfectly furious.

Dennis, by my direction, cut a strong pole twelve or fourteen feet long, which we laid across the brute's back, and pressed him down as tightly as we could, which, with the able assistance of Nep. kept my gentleman tolerably quiet till the old man cut and twisted a couple of withes, which he passed under the bear, near the hind and fore-legs, and secured him firmly to the pole, which my companions lifted on their shoulders, from which the beast now hung suspended, and commenced our march homewards.

I had great difficulty in keeping the dog off. He would rush in, every minute, in spite of all I could do, and seize poor Bruin by the side and shake him most unmercifully. I had enough to do with the help of a stout stick to keep him and the bear in order. The latter was equally violent—

striking with his fore-paws at the men who were—luckily for them—just out of his reach, and particularly so for Dennis, who marched in front, whose unmentionables not being in the best possible repair, appeared to excite Master Bruin's particular attention.

I very much wished to preserve this creature alive, that I might try and tame him. In this, however, I was destined to be disappointed; for what with the beating I was obliged to give him to keep him quiet, and the savage attack of the dog, he died just as we came within sight of the clearing. When we skinned him, we found his side much lacerated where the dog had bitten him. From the exaggerated description Dennis had given me of his size, I fully expected to find him as big as a bullock. He, however, only weighed a hundred and fifty-seven pounds, which, for a bear of two years old, which appeared to be his age, is, I believe, the average weight.

The summer of 1825 was warm, even for Canada, where this season is always hot. The thermometer often ranged above 90° in the shade. Such weather would be quite unbearable, were it not for a fine breeze which almost invariably springs up from the westward between ten and eleven o'clock in the forenoon, and continues till sunset.

The nights are cooler in proportion to the heat of the day, than in England.

This climate is subject to violent thunder-storms, accompanied by vivid forked lightning and heavy rain, which greatly tend to cool the air and make the country more healthy. Fatal accidents, however, sometimes occur, and houses and barns are burnt down by the electric fluid, and I have no doubt that, were it not for the proximity of the woods, a great deal more damage would be done.

The lofty trees serve as conductors, particularly the pine and hemlock, the former, from its great height above all the other trees of the forest, being much more likely to be struck by the lightning than any other. It is a curious fact that the electric fluid invariably follows the grain of the wood. I have often noticed in pines which had been struck, that the fluid had followed the grain in a spiral form, encircling the tree three or four times in its descent to the earth. I have myself witnessed some extraordinary effects produced by lightning. I remember that, not more than two years since, I had occasion to go out into the township of Douro to attend the sitting of the Council, of which I was then a member, and I had, on my way, to pass through a small clearing occupied by an Irish settler, one James Lynch.

This man, to save trouble, had left several large hemlock trees near his house. These trees had been dead for some years, consequently the wood was tolerably dry. * The day before, there had been a terrific thunder-storm which struck the largest, which was fully four feet in diameter, shivering it from top to bottom, and throwing the pieces around for upwards of sixty yards in every direction. If a barrel of gunpowder had been placed under the tree, greater devastation could not have been made. Lynch told me that the storm had been very severe in that neighbourhood.

" We were at dinner," he said, " when the dreadful flash came which shattered that tree. We were all knocked down by the shock, and narrowly escaped being killed, not only by the lightning, but by the pieces of timber which were, as you may observe, scattered in all directions."

After a thunder-storm, attended by heavy rain, a substance very much resembling sulphur is left floating on all the pools, which many people believe to be sulphur. This, however, is quite a mis-

* It is well known that dry timber offers a greater resistance to the electric fluid than the green.

take, for it is, in reality, nothing more than the farina from the cone of the pine trees. I have observed this substance equally abundant on the Huron tract, many miles from any pine grove. It must, therefore, from its lightness, have been carried up into the air, from whence it has been beaten down by the rain.

CHAPTER V.

CANADIAN HARVEST.—PREPARING TIMBER FOR FRAME-BUILDINGS.—
RAISING "BEE."—BEAUTY OF THE CANADIAN AUTUMN.—VISIT
TO OTONABEE.—ROUGH CONVEYANCE.—DISACCOMMODATION.—
LEARNED LANDLORD.—COBOURG.—OTONABEE RIVER.—CHURCH
OF GORE'S LANDING.—EFFECTS OF PERSEVERING INDUSTRY.

OUR harvest, with the exception of some late oats, was all carefully housed by the 18th of August. Very little grain is stacked out in this country : even the hay is put up in barns. As timber can be had for the cutting, log or frame-barns can be built very cheaply. I would certainly recommend frame in preference to log-buildings.

Square timber, fit for framing, can be purchased from four to five dollars per hundred feet, running measure. Twelve hundred feet are sufficient, varying in size from four inches to a foot square. This quantity will frame a barn fifty feet long by thirty feet wide, and sixteen in height, from the sill to the plate which supports the roof. Twelve thousand feet of boards and plank, at five dollars per thousand, superficial measure, will be enough to enclose the frame, and lay the threshing-floor, and board the roof ready for shingling.

The best and cheapest method of barn-building is as follows : In the winter season cut and square with the broad axe all the frame timber you require, and draw it home to the place you have fixed on for the building, and from the saw-mill all the lumber you require. As soon as the weather is warm enough hire a framer, whose business is to mark out all the tenons and mortices, and to make or superintend the making of them. When ready, the building is put together in what is called bents, each bent consisting of two posts, one on each side of the building, connected together by a strong beam running across the building. The foundation is composed of twelve cedar blocks, three feet long, sunk two-thirds of their depth into the ground, one under each corner of the barn, and under the foot of each post. These blocks support the sills, which are firmly united at the corner to the cross-sills. The bents, four in number, are then laid on this foundation, and are ready for raising, which is done by calling a " bee." Thirty-five men are ample for this service—more are only in the way. Every two persons should be provided with a light balsam or cedar pole, fifteen feet in length, shod at the end with a ring and strong spike. These pike-poles are laid in order in front of the bent to be raised, one between each person. All being ready, the framer gives the word "attention," when each man lays hold of the bent, one man being stationed at the foot of each post with a hand-spike, which he presses against it to prevent its slipping. "Yeo heave!" is then shouted by the framer, at which every man lifts, waiting always for the word, and lifting together. As soon as the bent is lifted as high as they can reach the pike, poles are driven into the beam, and the bent is soon in a perpendicular position. Several pikes are then stuck into the opposite side to keep the bent from being swayed over, until the tenons on the foot of the post is entered into the mortice on the sill : it is then secured by stays, until the next bent is raised, when the girts connect them together. In this manner all the bents are raised ; the wall-plates are then lifted upon the building, which connect all the bents. The tenon on the top of each post goes through the plate, and is firmly pinned ; the putting up the rafters completes the frame. The raising of a building of this size should not occupy more than three quarters of a-day. No liquor should be served out to the swarm of working bees till the raising is over, as many serious accidents having occurred for want of this precaution.

I am particular in giving these descriptions, because I flatter myself they may prove useful to the future colonist.

The first week in September we commenced sowing our fall-wheat, and finished on the tenth, which is considered in good season. I would by all means recommend early sowing, especially on old cleared farms. Late sown wheat is more liable to winter-kill and rust. In fact, you can hardly sow too early to ensure a good crop.

September is the most beautiful month in the Canadian year. The weather is neither too hot nor too cold. Nothing can be more delightfully pleasant; for, in this month, the foliage of the trees begins to put on that gorgeous livery for which the North American continent is so justly celebrated. Every variety of tint, from the brightest scarlet and deepest orange, yellow and green, with all the intermediate shades blended together, form one of the most beautiful natural pictures you can possibly conceive.

I received a very pressing invitation from my wife's brother-in-law, who resided near the foot of Rice Lake, in the township of Otonabee, to come and spend a few days with him. As an additional inducement, he promised to show me some capital duck-shooting. I was too fond of fowling to decline such an invitation as this. Besides, I wished to see that new settlement. The township lies north of Rice Lake, which forms its southern boundary : it is the largest in the county of Peterborough, with the exception of Harvey. Otonabee contains above eighty thousand acres, and is now the most populous as well as one of the most fertile townships in the county, which, at the time of which I am writing, had been just opened by the Government for location.

The only practicable road then to this settlement was from Cobourg, distant twelve miles from the southern shore of Rice Lake, leading over a chain of hills, the highest of which is, I believe, about seven hundred feet above the level of Lake Ontario, and from whence, on a very clear day, the opposite shore may be seen, though the distance is nearly sixty-five miles. I have heard this statement disputed, but I am perfectly convinced of the truth from having myself seen, on several occasions, the United States' shore of the lake from White's Hill, which is several hundred feet lower.

It was arranged that I should drive my wife as

far as Cobourg, and leave her with some friends till my return. I was to take out with me from Cobourg the gentleman's sister, Miss Jane W——, who was to return with me.

We left Darlington in a one-horse pleasure-waggon—so called, or rather mis-called, by the natives. For my part, I never could find in what the pleasure consisted, unless in being jerked every minute two or three feet from your seat by the unevenness of the road and want of springs in your vehicle, or the next moment being soused to the axletree in a mud-hole, from which, perhaps, you were obliged to extricate your carriage by the help of a lever in the shape of a rail taken from some farmer's fence by the roadside. You are no sooner freed from this Charybdis, than you fall into Scylla, formed by half a mile of corduroy-bridge, made of round logs, varying from nine to fifteen inches in diameter, which, as you may suppose, does not make the most even surface imaginable, and over which you are jolted in the roughest style possible, at the expense of your breath and injury of your person. I am happy to say that better roads and a better description of pleasure-carriages have superseded these inconvenient conveyances.

Since the institution of county councils, and

the formation of towns and townships into municipalities, great attention has been bestowed, and
large sums of money voted, for the improvement
of roads and bridges ; and several Joint-stock
companies, chartered by the Provincial Parliament, have completed sundry lines of plank and
macadamized roads, on which toll-gates have
been erected. What has already been done in
this way has added greatly to the wealth and settlement of the province. No one can understand,
indeed, except the early settler, what a blessing a
good road is, especially to those who are too far
back for the benefit of water communication.

The day was fine and clear when we started,
and we congratulated ourselves on the prospect
of a pleasant journey, which, I am sorry to say,
was not to be verified. Distant thunder soon
warned us that we might expect a storm. We
hurried on as fast as possible, in hope we might
be able to get through the nine-mile woods, in
the township of Clarke, before the bursting of the
storm. In this, however, we were disappointed ;
for, before we were half through the woods, the
rain fell in torrents, accompanied by the loudest
thunder and most vivid lightning I had ever seen.
After above an hour's most pitiless pelting, we
found ourselves suddenly before a small log-

house, in front of which, swinging between two upright posts, a cross-bar connecting them at the top, depended a sign, on which was described, in large characters, for the information of all way-worn or thirsty-travellers, " that good liquor, good beds, and good accommodations, both for man and horse, could be had from the proprietor, Thomas Turner Orton."

Although from the outward appearance of the premises we did not expect the best accommodation, we thought anything better than being exposed longer to the fury of the storm, so giving our horse and waggon to the charge of the ostler, we entered Mr. Orton's tavern, and demanded to be shown into a private room, which request we found it was out of the power of mine host to comply with, seeing he had only one apartment, which answered the treble purpose of parlour, kitchen, and bar-room. Besides this general apartment there were two small bedrooms on the ground-floor. Luckily for us, a good fire blazed on the ample hearth, its only occupant, in the shape of a guest, being a gentleman from Port Hope, who, like ourselves, had just taken refuge from the storm.

While our clothes were being dried, our hostess prepared dinner, which consisted of a boiled chicken, eggs, and fried ham, which we found excellent, and, as a preventive against catching cold, after the soaking we had got, I ordered some whiskey-punch, which I have always found very efficacious on such occasions. Some people recommend tea made from the boughs of the hemlock-pine, which, I dare say, is excellent for some constitutions; but it never agreed half so well with mine as the former antidote, which I can conscientiously recommend—but, like all other medicines, an over-dose may do more harm than good.

Our host, who appeared to make himself quite at home in his own house, joined in the conversation, and being very communicative about his own affairs, wanted us to be equally so about ours. His eccentricity greatly amused us. He informed me that he was by birth a Yorkshireman, and that he had been in business in London, where he had built some fine "place" or "terrace," which still bore his name. He spouted Latin occasionally, and showed me a Greek lexicon, which he told me was his constant companion. His real stock of Latin and Greek consisted only of a few words and sentences he had picked up, and which he quoted ostentatiously before the ignorant, who of course thought him a prodigy of learning.

As it continued to rain all the evening, I was obliged to give orders to have my horse put up for the night, and also to see what accommodation could be had for ourselves. I found on examination that this was bad enough—at least I thought so then, though many a time since I should have been happy to obtain any half as good.

We started early next morning, and reached Cobourg, without any farther adventure, about noon on the same day. We halted there three days. I left my wife with our friends, and took charge of Miss W—— to escort her to her brother's house.

We left Cobourg for Rice Lake, which was distant about twelve or thirteen miles from thence. It was a delightful morning in October ; and our road, though very bad, and in some places positively dangerous, where it descended into the deep ravines, was at the same time so picturesque that we were quite delighted with our drive, and particularly so when, emerging from the woods, we entered Hamilton-plains, and beheld in the distance the glittering waters of Rice Lake, and the gem-like islands which adorn its unruffled surface.

Rice Lake, or the Lake of the Burning Plains,

as it is called in the Indian language, is a fine sheet
of water, twenty-seven miles in length from east
to west, varying from two to three and a half miles
in width.　About six miles from its head on the
northern shore it receives the waters of the Otonabee river, which, rising near the head-waters of
the Madawaska, flows in nearly a westerly direction into Balsam Lake, where it takes a more
southerly direction, forming in its course a succession of beautiful lakes for upwards of sixty
miles.　Ten miles above Peterborough, and directly opposite my own farm in the township of
Douro, it suddenly contracts its channel and becomes a rapid and impetuous stream.　According
to a survey ordered by the government, it was
ascertained that from a point on my farm, at the
foot of Kawchewahnoonk Lake, and distant from
Peterborough nearly ten miles, there is a fall of
one hundred and forty-seven feet, affording an
unlimited water-power, which has already been
extensively applied not only in the town of Peterborough, where several fine flour and saw-mills
have been erected, but also in the townships
through which it flows.

At Peterborough the rapids cease, from whence
the river becomes navigable for steam-boats to
the Rice Lake, at the distance of twenty-one

miles, which it enters after a course of fully two hundred and fifty miles.

The Indian river takes its rise close to Stony Lake, from which it is only divided by a narrow ridge of granite : this ridge has been cut across at the sole expense of the Hon. Zacheus Burnham and Dr. John Gilchrist, for the purpose of obtaining a larger supply of water for the use of their mills at Warsaw, in Dummer and Keane, in Otonabee, thus connecting the two rivers by this canal. This river flows through the townships of Dummer, Douro, and Otonabee, its whole course not exceeding thirty-five or forty miles, with the exception of a few small streams. No other river of consequence flows into Rice Lake.

Our drive over the plains was truly delightful. New beauties presented themselves at every step. It can hardly be imagined what a relief it is to the eye, after travelling for miles through a dense forest, to see such a beautiful landscape suddenly burst on your sight.

For nearly three miles our road lay through natural park-like scenery, flowery knolls, 'deep ravines, and oak-crowned hills, with every now and then the blue waters of the lake glittering through the trees. Our path now entered a deep and finely-wooded ravine, which wound round the base of steep hills on either hand, rising to a considerable height, their summits crowned here and there with beautiful clumps of oak.

For nearly a mile we followed the sharp descent and windings of the beautiful valley, till a sudden turning of the road revealed to our sight the whole expanse of this fine sheet of water. Not a ripple dimpled the surface ; but, mirror-like, it lay with all its lovely islands thickly wooded to their summits with the sugar-maple, which rose, tree above tree, up the steep ascent of these conical islets, which, reflected in the clear lake, added new beauties to the scene.

A few minutes more brought us to the tavern, a small log-house, kept by one David Tidy, a very respectable Scotchman. The situation of this man's farm is one of the best on the lake shore. It is now the property of Mr. Alfred Hayward, whose good taste has added greatly to its natural beauties. Mrs. Hayward, who is an accomplished artist, has taken a view of the lake from her garden, and also one of Port Hope, both of which have been lithographed, and are much admired.

Tidy's tavern, and two other log-houses, were at this time the only settlements on the Rice Lake plains, which extend for nearly twenty miles along the south shore, forming the rear of the townships of Hamilton and Alnwick, but which are now dotted over with fine productive farms, substantial stone, brick, or frame-houses, full-bearing orchards, and possessing in fact almost every comfort and convenience a farmer could wish.

The pretty village of Gore's Landing is built partly on the lot formerly possessed by Tidy, and partly on the adjoining lot at present occupied by Captain Gore, from whom the village takes its name.   The gentlemen in this neighbourhood have, nearly at their own expense, built a very neat church, which is romantically situated on the top of a high hill overlooking the lake.   In summer time nothing can exceed the beauty of this spot, or be more suitable for the erection of a fane dedicated to Him

" Whose temple is all space ! "

This village contains two excellent taverns, a large steam saw-mill, two stores, and several other buildings.   Two steam-boats, the " Royal George" and " Forester," leave it daily for Peterborough, distant twenty-five miles, making their return-trip the same day.   Another steamer is being constructed to run from the village of Keane, on the Indian river in Otonabee down the Trent as far as Heely's Falls and back to Gore's

Landing. These boats meet Weller's line of mail-stages at one o'clock, P.M. A fine line of plank-road has been constructed from this place to Cobourg, avoiding all the high hills. The stage time is an hour and a half between lake and lake.

As nearly all the lumber and shingles manu-factured at Peterborough and the neighbouring townships, intended for exportation to the United States, must be either landed here or at Bewdley, at the head of the lake, whence it is conveyed across in waggons to Port Hope or Cobourg, this village bids fair to become a stirring little place.

One of my objects in writing this work is to point out what the country was twenty-seven years ago, and what it is now, showing clearly that what appeared to the pioneer of those days in-surmountable difficulties, have by persevering in-dustry been overcome, " and the howling wilder-ness made to blossom as the rose." The desolating torrent has been utilized and restrained; mills and factories have been erected ; bridges span our broadest rivers, and magnificent steamers plough our inland seas. Nor is this all : the first sod of a railway has been turned, which is ultimately intended to connect Lake Huron with Halifax and Boston, bringing the riches of the Far West through its natural channel to the sea.

Nothing, indeed, but industry and enterprise is needed to change the waste and solitary places of Upper Canada into a garden of Eden, which it is designed by the Supreme Architect to become.

CHAPTER VI.

WOOD-DUCK SHOOTING.—ADVENTURE ON RICE LAKE.—IRISH HOWL.
—ARRIVAL AT GORE'S LANDING.—GENERAL HOWLING FOR THE
DEFUNCT. — DANGERS OF OUR JOURNEY. — SAFE ARRIVAL AT
COBOURG. — SALMON-FISHING. — CANOE-BUILDING AFTER A BAD
FASHION.—SALMON-SPEARING.—CANADIAN FISH AND FISHERIES.
—INDIAN SUMMER.—SLEIGHS AND SLEIGHING.—DOMESTIC LOVE.

AFTER committing the care of my horse to our
landlord, I ordered dinner to be got ready immediately, as we had thirteen miles to row, and
I wished to reach Mr. W——'s before dark.
Our hostess exerted herself, and we soon sat
down to a sumptuous feast, consisting of a brace
of fine fat wood-ducks and fried black bass, two
dishes I am particularly fond of, and which at
this time of the year can always be obtained from
the lake.

The wood-duck is a delicious bird. It makes its
appearance early in the spring, as soon as the ice
breaks up. Its plumage is very fine—I should say
the most beautiful of any of its species. Its head
and upper part of the neck are dark green; from

the top of the head a long crest depends, richly
variegated with green, white, and dark purple
feathers. The lower part of the throat and
breast is cinnamon speckled with white, but
under the wings and sides towards the tail, grey,
speckled and fringed with black; the back of the
wings dark blue and black feathers. The wood-
duck frequents close-wooded streams, little bays,
and nooks, sitting upon old logs or the limbs of
trees which have fallen into the water. It feeds
on the wild rice, and is very fat from the middle
of August to November, when it migrates to a
warmer climate. This kind of duck is more
easily approached than any other. The sportsman should be seated near the centre of a small
canoe, his gun lying before him ready cocked,
when he should paddle very cautiously through
the rice, keeping his head as low as possible. A
person who understands the management of a
canoe can generally get within twenty-five or
thirty yards before he is seen, which gives him
ample opportunity to put down his paddle and
take his gun, in time to fire both barrels. In
this manner I have often killed from fifteen to
twenty brace in a few hours.

After dinner we hired a skiff and proceeded on
our voyage. The lake was calm, so we made

good progress, passing the Indian village belonging to the Mississauga tribe of Indians, a branch of the Chippewas, which I shall have occasion to speak of hereafter, Pantaush's point, Designs Bay, and the *embouchure* of the Indian river; and just at dusk landed opposite my friend's house, pretty well tired, though much delighted with our day's journey. We were received with a welcome such as only a backwoodsman knows how to give. In half an hour I felt as much at home as if I had belonged to the family.

During my stay here, which was upwards of a week, I amused myself with fishing and shooting. The fall and winter duck were beginning to come in from the north, a sure sign that hard weather was close at hand.

We had had an early spring and a long warm summer. Generally speaking, the ground does not close till about the middle of November; but this year the frost set in much earlier. It did not, however, continue, for the ground again opened, and we had nearly two weeks of beautiful Indian summer in the early part of November.

On the, 17th the ice was sufficiently strong to skate upon. On the 27th day of October the first hard weather commenced, and as there was some fear of the lake freezing, we determined to start for Cobourg the following morning. I accordingly made the necessary preparations, and hired an old man-of-war's-man, one Robert Redpath, to row us up the lake to Tidy's.

It froze hard during the night. The ice was fully half an inch thick on the bays, and along the margin of the lake we were obliged to break a passage for the skiff for upwards of fifty yards before we got into clear water. It was cold, and blew fresh from the north-west, and the wind being directly down the lake, caused a heavy swell, which increased every minute. As the gale freshened, our skiff shipped so much water that we thought it prudent to put across to the Alnwick shore, which was more under the lee, being sheltered by islands. While passing near one of these, I observed some person walking to and fro, apparently making signals of distress. I called Redpath's attention to this, and bade him " row to the shore that we might ascertain what he wanted." This our boatman positively refused to do, saying that " he had hired himself to ferry us to Tidy's, and he was not bound to go half a mile out of his way to hunt after every infernal Ingine (Indian) we might see on our road."

I, however, insisted on his immediately complying with my request. It was fortunate I did so, for on landing we found a man walking backwards and forwards, trying to keep himself warm. Indeed, the poor fellow looked nearly frozen. He seemed to have lost all power over his limbs, and was quite unable to articulate. I made Redpath light a fire, and in the meantime I gave the man a dram from our whiskey-bottle, which greatly revived him. We soon had a blazing fire, which had the desired effect of unloosing the tongue of our new acquaintance, and he informed us, " he was one of the Irish emigrants sent off by Government under the superintendance of the Honourable Peter Robinson ; that several hundreds of them had been forwarded from Cobourg to Rice Lake, a few days before, on their way to the new settlements up the Otonabee River, and were now camped at Tidy's. He and his friend, a man of the name of Daly, a tailor by trade, wished to settle in the township of Asphodel, on the River Trent. They had accordingly taken a boat and had rowed down the lake in the hope of reaching Crook's Rapids on the Trent before nightfall. Irishman-like, their only stores for the voyage consisted of a bottle of whiskey, to which it appears they applied themselves more diligently than to the navigation of their boat, which they let drift at the mercy of the winds and waves while they slept.

They did not wake up from their drunken slumbers till dark, when they found themselves stuck in a rice bed, and unable to extricate themselves from the dilemma in which they were placed; whereupon they again had recourse to the bottle, which this time proved fatal to Daly who, being very drunk, fell overboard. His companion, however, managed to catch hold of him and succeeded in getting him into the boat only to suffer a more lingering death, for he was frozen stiff before morning dawned. The survivor had covered his unfortunate companion with a blanket, the only one they had with them, in the hope it would keep him from perishing with cold during the night, which care, however, proved unavailing. He managed at dawn to extricate the boat from the rice bed, but not being able to row so large a boat, especially in his present condition, she drifted upon the point of the island on which we found him.

As soon as he was well warmed and refreshed, we proceeded to the place pointed out by him, where we found the boat thumping in the surf, on a ledge of rocks. After hauling it up, we proceeded to lift the blanket, when a shocking

sight presented itself. The dead man was
sitting upright on the seat, with his mouth and
eyes half-open. We lifted him out, laid him
under a tree, and spread the blanket over him.
We found our skiff too small to accommodate
another passenger, so we determined to leave it
behind and take the large boat, which we accordingly did ; and we put our new-comer to the oar
with Redpath, whilst I took the helm.

We had a long, tedious row against the head-
wind, which now blew a gale. Our new acquaintance, every now-and-then, would throw down his
oar, and howl and clap his hands to show his grief
for the loss of his departed friend. These pathetic
lamentations elicited no sympathy from Redpath,
who abused him for " a lazy lubber," and ordered
him " to pull and not make such an infernal howling, worse than a wild Ingin's yell."

We made the landing at Tidy's, just before
dark, and found several hundred emigrants in the
tavern, and camped round about it.

As soon as we came within hearing, our passenger commenced the loudest howl he had yet
perpetrated, which had the immediate effect of
bringing down to the landing the whole of his
countrymen, who, as soon as they learned the loss
of their friend, gave us a genuine Irish howl,

in which the women took the most prominent part.

On our way up to the house, we were met by the landlord, who, with a most woful look, informed us that our horse had strayed away from the pasture, and that he had searched the plains in every direction, and could hear no tidings of him, but as soon as he turned up he would send him home. "I am sorry, sir," he added, "this misfortune has happened, and particularly as I am unable to accommodate you and the young lady, for my house is full of drunken Irish, as you see. Indeed, the only chance you have of getting to Cobourg to-night is by an ox-cart, which will start about nine o'clock this evening."

I was very angry with the landlord for his carelessness, and told him I should look to him for payment unless my horse was forthcoming. I found the owner of the ox-cart, and made a bargain with him to set us down at my friend's house in Cobourg.

Our equipage was very unique of its kind, it having been constructed for the sole purpose of carrying barrels of flour and pork. The box was a kind of open rack, with two rows of upright stakes instead of sides: two long boards, laid on cross-bars, formed the bottom : we spread our buffaloes on these, and fastened a strong piece of rope across the cart, from stake to stake on either side, to hold on by.

Thus equipped, we commenced our journey. It was pitch-dark, so our driver let the cattle go as they liked, for guiding them was perfectly out of the question. I shall never forget the way our oxen galloped down those steep hills. Miss W. was dreadfully frightened. All we could do was to hold on and trust in Providence. Luckily, the oxen kept the track ; for had they deviated in the least, going down some of the steep pitches, the cart would have been upset to a certainty, and very likely we should have been seriously injured, or killed on the spot.

It was past one in the morning before we reached Cobourg, thoroughly fatigued with our expedition.

I heard no tidings of my horse for upwards of four months, and had given up all thoughts of beholding him again, when one morning I was surprised to see him, waggon, harness and all, drive into the yard. Upon inquiry, I found that the hard weather and snow had made him seek the clearings for food, when he was easily secured ; but one of his fetlocks was cut almost to the bone by the piece of rope he had been tethered with, and which was still upon him when he was found.

One of the most exciting amusements at this season of the year, is salmon-fishing. In order to enjoy this sport, I made a canoe sixteen feet in length, and two feet nine inches at its greatest breadth. It was my first attempt, and, certainly the thing looked more like a hog-trough than a boat. It, however, answered the purpose for which it was intended, and I can assure the reader I felt not a little proud of this, my first attempt at canoe-making.

Salmon-fishing commences in October, when the fish run up the rivers and creeks in great numbers. The usual way of catching them is by spearing, which is done as follows.—An iron grate —or jack, as it is called by the Canadians—is made in the shape of a small cradle, composed of iron bars three or four inches apart. This cradle is made to swing in a frame, so that it may be always on the level, or the swell would cause the pine-knots to fall out. Fat pine and light-wood are used to burn in the jack, which give a very brilliant light for several yards round the bow of the canoe. The fish can be easily seen at the depth of from four to five feet. One person sits in the stern and steers with a paddle, propel-

ling the canoe at the same time. The bowman either kneels or stands up with the spear
poised ready for striking. An expert hand will
scarcely miss a stroke. I have known two fishermen in this manner kill upwards of two hundred
salmon in one night. I believe, however, the
fishing is not nearly so productive as formerly.

Mr. Stephens showed me a small stream running
through his farm, which I could easily jump over.
He told me that one afternoon he was watering
his horses, when he perceived a shoal of salmon
swimming up the creek. He had no spear at
home, having lent it to a neighbour. He, however, succeeded with a pitchfork in capturing fifty-
six fine fish.

Thirty years ago, all the small streams and
rivers, from the head of the lake downwards to
the Bay of Quinte, used to abound with salmon.
The erection of saw-mills on the creeks, and other
causes, have tended materially to injure the
fisheries. White fish and salmon-trout are, however, taken in vast quantities, particularly the
former, which has become quite an article of
commerce. The most extensive fisheries are on
the Manitoulin island, in Lake Huron, and along
the Canadian shore of Ontario, opposite the township of Haldimand, Crambe, and Murray, in the

county of Northumberland, and part of the district of Prince Edward. Very large seine nets being used, many barrels of fish are often taken at a haul, which are cured and packed on the spot: the usual price of a barrel varies from five to six dollars.

Lake Ontario abounds with herring, of much the same flavour as the sea species, but not so strong and oily, nor so large. Sturgeon, pike, pickerel, black bass, sheep-heads, mullets, suckers, eels, and a variety of other fish, are plentiful in these waters : the spring-creeks and mill-ponds yield plenty of spotted trout, from four ounces to a pound weight : they are easily caught either with the worm or fly.

The best creek I ever fished in was the Speed, a branch of the Grand River, or Ouse, which runs through the township of Guelph. In winter you can catch them by fishing through a hole in the ice. The best way is to dig and store by in a box filled with earth, a quantity of worms, which must be kept in the cellar for use. A small piece of fat pork is commonly employed as bait, but is not nearly so good as the other.

A friend of mine, living near Colborne, told me rather an amusing story of a Yankee, who was fishing through the ice with the usual bait, a piece of pork. He had been very unsuccessful, and tired of the sport, he walked over to where my friend was throwing out the trout as fast as possible, when the following colloquy took place :

" Wal, how, under Heaven, did you get all them 'ere fish ? "

" Caught them."

" Wal, I s'pose you did ; but what kinder bait do you use ? "

" Worms."

" Varms ! Why, under Heaven, where do you get varms at this time of the year?"

" I got these out of my cellar."

" Get out ! how you do talk ! "

" You may believe me or not, as you like ; but I can assure you I did."

" Wal, do tell. I guess I never thought of diggin' in the cellar ; I will go to hum and try."

My friend met him a few days afterwards, when the Yankee said—" I calculate, Mister, you told me a tarnation lie, the other day, about them 'ere varms. I went and dug up every bit of my cellar, and, I do declare, I never got a single varm."

My friend laughed very heartily at this " Yankee diggin," but at the same time kindly informed his neighbour of the method he pursued, to provide worms for winter-fishing.

Before the winter fairly sets in, we generally have ten days or a fortnight of the Indian summer; indeed, it is the sure harbinger of winter. The air is mild and temperate ; a haze, resembling smoke, pervades the atmosphere, that at times obscures the sun, which, when visible, is of a blood-red colour. Various causes have been assigned for this appearance, but none very satisfactory.

Towards the end of November this year, the ice was strong enough to bear the weight of a man, and the ground was soon whitened with snow, but not in sufficient depth to make good sleighing. Just a week before Christmas, we had a fall of eight or ten inches, which made pretty good going : the sleighs were, of course, in immediate requisition.

A family sleigh is made to carry from six to ten persons ; the more stylish ones from four to six; a cutter, or single sleigh, two. These are all for pleasure, but every farmer is obliged to have a lumber-sleigh for general use. A much larger load can be drawn on runners in winter than on wheels in summer. Sleighing is, without doubt, the most delightful mode of travelling you can possibly conceive, but it takes several falls of snow to make the sleighing good. All the inequalities must be filled up and levelled, but the snow soon packs solid by the constant friction of the sleigh-runner. The horses are each provided with a ring of bells, the sound of which is not unmusical; and I am assured is delightful indeed to the ears of the anxious wife, watching for the return of her husband from a winter journey. Some years ago, when the country was unsettled, the females of the family had some cause for fear, since the absence of the father, son, or husband, was not always followed by his safe return; and the snow-storm, or the wolves, were thought of with alarm, till the music of the sleigh-bells announced the safety of the beloved absentee.

In no country on the face of the earth does the torch of wedded love beam brighter than in Canada, where the husband always finds " the wife dearer than the bride." I have seen many an accomplished and beautiful English girl, "forgetting with her father's house," the amusements of a fashionable life, to realize with a half-pay officer or "younger brother," the purer, holier pleasures of domestic love in this country, where a numerous issue, the fruits of their union, are considered a blessing and a source of wealth, instead of bringing with them, as in the old country, an increase of care.

CHAPTER VII.

EMPLOYMENTS OF A MAN OF EDUCATION IN THE COLONY.—YANKEE
WEDDING.— MY COMMISSION.—WINTER IN CANADA. — HEALTHI-
NESS OF THE CANADIAN CLIMATE.—SEARCH FOR LAND.—PURCHASE
WILD LAND AT DOURO. — MY FLITTING. — PUT UP A SHANTY.—
INEXPERIENCE IN CLEARING.—PLAN-HEAPS.

THE employments of a respectable Canadian
settler are certainly of a very multifarious character, and he may be said to combine, in his own
person, several professions, if not trades. A man
of education will always possess an influence, even
in bush society : he may be poor, but his value
will not be tested by the low standard of money,
and notwithstanding his want of the current coin
of the realm, he will be appealed to for his judgment in many matters, and will be inducted into
several offices, infinitely more honourable than
lucrative. My friend and father-in-law, being
mild in manners, good-natured, and very sensible,
was speedily promoted to the bench, and was
given the colonelcy of the second battalion of
the Durham Militia.

At this time there was no place of worship nearer than Port Hope, where the marriage cere- mony could be legally performed. According to the Colonial law, if a magistrate resides more than eighteen miles from a church, he is empowered to marry parties applying to him for that purpose, after three written notices have been put up in the most public places in the township, with the names and residences of the parties for at least a fortnight previous to the marriage. I witnessed several of these marriages during my stay in Darlington, some of which were highly amusing.

One morning a near neighbour presented him- self and a very pretty young woman, as can- didates for matrimony. He was an American by birth, and a shrewd, clever, sensible person. After the ceremony, the bridegroom invited me to partake of the wedding-dinner, and I went.

The dinner was very good, though not served exactly in the English fashion. We, however, managed to enjoy ourselves very much. After tea, dancing commenced, to the music of two fiddles, when country-dances, reels, and French fours were all performed with much spirit. The music was very good, the dancing but indifferent. I could not help thinking

" How ill the motion with the music suits,
  So Orpheus fiddled, and so danced the brutes."

During the pauses between the dances, some
lady or gentleman would favour the company with
a song. Then plays—as they are called—were introduced ; such as hunt the slipper, cross questions and crooked answers, ladies' toilette, and
several others of the same kind, in which forfeits
had to be redeemed by the parties making mistakes in the game—a procedure of course productive of much noise, kissing, and laughter.
Refreshments were handed round in great profusion, and the entertainment wound up with a
dance, which, I believe, is of purely American
origin. A chair is placed in the middle of the
room, on which a young lady is seated ; the company then join hands, and dance round her,
singing these elegant lines :—

" There was a young woman sat down to sleep,
  Sat down to sleep, sat down to sleep;
  There was a young woman sat down to sleep,
  Heigh-ho !—heigh-ho !—heigh-ho !

" There was a young man to keep her awake,
  To keep her awake, to keep her awake ;
  There was a young man to keep her awake,
  Heigh-ho !—heigh-ho !—heigh ho !

" John R—— his name shall be,
  His name shall be, his name shall be ;
  John R—— his name shall be,
  Heigh-ho !—heigh-ho !—heigh-ho !

The gentleman named walks up to the lady, salutes her, raises her from the chair, and seats himself in her stead, the rest dancing round, and singing as before, only substituting the gentleman, and naming the lady who is to release the gentleman in the same way, till all the ladies and gentlemen have been seated in their turn.

As soon as this queer species of Mazurka was concluded, the company broke up, seemingly well pleased with their entertainment. The introduction of English manners and customs during the last quarter of a century has tended greatly to improve society. It is now only amongst the lower orders that parties of this kind would be tolerated.

On my return home, I found an official letter from the Adjutant-general of the Upper Canada Militia, in which I was informed I was appointed by his Excellency Sir P. Maitland to an Ensigncy in the first regiment of Durham Militia. The effective militia of this province is, I believe, about 150,000 men. All persons, from sixteen to sixty, must enrol their names once a year, and all from sixteen to forty, must muster for general training on the 28th of June in each year. The officers, in time of war, receive the same pay and allowances as those in the line.

The winters of 1825 and 1826 were considered cold, even for Canada. The sleighing was good from the middle of December to the middle of March, with the exception of the January thaw, which continued for upwards of a week, and took away nearly all the snow. This thaw, though periodical, is not every year of the same duration, nor does it always take away the snow. Sometimes it is attended by strong gales of wind, from the southward, and with heavy thunder and lightning, which was particularly the case last January. The month of February is generally considered the coldest of the winter months. I have frequently known the thermometer range from 16° to 20° below zero, for a week together. On one day of the winter of which I am speaking, it was as low as 35°. This, however, is unusual.

The coldest day I ever remember was in the winter of 1833. It was called the "Cold Sunday." The quicksilver in Fahrenheit's thermometer was frozen in the ball, which marks 39° below zero. It was, however, stated in the papers, both in Canada and the State of New York, that the real cold was 40° below zero, or 72° below freezing point. I dined at a friend's that day, who resided three miles from my farm in Douro. The

day was clear, not a cloud being above the horizon.
The sun was of a dull copper-colour, and the horizon towards the north-west tinged with the same
hue.   Not a breath of wind was stirring.   The
smoke from the chimneys rose straight up into
the air, and appeared unable to disperse through
the atmosphere.   My horses were as white as
snow from the steam of their bodies freezing upon
them; the reins were frozen as stiff as rods;
the air seemed to cut like a knife.   I was only
a quarter of an hour upon the road, but even in
that time I felt the cold severely, and was very
glad when I got into the house to a large wood
fire.   The cold obliged the whole party at dinner
to take their plates upon their knees and sit
round the fire.   But, as I said before, this is only
an extreme case, and might not happen again
for twenty years.

The excessive cold seldom lasts more than
three days at a time, when it generally moderates,
though not sufficiently to soften the snow.   The
dryness of the atmosphere and snow makes you
feel the cold much less in proportion than in
England.   You do not experience that clinging,
chilly, damp sort of cold in Canada that you do in
the British Isles.   For my part, I much prefer a
Canadian winter, where the roads are good, the

sleighing good, and your health good. Sickness is scarcely known here in the winter months.

If I could have purchased land on the lake-shore, I should have liked to settle in Darlington ; but I found the farms I fancied much too high-priced for my pocket. So at last I made up my mind to go back to the new settlement of Peter-borough, and see what sort of a place it was, and what it was likely to become.

Accordingly, I started on my journey, and travelled east, along the Kingston road, parallel with the shore of lake Ontario for about twenty-four or five miles to the boundary line, between the townships of Hope and Hamilton. After this I walked for twenty-seven miles through Cavan and Monaghan, to the town of Peter-borough, which, at that time contained one log-house and a very poor saw-mill, erected some five or six years before by one Adam Scott to supply the new settlement of Smith with lumber.

I found several hundreds of Mr. Robinson's Irish emigrants camped on the plains. Many had built themselves huts of pine and spruce boughs ; some with slabs and others with logs of trees. Three or four Government store-houses and a house for the Superintendent, the Hon. Peter Robinson, were in course of erection. I had letters of introduction to that gentleman, and also to the Hon. T. A. Stewart, and Robert Reid, Esq. The two latter gentlemen resided in the township of Douro, and were at that time the only settlers in that part of Canada.

As I did not much like the appearance of the lodgings I was likely to obtain in the new town, I went on to Mr. Stewart's house, and presented my credentials. Nothing could have been more cordial than the welcome I received from him. This gentleman and his brother-in-law, Robert Reid, Esq., obtained a grant of land from the Colonial Government, on condition that they would become actual settlers on the land, and perform certain settlement duties, which consisted in chopping out and clearing the concession lines.* Before the Crown patent could issue, the party contracting to perform the settlement duties was obliged to appear before a magistrate, and make an affidavit that he or they had chopped and cleared certain concession lines opposite the lots of land mentioned in the certificate.

* Every township is laid out by the surveyor in parallel lines, sixty-six chains apart. These lines are sixty-six feet in width, and are given by government as road allowances, for the use of the public, and are called concession lines. Cross lines run at right angles with the former every thirty chains, and are called lot-lines: they subdivide the township into two hundred acre lots: every fifth cross line is a road allowance.

This was a bad law, because many of these lines crossing high hills, swamps or lakes, were impracticable for road-purposes : many thousand pounds consequently were entirely and uselessly thrown away : besides, it opened a door for perjury.

Land-speculators would employ a third party to perform their settlement duties; all they required to obtain the deed, or "lift" as it is called in Canadian parlance, was the sworn certificate for cutting the road, allowances, and the payment of certain fees to Government. The consequence of this was, that many false certificates were sworn to, as few persons or magistrates would be at the trouble and expense of travelling thirty or forty miles back into an uninhabited part of the country, to ascertain if the parties had sworn truly or not.

A magistrate in my neighbourhood told me that a Yankee chopper came to him one day and demanded to be sworn on a settlement duty certificate, which he did to the following effect, "that he had cut a chain between two posts opposite lots so and so, in the concession of ——township. The road allowances are a chain in width, and posts are planted and marked on each side of the concession, at the corners of each lot.

"I had some suspicion," he said, "in my

own mind that the fellow had sworn falsely, so I determined to ascertain the truth. I knew a person residing within a mile or two of the place, to whom I wrote for information, when I found, as I expected, that not a tree had been cut on the line. I therefore summoned the Yankee, on the information of the farmer, to appear before a brother magistrate and myself to answer for his delinquency.

"So, sir," I said, "you came before me and swore to a false certificate. Do not you know you have committed perjury, which is a very serious offence. What have you to say for yourself?"

"Wal, I guess, Mister, I han't committed no perjury. I swore I cut a chain between two posts opposite them lots, and I can prove it by Ina Buck, for he was with me the hul time I was doing on't."

"Now, Mr. Buck, what can you prove?"

"Wal, gentlemen, I was along with Jonathan Stubbs when he went to chop the settlement duties, and when we got to the posts opposite the lots, he said, 'Wal, this looks plaguy ugly any how! I calculate I must fix these duties the short way,' so he pulled out of his pocket a short piece of trace-chain which he laid on a stone in a line between the two posts, and with a stroke or two of his axe severed it in two. 'Now,' said he, 'Ina Buck, I guess you are a witness that I cut a chain between two posts, so they can't fix me nohow?'"

"He was, however, a little out of his calculation, for we did fix him, and sent him to jail, where I dare say he had ample time to plan some new device for performing settlement duties."

My new friend advised me to purchase land adjoining his grant, which was very prettily situated on the banks of the Otonabee, in the township of the same name, within a mile of Peterborough. The price asked was fifteen shillings per acre, which was high for wild land at that time, but the prospect of a town so near had improved the market considerably.

I took his advice, closed the bargain, and became a landed proprietor in Canada West. On the 16th of May, 1826, I moved up with all my goods and chattels, which were then easily packed into a single horse waggon, and consisted of a plough iron, six pails, a sugar kettle, two iron pots, a frying pan with a long handle, a tea kettle, a chest of carpenters' tools, a Canadian axe, and a cross-cut saw. My stock of provisions comprised a parcel of groceries, half a barrel of pork and a barrel of flour.

The roads were so bad that it took me three days to perform a journey of little more than fifty miles. We (that is to say myself and my two labourers) had numerous upsets; but at last reached the promised land without any further trouble. My friend in Douro turned out the next day and assisted me to put up the walls of my shanty and roof it with basswood troughs, which was completed before dark.

I was kept busy for more than a week chinking between the logs and plastering up all the crevices, cutting out a doorway and place for a window, casing them, making a door and hanging it on wooden hinges, &c. I also made a rough table and some stools, which answered better than they looked. Four thick slabs of lime-stone, placed upright in one corner of the shanty with clay well packed behind them to keep the fire off the logs, answered very well for a chimney with a hole cut through the roof directly above, to vent the smoke.

I made a tolerably good bedstead out of some iron-wood poles, by stretching strips of elm-bark across, which I plaited strongly together to support my bed, which was a very good one, and the only article of luxury I possessed.

I had very foolishly hired two Irish emigrants,

who had not been longer in Canada than myself, and of course knew nothing either of chopping, logging, fencing, or, indeed, any work belonging to the country, The consequence of this imprudence was, that the first ten acres I cleared cost me nearly 5*l.* an acre*—at least 2*l.* more than it should have done. Experience is often dearly bought, and in this instance the proverb was fully verified.

I found chopping, in the summer months, very laborious. I should have underbrushed my fallow in the fall, before the leaves fell, and chopped the large timber during the winter months, when I should have had the warm weather for logging and burning, which should be completed by the first day of September. So, for want of experience, it was all up-hill work with me.

This was the season for musquitoes and black flies. The latter are ten times the worse of the two. This happened to be a bad fly year, and I, being a new comer, was nearly devoured by them. Luckily, they do not last more than a month, and it is only before rain that they are so very annoy-

* The usual price for clearing land, and fencing it fit for sowing, is, for hard wood, from eleven to twelve dollars per acre; for evergreen, such as pine, hemlock, cedar, or where that kind of timber predominates, from twelve to fourteen dollars per acre. There is no fixed price for swamp.

ing.   I have seen children whose necks were one mass of sores, from the poisonous nature of their bite : sheep, calves, and foals, are sometimes killed by them.   Nor is this, indeed, an unfrequent occurrence.   It must be, however, borne in mind that, as the country is cleared up, and the woods recede, the flies disappear.   In the clearings along the front townships, the flies are not more troublesome than they are in England.

The farm on which I now reside used to swarm terribly with flies, lying, as it does, near the water ; but, for the last three years, it has been entirely free from them, especially from the black flies.*

A person who understands chopping, can save

* These insects are always much worse, and more numerous, when the spring is backward, and the floods are higher than usual. From close observation, I believe the larvæ are deposited during high water on the rocks, when, as soon as the water falls, the heat of the sun hatches the insects.   I have remarked large stones, which had been under water during the flood, covered over with small brown coloured cells, exactly the shape, and very little bigger than a seed of buckwheat.   From out of these cells, on a sunny day, the flies rise in clouds, for they bite through the envelope, and emancipate themselves.   Being provided with a sharp appetite, they will attack you the minute they are at liberty. These pests begin to appear between the 10th of May and 1st of June, according to the earliness or lateness of the season.   Towards the end of June, numbers of small dragon-flies make their appearance, which soon eat up all the black-flies, to which repast, you may be sure, they are heartily welcome.

himself a good deal of trouble and hard work by making what is called a plan-heap. Three or four of these may be made on an acre, but not more. The largest and most difficult trees are felled, the limbs only being cut off and piled. Then all the trees that will fall in the same direction, should be thrown along, on the top of the others, the more the better chance of burning well. If you succeed in getting a good burn for your fallow, the chances are, if your plan-heaps are well made, that they will be mostly consumed, which will save a great many blows of the axe, and some heavy logging.

CHAPTER VIII.

A LOGGING BEE. — LIME-BURNING. — SHINGLING. — ARRIVAL OF MY
BROTHER-IN-LAW. — BIRTH OF MY SON. — SAD JOURNEY TO DAR-
LINGTON. — LOSE MY WAY. — AM REFUSED A LIFT. — MY BOYISH
ANGER. — MY WIFE'S DEATH. — THE FUNERAL. — I LEAVE DAR-
LINGTON.

MY fallow was finished by the first week in
July, but I did not put fire to it until the first
week in August, because the timber was so green.
Indeed, I did not expect the fire would run at all.
I was, however, agreeably deceived, for I got a
very respectable burn, which gave me great help.

As soon as the ground was cool enough, I made
a logging Bee, at which I had five yokes of
oxen and twenty men, four men to each team.
The teamster selects a good place to commence a
heap, generally against some large log which the
cattle would be unable to move. They draw
all the logs within a reasonable distance in front
of the large log. The men with hand-spikes roll
them, one upon the top of the other, until the
heap is seven or eight feet high, and ten or twelve

broad. All the chips, sticks, and rubbish are then picked up and thrown on the top of the heap. A team and four good men should log and pick an acre a day when the burn has been good.

My hive worked well, for we had five acres logged and set fire to the same evening. On a dark night, a hundred or two of these large heaps all on fire at once have a very fine effect, and shed a broad glare of light for a considerable distance. In the month of July in the new settlements, the whole country at night appears lit up by these fires.

I was anxious to commence building my house, so that I might have it ready to receive my wife in before the winter commenced. My first step towards it was to build a lime-heap. I calculated I should require for plastering my walls and building my chimneys, about a hundred bushels.

We set to work, accordingly, and built an immense log-heap of all the largest logs I could get together. It took at least the timber growing on half an acre of land for this purpose, and kept five men and myself busy all day to complete it. We made a frame of logs on the top of the heap, to keep the stone from falling over the side. We drew for this purpose twenty cart-loads of limestone, which we threw upon the summit of the heap, having broken it small with a sledge-hammer ; fire was then applied to the heap, which was consumed by the next morning.　But it left such a mass of hot coals, that it was a week before the lime could be collected and covered.　This is the easiest and most expeditious way of burning lime ; but the lime is not so white, and there are more pieces of unburnt stone, which make it not so good for plastering.

I built my house of elm-logs, thirty-six feet long by twenty-four feet wide, which I divided into three rooms on the ground-floor, besides an entrance-hall and staircase, and three bed-rooms up stairs.　I was very busy till October making the shingles,* roofing, cutting out the door and

---

* Shingles are made either of pine or cedar.　I prefer the white pine, because it is less liable to gutter with the rain, and makes an evener roof.　Every settler in the bush should know how to make shingles, and how to choose a tree fit for that purpose, or much labour may be thrown uselessly away.　I do not know anything more annoying than, after cutting down a tree, perhaps more than four feet in diameter, and sawing a block eighteen inches long out of the centre, to find that it will not split fair, or (if it does) that the wood eats, which means, that the grain, though straight in the length of the shingle, makes short deep curves, which render it bad to split, and cause holes to appear in the shingle when you come to shave them.　The grain of most trees naturally inclines towards the sun, or the same way round the tree as the sun's course.　Consequently, a tree may be perfectly straight in the grain, where you chop it down, yet, ten or twelve feet up, it

window-spaces, and hewing the logs down inside the house.

I was anxious to complete the outside walls, roof, and chimneys before the winter set in, so that I might be able to work at the finishing part inside, under cover, and with the benefit of a fire.

As soon as my little fallow was ready for sow-

may wind so much as to be totally useless. To obviate this difficulty, attend to the following hints. :—First, select a good-sized tree, the larger the better, perfectly clear of outside knots for fifty or sixty feet. The head should be luxuriant, and the large limbs drooping downwards. Peel off with your axe a stripe of bark as high as you can reach. If, on examination, the grain is the least inclined towards the sun, reject it. If, on the contrary, it curves slightly in the opposite direction, or against the sun, you may proceed to try it by cutting out a piece a foot long, and three or four inches deep. Place your axe in the centre, and split it open. Continue to do so till you have reduced the piece to the thickness of two shingles, which again divide neatly in the middle. If the timber is good and fit for your purpose, the pieces will fly apart with a sudden snap, and will be perfectly clear in the grain on both sides, while, if the timber be not good, the grain of the one piece will eat into the other, or run off without splitting clear the whole length of the block. The blocks should be cut eighteen inches long, and split into quarters, and the sap-wood dressed off. It is then ready for the frow—as the instrument used for splitting shingles is called. A good splitter will keep two men shaving and packing. The proper thickness is four to the inch : the packing-frame should be forty inches long, and contain fifty courses of shingles, which make a thousand. The price varies from five shillings to seven and sixpence, according to quality. The upper bar of the packing-frame should be wedged down very tightly across the centre of the bunch, which will keep them from warping with the sun.

ing with wheat, I discharged my two Irishmen, of whom I was very glad to be rid. I would advise new colonists never to employ men who have not been some time in Canada : it is much better to pay higher wages than to be troubled with fellows who know nothing about the work of the country. Besides, these persons, though accustomed to bad wages and food at home, actually expect better provisions and wages than men who thoroughly understand their business : take the following for a fair example.

One day, a stout able-bodied fellow, a fresh importation from the emerald isle, dressed in breeches open at the knees, long worsted stockings, rucked down to the ankles, and a great-coat with at least three capes, while a high-crowned black hat, the top of which opened and shut with every breeze like the lid of a basket, completed his costume—rather a curious one for July, with the thermometer above 80° in the shade—accosted me with—" Does yer honor want to hire a boy to-day ?"

He stood at least six feet in his stockings.

" What can you do, and what makes you wear that great coat this hot weather ?"

" Why, sure, yer honour, it 's a good un to keep out the heat, and I can do almost anything."

" Can you log, chop, or fence ?"

" No."

" Can you plough ? "

" No ; but I think I could soon larn."

" Can you mow or cradle wheat ?"

" I can mow a trifle, but I don't know what the other thing is at all, at all."

" Pray, then, what can you do ?"

" Well, then, yer honour, I am illigant at the spade entirely."

" What wages do you expect ?"

" Twelve dollars, sir, and my boord, if it be plasing to you."

" No, no, my good fellow ; I do not please to do any such thing, and I do not think any one else in his senses will, either. I think you had better apply for work to the road-contractors, who require a good deal of spade-labour, which I think is at present all you are fit for."

Upon returning to my shanty in the evening, I was surprised to find that my brother-in-law had just arrived with the intelligence of the birth of my first-born son, and the dangerous illness of my dear wife. Little hope was entertained of her recovery. My poor Emma had been safely delivered of a fine boy, and was supposed to be progressing favourably, when some alarming symptoms appeared which made it necessary to send immediately for me.

Long before dawn I was some miles upon my sad journey to Darlington. I had no horse. The way was long and toilsome; and I had had neither time for rest nor appetite for food. I loved my amiable and excellent wife with all the warmth of a youthful husband united to the object of his affections. I am very fond of little children, and the idea of having one of my own to pet and work for had given a stimulus to all my labours. My first-born seemed dearly purchased now at the cost of his poor mother's peril. Still, my ardent temperament led me to hope that my dear wife would be spared. Her loss seemed an event too dreadful to realize, for the boy-husband had had no experience in sorrow then, and his buoyant spirits had never anticipated the crushing blow that had already annihilated his visions of domestic happiness. Fifty-five miles lay between me and my suffering wife. The roads were heavy from the effects of the late rains, and I had the misfortune to lose my way, which added three miles to my long pedestrian journey. Once I overtook a cart containing a boy and girl, whom I vainly entreated to give me a ride. I told them the painful circumstances which induced me to solicit their aid; but the boy was over-cautious, and the girl unusually hard-hearted for one of her kind and compassionate sex. I could easily have compelled them to give me a seat, but for a sense of moral justice which would not permit me to take that by force which they denied to pity. My boyish indignation, I recollect, was so great that I could scarcely help throwing stones after my unkind fellow-travellers.

It was evening by the time I reached Darlington Mills, and I was still five miles from my father-in-law's house. It was quite dark, and I was so overpowered with my fifty miles' walk, that to proceed without refreshment and rest appeared then to be impossible. I stopped at the tavern and asked for some tea.

I had scarcely been seated two minutes before some men entered, in whose conversation I became immediately and deeply interested. They were discussing what to them was merely local news, but the question, " When is the funeral to take place? " riveted my attention at once.

Putting down the much-needed but untasted refreshment, I demanded of the speaker " Whose funeral?" My heart at once foretold from its inmost depths what the dreaded answer would be.

Yes, she in whom I had placed my earthly hopes of a life-long happiness was, indeed, no more. She was snatched away in the bright morning of her existence with the rapturous feelings of maternity just budding into life. I never knew how I got out of the house, or in what manner I performed the last five miles of the journey. But I remember that in the excitement of that hour I felt neither hunger, thirst, nor weariness. Sometimes I doubted the truth of what I had heard. Indeed, it seemed really too dreadful to be true.

On my arrival at my father-in-law's house, I found that the information I had accidentally heard was unfortunately a sad reality. My brother-in-law had not left Darlington an hour on his journey to Otonabee before my wife breathed her last. I had not even the consolation of bidding her a last adieu. Few can comprehend my feelings on this trying occasion, except those who have suffered under a similar bereavement. I was not yet twenty-one years of age. I was in a strange country—the tie severed between me and my only friends in a manner so afflicting and melancholy—all my hopes and future prospects in life dashed, as it were, to the ground. I had expended all my little capital in providing a com-

fortable home for her, who, alas! was doomed
never to behold it; and I had a little son to
bring up without the aid of my poor Emma,
whose piety and sweet temper would have been
so invaluable to our child.

A nurse was obtained for my poor motherless
babe, the babe over whom I shed so many tears—
a sad welcome, this, to as fine a boy as ever a
father's eye looked upon !

I followed the remains of my beloved wife to
the grave ; and then tarried for a month in that
house of sorrow. My only consolation was derived from my knowledge that Emma loved her
Saviour, and put her trust in him while passing
through the valley of the shadow of death.

> " How many hopes have sprung in radiance hence ;
>   Their trace yet lights the dust where thou art sleeping.
>   A solemn joy comes o'er me, and a sense
>   Of triumph blent with nature's gush of weeping."

I left my little son in the care of his Irish
nurse, and quitted my friend's house, with a
heavy heart, for my new settlement at Otonabee.

CHAPTER IX.

RETURN TO OTONABEE.—BENEVOLENCE OF MY NEIGHBOUR.—SERI-
OUS ACCIDENT TO A SETTLER. — HIS SINGULAR MISFORTUNES.—
PARTICULARS OF HIS LIFE.

I RETURNED in sadness to my lonely and desolate home, feeling like a shipwrecked mariner, cast upon a desert shore.   In fact, I had to begin life again, without the stimulus of domestic love to quicken my exertions.   I had left my land un-sown, and therefore the prospect of a crop of wheat for the next year's harvest was, I felt assured, entirely gone.   Upon reaching my clear-ing, I was surprised to find my fallow not only sown but showing the green blade, for some friendly hands had been at work for me in my absence, that pecuniary losses might not be added to my heavy domestic bereavement.

On inquiry, I found I was indebted to the considerate kindness of my excellent neighbour Mr. Reid and his sons, for this act of Christian benevolence.   I hurried to his house to thank

him for the important service he had rendered
one, to whom he was almost a stranger.   He considered, however, that he had done nothing more
than a neighbourly duty, and insisted that I
should take up my abode with him, instead of
returning to my unfinished and melancholy home.

My residence under his hospitable roof increased my esteem for his character, which my
long experience of six-and-twenty years has never
diminished.   Mrs. Reid treated me with maternal
kindness ; and in their amiable family-circle my
bruised heart recovered its peace, and my spirits
their healthy tone.   The kindly disposition of my
host in all his domestic relations, his cheerful
activity, pure morality, and unaffected piety, presented an admirable example to a young man
left without guidance in a distant colony.   But
I did not at that time think about becoming his
son-in-law, though I had been several months
domesticated in his family, till the alacrity displayed by his eldest daughter in hastening to the
assistance of a wounded neighbour, through the
unknown intricacies of a Canadian forest, led me
to consider her character in a new and endearing
point of view.

A Mr. G. and his family had just commenced a
settlement, about four miles east of Mr. Reid's

clearing, when, early one morning, his eldest son, a lad of twelve or thirteen, with a face full of trouble ran to tell us " that his father had nearly cut his foot off with an axe while chopping logs to build his house, that his mother could not stop the bleeding, and that they were afraid he would bleed to death."

Mr. Reid's eldest daughter immediately volunteered to return with the boy, to render what assistance she could. Without any thought of fatigue, or danger, or trial to her feelings, she set out instantly with the proper bandages. Mr. Reid, his sons, and myself were all chopping in the woods when the lad came, so that Mary followed the spontaneous impulse of her own heart ; but as soon as we heard what had happened, her father sent over the river for our nearest neighbour, a stout canny Scotchman, to assist us in carrying the wounded man through the woods to his (Mr. Reid's) house.

John Morison readily obeyed the summons ; and had we required any additional help we should have had no difficulty, in a case like this, of finding plenty of volunteers. The only road leading to Mr. G.'s was from the town, a mere bush-road, and full three miles farther than if we could go straight back through the woods.

As the number of his lot was the same as the one* we resided on, we knew that a direct east course would bring us within call of his clearing. It was, therefore, agreed that Mr. Reid's eldest son should endeavour, with a pocket compass, to run a line in the direction which we wanted to go, and that I should blaze† out the line with the axe, while the rest chopped out the under-brush and levelled the path sufficiently wide to allow the passage of a litter.

We had some difficulty in avoiding one or two small swamps and a high hill, but finally succeeded in finding a good line of road; and so accurate was our surveyor and engineer in this, his first attempt, that his line actually struck the

---

* Each concession is divided into two hundred acre lots, numbering from the boundary line from number one upwards. According to the new survey, the lots run nearly east and west; therefore, number one in the first concession will have a corresponding number west, across every concession in the township.

† Blazing is a term used by the backwoodsman for chopping off a portion of the bark from each side of a tree to mark a surveyor's line through the woods. All concession roads, or lot lines are marked in this manner; wherever a lot line strikes a concession, a short post with the number of the lot and concession is marked on each side of the post. If a tree comes directly on the line where the post should be planted, the tree is substituted. A blaze is made on each side, about three feet from the ground, and the numbers marked. I have frequently in the matter of disputed lines seen the surveyor cut the old blaze off, perhaps, of twenty years' growth, and discover the numbers perfect, although the wood had made such a growth over the original blaze.

little chopping* of not more than a quarter of an acre where poor G. lay.

It was past three o'clock in the afternoon before the road was completed and the litter made, the last being effected by cutting two iron-wood poles eight feet long, and fastening them together by broad straps of bass-wood bark three feet apart. A blanket, doubled, was then laid over these straps, upon which we placed the poor man, whose bleeding wound had been stopped with some difficulty.

It appeared that a small twig had caught the axe, which caused it to glance in its descent, and struck the instep of his right foot, making a gash about five inches long, the edge of the axe coming out at the sole of the foot. It was a dreadful cut, —one of the worst I ever saw—and I have seen and dressed a great many axe wounds since my residence in Canada.

Mr. G. was a very heavy man, and as *only* four persons could conveniently carry him at once, we found it very hard work. I was completely done up when we reached the house.

Mr. Reid and his family did everything in their

---

* This gentleman, John Reid, Esq. is now a deputy provincial surveyor and county engineer. As a land-surveyor there are few better in the province.

power to make him and his wife comfortable. Mr. Stewart, his brother-in-law, kindly sent for two of the children : the other two remained with their father and mother.

It was ten months before the poor invalid was able to leave his hospitable host, and resume his settlement in the bush. I mention this little circumstance to show what kindly feelings exist between the settlers, especially in cases of this kind. I shall also relate some remarkable passages in this poor man's life which present an almost unparalleled train of misfortune. I shall tell his dismal story, as nearly as possible, in his own words.

The experience of life proves to a certainty, that some persons are compelled to drink deeper of the cup of adversity than others, nay even to drain it to the dregs.

We know that the Jews of old and the heathen world still suppose that such are visited for their sins by the judgment of Heaven ; but the Divine Teacher has taught us better things, and warned us against such rash conclusions, instructing us indeed that

> " There surely is some guardian power
>   That rightly suffers wrong ;
> Gives vice to bloom its little hour,
>   But virtue late and long."

Poor G. was one of these unfortunate persons, whose melancholy history I will now relate, in his own words.—He was, it seems, a native of Ireland, from which country he emigrated soon after the last American war, with his wife and two children, leaving three other children at home with his father and mother, who were the proprietors of a small estate in the county of Cork. He arrived safely with his family at the Big Bay in Whitby (Windsor,) and purchased a lot of land close to the lake-shore.

In those days, the emigrant's trials were indeed hard, compared with what they are now. The country was quite unsettled, excepting that here and there the nucleus of a small village appeared to vary its loneliness, for the clearings were mostly confined to the vicinity of the Great Lake. There were no plank, gravel, or macadamized roads then ; saw and grist-mills were few-and-far-between. It was no uncommon thing then for a farmer to go thirty or forty miles to mill, which cause indeed sometimes detained him a whole week from his family ; and, even more, if any accident had happened to the machinery. Besides this inconvenience, he had to encounter risks for himself and his cattle,—from bad bridges, deep mud-holes, and many other annoyances—I might say, with truth, "too numerous to mention." The few farms in that neighbourhood were then chiefly occupied by Americans, some of whom had found it highly desirable to expatriate themselves ; and might have exclaimed with the celebrated pick-pocket, Barrington, in a prologue spoken to a convict-audience in New South Wales, —

> " Friends, be it understood,
>   We left our country for our country's good."

I have no intention of reflecting here on the national honour of the American nation ; but it is a well-known fact, that many of the early frontier settlers were persons who had evaded the payment of their just debts or, perhaps, legal penalties for worse offences, by crossing the lines, and forming settlements in Canada. Such persons are not a fair specimen of American character. Individually, I have nothing to say against the Americans, but rather the contrary, for I have found them good and obliging neighbours.

I have heard it generally asserted, that the Yankees are the greatest rogues under the sun. If *smartness* in trading, or barter, be roguery, they richly deserve the epithet ; but I deny that their intentions are one whit more dishonest than those of the persons with whom they trade. That their natural shrewdness and general knowledge give them an advantage, I am quite ready to admit ; and perhaps they are not over-scrupulous in exercising it to the discomfiture of their less-gifted neighbours.

Unfortunately, Mr. G. purchased his land of a squatter, who had no title himself, and consequently could give none to the purchaser, who, after three or four years of hard labour upon it— when he had fondly hoped he had surmounted the greatest difficulties—found that the Government had issued a deed for the benefit of another person before he came into possession, who could not be induced to give up his legal rights to the unfortunate cultivator. He was so disheartened by this occurrence, that he determined to sell all he had and leave the country, which resolution he put into immediate execution.

He took a passage for himself and family in a ship, timber-laden, from Quebec, bound for Liverpool. It was late in the fall : the vessel was one of the last that sailed ; consequently, they experienced very rough weather, accompanied with snow and sleet. Mid-way across the Atlantic, they encountered a dreadful storm, which left the ship a mere wreck on the ocean. To add to their misfortunes, a plank had started, owing, it was supposed, to the shifting of some part of the cargo during the gale; and so quickly did the vessel fill, that they only saved two eight-pound pieces of salt pork and a few biscuits.

"I had," he said, "also in my pocket, a paper containing two or three ounces of cream of tartar. Luckily, a cask of water, lashed on deck, was providentially preserved, amidst the general destruction.

"Our ship's company consisted of the captain, mate, and six seamen, besides a medical man, myself, my poor wife, and two children, who were cabin passengers. We made several unsuccessful attempts to procure a supply of provisions; consequently, it became absolutely necessary to give out what we had in the smallest possible rations.

"The fourth night was ushered in by another storm, more terrific even than the last. A heavy sea struck the vessel, sweeping overboard the captain and three seamen; and the poor doctor's leg was broken at the same time, by a loose spar.

"We passed a fearful night; nor did the morning add to our comfort, for my daughter died from exposure and want, just as the day dawned.

"On the seventh morning, the doctor, who had suffered the greatest agony from his swollen leg, sank at last ; the paper of cream of tartar I had in my pocket being the only relief for his dreadful fever, during his misery. My poor wife and remaining child soon followed. We now had fine dry weather, which was some relief to our intolerable misery.

"On the twentieth day, the last of our provisions was consumed. I had an old pair of deer-skin mocassins on my feet : these we carefully divided amongst us. We had now serious thoughts of drawing lots, to see which of us should die, for the preservation of the rest. I, however, begged they would defer such a dreadful alternative to the latest minute.

"On the twenty-first night of our disaster, I had a most remarkable dream : I thought I saw a fine ship bearing down to our assistance, and that she was called " The London of London." I related my dream to my companions, in hopes it might raise their spirits, which, however, it failed to do ; for nothing was to be seen on that dreary waste of water, though we scanned the horizon in every direction. For upwards of two hours after, we scarcely spoke a word, when suddenly the sun, which had been obscured all the morning, shone out brightly and warm for the season of the year. I mechanically raised myself and looked over the bulwarks, when, to my astonishment and delight, I beheld a ship, the very counterpart of the one I had seen in my dream, bearing down directly for the wreck.

" It is not easy to describe our various feelings on this occasion : we could scarcely believe our senses when the boat came along side. We were so reduced by famine and exposure, that we had to be lifted into her. In this state of exhaustion every attention was paid us by the humane captain and crew.

" As soon as I was on board, I asked the name of the vessel, when I was surprised to find she was called the ' Portaferry of Portaferry.' Although the name was not that borne by the vessel of which I had dreamed, it must be considered at least a remarkable coincidence.

" Great care was taken to prevent us eating too ravenously at first : we received every kindness our weak condition required ; but, notwithstanding these precautions, two of my companions in misery died before we reached Ireland.

" When we arrived at Strangford, in the north of Ireland, I was entirely destitute—I had lost everything I possessed. Fortunately for me, I belonged to the honourable fraternity of Free and Accepted Masons, who kindly furnished me with clothing, and money sufficient to take me home, which I reached in safety.

" Like almost every person who has resided a few years in Canada, I found it impossible to content myself at home ; and, although I had no great reason to be fond of the country on account of the treatment I had experienced, still, there is that indescribable charm in the free life of a Canadian settler, which is wanting in a more civilized country : I, therefore, determined once more to try my fortune.

" I accordingly embarked with the young wife I had lately married, and the three children I had formerly left in Ireland with my parents. We sailed early in the spring of 1825. My ill luck still attended me ; for owing to the dense fogs we experienced on the banks of Newfoundland, we got out of our course, and our ship struck the shore near Cape Ray : fortunately the sea was smooth and the weather fine : so that when daylight broke we were able, without much difficulty, to be landed on that most inhospitable shore,

"Where the bones of many a tall ship lie buried."

"We saved little or nothing from the wreck; for, as the day advanced, the wind freshened into a gale, which blowing on shore, soon settled the fate of our gallant bark. The shore was soon strewn with casks, bales, and packages, some of which we were able to secure. Our captain chartered a small fishing-vessel, which landed us at last safely at Quebec. And now, you see, after enduring almost unheard-of sufferings, I am again prostrated by this unfortunate accident."

Such was the account given me by Mr. G——, who put into my hand, at the same time, an old Belfast newspaper, containing the account of his first wreck and sufferings. So I have no reason to doubt the entire truth of his statement.

After his foot healed he returned to his land, and, with the assistance of his family, cleared up a large farm. His location, however, was not well chosen; and, consequently, he was not a thriving settler. He, however, managed to bring up a large family, who are now sufficiently independent of him to maintain themselves and families comfortably.

On his father's death, about three years since, he returned with his wife to Ireland, where I believe he intends to pass the remainder of his days.

I'wish to make one remark before closing this chapter : does it not speak well for Canada, when a person, who was neither an active nor a clever person, and who had suffered almost unheard-of misfortunes, was still able to gain a living and see his family settled in comparative comfort ? Under such circumstances, what would have been the fate of these people in England or Ireland ? —Abject pauperism.

CHAPTER X.

PREPARATIONS FOR MY SECOND MARRIAGE. — DANGEROUS ADVEN-
TURE. — MY WIFE'S NOCTURNAL VISITOR.—WE PREPARE FOR
THE RECEPTION OF OUR UNINVITED GUEST. — BRUIN'S UNWEL-
COME VISIT TO AN IRISH SHANTY.—OUR BEAR-HUNT.—MAJOR
ELLIOTT'S DUEL WITH BRUIN.—HIS WOUNDS AND VICTORY.

I SPENT the spring of 1827 very pleasantly in
the company of my new friends. I used to go
down to my farm every morning, and return in
the evening to a cheerful fire-side and agreeable
society, which rewarded me for the toils of the
day. I had fenced in my fields, planted my
spring crops, Indian corn, and potatoes, which
looked promising ; and I had my house nearly
finished. I, therefore, considered it was time I
should go and reside in it, and not trespass
any longer on the hospitality of my kind and
generous friends. As, however, I did not like
the thought of living the life of a hermit,
and my little boy, for whom I had sent, was
weaned, and growing healthy and lovely under
the kind hospitality of my friends, required now a

watchful parental care, I proposed to, and was accepted by, my friend's eldest daughter, in whom I found what I sought—a faithful mother for my child, and the most devoted and affectionate wife for myself. A better woman, indeed, never existed. For upwards of twenty-two years she shared my various fortunes, and formed my greatest earthly blessing.   A few days before my marriage—an event to which I naturally looked forward for an increase of happiness — an accident occurred, which might have been attended with fatal results to myself, and actually was so to a lad who was in my service.   A kind Providence, however, watched over my life, and delivered me from this danger.

My farm was situated on the east shore of the Otonabee river, the town of Peterborough being on the west of that line; and there was no bridge communication between us and that place, so that we were obliged to cross in skiffs, canoes, or any other craft we could get.   When the river is flooded in the spring, it is dangerous for persons crossing, unless they are well acquainted with the management of a canoe. Several fatal accidents have indeed happened to the inexperienced at that time of the year, from this cause. Such was the state of the river, when I had to cross it to reach the store,

where I wanted to purchase some articles for my
intended marriage.   The stream was then at its
greatest height, running with extreme rapidity,
and I had, to contend with its force, only a small
log-canoe, about twelve feet in length, by thirty
inches at its greatest breadth, in which three of
us ventured upon the turbid water, namely,
John Fontaine, a French boy; Michael Walsh,
and myself.   We crossed a little above the new
mill-dam, which had been constructed at the
expense of the Government for the Irish emigration, and we managed to get over pretty well.
Not so, however, on our return.   I was near the
middle of the canoe, with a pair of small oars,
one of the boys at each end, and all seated at the
bottom for greater security.   In this manner we
got over the main channel ; but owing to the
swiftness of the current, we were carried down
much nearer the dam than we intended.   This
alarmed the boys a good deal.   I begged them to
sit still, assuring them I should be able to fetch
the canoe into an eddy a little lower down the
stream.   We were at this time close to an island,
which was deeply flooded, owing to the raising of
the water by the construction of the dam.   From
the point of this sunken island, a cedar tree had
fallen into the river.   It was therefore necessary

that we should drop below this, before we could make the eddy. In the act of passing, the boy Walsh—I suppose from fright—caught hold of the tree, which caused the canoe to swing round broadside to the current, and it instantly filled and upset.

A large quantity of timber had been cut on the island, for the use of the mill and dam. The workmen had piled the tops and limbs of these trees in large heaps, which now floated above the surface of the island. To one of these I immediately swam, and succeeded in getting upon it. I then perceived that Walsh had been swept from the tree to which he had clung, by the force of the current, into the middle of the river, and close to the edge of the falls. I saw at a glance, that his only chance was to swim for the opposite side, which I called on him to do, but he appeared to have lost all self-possession ; for he neither swam for one shore nor the other, but kept his head facing up the stream, uttering wild cries, which, in a few seconds, were silenced for ever.

In the meantime, John Fontaine, the French boy, had succeeded in getting partly across the canoe, which was floating past the heap on which I had taken refuge, and only a few yards from where I was standing. I immediately plucked a

long stick from the brush-heap, and swam near
enough to the lad for him to grasp one end of the
pole, bidding him leave the canoe, which I told
him would be carried over the dam to a certainty,
and him with it, if he did not abandon his hold. He,
with apparent reluctance, followed my directions,
but I had a hard struggle to regain my former place
of refuge, with the boy's additional weight. I
had some trouble to persuade him to trust himself
again in the water. And no wonder; for darkness
was fast approaching, and both the island and a
narrow channel of the river had still to be crossed.
However, trusting to the mercy of God, we again
committed ourselves to those wild, swollen waters,
which, by the providence of the Almighty, we
successfully accomplished. I was obliged to hold
the stick between my teeth whilst crossing the
channel, drawing along with me my terrified companion, it being necessary for our preservation,
that I should have the free use of both my arms.
I had on at the time a velveteen shooting coat,
the large pockets of which were filled with things
I had just purchased from the store ; among which
I remember there was a dozen cups and saucers,
which added no inconsiderable weight to the
swimmer.

As soon as we made the shore, we ran down to

the falls, to see if we could hear anything of the poor boy. We shouted, for it was now quite dark, but all in vain; indeed, I had not the slightest hope, as I had seen him carried backwards over the dam into the boiling rapids below, where the best swimmer would not have had the least chance. We failed to discover his remains then, but found his mangled body six days afterwards in a small lake, a mile and a half below the dam.

I was much concerned at the fate of my poor young servant, but felt deeply grateful for my own preservation and that of Fontaine.

A few weeks after my marriage, I was detained one night from home by business, leaving my wife, her little sister, and a small dog, called Suffolk— so named by me in honour of my native county— the sole occupiers of my house, of which the kitchen was still in an unfinished state, part of the floor only being laid. We, however, had to make use of it, until I could procure more boards to finish it, which, in those days, were not very easy to obtain.

In the middle of the night, my wife and her sister were awakened and dreadfully alarmed by a terrible noise in the kitchen, accompanied by the sharp barking of the little dog. They were quite sure by the low growls and the fury of Suffolk, that it was some wild animal, but whether a bear or wolf they could not tell. Towards morning, this unwelcome visitor took himself off, to their infinite joy. When I came home, they told me the story, at which I laughed very heartily, for I thought their fears had magnified the visit of some neighbour's dog into a bear, or some other wild beast ; but they appeared unconvinced, being both frightened and positive. My wife declared, that in the morning she found some of the salt-pork had been abstracted from the barrel, which stood in one corner of the kitchen, by the savage guest.

Now, I knew very well that master Bruin was fond of fresh pork, and I thought it possible that he might think the salt an improvement. At all events, I resolved to be prepared, in case he should pay us a second visit. Accordingly, before going to bed, I loaded my gun with ball, and tied Suffolk up in the vicinity of the pork-barrel. At midnight we were suddenly awakened by the piteous howlings of the poor dog, and by a noise, as if everything in the room had been violently thrown down. I jumped out of bed instantly, and seizing my gun, crept cautiously along the passage, till I came to the kitchen-door, which

I threw open, whereupon some large dark-looking object made a rush for the unfinished part of the floor. I immediately fired; but it was so dark, and the beast so quick in its movements, that I had little chance of hitting him. Whether or not, it had the effect of scaring him so much that he never resumed his nocturnal visitation. Indeed, I stopped his supplies from my larder by finishing the floor and building up the hole between the lower log of the house and the ground.

But to return to my story. As soon as the beast had made his exit, we lighted a candle and examined the room, which we found in confusion and disorder. The barrel of pork was upset and the brine running in miniature rivers over the floor, while poor little Suffolk was bleeding from his wounds—indeed nearly killed. From what I could make out of the footprints outside I am inclined to think my unwelcome visiter was a bear; but this, of course, will for ever remain a mystery.

I have heard many stories of their boldness, to some instances of which I have been an eye-witness. Not very long after the occurrence I have just related, the wife of an Irish emigrant saw a large bear walking very deliberately towards the shanty, which no doubt he mistook for a pigsty, and the inmates for pigs, for they were quite as dirty, therefore it was no great mistake, after all. The woman and her three children had barely time to get into the potato-cellar and shut down the trap-door, when his bear-ship made his forcible entrance through the feeble barrier the door opposed to his strength, much to the dismay and terror of the subterranean lodgers, who lay shaking and quaking for more than an hour, till the dying screams of their fatted pig told them he was after game of a more savoury nature.

In the fall of the year it is no uncommon thing for farmers to have their pigs killed by the bears, particularly in the new settlements.

Bears are, we know, very fond of good things. They are epicures in their way. They like honey, and love pork, and, you may be sure, often pay the settler a visit for the sake of his pigs. As Bruin makes very good eating himself, these visitations are sometimes made at the risk of his own bacon ; his warm jacket, which makes comfortable robes for the settler's sleigh, keeping him warm during his journeys on pleasure or business throughout the long Canadian winters.

One day, I was assisting my father-in-law and his sons in logging up his fallow, when we heard a great outcry among the pigs in a belt of woods between Mr. Reid's and Mr. Stewart's clearing, when, suspecting it was a bear attacking the swine, we ran for our guns, and made the best of our way towards the spot from whence the outcry proceeded.

Near the edge of the clearing we met Mr. B——, who was on a visit to his friend and relative Mr. Stewart, driving before him Mr. Reid's sow, which he had just rescued from the grip of an immense bear, that, alarmed by his shouts, dropped his prey and made off in the direction of a small cedar-swamp. We immediately proposed surrounding the place, as there were three of us provided with double-barrelled guns. Mr. B—— took up his station behind a large tree, close to where a small creek ran into the swamp. My brother-in-law John and myself went round to the opposite side, which we entered a few yards apart. We had not proceeded far, when an enormous brute popped up his head from behind some fallen logs and brush, for we had disturbed him in the act of devouring a pig. We both fired at the same instant, but apparently without effect; for he scampered off, passing within a few feet of where

B—— was hid, who fired only one of his barrels, reserving his second in case the bear should turn on him. We ran as fast as we could to the river, for we knew he had gone in that direction. Indeed, Bruin took to the water in fine style, swimming across gallantly. Before we could get another shot at him he had gained the opposite bank. There we gave him a second volley, which did not appear in the least to retard his ascent, so we concluded that it was a regular miss all round. B—— maintained, however, that he had hit him, and wanted us to cross the river and follow the track. We only laughed at him for not firing his second shot, and returned home very much crestfallen at the ill success of our expedition.

Had we but complied with B——'s wish, we should have found our hunt had been more successful than we imagined, for eight or ten days afterwards John Morison was going on the opposite side of the river to Peterborough, when, upon crossing a small creek, he came quite unexpectedly on the carcass of a large bear, not thirty yards from the bank we had seen him climb. No doubt B——'s shot was the fatal one, as he was not more than five or six yards from him when he fired. The stream, where the beast was found, is in the township of Smith, about a mile and a half from

Peterborough, on the river road, and is well-known by the name of Bear Creek to this day.

There is very little danger of being attacked by Bruin, unless you first molest him. An old she-bear, with cubs, is the most dangerous customer to meddle with.

Major Elliott, of the Canadian Militia, a gentleman with whom I was well acquainted, residing near Rice Lake, in the township of Monaghan, was out one day in the woods partridge-shooting, near the big swamp on the boundary line between Monaghan and Cavan, when he fell in with several old bears and their cubs. He had only one ball with him which he fired at the biggest fellow he could see among them, and wounded him very severely, though not enough to stop him from following his companions. But Elliott was not the man to be baulked without an effort to capture his wounded adversary ; so, being in want of a ball, he cut off from his waistcoat some open-work brass buttons, with which he loaded his gun, and followed the track of the wounded bear, which he soon overtook.

Bruin, however, being possessed of considerable pluck, immediately faced about and attacked the major, who gave him a taste of the buttons, as he advanced. But the bear, nothing daunted, returned to the charge, which Elliott met with a blow from the butt-end of his gun, that was instantly struck from his hand by his formidable antagonist, who immediately closed with him. It now became a regular stand-up fight between Major Elliott and Ursus Major. For a long time it was doubtful which would come off victorious. Elliott was severely wounded about the breast and arms ; notwithstanding which, he boldly maintained his ground, and ultimately succeeded in rolling the beast over the trunk of a large pine tree which lay on the ground beside them. Bruin was too much exhausted to climb over the tree, to renew the combat.

Luckily, Elliott received no internal injury, though his flesh was severely lacerated in the contest, which only ended with the bear's life. Ireland, indeed, never sent from her shores a bolder hunter, braver man, or more active backwoodsman, than Major Elliott.*

* This gentleman was afterwards returned as Member of the Provincial Parliament for the county of Durham.

CHAPTER XI.

CANADA THE POOR MAN'S COUNTRY. — DISADVANTAGES OF INEX-
PERIENCE.—TOWNSHIP OF HARVEY SETTLEMENT.— PAUPER EMI-
GRATION.—SUPERIOR ADVANTAGES OF THE LABOURER COLONIST.
— TEMPERANCE AND TEMPERANCE SOCIETIES. — A DRY ANSWER
TO WATERY ARGUMENTS. — BRITISH AND FOREIGN TEMPERANCE
SOCIETY.

THERE is no colony belonging to the British
Crown better adapted for the poor industrious
emigrant than the Canadas, particularly the Upper
Province, which is essentially the poor man's
country. Twenty-five years ago, the expense of
the voyage out to Quebec, and the difficulty,
delay, and additional outlay of the inland
journey put it completely out of the power of
the needy agriculturist or artizan to emigrate;
the very classes, however, who, from their having
been brought up from their infancy to hard labour, and used to all sorts of privations, were the
best fitted to cope with the dangers and hardships attending the settlement of a new country.
The impossibility of the working hand raising
funds for emigration, confined the colonists to a

set of men less calculated to contend with difficulties—namely, half-pay officers and gentlemen
of better family than income, who were almost
invariably the pioneers of every new settlement.

Many high-spirited gentlemen were, doubtless,
tempted by the grants of land bestowed upon
them by the Government, which made actual
settlement one of the conditions of the grant.
It followed, as a matter of course, that the majority of these persons were physically disqualified
for such an undertaking, a fact which many deserted farms in the rear townships of the county
in which I reside painfully indicate.

Eighteen or twenty years ago a number of
gentlemen located themselves in the township of
Harvey. The spot chosen by them was one of
great natural beauty ; but it possessed no other
advantages, except an abundance of game, which
was no small inducement to them. They spent
several thousand pounds in building fancy log-
houses and making large clearings which they
had neither the ability nor industry to cultivate.
But, even if they had possessed sufficient perseverance, their great distance from a market, bad
roads, want of knowledge in cropping after they
had cleared the land, lack of bridges, and
poor soil, would have been a great drawback

to the chance of effecting a prosperous settlement. In a few years not a settler remained of this little colony. Some stayed till their means were thoroughly exhausted; others, more wise, purchased ready-cleared farms in the settlements, or followed some profession more congenial to their taste, or more suited to their abilities.

The only persons fit to undertake the hardships of a bush-life, are those who have obtained a certain degree of experience in their own country upon the paternal estate or farm. Men who have large families to provide for, and who have been successful in wood-clearing, are generally willing to sell their improvements, and purchase wild land for their families, whose united industry soon places them in a better farm than they owned before. They are thus rendered greater capitalists, with increased means of providing for their children, who soon take up their standing in society as its favoured class. Indeed, I would strongly advise gentlemen of small capital to purchase ready-cleared farms, which can be obtained in most parts of the country, with almost every convenience, for half what the clearing of bush-land would cost, especially by an inexperienced settler. In fact, since grants of land are no longer given to the emigrant, there is less inducement to go so far back into the woods.

Since 1826, a steady influx of the working classes from Great Britain and Ireland has taken place. This has tended much to the prosperity of the country, by cheapening labour, and the settlement of vast tracts of wild land.

Several experiments have been made by Government in sending out pauper emigration : that from the south of Ireland, under the superintendance of the late Hon. Peter Robinson in 1824, was the most extensive, and came more immediately under my own observation. I have understood that some most obnoxious and dangerous characters were shipped off in this expedition—no doubt to the great comfort of landlords, agents, and tithe-proctors.

The Government behaved very liberally to these settlers. A grant of a hundred acres of good land was given to each head of a family, and to every son above twenty-one years of age.

A good milch cow, and rations of pork and flour were assigned to each emigrant family. These provisions they continued to receive for upwards of eighteen months, besides a variety of stores, such as axes, hammers, saws, nails, grindstones,

&c. A good log-shanty was also built on each settler's lot. These people have done as well as could be expected, considering the material of which they were composed. It has been observed that, whenever these people were located amongst the Protestant population, they made much better settlers than when remaining with Catholics.

In fact, a great improvement is perceptible in the morality, industry and education of the rising generation, who grow up more virtuous and less bigoted to their exclusive religious opinions.

As a general rule, the English, Scotch, and north of Ireland men make much better and more independent colonists than emigrants from the south of Ireland.

Seven years after the location of Robinson's emigrants, a colony of Wiltshire people settled in the township of Dummer under many more disadvantages than those placed by Government in the township of Douro.

The Dummer people had no shanties built for them, no cows, and were given much worse land; and yet they have done much more in a shorter time. An air of comfort and cleanliness pervades their dwellings, and there is a neatness about their farms and homesteads which is generally wanted in the former.

It must, however, be borne in mind that paupers sent out by the Government, or by their own parishes, are not a fair specimen by which to judge the working classes, who emigrated at their own expense. Of the latter, I know hundreds who, upon their arrival in the Upper Province, had spent their last shilling, and who, by persevering industry, are now worth hundreds of pounds. No person need starve in Canada, where there is plenty of work and good wages for every man who is willing to labour, and who keeps himself sober. The working man with a family of grown children, when fairly established on his farm, is fully on a par, as regards his prospects, with the gentleman, the owner of a similar farm, and possessing an income of 100*l.* per annum. The reason is obvious. The gentleman and his family have been used to wear finer clothes, keep better company, and maintain a more respectable appearance, and if he has children, to give them a more expensive education.

Then, again, the gentleman and his family are physically less qualified to undergo the hardships and toil of a practical farmer's life. On the other hand, the working man thinks it no degradation to send his sons and daughters out to service, and the united product of their wages amount, probably to eight or ten pounds per month. He is contented with home-spun cloth, while the spinning and knitting—and sometimes weaving—required by the family, are done at home. Labour, indeed, is money ; and hence in a few years the gentleman with his income is soon distanced, and the working hand becomes the man of wealth, while his children eventually form a part of the aristocracy of the country, if the father gives them a suitable education.

There is one thing, however, to be said in favour of the gentleman—namely, his education, which fits him for offices and professions which must remain for ever out of the reach of the half-ignorant. It is, therefore, only in agricultural pursuits, and mechanical operations, that the working man is able to obtain a superiority ; and then only if he be sober and industrious, for whiskey has been the great bane of the colony. Hundreds of our cleverest mechanics, and many of gentler blood, have fallen victims to its influence.

It is said that temperance societies have done a great deal towards checking this evil, and that the new society, the " Sons of Temperance," will complete what the others began. I am quite willing to admit it as a fact, because I believe that the practice of temperance has gained ground, both in Canada and the United States. But I am unwilling to allow that the means taken to effect that much-desired object are the best that might be adopted. Indeed, I think, in some instances, the endeavour to prohibit the use of fermented drink altogether, has been carried to unchristian lengths.

I believe that, if the same amount of money had been expended in propagating the gospel, as has been laid out by these total abstinence societies, more real converts to temperance would have been gained, because principle and true religion would have been the bases on which the reformation was founded.

Throughout the whole Bible and Testament, there is not a single command to abstain totally from either wine or strong drink ; but there is a positive one respecting the abuse, and dreadful denunciations against the drunkard. Then in respect to the prohibition, the false prophet has, in the Koran, forbidden his followers to use wine at all. Now, which do we profess to follow, —the precepts of Jesus Christ, or those of Mahomet ? But some will say, if your brother offends by his intemperate habits, you should abstain altogether, that you may become a good example to him. By the same rule, if my brother is a glutton, I should abstain from food also. Now, I believe with the Apostle, " that all the creatures of God are good," and lawful for us to use; but we are not to abuse them, " but to be temperate in all things," thus acting up to the rule of scripture, and setting a better example than if we wholly abstained from fermented drink. Any other rule, excepting in cases of notorious drunkenness, is, in my opinion, anti-scriptural, and therefore wrong.

The new American society, " The Sons of Temperance," which now takes the lead of all other temperance or tee-total societies, is a secret and benefit society, having its signs and pass-words. In the hands of clever leaders, and designing men, may not a society of this kind become a great political engine ?

Sometimes very ludicrous scenes occur at temperance meetings. A few years ago, when this question was first agitated in Canada, a meeting was held in a school-house on the English line, in the township of Dummer. The lecturer, on that occasion, was an itinerant preacher of the Methodist persuasion. After descanting some time in a very fluent manner, on the evils arising from intemperance, and the great numbers who had lost their lives by violent means, "for my part," said the lecturer, "I have known nearly three hundred cases of this kind myself."

This broad assertion was too much for one of the audience, an old Wiltshire man, who exclaimed, in his peculiar dialect, "Now, I know that 'ere be a lie. Can you swear that you did ever see three out of them three hundred violent deaths you speak on?"

"Well, I have heard and read of them in books and newspapers; and I once saw a man lying dead on the road, and a jar, half full of whiskey, beside him, which, I think, you will allow is proof enough."

"I thought your three hundred cases would turn out like the boy's cats in his grandmother's garden. Now, I will tell thee, that I did know three men that did kill themselves by drinking of cold water. There was John H——, that overheated hisself, walking from Cobourg, and drank so much water at the cold springs, that he fell down and died in a few minutes. Then there was that workman of Elliott's, in Smith, who dropped in the harvest-field, from the same cause; and the Irishman from Asphodel, whose name I forget. So, you see, that more people do die from drinking cold water than whiskey." Then he turned round to a neighbour, who, like himself, was not over-fond of cold water, and said, " I say, Jerome, which would you rather have, a glass of cold water, or a drap of good beer ?"

" I know which I would take," exclaimed Jerome ; "I would like a drap of good beer best, I do know."

This dialogue raised such a laugh against the apostle of temperance, that the meeting was fairly broken up, leaving the Wiltshire man triumphing in his victory over cold water and oratory, in the person of the lecturer. The dryness of his arguments prevailed against the refreshing and copious draughts of the pure element recommended by his discomfited opponent.

A good joke is not, however, a good argument, though it stood for one at this meeting. Total abstinence is the best plan to be adopted by habitual drunkards, who, if they can get at strong drink at all, seldom keep their pledge of sobriety. The British and Foreign Temperance Society, in fact, advises the habitually intemperate to abstain altogether, while, at the same time, it aims at bringing the man to repentance and reformation, by the renovating influence of the gospel. If I differ in some respects from that society, in its prohibition against the use of spirits altogether, in such a climate as Canada, I still must consider its views far more liberal, and more consistent with scripture rules, than that of any other for the promotion of temperance, as, indeed, possessing more of that charity, without which even the most fervent zeal is worse than useless.

CHAPTER XII.

WANT OF HOME-PASTURAGE IN CANADA.—DANGER OF BEING LOST
IN THE WOODS.—PLAIN DIRECTIONS TO THE TRAVELLER IN THE
BUSH.—STORY OF A SETTLER FROM EMILY.—AN OLD WOMAN'S
RAMBLE IN THE WOODS. — ADVENTURE OF A TRAPPER. —
FORTUNATE MEETING WITH HIS PARTNER.

ONE of the greatest inconveniences belonging
to a new settlement, for the first four or five
years, is the want of pasturage for your working
cattle and cows. Consequently, the farmer has to
depend entirely on the Bush for their support, for
at least seven months out of the twelve. The
inconvenience does not arise from any want of
food; for the woods, beaver meadows, and the
margins of lakes and streams yield an abundance,
and the cattle, towards the fall of the year, are
sure to grow fat. But it is the trouble of seeking
for your cattle.

Sometimes, indeed, in the midst of your greatest hurry, your oxen are nowhere to be found. I
have myself often spent two or three days in succession, searching the woods in vain; and it

not unfrequently happens that, while looking for the strayed beasts, you lose yourself in the woods.

As we generally carry a gun with us in these excursions, we often fall in with deer or partridges, which makes the way not only seem less fatiguing, but even pleasant, unless during the season of musquitoes and black flies, when rambling through the Bush is no pleasure to any one.

New-comers are very apt to lose themselves at first, until they get acquainted with the creeks and ridges ; and even then, on a dark day or during a snow-storm, they are very likely to go astray. If you have no compass with you, and the sun is obscured, the best way of extricating yourself is, to observe the moss on the trees, which —not every one knows—grows more luxuriantly and in greater quantities on the north side of the tree. It is of little use to look at any tree separately : this will perhaps only mislead you ; but if you observe the general aspect of the woods around, the indications may be of great service to you. Towards the north, the trunks of the trees will appear light and cheerful, while the south side will look dark and spotted. This plan, however, will only answer amongst hard woods.* The ridges mostly run north-east and

* Deciduous trees are called hard-wood.

south-west, and the swamps parallel with them, Then, again, in pine woods the general inclination of the timber is from the north-west. All these indications have been successfully followed, and should be borne in mind.

People who lose themselves in the Bush seldom persevere long enough in any one direction. They fancy they are going wrong, and keep changing their course ; till probably, after four or five hours' walking, they find themselves near the spot from whence they started. This has occurred to me more than once, and I shall relate a melancholy incident which happened only a few years ago, and which proves what I have just stated.

The person to whom I allude, resided in the township of Emily, and had been all the summer working at his trade in the village of Bowmanville, to earn money sufficient to pay for his land, which he had succeeded by the fall in doing. As the cold weather had set in, he determined to return home, and chop all the winter on his farm. He knew that by crossing the township of Darlington and Manvers in an oblique direction, twenty-five or six miles in length, he could reach his own house in half the time, the distance by the road being more than double that by which he proposed to travel. He therefore determined to try the short way, although he was well aware that the last eight or ten miles of his road was through the Bush, with not even a blazed line to guide him. He was, however, young and active, and moreover considered himself a good backwoodsman. He started one fine frosty morning early in December, expecting he should be able to reach his own house sometime before sundown.

For the first ten or twelve miles he got on pretty well, as he had a sleigh-track to follow, and as long as the sun shone out he made a good course. Unfortunately for him, a snow-storm came on and obscured his only guide. He, however, struggled on manfully through cedar-swamps and over ridges, with the snow half-way up to his knees, till the approach of darkness compelled him to look out for some place to shelter him from the storm, where he might best pass the weary hours of the coming night.

He selected a dry spot beneath some spreading cedars, and busied himself as long as daylight lasted in collecting as much fire-wood as would last till the morning. He then gathered a quantity of hemlock-brush for his bed, and by breaking off some large limbs from the surrounding evergreens, succeeded at last in forming a temporary shelter. For a long time he despaired of getting a fire, till he at length found some dry cedar-bark, which he finally succeeded in igniting with a piece of punk,* which every backwoodsman carries with him for that purpose. Though the poor fellow had only taken with him provisions for a day's journey, he made a hearty supper, merely reserving a portion for his breakfast, not suspecting that he should fail in reaching his destination. He fully expected he should see the sun in the morning, which would enable him to correct this course; for he knew that he was in the township of Manvers, and not more than seven or eight miles from his own home.

Wearied with his day's journey, he slept the greater part of the night, although awakened occasionally by the cold. At such times he would heap fresh fuel on the fire, and again compose himself to sleep.

To his infinite joy the morning beamed brightly—the sun shone out. With a light heart and renewed confidence he again shaped his course eastward, following the direction in which his house lay ; and there is no doubt, had the day remained clear, he would in a few hours have

* A substance obtained from the sugar-maple, similar to German tinder.

extricated himself from the dilemma into which he had fallen. His disappointment was great when he again beheld the sky overcast, and the snow falling thickly around him. He pushed on, however, bravely, till at length a thick cedar-swamp lay before him. For some time he travelled along its edge, in the hope of finding a narrow spot to cross, but in this he was disappointed, so he determined to attempt the passage. He fully believed, once on the other side, he should know the face of the country, from his having so often hunted game, or searched for his cattle in that direction.

For fully an hour he presssd on through a complete thicket of cedar ; but it was all random work, for the evergreens were so loaded with snow, that it was quite impossible to go one hundred yards in a straight course. At last he saw the tops of hard-wood trees before him, which again revived his sinking spirits, for he thought he had crossed the swamp. Alas, poor fellow ! he was mistaken. He had come out on the very side by which he had entered it, but of this he was not aware at the time. He, however, wondered that he did not recognize any part of the ground he was travelling over.

At length, to his great joy, he came upon the

fresh track of a man, which he had no doubt belonged to some person, who was then out from the settlement, still hunting ;* for he knew that Manvers was the most celebrated township for deer in the Newcastle District. As he observed that the footprints were going in a contrary direction to what he was, this circumstance gave him increased confidence. Two or three times, however, he thought some of the small swamps and ridges looked vastly like what he had traversed in the early part of the day. At last, about an hour before dark, he saw a thin wreath of blue smoke in a thicket before him. Judge of his disappointment and dismay, when, on his nearer approach, he found he had actually followed his own track, which had brought him back to the spot where he had passed the night. To describe his feelings on this occasion would be difficult and painful. He thought of his wife and his young children, who were hourly expecting his return, and who had, no doubt, prepared some little treat to welcome the wanderer home.

Bitter were his reflections during the waking hours of that long night ! Hungry, tired, and unrefreshed, the morning's light saw him struggling through the snow, but whither he knew

* Canadian term for deer-stalking.

not ; for though it had ceased snowing, the sky was still overcast, and continued so till the middle of the afternoon, when the wind suddenly veered round to the north-west, attended with intense cold. He now renewed every effort ; for once or twice he thought he heard the sounds of civilized life—the distant supper-horn or cattle-bell—but the fierce howling of the wind, which blew half a gale, rendered his hearing indistinct.

As long as daylight lasted he dragged on his wearied limbs, till utter exhaustion and coming darkness rendered his further progress impossible. To add to his misfortune, on attempting to kindle a fire, he found that his punk was damp, from the snow having come in contact with it when pressing his way through the swamp. He now gave himself up for lost, for the night was extremely cold, and he had neither fire to warm him, nor roof to shelter his head. To sleep thus he knew was certain death. He therefore paced up and down as long as he was able to stand, but his boots were frozen stiff, and his feet numb with the cold. After great difficulty he managed to pull off his boots, and having wrapped up his feet in his woollen cap, he lay down on the path he had beaten in the snow, for he could no longer resist the inclination to sleep.

While in the act of lying down, he distinctly heard a cock crow at no great distance. By a great effort he roused himself, and called as loudly as he was able. Once he thought he heard an answer to his cry—again the horn seemed to ring in his ears,—and then all was blank.

At daylight he was found by some of his own neighbours, one of whom was up early in the morning feeding his oxen, preparatory to a journey to the front, when he heard the shouts, which sounded to him like those of some person in distress. He immediately blew his dinner horn, that the sound might guide the lost person, and having collected three or four of his neighbours, they started into the woods in the direction from whence the shouts of the lost man had proceeded. Half a mile from the clearing, they came across his track, which they only followed for a few yards, when to their surprise they found their poor neighbour, whom at first they concluded to be dead. It was some time indeed before they could wake him, so overpowered was he with fatigue and the death-like sleep he had fallen into.

His friends lost no time in carrying him home; but unfortunately they placed him near a large fire, instead of rubbing his hands and feet with snow. The too sudden reaction of the blood caused him the most excruciating agony, for both his hands and feet were badly frozen. At length Dr. Hutchinson * was sent for from Peterborough, who found mortification had commenced, and that there was no chance of the poor fellow's recovery, which proved too true, for he expired the next day, a week from the morning he was found.

He, however, died in the arms of his afflicted wife, and was surrounded by his family, a privilege purchased at the expense of severe pain, but still one to the husband and father—even though he had been snatched from his pangless death-sleep to possess it, poor fellow !

The mischances consequent upon being lost in the woods, which were so frequent in the early settlement of Western Canada, are of rare occurrence now. Since, roads have been cut, and the clearings have brought the Bush-settlers nearer together. In my young time I have often searched for missing persons, and indeed have sometimes been lost myself.

I remember, the first summer I passed in Canada, making one of a party, who were for eight days looking for an old woman nearly eighty

* Dr. Hutchinson, is a medical practitioner of great note, and one of the first settlers and oldest magistrates in that section of the country. I had the particulars of this story from him ; though, as it was some years ago, I may have made some mistake as to the exact locality.

years of age, and her little grandson, who were lost in the Bush.

The old lady was going by a foot-path across a piece of woodland between her son-in-law's house and a neighbour's, which, by-the-by, were almost within sight of each other. The little boy, it seems, ran a short distance off the path to gather some wild-flowers, and was followed by his grandmother, who, either from her defectiveness of sight, or, more probably, from having crossed without perceiving it, was unable to regain the track. Her friends finding that she did not return, went over to their neighbour's house to see if she was there; but they only learned that neither she nor her grandson had found their way thither. Search was instantly made till night came on, but without success.

The next day, all their friends and neighbours turned out, myself among the number, to search for the unfortunate woman and the boy. We concluded, from her advanced age and the tender years of the child, that they could not be very far off; consequently we confined our search for several days within a radius of two or three miles.

On the fifth day, tracks were discovered near the edge of a small creek, which, from being the prints of a small and large foot, left no doubt as to whom they belonged. Strange as it may appear, this was the only sure indication of the lost ones that we had yet seen. No further trail was seen till the evening of the seventh day, when fresh signs were found. Our party therefore determined to camp out all night, and follow these new indications early in the morning, which object they succeeded in effecting. The lost ones were then found, and both were discovered alive.

The old woman had suffered the most; but the two had sustained themselves by eating roots and beech-mast: the little boy was quite frightened when he saw the men coming, and hid himself; such were the consequences of solitude and privation on his mind.

The place where they were found was in the township of Beach, at least fourteen miles due east from the place where they were lost; and it is more than probable, in their wanderings, that they had more than doubled that distance— a most extraordinary circumstance, when the ages of the parties are considered.

About three years since, two young men, with whom I was well acquainted, went back into the uninhabited township of Methuen, to trap for fur, and hunt deer. They set a line of marten-traps,* extending upwards of three miles. One or other of them used to go every alternate morning, to examine these traps — to re-set any that were sprung ; and bring back to their camp any furry animal that might chance to be captured.

One morning, the less-experienced trapper of the two, this being his first season, went along the line to look at the traps, as usual. He had his gun with him, but only two or three charges of powder. After proceeding to the extreme end of the line, he thought he would go on and look for some partridges, which he heard " drumming"† some little distance a-head.

---

* The method pursued by the trappers and Indians is to blaze a line through the bush for several miles. Along this line is set, at intervals of one or two hundred yards, a kind of trap, called a dead fall, which is constructed thus :—Two rows of short sticks are driven into the ground about one foot apart, open only at one end, the top being covered with brush-wood at the entrance. A piece of wood two or three feet long is bedded into the ground, or snow, as the case may be. The falling pole is supported immediately over this by three pieces of stick notched together in the form of a figure of four. The centre-piece is made long and sharp at the point, to which the bait is attached, and projects well into the miniature house. The marten or fisher, allured by the bait, reaches in to snatch it, which springs the trap, and causes the pole to fall across the neck of the animal, which is instantly killed by the blow.

† This sound is made by the Canadian partridge (a species of grouse) during its season of courtship. The cock-bird perches himself on the top of a large hollow log, or fallen tree, and with

In the pursuit of his game, he was induced to go further than he had at first intended. He never doubted that he should easily find his way back to the line. In this, however, he was woefully deceived, for the day was cloudy, and the face of the country was very rough, It formed, indeed, a part of the great granite range, which is said to cross the St. Lawrence, at the Lake of the Thousand Islands, traversing the rear of the Midland District and the counties of Hastings and Peterborough, through the un-surveyed lands north of Lake Simcoe, to the shores of Lake Huron. This granite formation is supposed to have an average breadth of ten or twelve miles, being intersected with small lakes, deep ravines and precipitous rocks. The woods of this region being composed principally of pine, hemlock, and cedar, are of a peculiarly gloomy character. In such a difficult country as this, it was no wonder that our inexperienced trapper went astray.

After an hour's fruitless search for the line, he came to the conclusion that he was lost, and that his only chance was to fire off his gun, in the hope that his companion would hear and

his wings produces a vibratory sound, like the distant roll of a drum, which, in still weather, can easily be heard at the distance of a mile in the woods.

return it. As no answering sound greeted his ear, he durst not fire his only remaining charge of powder, for it was all he had to defend himself from wolves, or to obtain some animal or bird whereupon to sustain his life.

For four days and three nights did this poor fellow wander through these rugged wilds. On the afternoon of the fourth day he came upon a ridge of land, which appeared better timbered and more open ; so he determined to follow this route, expecting it might lead him to the lake-shore, where his camp was situated.

He had not walked a hundred yards in this new direction, when to his surprise he saw quite a fresh blaze on a tree, and within a few yards of the spot on which he stood, a newly-constructed marten-trap. Words cannot express the joy he felt at this discovery ; it was his own line he had so fortunately come upon. Had he only gone the smallest distance to his left, he would have missed it altogether ; but he came, providentially, upon the very spot where he had set his last trap, and within a few feet of the place he had left four days before.

On his way to the camp, a sudden fear came over him ! Had his companion left it, supposing him to be irrecoverably lost ? If so, what was to become of him on the north shore of Stony Lake, without a canoe to cross over to the settlement, food, or ammunition to procure any for his support. His fears were, however, groundless, as the report of a gun, and soon after the appearance of his companion convinced him; but the danger had been great; for, from the statement of his fellow-trapper, he found that the latter was then on his way to the end of the line, hoping that he might see or hear something of him before he broke up their camp, which he intended to have done in the morning, if he had not unexpectedly fallen in with his friend. Thus had Providence again interposed in his behalf, and a few days of rest restored him to his wonted health, spirits, and activity.

CHAPTER XIII.

DIRECTIONS FOR ASCERTAINING THE QUALITY OF LAND IN THE BUSH.— SITE OF LOG-SHANTY.— CHOPPING.— PREPARATION FOR SPRING-CROPS.—METHOD OF PLANTING INDIAN CORN.—PUMPKINS AND POTATOES.—MAKING POT-ASH.

I SHALL now endeavour to give the emigrant some information to guide him in the selection of his land, and other matters connected with a settlement in the bush. In the first place, the quality of the land is the greatest consideration, and to make a good choice requires a practical knowledge as to the nature of the soils, and the different kinds of timber growing thereon.

The best land is timbered with oak, ash, elm, beech, bass-wood, and sugar-maple. A fair mixture of this species of trees is best, with here and there a large pine, and a few Canadian balsams scattered among the hard-wood. Too great a proportion of beech indicates sand or light loam : a preponderance of rock-elm is a sign of gravel or limestone-rock near the surface.

The timber should be lofty, clean in the bark and straight in the grain, and of quick growth. The woods should be open, free from evergreens, and with little under-brush. Generally speaking, the soil is of excellent quality, when timbered in the manner described.

It however, often happens, that the best land is full of boulders, which are both troublesome and expensive to remove. Two-thirds of these stones are not visible above the surface, and the remainder are so covered with moss and leaves, that they require a practised eye to detect them. I have no objection to a small quantity of stones, as they are useful to construct French drains, or to roll into the bottoms of the rail-fences.

When limestone-flag is near the surface, the stems of the trees will be shorter, their heads more bushy, and the roots spreading along the top of the ground. Such land is apt to burn in hot weather, and soon becomes exhausted. White pine, or hemlock ridges, are almost always sandy, and good for little—except the timber, which is valuable, if near enough to water. White-pine, mixed with hard-wood, generally indicates strong clay land, good for wheat ; but the difficulty of clearing off such heavy timber, and the long time it takes to get rid of the stumps, render such a selection unprofitable, and add additional toil to the emigrant.

The best land for wheat should be gently undulating soil, rich loam, on a clay bottom. In the summer months you can judge the quality of the land by the freshly turned-up roots of trees, which have fallen by the wind.

In winter, when the surface of the ground is covered with snow, and frozen hard, the growth and quality of the timber, as before described, are your only mode of judging correctly.

A constant supply of water is absolutely necessary, in a country liable to such extreme heat in summer. Canada West, abounding, as it does, in small spring-creeks, rivers, and lakes, is, perhaps, as well watered as any country in the world; and, in almost every section of the country, even on the highest ridges, good water can be obtained by digging wells, which seldom require to be sunk more than twenty feet; and in many townships, not half that depth is required.

After the emigrant has selected a proper location, his next object is to choose the best situation to build his shanty, and chop his first fallow. Most settlers like to commence as near as possible to the concession-line or public road;

but sometimes the vicinity of a stream of water or good spring is preferred. In fact, circumstances must, in some measure, guide them in their choice.

The best time of the year to commence operations is early in September. The weather is then moderately warm and pleasant, and there are no flies in the Bush to annoy you.

A log shanty, twenty-four feet long by sixteen, is large enough to begin with, and should be roofed either with shingles or troughs. A small cellar should be dug near the fire-place, commodious enough to hold twenty or thirty bushels of potatoes, a barrel or two of pork, &c.

As soon as your shanty is completed, measure off as many acres as you intend to chop during the winter, and mark the boundaries by blazing the trees on each side.

The next operation is to cut down all the small trees and brush—this is called under-brushing. The rule is to cut everything close to the ground from the diameter of six inches downwards.

There are two modes of piling, either in heaps or in wind-rows. If your fallow is full of evergreens, such as hemlock, pine, balsam, cedar, and such description of timber, then I should say windrows are the best ; but when the timber is deciduous, heaps are better.

The brush should be carefully piled and laid all one way, by which means it packs closer and burns better. The regular price for underbrushing hard-wood land, and cutting up all the old fallen timber—which is always considered a part of the underbrushing—is one dollar per acre, and board. Rough land and swamp vary from seven shillings and sixpence to ten shillings. Your under-brush should be all cut and piled by the end of November, before the snow falls to the depth of four inches, for after that it would be both difficult and tedious.

The chopping now begins, and may be followed without any interruption until the season for sugar-making commences. The heads of the trees should be thrown upon the heaps or wind-rows. A skilful chopper will scarcely ever miss a heap when felling the timber, besides it saves a great deal of labour in piling the limbs.

The trunks of the trees must be cut into lengths, from fourteen to sixteen feet, according to the size of the timber. Now and then a large maple or beech, when felled, may be left without cutting up, with the exception of the top, which is called a plan-heap, and is left to log against :

this is only done when the tree is too large to be cut through easily with the axe.

All timber fit for making rails should be left in double and treble lengths, as it is less likely to burn.

A good axe-man should be able, with fair chopping, to cut an acre in eight days after the under-brushing is done. The regular price of chopping is five dollars per acre, with board, or six without.

The emigrant should endeavour to get as much chopping done as possible during the first three years, because after that time he has so many other things to attend to, such as increase of stock, barn and house-building, thrashing, ploughing, &c., which, of course, give him every year less time for chopping, particularly if his family be small, in which case fifty or sixty acres are enough to clear at first, till his boys are old enough to give him assistance.

Clearing up too large a farm, when labour is so high, is not wise, for it will not answer to disburse much for hire, at the present prices. If, therefore, you are not able to cultivate what you have cleared properly, it will grow up again with raspberries, blackberries, small trees, and brush, and be nearly as bad to clear as it was at first.

The size of the farm must, however, depend on
the resources of the emigrant, the strength and
number of his family, and the quantity of acres
he may possess.

In the month of May the settler should spring-
burn three or four acres, and log them up for his
spring-crops, such as potatoes and Indian-corn.
The Indian-corn should be planted with the hoe
in rows, three feet apart and thirty inches in the
row.   A pumpkin-seed or two should be sown in
every second or third hole in each third row. The
corn must be earthed or hilled up by drawing
the mould close round the roots, and five or six
inches up the stalks, which should be done when
the plants are fifteen or sixteen inches high.   No
further cultivation is necessary until the time of
cutting, except breaking off some shoots from the
roots, if too many are thrown out.

Potatoes on the new land are also planted with
the hoe, and in hills of about five thousand to
the acre.   A hole is scraped with the hoe, in
which four or five sets, or a whole potato is
dropped.   The earth is then heaped over them
in the form of a mole-hill, but somewhat larger.
After the plants have appeared above the surface,
a little more mould is drawn around them.   Very

large crops of potatoes are raised in this manner. Two hundred and fifty bushels per acre are no uncommon crop. I have assisted in raising double that quantity; but of late years, since the disease has been prevalent, but poor crops have been realized.

Both white turnips and swedes do well, and grow to a large size, particularly on new land: the roots must be either pitted or put in a root-house, or cellar, as the winter is too severe for them to remain unhoused.

The remainder of the fallow should be burnt off and logged up in July, the rail-cuts split into quarters and drawn off to the site of the fences, ready for splitting into rails. After the log-heaps are burnt, you should either spread the ashes or rake them while hot into heaps, if you intend to make potash,* with which, by the by,

* This article is very extensively made in nearly all the new settlements, and may be considered one of the staples of the country. The process is very simple; but great care must be taken in collecting the ashes clear of sand or dirt of any description. If your ashes are well saved and from good timber, ten acres should produce at least five barrels of potash, each barrel containing five hundred weight. Several things should be considered before the emigrant attempts the manufacture of this article. Firstly, his land should be well timbered with oak, elm, maple, and bass-wood. Secondly, it must have a stream of water, near which he may erect his works. And, lastly, it ought to be

I should advise the new-comer to have nothing to do until he has made himself thoroughly acquainted with the process.

As soon as the settler has cleared up fifteen or twenty acres, his first care should be to erect a frame or log-barn ; I should strongly recommend the former, if boards can be obtained in the neighbourhood, as it is undoubtedly the best and cheapest in the long run. If I were commencing life again in the woods, I would not build anything of logs except a shanty or a pig-sty ; for experience has plainly told me that log buildings are the dirtiest, most inconvenient, and the dearest when everything is taken into consideration.

As soon as the settler is ready to build, let him put up a good frame, roughcast, or stone-

within reach of a market and a remunerating price, which, to pay the manufacturer, should not be less than twenty-five shillings, Halifax currency, per cwt.

The best situation to erect an ashery upon, is the side of a bank, beside a running stream ; and if there should be fall enough in the creek to bring a supply of water over head into the leaches, a great deal of labour will be saved. An ash-house, six or eight leach-tubs, a pot-ash kettle, and three or four coolers are all the requisites necessary. Most persons use a small portion of common salt and lime in the manufacture of pot-ash. After the lye is run off it is boiled down into black salts, which are melted into pot-ash, cooled off, and packed into air-tight barrels ready for market.

house, if he can possibly raise the means, as stone, timber, and lime, cost nothing but the labour of collecting and carrying the materials. When I say that they "cost nothing," I mean that no cash is required for these articles, as they can be prepared by the exertion of the family.

With the addition of from a hundred to a hundred and fifty pounds in money to the raw material, a good substantial and comfortable dwelling can be completed. Two or three years should be spent in preparing and collecting materials, so that your timber may be perfectly seasoned before you commence building.

Apple and plum orchards should be planted as soon as possible, and well fenced from the cattle and sheep. The best kind of grafted fruit-trees, from three to seven years old, can be obtained for a shilling a tree ; ungrafted, at four shillings the dozen.

The apple-tree flourishes extremely well in this country, and grows to a large size. I gathered last year, out of my orchard, several Ribstone pippins, each of which weighed more than twelve ounces, and were of a very fine flavour. The native plums are not very good in their raw state, but they make an excellent preserve, and good wine.

Some of the particulars mentioned in this chapter have been glanced at in an earlier portion of the work ; but I make no apology for the repetition. My object is, to offer instruction to the inexperienced settler, and to impress these important matters more firmly upon his mind and memory, that he may have his experience at a cheaper rate than if he purchased it at the expense of wasted time, labour, and capital.

CHAPTER XIV.

MY FIRST SHOT AT A BUCK.—HUNTING AND SHOOTING PARTIES.—
DESTRUCTIVENESS OF WOLVES. — LOSS OF MY FLOCKS. — COW-
ARDICE OF THE WOLF. — THE LADY AND HER PET. — COLONEL
CRAWFORD'S ADVENTURE. — INGENIOUS TRICK OF AN AMERICAN
TRAPPER. — A DISAGREEABLE ADVENTURE. — HOW TO POISON
WOLVES.—A STERN CHASE.

MY father-in-law had a large field of fall wheat, upon which, during the night, the deer were very fond of grazing. Just before dark, the herd used to make their appearance, and we tried repeatedly to get a shot at them, but in vain. At the least noise, or if they winded us, up went their tails, and they were off in an instant. I was deter- mined, however, not to be so continually balked. I had observed, by the tracks, the direction they took in their way to the field ; so, an hour before their usual time of coming, I sallied out, and concealed myself in the top of an old fallen tree which lay a few feet from the ground, and about twenty yards from a path which I suspected had been beaten by the deer, going backwards and forwards to the field.

The place I had selected to watch for them was an old settlement duty-road, which had been cut out some years before, but was now partially grown up again with a second growth of timber and underbrush. Having seated myself very snugly, I took out of my pocket a volume of Shakspeare to pass away the time. I had not been half-an-hour so employed, before my attention was suddenly aroused by hearing a stick break near me, when upon looking up I beheld the head and horns of a large buck projecting from behind a thicket of trees. He appeared to be in a listening attitude, so I durst not stir till he should have lowered his head, as I knew the least movement then would make him start off in an instant. Luckily, however, the wind was blowing from his direction to mine. Presently, he walked into the open space ; and whilst I was cautiously raising my gun, he disappeared beneath the brow of a small hill ; but almost immediately, from the inequality of the ground, his head and shoulders again became visible. On this, I instantly fired.

Astonished and mortified was I, when I saw him scamper off with his tail up, as if nothing had happened. Still, I was sure I must have hit him, as he was not forty yards from where I sat,

his broadside being towards me. So I followed
the track for about two hundred yards, but without seeing any blood ; and was in the act of
turning back, concluding, that as he had hoisted
his tail, I had missed him altogether. Indeed, I
had often heard, that if they show the white
feather, as putting up their tail is called by Canadian sportsmen—they are not hit. This, however, is a mistake ; for, in the act of turning
round to retrace my steps, I saw a small drop of
blood upon a dry leaf. I now felt quite certain that
I had struck him. On proceeding a few yards further, I saw several large splashes of blood. There
was now no room left for doubt; and, in another
minute I was standing beside the first buck I
had ever killed. On opening him, I found I had
put a ball and five buck-shot into him, which
had entered just behind the fore-shoulder; and
though two of these shots had lodged in the
lungs, he had, notwithstanding this, continued
to run on the full jump, more than two hundred yards.

Not long after this adventure, my brother-in-
law shot a deer through the heart, which ran full
a hundred yards before he dropped.

Two or three years after, in the township of
Douro, where I now reside, I was walking down

to the saw-mill about half a mile from my house, with my American rifle in my hand, when, on coming close to the river, I saw a large buck swimming down the middle of the stream near the mill-dam. I ran down to the spot as fast as I could, for I expected he would land on the opposite shore, at the corner of the dam. The surmise proved to be correct. He was in the act of climbing up the bank when I fired, and he fell back into the river. Recovering himself, however, he scrambled out and made off. I crossed the bridge and went round to the spot where he landed, and followed on the track.

While in chase I was joined by an old hunter, who had been out since day-light, still-hunting (deer-stalking); so he agreed to go with me and examine the track, which we followed for about half a mile without seeing any blood. But at last we came to a place where the buck had stood and pawed up the ground. My companion, remarking upon the circumstance, said—

" He was quite satisfied the fellow was hit; and you will find," added he, " if we get him, that he is hit on the top of the back, and that is the reason there is no blood to be seen."

The track led us round nearly in a circle; for we came back to the river within a few yards of where I had fired at the buck. My companion now suggested that we should recross the river and follow up the stream on the opposite bank. " For," said he, " we shall probably find him on one of the islands opposite your house."

Acting on his suggestion, we retraced our steps, and found, as he had predicted, that the buck, after taking the water, had swum up the river and taken refuge on the west side of the lower-island. We saw him standing near the edge of the water, partially hidden by the trunk of a fallen pine, when we both fired our rifles at the same instant. This did not, however, drop him, for he bounded across the island, and took the opposite channel in gallant style.

As the distance from which we fired was less than a hundred yards, we concluded that one of us at least had hit him. Reinforced by my old hound Towler, who, attracted by the firing, had joined us, we recrossed the river, and put the dog on the track. Towler was in high spirits, and soon made the wood ring with music pleasant to the hunter's ear.

We momentarily expected to see our quarry again take the water ; but from the continued howling of the hound in the same spot, I began to think the buck was standing at bay, which was really the case ; for on my near approach he was busily employed with his head down, keeping off old Towler by making sudden plunges at him every now and then. The moment he saw me, he made a rush for the river, but as he passed me on the full bound, I fired at his fore-shoulder ; and though he still continued his course to the river, I knew by the jet of blood which followed my shot that his fate was sealed. Near the river he made a sudden turn, striking his head against a hemlock tree, and at the same instant a shot from my companion stretched him lifeless on the ground. And thus concluded an exciting chase of more than two hours.

This was the largest buck I ever killed, for he weighed, after he was skinned and dressed, two hundred and thirty pounds. We found that four out of the five shots had hit him. The last shot I fired, cut away the small end of his heart, though he actually managed to run thirty or forty paces afterwards.

Deer-hunting is a very exciting sport; but I prefer still-hunting (or deer-stalking, as it is called in the Highlands of Scotland) to driving them into the lakes and rivers with hounds.

The deer are not now nearly so numerous as they formerly were. Civilization has driven

them back into the unsurveyed lands or less populated townships.   To give my readers some
idea how plentiful these wild denizens of the
forest were, some years since, I need only mention that a Trapper with whom I was acquainted,
and four of his companions, passed my house on
a small raft, on which lay the carcasses of thirty-
two deer—the trophies of a fortnight's chase near
Stony Lake.   The greater number of these were
fine bucks.

I once had seventeen deer hanging up in
my barn at one time—the produce of three days'
sport, out of which I had the good fortune to
kill seven.   Parties are now made yearly every
October to Stony Lake, Deer Bay, or the River
Trent.   I do not know anything more pleasaut
than these excursions, especially if you have
agreeable companions, a warm camp, and plenty
to eat and drink.   Indeed, poor hunters must
they be who cannot furnish their camp-larder
with wild-ducks and venison.   This is one of
the great charms of a Canadian life, particularly
to young sportsmen from the mother-country,
who require here neither license nor qualification to enable them to follow their game ; but
may rove about in chase of deer, or other game,
at will.

The greatest enemy the deer has to contend with is the wolf. In the spring of the year, when the snow is in the woods, and a crust is formed on the surface, the deer are unable to travel any distance, the snow not being sufficiently hard to bear their weight. Consequently, great numbers of them are destroyed by their more nimble adversaries, who from their lighter make and rounder-shaped feet, are able to run on the top of the crust, which gives the deer but little chance of escape.

The wolves commonly hunt in packs, and generally at night. The deer, when pursued, always make straight for the water, which, if they succeed in reaching it, saves them for that time.

When the wolves reach the shore and find their prey gone, they utter the most diabolical yells. One night I was awakened by a pack of these rascals, who were in chase of a deer. They ran through my wood-yard within sixty feet of the house in full chorus. I think I never heard in the stillness of the night a more wild and unearthly din.

For some years, till the country became more settled, I was obliged to shut up my sheep at night for fear of these prowling wretches. The first flock I ever had were all killed by these

thieves.   One night I was awakened by my dog
barking furiously, and from the manner in
which he kept rushing against the door I was
sure some wild animals were about the premises.   At first I thought it was useless to get
up; for the night was dark, and I knew the
sheep were housed.   However, the increased fury
of my dog Grouse, who seemed intent on getting
into the house, as if he were frightened, obliged me
to dress and turn out.   On my opening the door,
Grouse rushed in looking dreadfully scared, so
with a lantern in one hand and a gun in the other,
I marched towards the sheep-pen, the door of
which not having been securely fastened by my
lad, I found open, and six sheep out, and for
these I now commenced a cautious search.

About twenty yards from the pen, I found one
of my best sheep lying on the grass with his
throat cut very scientifically just behind the ear.
A few paces further on, I found another, and so
on, till five were forthcoming.   The sixth I did
not get till the morning, which was the only one
that escaped the teeth of the marauders.   It
seems that my appearance with the light drove
the wolves from their prey.

Luckily for me, the weather was cold, my
sheep fat, and well-butchered, as far as bleeding

was concerned, so that I was no great loser, except by having a rather larger supply of mutton at one time than was quite convenient for the housekeeping department.

About eleven or twelve years since, I lost in one season a flock of sheep by the wolves. This misfortune occurred, unluckily for me, in the hottest month of the Canadian year, July. I had not housed my sheep, because I found that, in very sultry weather, during the fly-season, they would not feed in the day-time, but would creep under the fences and into the Bush for shade. I, therefore, thought it best to risk losing some, than to spoil the whole flock; for I knew the only time they would graze was during the night, or very early in the morning. Consequently, for three or four years previously, I had allowed them to run at large during the summer months.

One morning, I observed from the veranda in front of my house, a sheep, which was standing on the opposite bank of the river. As I knew there was no farm within two or three miles of the river in that direction, I thought I would go over in a canoe, and see what brought it there. I had not gone half way to the river when I discovered the mangled carcass of one of my own sheep, and on further search found ten more, lying, half-devoured, in different directions—the murder was now out. The sheep I had seen on the opposite shore was one of my own, which had taken to the water, and had thus escaped the fangs of the wolves. I saw two more of my luckless flock on a shoal more than a mile down the river, which—less fortunate than their companion—had been swept down by the current and drowned. Exactly a week afterwards, I had a similar number destroyed by the wolves. As far as I was personally concerned, I may 'say that they were a total loss; for the weather was too hot to keep the meat any length of time, so I gave the greater part of the mutton to my neighbours. Since that time, I have had better luck, not having lost any part of my flock, although I have invariably left my sheep abroad during the night.

Notwithstanding his ravenous propensities and cruel disposition, the wolf is a very cowardly animal in his solitary state. Indeed, it is only when he hunts in a pack, that he becomes formidable to man. Nature has, in some measure, checked his evil disposition, by rendering him timid. If he falls into a snare, he never attempts to get out of the scrape ; but crouches in a corner, awaiting his fate, without the least intention of displaying any pluck to the trapper.

That the cowardice of the wolf is very great, the following anecdote will sufficiently prove.

My wife's youngest sister had a pet-sheep that she had brought up from a lamb, and to which she was much attached. One afternoon she was going down to the spring for a pitcher of water, when she saw a large dog—as she thought—worrying her sheep, upon which, being naturally courageous, she picked up a large stick and struck the beast two or three strokes with all her strength, thus compelling him to drop her favorite. This, however, he did very reluctantly, turning his head at the same time, and showing his teeth with a most diabolical snarl. She saw at once, when he faced her, by his pricked ears, high cheek-bones, long bushy-tail, and gaunt figure, that her antagonist was a wolf. Nothing daunted, she again bravely attacked him; for he seemed determined, in spite of her valiant opposition, to have her pet, which he again attacked. She boldly beat him off the second time; following him down the creek, thrashing him and calling for aid with all her might; when, fortunately, one of her brothers, attracted by her cries, ran down with the dogs and his gun, but was not in time for a shot; for when the felon wolf saw the reinforcement, he scampered off with all his speed.

There are few dogs bred in the Canadas fit to cope with the wolf ; indeed, they seem in general to have a great dread of him.

Colonel Crawford, a gentleman with whom I am well-acquainted, for he was many years one of my nearest and best neighbours, was one day partridge-shooting, near Buckhorn Mills, in the township of Harvey, when his sporting-dog, which had been ranging the bush a little in advance, came running towards him, yelping in a most piteous manner, followed by a large wolf. So intent was the beast on his prey, that he did not perceive the gallant colonel, who met his advance with both barrels, which stopped his earthly career, and rescued poor Carlo from his impending fate. The colonel was very proud of this exploit, both because he had killed so large an animal with partridge-shot and had saved his dog at the same time.

According to an act of the Provincial Parliament, six dollars must be paid by the county treasurer for every wolf-certificate, signed by a magistrate. No certificate now will be granted, unless the scalp of the animal is produced, which is then taken possession of by the magistrate. This precaution is absolutely necessary ; for, previously to this arrangement, it was found that double the number of wolves were killed, or, rather twice the number of scalps were brought in—one wolf often furnishing two pates—a curious feature in Natural History.

Many petty frauds of this kind have been brought to light ; amongst other cases, that of a magistrate, not a hundred miles from the county town, who forged seventeen wolf certificates, and succeeded in getting the money for them ; and, most likely, emboldened by his success, would have continued to drive a flourishing trade, had not his career been suddenly stopped in the following manner.

One of the persons, whose name had been made use of in one or more of the certificates, was congratulated on his recent success.   He, however, denied that he had either shot or trapped a wolf during the last year, and declared, " that there must certainly be some mistake."   An inquiry was accordingly made, whereupon the whole nefarious transaction was brought to light.

Our magistrate was not long in availing himself of the proximity of the United States ; for the next day saw him an inhabitant of the good city of Rochester, in the State of New York, where, I make no doubt, over gin-cocktail, or mint-julep, he entertains the free and enlightened citizens with an account of his adroit manner of "sloping" the British Government. Luckily for Rochester, there are no wolves in that neighbourhood.

A celebrated wolf-trapper, in the township of Smith, once caught a fine she-wolf, big with young. Her fore-paw broken below the knee, was the only injury she had sustained. So he thought, if he could but keep her alive till after her accouchement, he should be able to demand the bounty for every scalp ; for he considered that as there was no mention made in the act respecting the size the wolves must be, he might as well have the benefit of that oversight. He put his scheme, accordingly, into effect, and it proved quite successful. Her wolfship in a few days was safely delivered of five fine whelps, whose scalps, with that of their mother, were duly presented to the magistrate. At first he demurred respecting the certificate, but upon referring to the statute, he found there was no provision to meet a case of this kind. He, however, satisfied his moral justice by the reflection, " that if the dam had remained at large a few days longer, and whelped in the Bush, it would have amounted to the same thing, and that, perhaps, many sheep had been saved from the greedy fangs of the growing family, by the ingenious plan of the trapper." It was a clever trick, no doubt—a real Yankee shave ; but one for which the sternest moralist can scarcely get up an effective lecture.

The Canadian wolf is not nearly so ferocious as the European animal, nor I believe quite so large. I have heard of very few well-authenticated accounts of persons having been destroyed by these creatures, though I must say I should not like again to be in their vicinity in a dark night, as more than once I have been. I was returning from Whitby after dark, and had just entered the woods, through which my path lay for a full mile and a half. The night being dark, and the road not particularly good, I gave Prince the rein, and allowed him to choose his own pace. Presently, I thought I heard a pattering on the leaves, like the tread of animals, at which sound my horse pricked up his ears, snorted, and shied nearly across the road, so suddenly that I was nearly thrown out of the saddle. Well for me was it, however, that I kept my seat ; for instantly such an infernal howling was raised all round me as made my heart leap up to my mouth, and I must candidly own I felt horribly afraid I should fall into the clutches of devouring wolves. My good steed Prince, I fancy, was as scared as myself, for he galloped off, followed by the pack, who fairly made the woods ring with their unearthly yells. They did not chase us far, and ceased howling, having seemingly lost the scent; but in a few minutes a fresh burst in the direction of the lake-shore plainly told me they had regained it, and were on the track of a deer, which most probably had crossed the road at the time when I first heard their chorus. It is not very easy to describe one's feelings on such occasions.

There is something particularly appalling in the full cry of a pack of wolves, especially when alone in the woods, and at night. I have frequently heard them at such times, when camped out on hunting expeditions. However, we mustered strong and were well armed, so we cared little for them or their yells.

The only instance of any one being killed by wolves, to which I can speak with certainty, occurred a few years back in the township of Douro. A young lad of the name of M'Ewen was sent by his father to a shoemaker, one George Disney, for his shoes. The distance was not more than a mile by a path through the woods, and the boy was well acquainted with the road. It appears, he went to Disney's, and waited for his shoes till nearly dark, when he started for home. But nothing more was ever heard or seen of him till the thaw in the spring, although diligent search was made at the time. Owing to a snow-storm which fell the same night, he was lost. It was impossible to follow the boy's tracks, and as a pack of wolves had been heard the same night in the immediate neighbourhood, no doubt was entertained that he had been attacked and eaten by these ravenous monsters. Some bones and pieces of clothing, supposed to have belonged to the unfortunate youth, were the only memorials found of him.

I have heard the old settlers say, that very few instances have occurred like this in their recollection, though from the many persons lost in the woods and never again discovered, it is more than probable that some of them, when weakened by fatigue and hunger, and no longer able to defend themselves, may have fallen victims to their insatiable maws.

Several plans have been devised by the inhabitants for the destruction of these animals. That most commonly resorted to, and which is considered the least troublesome and the most efficacious, is poison. The best and surest for that purpose is strychnine, one grain of which, if genuine, will kill the largest wolf in Canada. I have used this poison myself, when baiting for foxes. The properest method in the winter-season, is to take a piece of hog's-lard, about the size of a walnut, make a hole in the centre, and insert it carefully with a quill or the point of a small knife, taking care not to spill any on the outside, then to fill up the puncture with some fresh lard.

If you have heard, or have reason to know, that wolves are in the vicinity, your best way is to bait with pieces of carrion of any description. This must be done at some distance from the clearing, or you will be sure to lose your own dogs, or kill those of your neighbours, when you come to lay your poison, which you need not do till you see some of your bait taken, and observe their fresh tracks.

I know a gentleman who had lost an ox, which he had drawn away some distance into the Bush. In a few days, finding the wolves had paid their respects to the carcass, he laid out several poison-balls, and actually killed six of them before the carcass was eaten. The value of the wolves, including their skins and the bounty-money, amounted to forty-four dollars, a nice little sum for a few hours' trouble, not to speak of the satisfaction of having contributed to extirpate this devouring crew. I must, however, caution the uninitiated to be very careful in the use of this deadly poison : indeed it should only be used by the most experienced trappers, and then at some distance from the settlement.

The price of the wolf-skin varies from 5s. to 7s. 6d. Halifax currency, according to size and quality : they are always in good demand for sleigh-robes.* Those made of this species of fur are considered the most elegant and *distingué*.

A perilous adventure once befel my brother-in-law, James. He was a bold brave boy, of ten years old at the time, and was on his return

---

* Sleigh-robes are commonly made of bear or buffalo skins dressed with the hair on. The most fashionable are racoon or wolf. Several of these skins are sewn together, with the tails of the animals stitched to the bottom of the robe. The inside lining is generally scarlet or purple cloth. A well equipped sleigh should have two robes for each seat, one of which should cover the cushions, and fall gracefully over the back of the seat, whilst the other is drawn over the passengers, and wraps them securely from the cold.

home with a pair of oxen, with which he had been assisting a neighbour residing about six miles from his father's house. His road lay by the river shore, which was dreary enough at the fall of the year and in the evening hour ; but the child was fearless, and saw the deepening shades sink into night without experiencing anything like apprehension.

He was trudging on steadily, singing cheerfully as he walked, when a sound came on the night-air that sent a shiver through the young pedestrian's frame—the war-cry of the wolves. At first he hoped he was not the object of pursuit; but the hideous uproar came nearer and nearer, and then he knew that he must instantly adopt some plan for his escape.

His route lay by the river shore, and he could swim well ; but the night was dark, and he might be hurried into the rapids ; and to be dashed to pieces on the rocks was scarcely less dreadful than to be mangled and devoured by wolves. In this extremity, the child lifted up his brave young heart to God, and resolved to use the only chance left him of escape. So he mounted Buck, the near-ox, making use of his goad, shouting at the same time to the animal, to excite him to his utmost speed.

In most cases, the horned steed would have
flung off his rider, and left him for wolves'-
meat, without hesitation ; but Buck set off with
the speed of a race-horse, as if fully aware of his
young rider's peril. Nor was his companion
less tardy. Fast, however, as the trio fled, still
faster came upon them the yelling pack behind ;
and James could ever hear—

> " Their long hard gallop which could tire
> The hound's deep hate and hunter's fire."

Fortunately for him, old Buck heard it too,
and galloped on and on ; but still the wolves
came nearer and nearer. James shouted to
keep them off; the oxen almost flying; their
chains rattling as they went. This clanking
sound, to which the hateful pack were unaccustomed, made them pause whenever they came
close upon the oxen, whilst the latter redoubled
their speed, till at length these gallant racers
left the wolves behind, and finding themselves
within a short distance of home, never stopped
till they brought the brave little fellow safely
to his own door.

He had felt afraid but once ; and that was
when those dismal yells first broke upon his
ear—and *never* lost his presence of mind. He

trusted in God, and used the means within his reach for his preservation, and arrived safe at last.

Few boys would have displayed so much sense and spirit—but the boy is almost always the father of the man ; and what James was then, he is now.

CHAPTER XV.

FORMATION OF THE CANADA COMPANY. — INTERVIEW WITH MR. GALT.—HIS PERSONAL DESCRIPTION AND CHARACTER.—GUELPH. —DR. DUNLOP.—MY MEDICAL SERVICES AT GUELPH.—DR. DUNLOP AND THE " PAISLEY BODIES."—AN ECCENTRIC CHARACTER.— AN UNFORTUNATE WIFE.

I REMEMBER on my first visit to the mouth of the river Maitland, now the site of Goderich, a bridle-path for seventy miles through the trackless forest was the only available communication between the settlements and Lake Huron. This was only twenty-four years ago. This vast and fertile tract of more than one million acres, at that time did not contain a population of three hundred souls; no teeming fields of golden grain, no manufactories, no mills, no roads; the rivers were unbridged, and one vast solitude reigned around, unbroken, save by the whoop of the red-man, or the distant shot of the trapper.

Reverse the picture, and behold what the energies and good management of the Canada

Company have effected. Stage-coaches travel with safety and dispatch along the same tract where formerly I had the utmost difficulty to make my way on horseback without the chance of being swept from the saddle by the limbs of trees and tangled brushwood. A continuous settlement of the finest farms now skirts both sides of this road, from the southern boundary-line of this district to Goderich.

Another road equally good, traverses the block from the western boundary. Thriving villages, saw and grist-mills, manufactories, together with an abundance of horses, cattle, sheep, grain, and every necessary of life enjoyed by a population of 26,000 souls, fully prove the success caused by the persevering industry of the emigrants who were so fortunate as to select this fruitful and healthy locality for their future homes.

Much of this prosperity is due to the liberality and excellent arrangements of the Canada Company, who have afforded every facility to their settlers in regard to the payments for their land : I particularly refer to their system of leasing, which affords the best chance possible to the poor emigrant.

"This spirited and enterprising" Company's principal tract of land lies nearly in a triangular form, commencing in latitude 43°, and extending about sixty miles along the coast. In 1824, this incorporated company contracted with Government for this line of country and some others, as well as for a portion of the clergy reserves, comprehending in all about two million acres, payable in fifteen years.*

In the spring of 1827, a memorable year for Canada, the Company commenced their operations at Guelph, under the superintendence of John Galt, Esq.

I had heard a great deal about the fertility of their lands, especially of those in the Huron tract, containing a million of acres in one block, of which I shall hereafter speak more particularly.†
As I was enterprising, and fond of an active life, I resolved to go and judge for myself; and as I heard the superintendent was then at Toronto, I

* M'Gregor's "British America."

† The territory from which the Huron tract has been selected, was explored previously to the selection being made, and the reports which were received from the parties employed on that mission were of the most satisfactory nature. This tract is bounded on the west by Lake Huron, along which it runs for nearly sixty miles, having within its limits one considerable river, at the mouth of which is a good harbour; another river, which may probably be rendered navigable, and numerous creeks and streamlets, many of which are large enough, and have fall sufficient to drive mills or machinery of any description.—MAC TAGGART's " Three Years in Canada."

determined to call upon him there and collect all the information in my power.

My first interview with Mr. Galt, the celebrated author of "Laurie Todd," took place at the Old Steam-boat Hotel, in February, 1828. He received me with great kindness, and asked me many particulars of Bush-life, connected with a first settlement.

I suppose my answers were satisfactory, for he turned towards me abruptly, and asked me, " If I would like to enter the Canada Company's Service ; for," said he, "I want a practical person to take charge of the out-door department in the absence of Mr. Prior, whom I am about to send to the Huron tract with a party of men to clear up and lay off the New-town plot of Goderich. You will have charge of the Company's stores, keep the labour-rolls, and superintend the road-making and bridge-building, and indeed everything connected with the practical part of the settlement."

This was just the sort of life I wished ; so I closed at once with his offer. No salary was to be named, till I had been three months in the Company's employ. Indeed, I left everything to Mr. Galt, who, I felt certain, would remunerate me according to my deserts.

In person, Mr. Galt was, I should think, considerably above six feet in height, and rather of a heavy build; his aspect grave and dignified, and his appearance prepossessing. His disposition was kind and considerate; but at the same time he commanded respect; and I can say with sincerity, I always found him an upright and honourable gentleman.

Of Mr. Galt's fitness for the office of superintendent of the Canada Company, it would, perhaps, be considered presumptuous in me to give an opinion. His position was an unfortunate one, and from his first residence in the country till his resignation, there appears to have been a serious misunderstanding between him, the Governor, and the Executive-council, in consequence of which, Galt's character was misrepresented at home as that of a meddling politician and troublesome person. Other charges regarding the wasteful expenditure of money in forming the new settlements were laid before the Directors, and these repeated complaints against him left him no other alternative than to resign his situation.

My own opinion is, that Galt was ill-used by the Canadian Government. He says in his " Autobiography," that his whole and sole offence consisted in having accepted a file of the "Colonial Advocate," and shaken hands with the editor, the notorious William Lyon Mackenzie. In those days of ultra-toryism, such an instance of liberality and freedom from party-prejudice was sufficient to excite the displeasure of the Governor and his council. There is no doubt that Galt acted imprudently in this matter, though I fully believe without any intention of opposing the Government.

In regard to the Company's affairs, more might be said to his prejudice—not in respect of his integrity, for, I believe him to have been a most honourable man, and incapable of any meanness— but in regard to his management. Although, as the original projector of the Canada Company, he evinced much cleverness, and afterwards displayed considerable judgment in the choice of the best situations for building towns and villages, yet he committed some grievous mistakes. His ideas were generally good ; but often not well carried out in detail.

His first error was in the selection of persons to fill the various offices belonging to the Company. For, instead of appointing men who had long experience in the country, and who were, therefore, practically qualified to superintend the

workmen by their experience of all the requirements of a new settlement, he filled these
situations, for the most part, with inexperienced
young men, recently arrived from the old country, who, of course, could know nothing of road-
making and bridge-building, and were, therefore,
incapable of directing a number of workmen.
Then, again, most of the hands employed on the
Company's works were new settlers, and, of course,
knew nothing of chopping, house-building, or
clearing land ; and yet these men were paid just
as much as if they had served a long apprentice-
ship in the country. If Mr. Galt's appointments
had been judicious, there is no doubt, in my
mind, that half the outlay would have produced
greater results.

It was arranged that I should meet Mr. Galt at
Toronto, in April, at the commencement of the
spring operations. At the appointed time, I
again waited upon him, when he ordered me to
Guelph, to take charge of the department, as
formerly agreed upon between us. He then introduced me to Dr. Dunlop and Mr. Prior, who
kindly invited me to take a seat in their waggon,
which would leave for Guelph in a few hours. The
former gentleman is well known in the literary
world, as the author of the " Backwoodsman."

During our journey, I found that he deserved his celebrity for good companionship, which was fully borne out on this occasion. He could, indeed, speak well on any subject. He was full of sound information, and overflowed with anecdote —in fact, his way of telling a story was inimitable. He had a fund of wit, which seemed almost inexhaustible.

My fellow-travellers left me at Mr. Galt's house, near Burlington Heights, where, after taking some refreshment, I again proceeded on my journey, and ultimately reached Guelph on the afternoon of the second day.

The situation of the town I found exceedingly pleasant, and well watered. It was built in an angle, formed by the confluence of the rivers Speed and Eramosa. The town-plot also abounds with copious never-failing springs, of the purest water.

I found some twenty or thirty log-houses, about as many shanties, a large frame-tavern building, a store, two blacksmiths' shops, and the walls of two stone-buildings, one of which was intended, when finished, for the company's office. Besides these edifices, Dr. Dunlop and Mr. Prior had each a good house, and there was the Priory, a large log-building, afterwards occupied by the superintendent. This was pretty well, considering that a year only had elapsed since the first tree was felled.

Mr. Galt, in his "Autobiography," has given an account of the founding of the town of Guelph,* and how Mr. Prior, Dr. Dunlop, and himself, cut down the first tree-—a large sugar-maple, whereupon the Dr. produced a flask of whiskey, and they named and drank success to the new town. This was on St. George's day, April 23rd, 1827. Eighteen months after this, by Mr. Galt's orders, I had the stump of that tree inclosed by a fence, though, I make no doubt, it has long since decayed. The name of the founder will, however, remain,—a better and more enduring memorial.

On my arrival, I drove up to the only tavern in the place, a small log-house, kept by one Philip Jones, an Englishman—or, rather, by his wife—a buxom, bustling body, who was, undoubtedly, the head of the establishment. In answer to my inquiry for lodgings, she courteously informed me that she had neither bed nor blanket, but what

---

* "This name was chosen in compliment to the royal family, both because I thought it auspicious in itself, and because I could not recollect that it had ever been before used in all the king's dominions."—Galt's "Autobiography."

was doubly occupied, and, moreover, that she was sure I could not obtain one in town, as every house was full of emigrants; but as the most of her lodgers would leave for the Huron tract on the morrow, she should be able and happy to accommodate me after their departure. With this promise I was obliged to be satisfied.

I might, perhaps, have succeeded in obtaining a share of a bed, but as I did not know what population I might gain, or, indeed, what might be the unpleasant results of such an arrangement, I preferred a hay-loft, in which I slept soundly till the break of day.

The superintendent and his staff arrived the next morning, when I was duly installed in my office. Mr. Galt's coach-house being unoccupied, I took immediate possession, and converted it into a very respectable store-house and office, till a building was completed for that purpose. I was thus fairly established as an *employé* in the service of the Canada Company.

The township of Guelph contains upwards of forty thousand acres of land, of a fair average quality, well timbered, and well watered. I believe the Company have disposed of all their saleable lots in this township. I was fully employed the whole summer in constructing two bridges, one over the Speed, and the other over the Eramosa branch, and also in opening a good road to each. These bridges were built of cedar logs, and on a plan of my own, which Mr. Galt highly approved. I should, however, have preferred square timber, framed in bents, which, I think, would have been more durable, and better adapted for the stream they were intended to cross.

Amongst the men under my charge, I had two Mohawk Indians, both of whom were excellent choppers, and behaved themselves remarkably well. One of them was called Henhawk, and the other William Fish. The Mohawks are more civilized, and make better farmers than the Chippewas, and I think are a finer-looking race of men.*

My time passed pleasantly enough at Guelph, for I had plenty of work to do, and in all labour there is profit. And what could be better for a healthy, active young man than the

* Benjamin West, the celebrated American painter, on being shown the Apollo Belvidere, astonished a number of Italian cognoscenti by comparing that *chef d'œuvre* of ancient Greek art to a young Mohawk warrior. But the fine proportions of these savage warriors, and their free and graceful action, rendered the remark of this great artist a just and beautiful critique, and of a complimentary not a depreciating character.

employment of assisting in settling a new country ?

The only drawback to my comfort was the temporary loss of the society of my wife ; a pretty, sensible young woman, whose mental and personal charms had, since my union with her, formed the happiness of my life. We cannot, however, have every blessing at once, and I worked on cheerfully in the hope of getting things comfortably round me for my dear girl against the moment when she would join me.

Besides the services rendered to the Company, I performed *con amore* some gratuitous ones for the benefit of the township of Guelph, which will, doubtless, both surprise and astonish my readers. We had no medical man in Guelph for some months after my arrival, so, for want of a better, I was obliged to turn physician and surgeon, and soon became very skilful in bleeding and tooth-drawing, and, as I charged nothing, you may be sure I had plenty of customers. And so well-pleased was Dr. Dunlop with my proficiency, that he invariably sent all his patients to me.

I remember one time in particular, he came over to my office and inquired for me, when, on the store-porter telling him I had just gone out, he said,

"Tell him when he comes back, to take the calomel and jalap down to my house, and treat those Paisley bodies with a dose apiece."

"What! all of them, sir?"

"Yes, to be sure; they are but just arrived, and have got as fat as pigs on the voyage. Some of their bacon must be taken off, or with this heat we shall have them all sick on our hands. And tell him not to spare the jalap."

When I returned and heard the message, I literally obeyed his order by administering forty-two doses of various strengths to the men, women and children, designated by the Doctor as the "Paisley bodies."

This wholesale way of medical treatment was in this instance attended with a good effect; for there did not occur a single case of sickness amongst them during the summer.

Shortly after this, a medical man, a Mr. W——, applied for a town-lot and commenced practice. This gentleman was certainly a great oddity. He never had but two patients that I ever heard of, and they both died. The settlers used to call him the "mad doctor," and I believe not without good reason. He built a log-house without any door, his mode of entrance being through a square hole he had cut out of the end of the house about six feet from the ground.

I walked over to his place one day to speak to him on some business, and found him very busy in his garden, driving into the ground a great quantity of short sticks.

I asked him " what all those sticks were for."

" Why you see, sir, I have planted part of my garden with Indian corn, and I am putting sticks down to mark the places where I have planted them."

A day or two afterwards I met him wearing his coat turned inside out, the rough seams and red-edging of which had a very curious effect. I inquired " what might be his reason for going about in such a costume ?"

" Well, you see I call this my morning attire ; in the evening I have nothing to do but turn my coat, and, lo! I am dressed ; a very capital arrangement, and quite good enough for the Bush. Do not you think so ?"

" As far as regards economy," I replied, " it may do well enough, and as you do not appear to care about being laughed at, your plan will answer : and who knows but that you may have the pleasure of introducing a new fashion into the colonies ? "

Amongst other odd characters I had to deal with, was a Mr. W——, I believe a portrait and miniature painter by profession, who had travelled a good deal in Russia, and understood that language well. He purchased a lot of land from the company on the Waterloo-road, about a mile from the village. Under the ground-plot chosen by him to build on, he found there existed a good quarry of limestone ; so he made up his mind to build a stone-house, although he had spent his last dollar, and his profession in a new and poor settlement would avail him little.

However, he went to work, excavating the stone which he had found when digging his cellar, for building the walls of his house : his only assistant in the undertaking was a delicate lady-like young woman, whom he had married in the United States, and brought here as a bride. He treated his unfortunate partner like a slave. She had to mix and carry all the mortar, and help him to raise the stone.

I often, on an evening, walked down to see how they were getting on with their job, and was quite astonished to find how well they progressed. But, at the same time, I pitied the poor wife exceedingly, whom the neighbours said he treated very harshly, notwithstanding her conjugal devotion to him.

At the end of three months his creditors began to threaten him. His land was still unpaid for, and the walls of his house unfinished. When too late, he counted the cost of completion, and found his best plan was to take a Yankee leave, and clear out, leaving his unfinished home as a legacy to his creditors.

How to beat a retreat, and take his goods and chattels with him, without discovery, was a difficult matter. He, however, set his wits to work, and adopted the following plan, which, in theory, looked feasible enough, but, when put in practice, was found not quite so easy as he had anticipated.

He knew that the river Speed, which ran at the rear of his lot, after a course of fourteen or fifteen miles, debouched into the Grand River, and was, from thence, navigable for boats to Lake Erie, a distance of some seventy or eighty miles further. He, therefore, conceived the plan of building a small scow,* large enough to hold his wife, himself, and his effects, and silently drop-

---

* A long-shaped flat-bottomed boat of the same width the entire length, rising gently at each end, built of two-inch plank, and much used on shallow rivers and creeks.

ping down with the current, bade adieu to their sylvan retreat, and the great city of Guelph, which, however, he was destined to see again, much sooner than he expected.

He built his boat close to the river's edge, having, with the assistance of his wife, carried the planks down for that purpose. I suppose he took a lesson from Robinson Crusoe, not to build his scow too far from the water.

Everything being ready, the boat was launched and freighted, our hero in the stern, with steering paddle in hand, and his patient *compagnon de voyage* acting as bowman.

The Speed is a shallow, swift, running stream, seldom exceeding three feet in depth during the dry season. For the first mile they got on pretty well, till they came to a jam of drift wood; over this with great difficulty they hauled their scow; every few yards fresh obstructions occurred in the shape of snags, fallen trees, and drift wood, which caused them to upset twice before they had accomplished the second mile, till at last an extensive jam across the river many yards in length, put a complete barrier to their further advance.

Wet and weary, half the day gone, and no chance of proceeding down the stream, they determined to retrace their course.   This was not easy to accomplish, for the current was too swift to paddle against ; so, tying a short piece of rope to the stem of the scow, he ordered his unfortunate wife to take the water and tow the boat, whilst he sat in state in the stern assisting with his paddle.

In the evening, I was walking out with my wife; and as we were passing I thought we would look in and see how their work progressed, when to my astonishment I saw Mrs. W—— sitting on a stone, weeping bitterly.   I perceived at once that something extraordinary had occurred, for her dress was sadly torn and saturated with wet.   Upon making an inquiry respecting her appearance, and the causes of her grief, she told me the sad story I have just related, adding, that they had only just got back from their expedition, and that all her clothes, bed, and blankets were wringing wet.

My wife, who had lately joined me, and was of a most kind disposition, always ready to help those in distress, offered her an asylum for a few days, and a change of apparel, which she thankfully accepted.   Her brutal husband cleared out the next day, and she joined him the week following.

Some time afterwards, I was told that Mrs. W —— had committed suicide, goaded, doubtless, to desperation by the ill usage of her partner, and the hardships she had to endure. As this, however, is only hearsay, I will not vouch for its truth ; though from my knowledge of the parties I am afraid it was only too true.

CHAPTER XVI.

PORCUPINE-CATCHING.—HANDSOME BEHAVIOUR OF MR. GALT.—
OWLINGALE.— INTRODUCTION TO THE SON OF THE CELEBRATED
INDIAN CHIEF, BRANDT. — EXPEDITION TO WILMOT. —SHAM
WOLVES.— NIGHT IN A BARN WITH DR. DUNLOP.—THE DOCTOR
AND HIS SNUFF-BOX.—HIS BATH IN THE NITH.—LOUIS XVIII.
AND HIS TABATIERE.—CAMP IN THE WOODS.—RETURN TO
GUELPH.

ONE day, being out in the woods with an emigrant, examining a lot of land, I was attracted by the barking of my dog, who had treed some animal, which, upon coming up, I discovered was a porcupine. We cut down the tree, a small beech, in which he had taken refuge, and secured him alive. I did not notice my dog till I got home, when I found his mouth was full of quills, which the porcupine, in self-defence, had darted into him. The manner in which they accomplish this is, by striking the object that offends them with their tail, when the outside points of the quills, being finely barbed, if inserted ever so slightly, retain their hold, and are easily detached from the porcupine without pain.

I once lost a fine Irish greyhound, who was stuck full of quills in this way, although I pulled out hundreds of them from his mouth, head, and different parts of his body, with a pair of pincers. In fact, some of these barbs had worked into him nearly their whole length, so that I had a difficulty in getting hold of the end of the quills to extract them ; and I have no doubt, as the dog died, that many of them had completely buried themselves in some vital part, and caused his death.

I took home my prize, and put it into a barrel in a dark corner of the store, which was half full of nails. A few minutes afterwards, Dr. Dunlop, as he often did, came in to see me, and drink a glass of cider, of which I had at that time some of excellent quality in bottle. The Doctor, as he said, used to " improve" it, making what he called, " a stone-fence," by inserting a small *soupçon* of brandy from a pocket-pistol, which he was too much in the habit of carrying about with him in hot weather.

" Now," said I, " Doctor, I know you like a bit of fun. When Fielding, the porter, comes in, ask him to go to that barrel in the corner and fetch you a nail; for I have got a live porcupine in it that I have just brought home from the woods."

The Doctor was mightily tickled with the

notion ; so, as soon as poor Fielding made his appearance, he sent him off to the barrel. Quite unsuspiciously the man put in his hand for the nail, and as quickly drew it out again, with the addition of some half a score quills sticking to his fingers, to the no small delight of the Doctor, who greatly enjoyed Fielding's consternation, for the porter thought the devil himself was in the tub.

Every one who came into the store during the afternoon was served the same trick by the Doctor, and it was certainly amusing to watch their countenances and hear their remarks, those who showed the most anger being of course the most laughed at for their pains.

Shortly after, a Mr. Smith, an accountant, was sent out by the directors to examine the accounts, and report on the state of the Company's affairs in the colony. A few days after his arrival, he went round with the superintendent, and examined the works that had been completed, and those in progress. Mr. Galt and the accountant both expressed themselves much pleased with what I had done, especially with the bridge connecting the clergy-block (now called the township of Puslinch) with the town of Guelph.

In the afternoon, Mr. Smith called upon me and

said he was authorized by the superintendent to arrange with me as to the amount of salary I was to receive. He then informed me the amount that Mr. Galt had instructed him to offer me— a liberal income, and the use of a house rent-free, desiring him at the same time to express his satisfaction at the manner in which I had conducted the operations since my engagement with the Company, in which, he said, from what he had seen, he fully concurred.

As this result was entirely unsolicited by me, and as it was generally understood that the accountant had been sent out partly as a check on the superintendent, to prevent extravagant expenditure, I took this as a compliment paid by both to my abilities and integrity.

Several of the clerks had light neatly-made boats, in which we used to make excursions up the Speed for the purpose of trout-fishing. I think, without exception, this stream is the best for that species of fish I ever saw. I have frequently caught a pailful of these delicious trout in the space of two or three hours. For my own part, I found a small garden-worm the best bait ; but one of our clerks, a Mr. Hodgett, was skilful with the fly, and consequently used to catch his fish in a more scientific manner.

My native county, Suffolk, with the exception of that part watered by the Waveney, is not famed for its fly-fishing: therefore I was no adept in the gentle art, but in ground-bait angling I consider myself no contemptible performer.

The small streams and creeks are so over-arched with trees in Canada, that it is almost impossible, except in odd spots, to make a cast with the fly without endangering your tackle.

The speckled trout in the river Speed vary in size from four ounces to a pound and a half, though it is seldom that one of the latter size is captured.

Guelph I consider to be remarkably healthy, and for an inland town very prettily situated. I think, however, that the town-plot was laid out on too large a scale—especially the market-place, which is large enough for a city containing fifty thousand inhabitants. I have not been there since 1832. It has since become the assize-town for the Wellington district, and consequently has greatly increased both in size and population.

Although I had been several months a resident in Guelph, I had neither seen nor heard a clergyman of the Established Church. Why are we always the last to send labourers into the vine-

yard ?   No sooner does a small village, composed
of a mill, a black-smith's shop, and a few houses,
spring up in the woods, than you find a Presby-
terian, Methodist, or Baptist Church—or perhaps
all three—settled there immediately.   No wonder,
then, that our church is losing ground when so
little energy is displayed either in building
churches or sending active and zealous men to
preach the gospel.

The first person I heard preach in Guelph was
a tailor, who had made a professional visit to the
city, and who had the reputation of being considered a very eloquent man.   Due notice having
been given, a large congregation assembled to
hear Mr. H——, who, to do him justice, was
eloquent enough, though his sermon was all in
his own praise from beginning to end.

He said that " he had once been a great infidel and an evil liver, but now he was converted,
and was as good as he formerly had been wicked ;
and he hoped that all his hearers would take example from him and do as he had done—forsake
the crooked paths and steadfastly follow the
straight."   After this autobiographical discourse
was at length over, and a brother snip invited him
to dinner, I was also honoured with an invitation.
which my curiosity induced me to accept.

I found that the party consisted of a magistrate and his wife, from E——, the mad Doctor, and Mr. Y——, one of the Company's clerks. Our host-tailor, No. 1, took the head of the table ; the preacher, tailor No. 2, sat at the foot. The dinner itself was quite a professional spread, and consisted of a fine fat roast goose at the top, and another at the bottom—a large dish of cabbage in the centre, and a plate of hard dumplings on each side. Mr. Y——, who sat opposite, gave me such a comical look when the second goose made its appearance, that I found it impossible to suppress my risibility, which, unfortunately for me, exploded just as the preacher—who, of course, mentally consigned me to perdition — commenced a long grace ; but if the Governor-General himself had been present, I do not think I could have restrained my inclination to laugh.

The dinner was certainly excellent of its kind ; and in a new settlement where nothing but salt pork and beef could be obtained, I might with truth say, that it was a great treat. After the cloth was removed, it was proposed by the magistrate's lady, that the company should sing a hymn, upon which the mad Doctor, who was considered the most pious, as well as the most scientific, singer of the company, sang like an *owl*ingale, Pope's celebrated lines :—

> " Vital spark of heavenly flame,
> Quit, O quit, this mortal frame.

I am ashamed to say that I was obliged to stuff my handkerchief into my mouth to keep from laughing outright ; and no wonder, for I never heard such an insane screeching in all my life.

In the course of the summer, Mr. Buchanan, the British Consul, visited Guelph, when the superintendent gave a public dinner at the Priory, to which I had the honour of an invitation. Amongst other guests was John Brandt, the chief of the Mohawks, and son of the celebrated chief whom Campbell the poet, in his " Gertrude of Wyoming," has stigmatized as—

> " The monster, Brandt,
> With all his howling, desolating band."

And again—

> " Accursed Brandt ! he left of all my tribe,
> Nor man, nor child, nor thing of living birth."

It is said that John Brandt was very angry when these lines were pointed out to him.*

On his health being drunk, he acknowledged the courtesy in a short but eloquent speech. He was not handsome, though rather a fine-looking man. I believe he died of cholera in 1832.

* Campbell subsequently made an apology to him.

One day, Dr. Dunlop came to my house, and informed me that I was to accompany him on an expedition to the township of Wilmot, joining the Huron tract, to examine the site, and make a report of the probable cost of building a bridge over the river Nith—or " Smith's Creek," as it was then called—one of the tributaries of the Grand River. "The accountant," he said, " has taken it into his head that he will accompany us ; and, as he has never been in the Bush before, won't we put him through his facings before he gets back ? that is all. Mind, and keep your eye on me. When I am ready to play him off, I will give the signal to you."

" Well, Doctor," said I, "if you will take the blame, I have no objection to the fun ; but remember ! I am a very young man, and if Mr. Smith should complain to the Company— "

" Oh, never fear," was his reply, " for I will make it all right with Galt, if he do. In the meantime, order my man to saddle the horses. Let the Cockney have the roan-mare. You can take your own pony ; and do not forget to tell Hinds to bring the brandy. Should we have to camp out all-night, a small *soupçon* of the creature will do us no harm."

Everything being in readiness, we started about

two o'clock, P.M.   Our route lay through the new
settlement of Guelph and the fine townships of
Upper and Lower Waterloo.   This tract of land
was originally bought and settled by a company
of Dutch Pennsylvanians, upwards of fifty years
ago.   The Grand River, or Ouse, intersects these
townships—a fine stream, spanned by several substantial bridges.   This part of the country is
densely populated and very fertile.   The soil, for
the most part, is a light rich loam.

As soon as we had crossed the open country,
we entered a narrow bush-road, only just wide
enough for two persons to ride abreast.   It must
be remembered that Smith was a very bad rider,
and looked as if he had never been on horse-back
before ; for every time he rose in his saddle you
could see his horse's head under him.

The Doctor now gave me the wink to fall into
the rear ; then riding up abreast of Smith, he
commenced operations by slyly sticking his spur
into the roan mare, exclaiming at the same time,
" Come, man, if we don't push on a little, we
shall not reach Blenheim to-night."

As soon as the roan mare felt the spur, off she
went at a rattling pace, the Dr. keeping close
along-side, and applying the spur whenever he
could get a chance.   At first, Smith tried hard

to pull in the mare ; then he shouted to the Doctor to stop her ; instead of which, the spur was only applied the sharper.   At last, quite frightened, he seized the mane with both his hands. And then commenced a neck-and-neck race for nearly two miles—myself and the Doctor's man, John Hinds, bringing up the rear, and shouting with laughter. Smith was so frightened, and so intent on stopping his run-away steed, that he never suspected his persecutor who, looking quite grave, said, "He never remembered his roan running off in that extraordinary manner before ; but," he added with a grin, "I suspect, Smith, she knew you were a Cockney."

After this exploit, we went on soberly enough, until we entered the township of Blenheim.   We had still some distance to travel through a dense forest, before we should reach Springer's—a farm-house where we intended to stop all night, and where the Doctor kept a store of good things, under the charge of Mrs. Springer ; for this was always his halting-place, on his various journeys to Goderich.

Darkness fell as we entered the Blenheim woods, and now the Doctor took the opportunity of asking me, "If I thought that I could howl ? I expressed confidence in my abilities that way.

The Doctor then said, " Second any move of mine for pushing you on to Springer's. But mind," continued he, " you are to stop within half a mile of his clearing ; and when you hear us coming, you must howl with all your might, and leave the rest to me."

After a while, when it was quite dark, so that we could scarcely see our horses' heads, the Doctor proposed that I should take Hind's, and " ride on as hard as we could, and tell Mrs. Springer to have supper ready for us; and," said he, " let the old man tap the whiskey I forwarded to his house last week. We will follow you at our leisure ; for my friend is not used to travel after dark on such roads as these."

We accordingly rode on smartly, till we could perceive a slight glimmering of light through the trees, which we knew to be Springer's clearing. We then halted, one on each side of the road, but entirely concealed from view by the thick underbrush. As soon as we heard the party coming, we set up a most unearthly yell, which made the woods fairly ring again. We could hear the Doctor cry out, "The wolves ! the wolves ! ride for your life, man," and he then galloped off in the direction from which they had just come.

Poor Smith shouted after him at the top of his voice, imploring the Doctor, for God's sake, not to leave him. "Oh Lord!" we heard him say, as he rode after the Doctor, "I shall surely be devoured by the ravenous wretches. Help— help! Doctor—stop!" and such like piteous ejaculations.

The Doctor, who had riden ahead, as soon as he heard his victim approach, commenced in the same key as we had done before, and a dismal howling we all made. Fear now compelled poor Smith to wheel the mare round and ride back, whereupon we again greeted him with a second edition, even— if that were possible—more diabolical than the first, which terminated the fun sooner than we expected; for, losing all presence of mind, he let his steed get off the track into the woods, and, consequently, he was swept off by the branches. We heard him fall and roar for help, which we left the Doctor to administer, and made the best of our way to Springer's, where, half an hour after, we were joined by our fellow-travellers, one of whom had scarcely recovered from his fright, and still looked as pale as a ghost. Two or three glasses of whiskey-punch, however, soon restored him to his natural complexion.

I do not know if he ever found out the trick

we had so successfully played him ; but if he did, he kept it to himself, rightly judging that if the story got wind he would never hear the last of it.

Springer had only one spare bed, which we resigned in favour of the accountant, as some little compensation for the fright he had sustained.   The Doctor and I took possession of the barn, where we found plenty of fresh hay, which we infinitely preferred to the spare bed and its familiars.   There we slept delightfully, till a chorus of cocks (or *roosters*, as the more delicate Americans would call them) awakened us from our repose, to the wrathful indignation of Dunlop, who anathematized them for "an unmusical ornithological set of fiends."

We made an early breakfast off fried sausages, and the never-failing ham and eggs, and were soon again in the saddle.   We took the nearest road to Plum Creek, where we left our horses, and proceeded for the remaining four miles on foot, through a magnificent forest.

We were now in that part of the township of Wilmot belonging to the Canada Company, which did not then contain a single farm, but has been since completely settled.   At length, we came to a narrow valley, some fifty or sixty feet below the level of the country through which we had been travelling, in the centre of which flowed the Nith, sparkling in the sun : the wild grapes hanging in rich festoons from tree to tree, gave an air of rural beauty to the scene. For the convenience of foot-passengers, some good Samaritan had felled a tree directly across the stream, which at that place was not more than fifty feet wide. The current was swift, though not more than four or five feet deep.

Here a small misfortune happened to the Doctor, who was an inveterate snuff-taker, and carried a large box he called a coffin—I presume from its resemblance to that dreary receptacle.

While in the act of crossing the temporary bridge, and at the same time regaling his olfactory nerves with a pinch of the best Irish, his famous coffin slipped from his grasp and floated away majestically down the swift-flowing waters of the sylvan Nith.

The Doctor was a man of decision : he hesitated not even for a moment, but pitched himself headlong into the stream, from which he quickly emerged with his recovered treasure. It is but justice to my friend Dunlop, to remind the reader that his extravagant affection for his snuff-box is not without a parallel in history, since Louis XVIII. has recorded with his own royal hand an attachment to his *tabatière*, equally eccentric and misplaced.

Scarcely had this Prince escaped three miles from Paris and its democrats, when, on putting his hand into his waistcoat-pocket, in order to take a consoling pinch, he missed his snuff-box, which, in his hurry, he had left upon his toilette, at the discretion of the mob. " Mon Dieu, ma tabatière !" was his horrified exclamation, as he deliberated for a moment upon a misfortune so overwhelming.

To go back to Paris was only to risk his life, while to proceed on his journey was to lose his snuff-box. His philo-tabatièrishness triumphed : he returned, snatched up his beloved box, and made it the companion of his flight ; and, in all his vicissitudes, from exile to a throne, he considered the possession of his favourite *tabatière* as his principal consolation. The Doctor was no less rash than the French monarch, and in reco- vering his *tabatière* equally fortunate.

A good fire and some brandy soon made the Doctor all right again, after his cold bath in the Nith. We now prepared our camp for the night : this we had no trouble in doing, for we found plenty of poles and bark, which had been used by the labourers, whilst cutting out the road to the

Huron tract. The Doctor's man had brought a bundle of blankets and an axe, from Springer's, and I, like Dalgetty, carried the provender.

While Hinds was cooking the supper, I prepared our bed, by breaking a quantity of fine hemlock-brush to thatch the bottom of the camp, to keep us from the damp ground, which it did quite effectually. I have camped out, I dare say, hundreds of times, both in winter and summer; and I never caught cold yet. I recommend, from experience, a hemlock-bed, and hemlock-tea, with a dash of whiskey in it, merely to assist the flavour, as the best preventive.

The Doctor was in first-rate humour, and seemed determined to make a night of it; and even the Cockney appeared to enjoy himself amazingly. I knew, by the wicked eye of the Doctor, that he was bent on mischief. Hinds was kept busy after supper in making brandy-punch, the Doctor keeping us in a roar of laughter with his amusing anecdotes. I knew by the long Latin quotations that Smith indulged in, that he was fast verging on intoxication. For my part, tired and drowsy, I soon fell into a state of pleasing forgetulness, leaving my two companions in the middle of some learned discussion, the subject of which I have long forgotten.

In the morning we examined the proposed site for building the bridge, which we found presented no unusual difficulties. I have since been informed that excellent mills and a thriving village now occupy the very spot where we bivouacked on this memorable occasion.

At Plum Creek we again resumed our horses, and, at the village of Galt* we parted company. The Doctor and his man went on to Flamborough† West; whilst Smith and I returned to Guelph, which we reached a short time after dark, without inflicting on him any more adventures.

* Galt is a thriving town, situated on the west bank of the Grand River, in the township of Dumfries. The town-plot originally belonged to the Honourable William Dixon, who gave it that name in compliment to the superintendent of the Canada Company.

† One of the prettiest situations in Canada West, commanding a fine prospect of Ancaster and the surrounding country; and also the seat of the Hon. James Crooks.

CHAPTER XVII.

A NEW WAY OF KEEPING A BIRTHDAY.—LOST IN THE WOODS.—
KINDNESS OF MR. GALT. — ADVICE TO NEW SETTLERS. — UNEX-
PECTED RETIREMENT OF MR. GALT.—I ACCOMPANY HIM TO THE
LANDING-PLACE. — RECEIVE ORDERS TO LEAVE GUELPH FOR
GODERICH.—WHIRLWINDS AT GUELPH AND DOURO.

THE 6th of November was my birthday, so I
determined to give myself a holiday, and go out
still-hunting. I had been told by some of the
workmen that deer were very plentiful in the
Clergy-block, so I started early in the morning
without waiting for my regular breakfast, merely
taking a biscuit, as I was too eager for the sport
to have much appetite ; besides, I intended to be
home to an early dinner. The sky was overcast,
and a few flakes of snow were falling, but I did
not dislike these signs ; for I prefer a little damp-
ness on the leaves, which causes less noise from
the tread—an important point to the hunter ; for
when the leaves are crisp and dry, it is useless to
attempt approaching the deer, who are sure to
hear you long before you get within range.

I considered myself a tolerably good woodsman, and was, therefore, not much afraid of being lost ; but I reckoned without my host in this instance. After crossing the river, I proceeded for some distance along a hard-wood ridge, till I came to a thicket of brush-wood, out of which sprang three fine deer, a buck and two does. I fired at the buck as he scampered off, and had the satisfaction of finding blood on the track, which I followed for more than two miles. But I lost him at last in the middle of a cedar-swamp, owing to the quantity of soft snow, which was by this time falling heavily. I, therefore, thought it best to return home, and put off my hunt to a more propitious day.

On emerging from the swamp, which I did on the wrong side—for I had no sun to guide me—I saw a fine doe within fifty yards of me, feeding on the side of a hill. I thought I was sure of this one at any rate ; but, in this also, I was woefully disappointed ; for the powder in the pan of the lock had got damp by the wet snow, and only flashed in the pan. My gun had the old flint-lock, percussion-caps being then hardly known in the colonies.

My second disappointment decided me to return home. This, however, was sooner said than done; for, after walking for more than two hours, I found I had lost my way, a conclusion as to which there could be no mistake. At first, I thought it would be best to take my back-track, but I found this would not answer; for the snow was melting as fast as it fell. I could not even avail myself of the common indications for finding my way, because the under-brush was still loaded with snow, so that it was quite impossible to see fifty yards in any direction.

Whilst I was debating what I had best do to extricate myself from this dilemma, I came upon a tolerably fresh blazed line, which I suspected was the boundary between the townships of Guelph and the Clergy-reserve-block of Puslinch. In this idea I was perfectly right; but the question now with me was, in which direction I should follow the line. After considering for some time, as ill-luck would have it, I took the wrong route, and, having walked at least three miles, came to the end of the blaze, where I found a surveyor's post, on which was legibly written, in red chalk, on each side, the names of the four townships, of which it was the corner-post; viz. Guelph, Puslinch, Nasagiweya, and Eramosa; and lower down on the post, "*seven miles and a half to Guelph*." I had, therefore, nothing for it, but to turn back on the line and retrace my steps. This I did in a smart run, for I saw the shades of night fast gathering around me.

In less than an hour I had passed the place where I first found the blaze, but soon after came to a windfall,* where I found it impossible to follow the line through. I was, therefore, compelled to leave the blaze—my only sure guide—which, however, I still hoped to re-find, by keeping round the edge of the windfall, till I again struck the line. Just before dark, I saw a partridge sitting—on a log, I believe. I fresh primed, and snapped half a dozen times at him, without effect, but the gun had got so wet, that at last I gave it up as a bad job ; though I should have liked him very much for my supper, for which I had a ravenous appetite.

Presently, I came to a nice little spring creek running under some fine shady cedars. The ground looked dry and mossy ; and as it was nearly dark, I thought the best thing I could do was to camp for the night, for I knew it was impossible to find my way after dark. I immediately collected a large quantity of dry balsam-fir, which lay about in great profusion, and chose a cluster of spreading cedars for my camp. After

* A heap of great trees blown down by the wind.

this, I piled a large heap of wood against one of the trees; and rubbing some dry cedar-bark quite fine, put it under my wood. In order to light my fire, I tore up a piece of a cotton handkerchief, which I laid over the pan of my gun, newly primed. Having fired the cotton in this manner, I enclosed it in the cedar-bark, keeping up the flame—not by using that primitive bellows, my mouth—but, by waving the bark to and fro, after the method used by the Indians. Thus, I soon had a large cheerful fire, which I much needed, for I was thoroughly wet.

My first care was to dry my gun and reload it, in case of wolves. Whilst I was busy doing this, I heard a shot, and then another; but the gunners were a long way off, as I knew by the sound—certainly not less than three miles; and as I was quite aware it was useless for me to attempt to make my way out, I contented myself with firing my gun in answer to their shots, which, not being repeated, I also ceased firing, though I had no doubt my neighbours were searching for me, but not near enough to find me out. However, I discovered the direction in which Guelph lay, by the sound of their volleys, so I did not despair, as I felt sure of being able to regain my home in the morning.

The snow soon ceased to fall, and the night came out fine and clear, though rather sharp. I had a famous fire, and slept tolerably well, though awaking occasionally with the cold ; when I would replenish the fire and turn my chilled side to the blaze, by which means I managed to pass the night as well as I could expect under the circumstances, considering, too, that I had eaten nothing from six o'clock the previous morning.

By day-break, I was on my march in the direction in which I supposed Guelph to lie. The sun rose clear and bright, which enabled me to make a true course in half an hour ; for I began to recognize ridges I had before traversed in former hunting excursions ; and was soon confirmed in this opinion, by the firing of guns and blowing of horns in the direction I was going. In a few minutes, I heard two men in conversation, one of whom was a native of Somersetshire, living close to me. I stepped behind a large tree, directly in their path, when I heard my neighbour say to his companion—

" This is the way he generally takes ; I will warrant we shall find he." At that instant, I fired my gun close to them, which made them start with surprise. They then informed me that Mr. Galt had sent out all the workmen in search of me. This I was well-aware of, from the continual volleys which rang in all directions. We were soon out on the main-road leading to the bridge, where I found more than fifty of the inhabitants looking for me.

This birthday hunting excursion turned out anything but a frolic ; for the result was, twenty-six hours' starvation and the loss of a fine buck; besides my being hungry, weary, and stiff, from sleeping all night in the woods. Moreover, in common gratitude, I was bound to treat my neighbours and the workmen sent to look for me, and the treat cost me five gallons of whiskey. To add to this chapter of accidents, two of the party who turned out to hunt for me in the woods, lost themselves, and spent the night in as disagreeable a manner as I had myself done.

I would advise all new settlers to provide themselves with a pocket-compass, which can be procured for a few shillings. This should be suspended round the neck by a ribbon, in the same manner as a watch—and I need not add that in the Bush it is of infinitely more use.

My employments in the Company's service often obliged me to leave home and take long journeys —fatiguing enough, indeed, they often were. But youth is the season of enterprise, and I always have accustomed myself to look upon the bright side of everything, leaving to the grumblers the reverse of the picture, upon which I fear they are only too fond of dwelling. But I am sure a cheerful spirit is the best assistant in carrying a settler through every difficulty.

Early in the spring of 1829, I made a tour of the Newcastle district, selling land and receiving payments for the Company. Whilst so employed, I received a letter from the superintendent, informing me of his resignation, and appointing me to meet him in Toronto with what money I had collected.

I was very sorry to hear of Mr. Galt's retirement. He had always acted in a kind and liberal manner towards me; and, indeed, when he left the Company, I considered that I had lost a true and affectionate friend. I could not help, therefore, noticing with regret that, although most of the clerks belonging to the office were at that time in Toronto, only Dr. Dunlop, Mr. Reid * and myself accompanied Mr. Galt to the landing-place to see him depart and cry " God speed!" But this is the way of the world. Those who should be most grateful when

* Mr. Galt's friend and private secretary.

the hour of adversity dawns on their benefactor, are often the first to desert him.

On the same day the Doctor introduced me to one of our new Commissioners, Thomas Mercer Jones, Esq., a fine gentlemanly-looking person. The other Commissioner was the Hon. William Allen. These gentlemen were appointed by the directors to supersede Mr. Galt in the direction of the Company's affairs in Canada. On my return to Guelph, I received an intimation that I must prepare to take up my residence in Goderich, as my services in future would be required in the Huron tract.

A few days before my departure, I witnessed the most appalling land tornado (if so I may term it), I ever saw in my life. As this is a phenomenon seldom if ever witnessed in England, I think a particular description may possibly interest those readers who are unaccustomed to such eccentricities of Nature.

In my hunting excursions and rambles through the Upper Canadian forests, I had frequently met with extensive windfalls; and observed with some surprise that the fallen trees appeared to have been twisted off at the stumps, for they lay strewn in a succession of circles. I also remarked, that these windfalls were generally narrow, and had the appearance of a wide road slashed through the forest.

From observations made at the time, and since confirmed, I have no doubt Colonel Reid's theory of storms is a correct one, viz. :—" That all wind-storms move in a circular direction, and the nearer the centre, the more violent the wind." Having seen the effects of several similar hurricanes since my residence in Canada West, I shall describe one which happened in the township of Guelph, during the early part of the summer of 1829.

The weather, for the season of the year (May) had been hot and sultry, with scarcely a breath of wind stirring. I had heard distant thunder from an early hour of the morning, which from the eastward is rather an unusual occurrence. About ten A.M. the sky had a most singular, I may say, a most awful appearance ; presenting to the view a vast arch of rolling blackness, which seemed to gather strength and density as it approached the zenith. All at once the clouds began to work round in circles, as if chasing one another through the air. Suddenly, the dark arch of clouds appeared to break up into detached masses, whirling and eddying through each other in dreadful commotion. The forked lightning was incessant, accompanied by heavy thunder. In a short space the clouds seemed to converge to a point, which approached very near the earth, still whirling with great rapidity directly under this point; and apparently from the midst of the woods arose a black column in the shape of a cone, which instantly joined itself to the depending cloud: the sight was now grand and awful in the extreme.

Let any one picture to the imagination a vast column of smoke of inky blackness reaching from earth to heaven, gyrating with fearful velocity; bright lightnings issuing from the vortex—the roar of the thunder—the rushing of the blast—the crashing of timber—the limbs of trees, leaves and rubbish, mingled with clouds of dust, whirling through the air—a faint idea is then given of the scene.

> " Through all the sky arise outrageous storms,
>   And death stands threatening in a thousand forms;
>   Clouds charged with loud destruction drown the day,
>   And airy demons in wild whirlwinds play;
>   Thick thunder-claps, and lightnings' vivid glare
>   Disturb the sky, and trouble all the air."

I had ample time for observation as the hurricane commenced its desolating course about two miles from the town, through the centre of which it took its way, passing within fifty yards of the spot where a number of persons and myself were standing watching its fearful progress. As the tornado approached, the trees seemed to fall like a pack of cards before its irresistible current. After passing through the clearing made around the town, the force of the wind gradually abated, and in a few minutes died away entirely.

As soon as the storm was over, I went to see what damage it had done. From the point where I first observed the black column to rise from the woods and join the cloud, the trees were twisted in every direction. A belt of timber had been levelled to the ground about two miles in length, and about one hundred yards in breadth : at the entrance of the town it crossed the river Speed, and up-rooted about six acres of wood which had been thinned out and left by Mr. Galt as an ornament to his house.

The Eremosa road was completely blocked up for nearly half a mile, in the wildest confusion possible. In its progress through the town, it unroofed several houses, levelled the fences to the ground, and entirely demolished a frame-barn : windows were dashed in, and in one instance the floor of a log-house was carried up through the roof. Some hair-breadth escapes occurred, but, luckily, no lives were lost.

About twelve years since, a storm of this kind occurred in the north part of the township of Douro, though of less magnitude. I heard an intelligent settler who resided some years in the township of Madoc state that, during his residence there, a similar hurricane to the one I have described, but of a more awful character, passed through a part of Marmora and Madoc, which had been traced in a north-easterly direction upwards of forty miles into the unsurveyed lands, the uniform width of which appeared to be upwards of three quarters of a mile.

It appears very evident that storms of this description have not been unfrequent in the wooded regions of Canada ; and it becomes a matter of interesting consideration, whether the clearing of our immense forests will not, in a great measure, remove the cause of these phenomena.

Dark, heavy clouds were gathering in the west,
  Wrapping the forest in funereal gloom ;
Onward they roll'd and rear'd each livid crest,
  Like death's murk shadows frowning o'er earth's tomb :
From out the inky womb of that deep night
  Burst livid flashes of electric flame :
Whirling and circling with terrific might,
  In wild confusion on the tempest came.
Nature, awakening from her still repose,
  Shudders responsive to the whirlwind's shock
Feels at her mighty heart convulsive throes ;
  Her groaning forests to earth's bosom rock.

But, hark ! what means that hollow rushing sound,
　　That breaks the sudden stillness of the morn ?
Red forked lightnings fiercely glare around :
　　What crashing thunders on the winds are borne !
And see yon spiral column, black as night,
　　Rearing triumphantly its wreathing form ;
Ruin 's abroad, and through the murky light,
　　Drear desolation marks the spirit of the storm.
　　*　　*　　*　　*　　*　　*
How changed the scene ; the awful tempest 's o'er ;
　　From dread array and elemental war
The lightning's flash hath ceased, the thunder's roar—
　　The glorious sun resumes his golden car.*

---

* My description of this whirlwind, and the accompanying
lines, have already appeared in the " Victoria Magazine," published in Canada West, under the signature of " Pioneer."

CHAPTER XVIII.

THE HURON TRACT. — JOURNAL OF DR. DUNLOP. — HIS HARDSHIPS. — I LEAVE GUELPH FOR GODERICH. — WANT OF ACCOMMODA- TION.—CURIOUS SUPPER. — REMARKABLE TREES.—THE BEVERLY OAK.—NOBLE BUTTER-WOOD TREES.—GODERICH.— FINE WHEAT CROP.—PURCHASE A LOG-HOUSE.—CONSTRUCTION OF A RAFT.

I HAD always wished to go to the Huron tract, whose fine lake, noble forests, and productive soil, have made it a source of wealth to many a settler. The climate too, was mild, and I had heard a great deal about it from my gifted and facetious friend Dr. Dunlop, whose services in exploring that part of their possessions were not only useful but inestimable to the Company, and, in fact, to emigration in general.

" Dr. Dunlop, the Warden of the Company's Woods and Forests, surveyed the great Huron tract in the summer of 1827, assisted by the Chief of the Mohawk nation, and Messrs. Sproat and MacDonald. They penetrated the huge untravelled wilderness in all directions, until they came out on the shores of the Huron, having experienced and withstood every privation that wanderers can possibly be subject to in such places."*

The Doctor himself has given a very accurate account of the valuable resources of the Huron tract. He says in his journal—" I have already adverted to its nature and fertility, and think I may be justified in adding, such is the general excellence of the land, that if ordinary care can be taken to give each lot no more than its own share of any small swamp in its vicinity, it would be difficult, if not impossible, to find two hundred acres together in the whole territory, that would make a bad farm. Although the land may be capable of raising any kind of produce usual in that country, yet some spots are more particularly advantageous for particular crops. The black ash-swales (a kind of swamp) make the best ground for hemp ; as by the scourging effect of two or three crops, the ground will be made more fit for the raising of wheat, for which, in the original state, it is too strong. The rich meadows by the side of the rivers, (more especially such as are annually overflowed,) are ready without farther preparation, for tobacco, hemp, and flax. The lower meadows, and meadows adjoin-

* Mac Taggart's " Three Years in Canada."

ing Beaver dams, which are abundant, produce at this moment enormous quantities of natural hay and pasture; and the rest of the land, for the production of potatoes, Indian corn, wheat, and other grain, is at least equal, if not superior, to any other land in the Canadas. Independent of the swamps, the timber on the land is very soon described.

"The sugar-maple is the principal growth, and the size and height which it, as well as other trees, attains, sufficiently evince the strength and power of the soil. Next to this come the beech, elm, and bass-wood, in various proportions. In some instances, the beech and elm predominate over the maple, but this is rare. Near the streams the hemlock is found; and interspersed through the whole is the cherry, butter-nut, the different species of oak, and the birch." *

In exploring this, then unknown, wilderness, Dr. Dunlop encountered many difficulties, and was more than once in danger of starvation—though an Indian Mohawk Chief shared his risks and perils.† As he told a story admirably well, I was delighted to hear him discuss his peregrinations over a glass of brandy-punch, of which he was very fond. Whatever

Mac Taggart's "Journal of Dr. Dunlop."

might have been his feelings at the time, he only made a joke of his trials at the period in which he related them to me.

I should have experienced some regret in quitting Guelph, if the society had been more to my taste. The only persons of education in that town were, in fact, the Company's officers, many of whom I might reasonably expect to meet again at Goderich. Of course, I found some exceptions, but the average was not in favour of Guelph. Besides, the water was an attraction to me, as my Suffolk home was within a short distance of the German Ocean. Brought up so near a sea-port, my natural inclinations made me dislike an inland situation; and if I were not going to have a sea-side residence, at least the shores of the mighty Huron Lake came the nearest to it in my estimation.

I left Guelph early in June with Mr. Prior, the Company's agent at Goderich. Our road after leaving Springer's in Blenheim lay through the township of Wilmot to the southern boundary of the Huron tract, and from thence nearly in a straight line to the town of Goderich at the mouth of the river Maitland, on Lake Huron, on our route for a distance of nearly seventy miles, being bounded on the east by the townships of North Easthope, Ellice, Logan, M'Killop, Hullett, and

the east part of Goderich to the west, by South
Easthope, Downie, Fullarton, Hibbert, Tucker
Smith, and the west part of Goderich.

This road was a mere sleigh-track through the
woods, newly cut out, and rarely exceeding twelve
feet in width. At this time we saw only three
log-cabins during the whole way, these being
about twenty miles apart from each other. These
three were kept by Dutch or German emigrants,
who supplied travellers with whiskey and provisions—when they had any—which was not always
the case. Indeed, I can testify, to my sorrow, to
the uncertainty of finding a decent table provided
for guests by these foreigners; for I once had to
stop at old Sebach's, the centre house, for the
night, and being tired by a long day's march
through the snow, I had calculated on making a
capital supper. Not that I expected anything
better than tea, fried pork and bread and butter,
to which, hungry as I was, I should no doubt have
done ample justice. Judge, then, of my astonishment and disappointment, when mine hostess
placed before me a piece of dirty-looking Indian
meal-bread, and a large cake of beef-tallow, and,
to wash down this elegant repast, a dish of crust
coffee without either milk or sugar, assuring me
at the same time in her broken English, "That

she had nothing better in the house till the return of her husband, who had gone fifty miles to the mill and store for a supply of flour, groceries, and other fixings."

Not being a Russian, I rejected the tallow with disgust, and made but a sorry meal of the other delicacies.

On our route, we crossed several pretty streams, the principal of which are the Avon, then called the Little Thames, the Big Thames, and the Black Water. The Bayfield does not cross the road, though it makes a bend close to it, and within sight. I believe I am correct in saying, that we did not cross a single cedar-swamp from the time we entered the Huron tract * till we reached

* " This interesting portion of the Company's possessions contains a million of acres in one block, within the compass of which a bad farm could scarcely be found. The soil is a rich black loam, on clay or limestone ; and as it is entirely timbered with the best kind of hard wood, no land in the Province is so well adapted for the manufacture of potash, an object of considerable importance to the industrious settler. It is bounded, for an extent of sixty miles, by Lake Huron ; is a separate district ; and Goderich, its principal town, where the district courts are held, is situated at the confluence of the river Maitland with Lake Huron, where it forms an admirable harbour. The population of the town is seven hundred, and there are several good stores and shops in it ; mechanics carrying on some useful trades. There are also an episcopal church and other houses of religious worship, and a good school, where the higher branches of the classics are taught, as well as the more ordinary routine of education."— Statistics published by the Canada Company.

Goderich, a distance of sixty-seven miles. I consider this block the finest tract of land I ever travelled over in Canada West.

The land is well timbered with the best description of hard wood, amongst which is to be found in considerable abundance, the black cherry. This tree grows often to a large size, and is used extensively for furniture, particularly for dining-tables : if well made and polished, it is little inferior to mahogany, either in appearance or durability.

I remember, on this very journey, that Mr. Prior and myself were much struck by the size and magnificent appearance of one of these cherry-trees, which grew close to the road side, not far from the Big Thames. Two years afterwards, passing the same tree, I got out of my sleigh and measured the circumference as high as I could reach, which I found to be ten feet seven inches, and, I should think, it was not less than fifty feet in height from the ground to the first branch : it is a great pity to see such noble trees as these either burned or split up into fencing-rails.

I think the largest tree of the hard wood species I ever saw in this country, was near Bliss's Tavern, in the township of Beverly, and it was called the Beverly-oak.* I was induced to visit this giant of the woods from the many accounts I had heard of its vast dimensions, and was, certainly, astonished at its size and symmetry. I measured it as accurately as I could about six feet from the ground, and found the diameter to be as nearly eleven feet as possible, the trunk rising like a majestic column towering upwards for sixty or seventy feet before branching off its mighty head. Mr. Galt, who was induced to visit this tree from my description has, in his "Autobiography," mentioned the height of the trunk from the ground to the branches, as eighty feet; but I think he has overrated it. I was accompanied to the tree by the landlord, who remarked, "that he calculated that he should cut that 'ere tree

* " On the road to Guelph, a short distance from Galt, there is an uncleared portion of the primeval forest, on the edge of the township of Beverly, where, in those days, a small tavern, convenient to rest the horses of travellers, was situated. One day, when I stopped at this house, while my horse was taking his corn, I strayed into the woods, not many hundred yards, and came to a tree, the most stupendous I had ever seen.

"At the first glance, the trunk reminded me of the London Monument, an effect of the amaze which the greatness of its dimensions produced. I measured its girth, however, at the height of a man from the ground. and it was thirty-three feet, above which the trunk rose without a branch to the height of at least eighty feet, crowned with vast branches.

" This was an oak, probably the greatest known, and it lifted its head far above the rest of the forest. The trees around, myr-

down some day, for he guessed it would make enough rails to fence the side of a ten acre field."

I replied, " Surely, you would not be such a Goth as to cut down such a splendid oak merely for fence-wood, when you have plenty of rail-timber which will answer that purpose equally well ; and, besides, it may be the means of drawing customers to your tavern."

" I do not know what you mean by a Goth ; but I do know, if I could get a cross-cut saw long enough to cut that tree, I would not let it stand there long ; for you see it is mighty straight in the grain, and would split like a ribbon."

Thus was this gigantic specimen of the primeval forest preserved for a time, because there was not a saw long enough to cut it through in Canada. I dare say there are many old oaks in

midons of inferior growth, were large, massy, and vigorous, but possessed none of the patriarchal antiquity with which that magnificent ' monarch of the woods ' was invested. I think, therefore, that I was not wrong in imagining it the scion of a forest that had passed away, the ancestral predecessor of the present woods.

" Had I been convinced it was perfectly sound, I would have taken measures for cutting it down and sending home planks of it to Windsor Castle. The fate that awaited it would have justified the profanation. The doubt of its soundness, however, and the difficulty of finding tools large enough to do it justice, procrastinated the period of its doom. I recommended the landlord of the tavern to direct his guests, from time to time, to inspect this Goliath of oaks."—Galt's " Autobiography."

England that exceed this in diameter; but I do not believe one is to be found whose length of trunk can be at all compared to it.

On the flats about a mile from the mouth of the Maitland, are some very large button-wood trees.   There is one, in particular, growing near a fine spring of water, the circumference of which appeared very vast, though I did not measure it; but the tree was a complete shell, and had a sort of natural arched doorway, just high enough to admit a full-sized man.   I was once inside this tree with Dr. Dunlop and eleven other persons, at the same time.   The trunk of this tree forked at twelve or fourteen feet from the ground.   There are several others of this species near to the one I have described, of very large growth, which apparently are sound, but not equalling it in size.

I left a noble oak-tree standing in the middle of one of my fields in the township of Douro, which I hoped I should have been able to preserve, as it was such a remarkably fine tree.   It, however, was doomed to destruction; for in the summer of 1838, it was twice struck with lightning in the space of a week.   The first time, the bark only was furrowed by the electric fluid, but at the second stroke it was split from the top to the bottom, and thrown down by the violence of the shock. I measured this tree correctly, and found the diameter, twenty-four feet from the ground, to be five feet three inches. The length of the trunk was forty-eight feet up to the first branch, and it was perfectly sound to within three or four feet of the soil.

Generally speaking, the white or American pine, from its vast length of trunk, contains a larger number of cubic feet than any other tree in the Canadian forest. I have seen several of these pines sold for masts, the trunks of which were upwards of one hundred feet in length, and full three feet in diameter, a third of the way up from the butt-end. There is very little pine-timber on the Huron tract, which, though a disadvantage in regard to building, is all the better in respect to the land, hard wood being the best indication of a good soil.

I did not—as I have said—regret my transfer to Goderich, though that flourishing town was then in its infancy, the most unpleasant aspect in which any Canadian settlement can be viewed. Still, I am pleased that I have had the opportunity of tracing some of these important places from their dawn to their present prosperous condition.

I found the general aspect of the country level.

There is scarcely a rise of land sufficient to justify the appellation of hill from Wilmot to Goderich ; but as you approach the lake, the land becomes more rolling, and better watered by fine spring streams.

I was quite delighted with the situation of Goderich, though the town-plot was only just surveyed. Three frame-houses were in process of building. A log-house, beautifully situated on a bold hill, overlooking the harbour, called by Dr. Dunlop, the Castle,* and a dozen or so of log-cabins, comprised the whole town of Goderich, most of the latter being inhabited by French Canadians and half-breeds. The upper town is situated on a fine cliff fronting the lake and harbour, and upwards of one hundred feet above the level of the water.

* " In the afternoon of the following day, we saw afar off, by our telescope, a small clearing in the forest, and on the brow of a rising ground a cottage delightfully situated. The appearance of such a sight in such a place was unexpected, and we had some debate, if it could be the location of Dr. Dunlop, who had guided the land-exploring party already alluded to. Nor were we left long in doubt ; for on approaching the place we met a canoe, having on board a strange combination of Indians, velveteens and whiskers, and discovered within the roots of the red hair, the living features of the Doctor. About an hour after, having crossed the river's bar of eight feet, we came to a beautiful anchorage of fourteen feet water, in an uncommonly pleasant small basin. The place had been selected by the Doctor, and is now the site of the flourishing town of Goderich."—Galt's " Autobiography."

The lower town comprises a few acres of alluvial flat, only a few feet elevated above the river. This piece of land was destitute of trees or stumps, and had evidently been cleared many years ago by the Indians, who had cultivated it with Indian corn. I ploughed up this flat of land for the benefit of the Company, and sowed it with oats in the spring of '29 ; and, therefore, I can justly claim the honour—for the sake of which I did it—of putting the first plough into the ground of the Huron tract. I also put in four acres of wheat on the top of the hill near the castle, in the fall of the same year, the yield of which was upwards of forty bushels to the acre—a good yield for any country, especially when it is considered that at least one-twelfth of the ground may be fairly deducted for stumps of trees, stones, and other obstructions, usually found in all new clearings. I believe, however, I may say without exaggeration, that the Company's tract may safely challenge any other block of land of the same dimensions either in Canada East or West, for fertility of soil, average yield per acre, or healthiness of the climate.*

* " The Canada Company's Huron tract is known to be one of the most healthy and fertile settlements in Canada. The tract in the year 1842 contained 7101 souls. In June last year (1849), the Huron district numbered 20,450 souls, according to the official

I bought a small log-house and town-lot, or rather the good-will of them, from a French Canadian, putting myself in his place with the Company, with whom I completed the purchase. The situation was very pretty, commanding a fine view of the Lake. I immediately prepared to build a suitable house, to receive my wife and family, whom I had been under the necessity of leaving behind me in Guelph, till I could make suitable preparations to receive them here.

At this time, there was only one saw-mill* in the whole Company's tract, and that was ten miles up the river, situated near the mouth of a large creek, which flowed into the Maitland. This mill was built close to one of the finest pine-groves in the block.

reports, exclusive of the townships of Bosanquet and Williams. The Canada Company's tract now contains a population of 26,000 souls, showing an increase of 18,900, and that the population has nearly quadrupled itself in seven years—a progress of settlement of a tract of country scarcely exceeded in any part of North America."—"Information to Emigrants," by Frederick Widder, Esq.

* "In no situation can settlers be distant from a mill, as there are at convenient places distributed throughout the tract twelve grist-mills and twenty saw-mills, and the facilities for communication are very great; for seventeen of the townships are bounded on the one side by the great roads traversing the tract in two directions for one hundred miles in extent, and six of them are bounded by the Lake on the other side."—Statistics published by the Canada Company.

I hired a man, who had been a raftsman on the Delaware, to go with me by land up to the mill, for a few thousand feet of boards, that I required for my new house. It was only seven miles to the mill by a new cut-out sleigh-track, through the township of Goderich as far as the Falls, which we crossed by wading the river just above them, which at that time we were able to do, though not without some caution ; for, although the spring-floods were considerably abated, the water ran with great rapidity, and in some places was up to our middles ; but with the help of a strong setting-pole, we got over with safety.

We made our little raft in three cribs, of a thousand feet of boards in each crib, which we connected together by short pieces of scantling, which are bored near each end with a two-inch auger and strung on the corner-pickets of each crib, thus uniting them in one length. At each end of the raft, a long oar is securely fixed, in temporary rowlocks for that purpose.

The whole course of the river, from the mill to the harbour at Goderich, is a strong rapid : two perpendicular falls occur in its course to the lake. The Upper, or Big Fall, is about six feet, and the Little Fall three. We made a capital run down, though in plunging over the first Fall we were up

to our arm-pits in water.   But our little raft rose
gallantly to the surface ; and we encountered no
further difficulty.

I enjoyed my trip down the river amazingly.
I do not know anything more delightful, when
all goes well, than being borne over the foaming
rapids at the rate of eight or ten miles an hour
The channel of the Maitland is wide, and the.
banks picturesque.   Our voyage did not exceed
an hour, though the distance was above nine
miles.

CHAPTER XIX.

MY NEW HOUSE AT GODERICH.—CARPENTRY AN ESSENTIAL ART.—
AMERICAN ENERGY.—AGREEABLE VISITORS.—MY WIFE'S DIS-
ASTERS.—HINTS FOR ANGLERS.—THE NINE-MILE-CREEK FROLIC.
—THE TEMPEST.—OUR SKIPPER AND HIS LEMON-PUNCH.—SHORT
COMMONS.—CAMP IN THE WOODS.—RETURN ON FOOT.—LUDI-
CROUS TERMINATION TO OUR FROLIC.

MY new house at Goderich was constructed
with cherry-logs neatly counter-hewed both inside
and out, the interstices between the logs being
nicely pointed with mortar.   I had no upstair-
rooms, excepting for stowage.   The ground-story
I divided into a parlour, kitchen, and three bed-
rooms.   After office-hours I used to work a good
deal at the carpenter's bench—for I was always
fond of it when a boy.   I had made some useful
observations, as well as tormenting our workmen
on repairs at home, with the usual amount of
mischief, and I now reaped the benefit of my ju-
venile experience.   I was able to make the doors,
and do nearly all the insidework of my house
myself.   Indeed, it is really essential for the well-

doing of the emigrant, that he, or some members of his family, should have some knowledge of carpentry—in fact, be a jack-of-all-trades ; and, in that excellent profession, educated persons, healthy in mind and body, excel the most.

There is a very true saying, that necessity is the mother of invention, and in no country is it better exemplified than in Canada. The emigrant has there, especially when distant from a town or settlement, to make a hundred shifts, substituting wood for iron, in the construction of various articles, such as hinges for barn-door gates, stable and barn-shovels, and a variety of other contrivances whereby both money and time are saved.

I have often heard young men say, they " could not" do this or do that. "Did you ever try ? " is a fair question to such people. I believe that many persons, with average capacities, can effect much more than they give themselves credit for. I had no more been bred a carpenter than a civil engineer, in which last capacity I was holding office satisfactorily. My education had consisted of Latin, Greek, and French, and the mathematics. My time had been spent in my own country; riding, shooting, boating, filled up with a little amateur gardening.

Want of energy is not the fault of the Americans; they will dash at *everything*, and generally succeed. I had known them contract to do difficult jobs that required the skill of the engineer or regular architect, and accomplish them cleverly too, although they had never attempted anything of the kind before; and they generally completed their task to the satisfaction of the parties furnishing the contract. " I cannot do it" is a phrase not to be found in the Yankee vocabulary, I guess.

It is astonishing how a few years' residence in Canada or the United States brightens the intellects of the labouring classes. The reason is quite obvious. The agricultural population of England are born and die in their own parishes, seldom or never looking out into a world of which they know nothing. Thus, they become too local in their ideas, are awake to nought but the one business they have been brought up to follow; they have indeed no motive to improve their general knowledge.

But place the honest and industrious peasant in Canada, and, no matter how ignorant he may be, when he sees that by his perseverance and industry he will in a short time better his situation in life, and most likely become the possessor of a freehold, this motive for exertion will call forth the best energies of his mind, which had hitherto, for want of a proper stimulus, lain dormant. Having to act and think for himself, and being better acquainted with the world, he soon becomes a theoretical as well as a practical man, and consequently a cleverer and more enlightened person, than he was before in his hopeless servitude in the mother-country.

When I left Guelph, I had arranged with my wife that as soon as I could get the new house ready, I would send for her. I did not think that this could possibly be done before sleighing-time, as the newly-cut road was almost impassable for waggons. Judge, then, of my surprise when, on returning home from the store-house one day, I noticed the door of my log-cabin open, and saw a lovely curly-headed child sitting in the doorway. I could hardly believe my eyes—it was my own little Maria. My dear little boy had remained at Douro with my wife's sister Eliza, of whom he was so fond that my wife did not like to separate such friends from each other. On my entrance I found my wife surrounded by a pile of luggage, laughing heartily at my astonishment.

She told me, she felt so lonely that she determined to brave all the dangers of the road in order to join me. Accordingly, she hired a settler who was the owner of a waggon and a yoke of oxen, which she loaded with the most useful articles we required—bedding and bed-clothes, &c.,—reserving room in the waggon for herself, the child, and nursemaid.

During the whole of the first day's journey and part of the next, all went on smoothly enough, their route lying through settlements; but as soon as they entered the newly-cut road their difficulties commenced, and before they had traversed five miles, the waggon was twice upset. This so alarmed my poor wife, on account of the baby, that she durst not ride another step of the way, although the travellers had still upwards of sixty miles to go. Moreover, she was obliged to carry the child the entire distance ; for the teamster had enough to do to look after and guide his cattle, and the servant girl was too young and too tired to render much assistance.

Fifteen miles a day was the outside distance they could persuade the oxen to travel, consequently, they were compelled to camp out two nights out of the six in which they were on the road. Luckily, the weather was dry and warm. At night the musquitoes were dreadfully annoying, as my poor little Maria's neck and arms too plainly showed.

During the afternoon of the second day, when within six miles of Trifogle's tavern, their intended resting-place for the night, they were overtaken by a man who was going in the same direction, who very politely—as my wife thought—offered to carry her baby part of the way. She was, of course, very glad to avail herself of his kind offer ; nor did she perceive, till after he had got possession of the bairn, that he was intoxicated. She immediately demanded back her little treasure, but no inducement could persuade him to relinquish it, and he set off with the infant as fast as he could. In vain the poor mother besought him to stop—in vain she sobbed and cried. On he went, followed by my Mary, who found great difficulty in keeping up with him, which she did at first, till, at length, exhausted by the unusual fatigue, maternal anxiety, and the roughness of the road, she lost sight of him when about a mile from the tavern. He had walked off with his little burden.

She was now dreadfully alarmed, for night was fast coming on, and she did not know whether she was on the right track or not. Fortunately, a light through the trees extricated her from this dilemma : her only uneasiness was now for her child. She was soon, however, relieved from this uncertainty; for, on entering the house, there sat the man with the baby on his knee. The child appeared to be on very friendly terms with him, and had, no doubt, enjoyed herself amazingly while her bearer was running away with her.

He at once restored the child to her mother's arms, observing, "that he hoped she would give him the price of a quart of whiskey for his trouble, for the child was main heavy, God bless her."

My wife, of course, did not dispute the payment. She was only too glad to recover her little pet, whom she took good care not again to trust to masculine keeping, however tired she might be. So Maria remained safely in her mother's arms, for the remainder of the journey.

At length, when down-hearted and weary, the bright waters of the Huron gladdened their eyes, on the morning of the sixth day, and a few minutes afterwards they took possession of my log-cabin, and gave me the happy surprise already recorded.

"I wonder you were not afraid of encountering such hardships, and even danger, in travelling so many miles through the wild woods and on foot, and with that heavy child to carry in your arms," was my remark to my enterprising wife. She replied, " that there had certainly been more difficulties than she had anticipated ; but had they been double, it would not have prevented her from joining me." So much for woman's love and devotion.

During the summer months, we were plentifully supplied with fish. On some days the harbour appeared to swarm with them. When the sun shone brightly, you could see hundreds lying near the surface. There was no difficulty in catching them, for the moment you threw in your bait, you had a fish on your hook.

In the early part of the season, I used to make an imitation mouse of a piece of musk-rat fur. This is a killing bait for trolling either for black bass or maskilonge—as the season advances, a red and white rag, or a small green-frog. But the best bait for the larger fish, such as salmon-trout and maskilonge, is a piece of brass, or copper, about the shape and size of the bowl of a tablespoon, with a large hook soldered upon the narrow end. If properly made, and drawn fast through the water, it will spin round and glitter, and thus is sure to attract the fish. I have caught hundreds by this method, and can therefore recommend it as the most certain. Your trolling line, which is attached to your left arm, should not be less than eighty or a hundred feet in length, and sufficiently leaded to sink the bait three or four feet beneath the surface, this line following the canoe as you paddle it swiftly through the water.

The scenery up the Maitland, from the harbour's mouth to the flats, or natural meadows, two miles from the lake, is very pretty and interesting. I think it would be difficult to find for a summer residence a more charming situation than the town of Goderich, and I might say with equal confidence, a more healthy one. The water is excellent, and the town-plot abounds with copious springs.

About a mile from the town, there is one of the largest and purest springs of the coldest and best water I ever drank. It gushes out of the side of a hill, and rushes down the declivity with great swiftness over its pebbly bed, till it is joined in its course, a few yards below the hill, by another spring of nearly equal size, within half a mile of its source, turning a grist-mill on its way to swell the waters of the Maitland.

Nine miles up the lake-shore, east of Goderich, a fine little stream empties its bright waters into the mighty Huron. A party of us had often expressed a wish to explore the outlet of this stream, and at length a day was fixed for the expedition. As we intended merely to pass one night at the river, and return the next day, we only supplied ourselves with as much provisions and grog as would last for that time—a great mistake, as it afterwards proved. However, I will not anticipate.

A large piece-log canoe was furnished by Mr. W. F. Gooding, our Goderich store-keeper, who was one of the party, which consisted of nine persons, including myself. All things being in readiness, Mr. Fullarton was dubbed Captain for the occasion. At an early hour one fine sunny morning in June, we stood out of the harbour with a light breeze, having rigged up two blankets as sprit-sails. They answered very well, as long as we had any wind, which, however, unfortunately soon died entirely away.

"Come, boys," said the Captain, "this won't do. We must raise a white-ash-breeze (meaning that we must have recourse to our paddles) or we shall not see the Nine-Mile Creek this day, I can tell you." The impetus given to our canoe by the vigorous application of eight paddles, independent of our steersman, made the De Witt Clinton (the name of our canoe) fly through the water, which was now as calm as a mirror. After the wind fell, the heat was intense; and, towards noon, huge double-headed thunder-clouds showed themselves, slowly emerging out of the still waters of the Huron, far away to the north-west—a certain indication of a thunder-storm and change of wind.

About noon, we entered the creek by a very narrow channel, not ten feet in width. Indeed, the lake has choked up the entrance of the little harbour with sand and gravel, which, the water, descending the creek in summer-time, is not sufficient to disperse. I think, however, by clearing out, and piling the channel, and erecting two piers a short distance from each other, carried out upon the lake, and curving towards each other, until only sufficient space is left between them for the entrance of steam-boats and schooners, it might yet be made navigable. The harbour at Cobourg has been built something on this plan, which answers tolerably well; but if it had had a creek only the size of this I am describing, it would have been much better, as the current is a great help in clearing out the sand and gravel.

On crossing the bar, we found ourselves in a snug little basin, sufficiently deep for a vessel drawing six or seven feet water. We landed on a little peninsula, between the lake and the harbour, and commenced operations for cooking.

After dinner, we paddled through the harbour, and up the river, as far as we could go, which was only a very short distance, the navigation being interrupted by a pretty fall of water, which tumbled from ledge to ledge, like a succession of stone stairs, stretching from bank to bank across the stream, and forming, as the Americans would say, an elegant mill-privilege.

Since I left Goderich, a township, called Ashfield, has been laid out north of the Company's township of Colborne ; the principal place of which is the village of Port Albert—the very spot we went to explore.

What a difference a few years make in a new country like Canada! With the aid of a compass, or by following the course of some unknown stream, with much toil and difficulty we make our way back for miles, through dense forests, swamps, and creeks ; scale the rocky precipice, or launch the light bark-canoe on some far distant lake. We travel the same route twenty-five years afterwards, and the forests have bowed their lofty heads—the swamps are drained—the rivers bridged, and the steamer ploughs the inland wave, where shortly before glided the canoe of the hunter. Such is no over-coloured picture. I have seen it in my day realized many a time. The Huron tract, and the county of Peterborough, are the proofs of my assertion ; and various other settlements I could name, would equally bear me out.

But to return to our expedition—or as I might with greater truth say—our *pic-nic*, for we did little else than paddle up and down the creek, ramble about the falls, and eat and drink whenever we felt inclined. In this manner we spent the first day ; till the coming night, and the distant growl of the thunder, warned us to prepare for our night-bivouac.

One of our party, Mr. Brewster—the professor, as we generally called him—from the circumstance of his being a near relation of Sir David Brewster, the talented author of "Natural Magic," had a small tent-cloth with him, but not sufficiently large for the whole party. It was, therefore, determined that four of us should sleep under the canoe, and the remaining five under the tent. Quite a contention now arose between us, as to who should be the favoured possessors of the tent.

Not liking the appearance of the weather, I resigned any pretensions I might have had to the canvas, knowing the canoe was, from its length and size, capable of effectually sheltering four persons. We, accordingly, turned the canoe bottom upwards, and raised one side of it sufficiently high to allow us to creep under. To keep it in that position, we supported the raised edge on some forked sticks; and a quantity of hemlock brush and fern, spread evenly under it, made as good a bed as I would care to sleep on in hot weather. Our companions pitched their tent close beside us, so that we might be more sociable. After supper, we amused ourselves by singing songs, telling stories, and—if the truth must be told—drinking whiskey-punch.

The lightning was now incessant, illuminating the harbour and lake, and revealing dark masses of clouds, piled upon one another in endless succession. Few spectacles are more grand than the coming storm, or more awful when it bursts in its wildest fury. Such was its appalling character on this night. For the last hour I had been watching its progress, and admiring the brilliant forked lightning, and listening to the deep-toned thunder, which woke the lone echoes of the wood-crowned heights.

A few large drops of rain warned us to seek the friendly shelter of our respective camps. I had just settled myself snugly, when our skipper came to me with a jug of lemon-punch fresh mixed. I declined taking any more. He was too old a stager, however, to be put off that way, and was proceeding to show me the necessity of taking a night-cap, when he was saved all the trouble of any farther solicitation, and me of refusal, by a blinding flash of lightning, followed by a succession of deafening reports. At the same instant, the wind burst upon us like a whirlwind, prostrating in its irresistible fury our unfortunate skipper, punch, and all. As for the tent, it was whisked half across the harbour, in one blast, and the unfortunate inmates were left exposed to all the pelting of the pitiless storm, which raged with unmitigated violence till the dawn of day. We made room under the canoe for the professor and our skipper, the utmost we could accommodate. The three remaining unfortunate fellows were left to brave the tempest as they best might.

The next morning, the lake was white with breakers. The storm of the preceding night had brought a strong north-wester in its train, so that we found it impossible to launch our canoe—and, indeed, if we had, it would have been unsafe to have attempted the passage therein ; there was nothing else for us but patience. But the worst part of the business was, that we had barely sufficient provisions for breakfast, and what the professor said—" Was worse than all—there was not a single horn of whiskey left in the jar."

The merchant and three of our party now determined to take the woods, and endeavour to reach Goderich by that route, leaving us to follow with the canoe if the wind should fall, of which, however, there appeared but little chance.

It now became expedient that we should look out for food of some description, as there was no doubt we should have to pass another night. On examining the state of our larder, we found that our whole stock consisted of half a loaf of bread, and a few ounces of sugar—rather short commons for four hungry men, even for a single meal.

We had no gun with us, or any fishing-lines. I had, it is true, a spear, but there was too much wind to fish in the harbour. Luckily, I bethought myself of the falls up the creek, where there was a pool sheltered by the woods. Thither we went with the canoe, and succeeded in spearing a number of suckers, which are, without exception, the softest and worst of all Canadian fish, especially in the hot months; but even bad suckers are better than nothing. Our first starvation-dinner consisted of a dish of boiled fish, a little bread, and a cup of hemlock-tea ; our supper, boiled fish without bread, and hemlock-tea without sugar.

To amuse ourselves, we built a nice camp on a wooded point overlooking the harbour, and arranged everything comfortably to pass the night ; and, although we had such bad commons, we were merry enough, considering we had nothing stronger to drink than hemlock-tea.

In the morning, as appearances were no better in respect to the weather, and as we were heartily sick of boiled suckers, we determined to do— as some of our party had done previously—take the bush-route for Goderich.

Accordingly, we crossed the harbour in the canoe, which we hid amongst the bushes, and commenced our journey along the lake-shore. In some places we found tolerably good walking, while in others we were compelled to mount the cliffs to avoid the break of the surges, where headlands jutted out into the lake. For the most part, however, we were enabled to travel upon natural terraces about half way up the bank, which I should think averages nearly one hundred feet in height.

To our great delight, we discovered an abundance of fine wild strawberries, the largest and most delicious I had ever seen. We found this a very seasonable refreshment. The day was fine, and we enjoyed the prospect, which, viewed from some of the highest points of land, was truly magnificent.

About four o'clock in the afternoon we reached Goderich, weary and half-starved. Thus ended our memorable pic-nic to the Nine-Mile Creek.

CHAPTER XX.

CHOICE OF A LOCATION.—THE COMPANY'S LANDS.—CROWN LANDS.
—TABLES PUBLISHED BY THE CANADA COMPANY.—PROGRESSIVE
IMPROVEMENT OF THE HURON TRACT.

AFTER twenty-seven years' residence in Canada West, it may be reasonably inferred that
I am justly entitled, from my long experience,
to give a fair opinion as to the best chances
of location at present available to the emigrant.

On mature consideration, I must give the preference to the Huron tract, as affording a greater
facility for settlement, and this for three reasons.
First, on account of the excellent roads constructed
by the Company—an inestimable boon, which
none but the early pioneer can fully appreciate.
Secondly, because of the excellent quality of the
soil, which is remarkably free from surface-stone,
that every old settler knows is both troublesome and expensive to clear away. And, thirdly
the low price of these lands, and the facility of

payment. Indeed, their system of leasing affords the poor man every chance. I shall copy a table of the yearly rent of farms leased on this plan by the Company, for the information of those of my readers who contemplate emigrating to Canada West. The present price of the Company's lands in the Huron tract, is from 12s. 6d. to 20s. currency per acre.

The Company dispose of their lands, according to quality and situation, for ready cash, or by lease for a term of ten years. In the latter case no money is required to be paid down, the lease being granted upon the following terms :—

		s. d.			£ s. d.	
100 acres,	at	2 0	per acre,	ann. rent	0 10 0	and no more.
,,		3 6	,,	,,	0 12 0	,,
,,		5 0	,,	,,	0 18 0	,,
,,		6 3	,,	,,	1 4 0	,,
,,		7 6	,,	,,	1 10 0	,,
,,		8 9	,,	,,	1 17 6	,,
,,		10 0	,,	,,	2 5 0	,,
,,		11 3	,,	,,	2 12 0	,,
,,		12 6	,,	,,	3 0 0	,,
,,		13 9	,,	,,	3 7 6	,,
,,		16 3	,,	,,	3 15 0	,,
,,		17 6	,,	,,	4 2 6	,,

The rent is payable on the first day of February in each year, full power being reserved to the settler to purchase the freehold, and take his deed for the land he occupies, at any time during the lease, an arrangement, of course, saving all future payment of rent.

Many persons unacquainted with the country, might object to pay from twelve shillings and six-pence to twenty shillings for the Company's lands, when they see that the Government price on the wild lands belonging to the Crown, in most town-ships, is only eight shillings per acre.

However, they must recollect, that all the choice lands belonging to the Crown have long since been located ; and unless the emigrant is prepared to go back into the remote townships, he cannot expect to get land as good as that be-longing to the Canada Company.

Indeed, the only Crown-lands which could at all compete with the Company's lands are the townships lately surveyed north of the Huron track to the River Saugeen, and the new settle-ments of Owen's Sound and the Queen's-Bush.

In a report, drawn up and published by Daniel Lizars, clerk of the peace for the united coun-ties of Huron, Perth, and Bruce, May, 1851, he says,—

" In this favoured portion of ·the province of Upper Canada, blest with a salubrious climate and a fertile soil, watered with crystal springs and brooks in every direction, reposing upon a

table-land whose natural drainage flows uninter-
ruptedly onwards to the streams and great rivers
which intersect it in every quarter towards the
noble Huron, or Lake St. Clair, the energies of
the people have been steadily devoted to practical progress and improvement ; having, in the
short period above alluded to, brought upwards
of eighty thousand acres of the wilderness into
cultivation, erected five thousand dwelling-houses,
fifty-six schools, fourteen churches, twelve grist-
mills, with nineteen run of stores, five oat and
barley-mills, five distilleries, two breweries, eight
tanneries, and twenty-four pot and pearl-ash factories."

" Among other matters which crowned their
industry in 1850, I may state the following productions :—

Wheat	.	.	.	.	292,949 bushels.
Barley	.	.	.	.	13,012 ,,
Rye	.	.	.	.	2,181 ,,
Oats	.	.	.	.	215,415 ,,
Peas	.	.	.	.	54,657 ,,
Indian Corn	.	.	.	.	5,352 ,,
Potatoes	.	.	.	.	210,913 ,,
Buck-wheat	.	.	.	.	673 ,,
Mangel-wurzel	.	.	.	.	297 ,,
Turnips	.	.	.	.	143,725 ,,
Hay	.	.	.	.	12,823 tons.
Flax or Hemp	.	.	.	.	7,359 pounds.
Maple Sugar	.	.	.	.	351,721 ,,

Wool				54,347 pounds.
Fulled Cloth				10,303 yards.
Linen, or Cotton Cloth				1,197 ,,
Flannel, or other unfulled Cloth				41,397 ,,
Cheese for Market				7,761 pounds.
Butter for Market				58,873 ,,
Beef, or Pork for Market				1,308 barrels.

" And they further rejoice in the possession of the following stock :—

Neat Cattle				26,260
Horses				2,646
Sheep				20,022
Hogs				14,655

" The above gratifying examples speak loudly for the industry of the settlers ; and where hired labour can, with difficulty, be obtained at a high remuneration, notwithstanding the yearly increased ratio of new comers, and, moreover, where all are diligently employed in the onward march to happiness and independence, we may truly be thankful to a superintending Providence, that prosperity is in the ascendant."

Mr. Lizars states in another part of his Report, that the population of the Huron district

In 1841, was			5,600		
In 1847, six years afterwards		.	16,641	increase	11,043
In 1848, one year do.	.	.	20,450	,,	3,807
In 1850, two years do.	.	.	26,933	,,	6,483

According to this ratio of increase, we may

safely infer the population at the present time (1852), to exceed thirty-two thousand souls ; an increase almost incredible ; as, upon reference to Smith's Work on Canada, it will be found that the Huron district has made more rapid progress since its first settlement in 1827, than Lower Canada did in one hundred and four years ; its population then being (in 1721), 24,511.

Many contradictory statements have been made and published in respect to what is the real actual grain average of Canada West. My own opinion is, that even could a truthful average be obtained, it would throw very little light on the real capability of the land—and for this reason. One-half of the emigrants who settle upon land in Canada, and adopt cultivation as their employment, are weavers, tinkers, tailors, sailors, and twenty other trades and professions. It must be the work of years to convert such settlers into good practical farmers. In such cases, how can a fair yield be extracted from land ignorantly cultivated ? But I will venture to affirm, that wherever good farming is in practice, as good an average yield will be obtained, as in any country in the world.

"The following average of ten years for the Huron tract, has been published :—Wheat, 25

bushels ; barley, 30 bushels ; oats, 40 bushels ;
rye, 30 bushels ; potatoes, 250 bushels per acre.
Swedish turnips, mangel-wurzel, and other roots
of a similar kind, are not yet sufficiently cultivated, to enable an average yield to be given;
but it may very safely be said, that, with similar
care, culture, and attention, the produce will not
be less per acre than in England.   Indeed, it may
be said with truth to apply to every grain except
beans, which do not thrive well in the Canadian
climate."

CHAPTER XXI.

THE KING PROCLAIMED IN THE BUSH. — FETE AND BALL IN THE
EVENING. — MY YANKEE FELLOW-TRAVELLER. — AWFUL STORM.
—MY LONELY JOURNEY.—MAGICAL EFFECT OF A NAME.

I WAS busy in the storehouse one afternoon, when Mr. Prior entered with a newspaper in his hand, which he had just received from the old country.

"I see by this paper, Strickland, that George IV. is dead; and that his Majesty King William IV. has been proclaimed. Now, I think, we must give the workmen a holiday on this memorable occasion."

"In what manner do you intend to celebrate the day?" was my rejoinder.

"I have been thinking," he replied, "of making a litte fête, and inviting all the settlers within reach to assemble on the Button-wood Flats. We will have some refreshments served round; and if the day is fine, I have no doubt we shall enjoy ourselves much."

Due notice having been given, upon the appointed day every-one within ten miles assembled on the Flats, dressed in their best attire; and ready to show their loyalty in any way Mr. Prior might think proper to recommend.

As soon as the squire made his appearance, he ascended a large stump; and, in a patriotic and loyal speech, informed us "that he had called this meeting to hear him proclaim his most gracious Majesty King William IV."

He then read the proclamation, which was received with nine rounds of British cheers. Our party then formed a large circle by joining hands; and sang the national anthem, accompanied by the Goderich band, which was composed of two fiddles and a tambourine. "Rule Britannia" for our sailor-king was also played and sung—I was going to say in good style, but at all events with great loyalty and enthusiasm.

As soon as this ceremony was over, a pail of whiskey, with a tea-cup floating on the surface, was handed round, followed by another pail containing spring-water. Every person present drank his Majesty's health; even the fair sex, on this propitious occasion, did not disdain to moisten their pretty lips with the beverage.

The eating and drinking part of the festival

now commenced in earnest, We had seated ourselves on the grass, under the shade of four or
five immense button-wood trees, which effectually
sheltered us from the scorching rays of the
sun. In the centre of the group, the union-
jack of Old-England waved gracefully above our
heads—

> " The flag that braved a thousand years
> The battle and the breeze."

As soon as we had eaten and drunk to our
satisfaction, a dance was proposed and acceded
to by the party. The band struck up "The
Wind Shakes the Barley:" country dances,
Scotch reels, and "French fours," were kept up
with great spirit on the level turf—"All under
the greenwood tree."

> "For all that day to the rebeck gay
> They danced with frolicsome swains."

Those of our party who did not patronize the
dance, amused themselves with ball-playing and
a variety of old English games.

The day was lovely ; and the spot chosen for
our sports is one of the most beautiful natural
meadows I ever beheld. We kept our fête in
honour of King William on a smooth green semi-
circular meadow, of large extent, ornamented

here-and-there with clumps of magnificent but-ton-wood trees.* Towards the north, skirting the meadow, a steep bank rises in the form of an amphitheatre, thickly-wooded—tree above tree, from the base to the crown of the ridge. The rapid waters of the Maitland form the southern and western boundary of this charming spot,— then not a little enhanced by the merry groups which dotted the surface of the meadow, and woke its lone echoes with music and song.

I was much amused by a Yankee mill-wright, who had contracted to build a large grist-mill for the Company, both in Guelph and Goderich. He appeared enchanted with the whole day's proceed-ings.

"I do declare," he said, "if this don't almost put me in mind of the 4th of July. Why, you Britishers make as much fuss proclaiming your king as we do celebrating our anniversary of Inde-pendence. Well, it does me good to look at you. I vow if I don't feel quite loyal. Come, let us drink the old gentleman's health agin. I guess, I feel as dry as a sand-bank after so much hol-lering."

The setting sun warned us to discontinue our

* Both the wood and the growth of this tree greatly resemble the sycamore.

pastime and prepare for a move. Before doing so, however, the squire again came forward, and after thanking us for our attendance, loyalty, &c., he proposed "we should give three cheers more for the King, and three for Queen Adelaide," which were given with all the power of our lungs, not a little aided by sundry potations imbibed by the loyal in drinking their Majesties' healths during the day's proceeding.

Three cheers were then given for the Canada Company, three for the Commissioners, and three for the old Doctor. Thus terminated the proclamation of our sovereign in the Bush.

Mr. Prior had kindly issued invitations to the *élite* to a ball and supper at Reid's Hotel, which was well attended. The refreshments were excellent, the supper capital ; and the dancing was kept up with great spirit till day-light warned us to depart.

The next day, I started for Guelph with the Yankee mill-wright, whom I found a clever, shrewd man. He told me he had travelled over a great part of the Western States and Canada ; but in all his wanderings he had never seen a section of country, of the same size, that pleased him equal to the Huron tract.

"I guess, when this country of your'n is once

cleared up, and good roads made, and the creeks bridged, there won't be such another place in all creation."

" What makes you think so?" I enquired.

"Wal, just look what a fine frontage you have on that 'ere big pond (he meant Lake Huron) and good harbours and land that can't be beat not no how. All you want is 'to go a-head,' and you may take my word for it that this will be the garden of Canada yet."

We had only one horse between us, which belonged to the Doctor, so that we were obliged to ride turn about. In this manner we got on pretty well, so that by four o'clock we were within two miles of old Sebach's. The day had been excessively hot, and for the last hour we had heard distant thunder. We, therefore, pushed on with redoubled energy, in hopes of escaping the storm.

Ever since I had witnessed the devastating effects of the whirlwind which passed through Guelph, and which I have described in a previous chapter, I had a dread of being exposed in the woods to the fury of such a tempest. In this instance, however, we had the good fortune to reach the shanty just as the rain commenced ; and well for us it proved that we had gained a shelter for ourselves and steed ; for I seldom witnessed a more terrific storm. The lightning was awful, accompanied by the loudest thunder I ever heard. The volleys of heavy hail-stones on the shingled roof, together with the rushing sound of the wind, and the crash of falling trees, made it impossible for us to hear a word that was said. Indeed, I did not feel much inclined for conversation; for I could not help meditating on the peril we had escaped. Had the storm commenced an hour or two earlier or later, we should have been exposed to its utmost fury, as there was no place of refuge nearer than twenty miles either way.

To show the terrible danger we had avoided, I counted a hundred and seventy-six large trees that had fallen across the road between Sebach's and Trifogle's—a distance not exceeding twenty miles.

What a contrast this road now presents to what it was when I used to be in the habit of travelling over it! I remember, once having been sent on some important business to the settlement, which admitted of no delay. It was late in November; the snow had fallen unusually early, and there was no horse then to be procured at Goderich; so that I was obliged to walk without even a companion to cheer the solitary way. I found the walking exceedingly laborious: the snow was fully a foot deep and unbroken, save by the foot-marks of some lonely traveller.

I was very curious to learn who the person could be who had been necessitated to take such a long journey through the wilderness alone. The second day of my journey, my curiosity was gratified by seeing the name of the person written in large characters in the snow. I stopped and read it with much interest : it was that of a Scotchman I knew,—one James Haliday. After reading that name, it appeared as if half the loneliness of the road was gone; for I knew from the freshness of the track, that a human being was travelling on the same path, and that he was, perhaps, not far ahead.

Not many minutes after this occurrence, whilst descending a slight hill, I saw nine fine deer cross the road, within a short gun-shot of the spot where I stood. I had no gun with me ; for I thought, if I did kill a deer, I should be obliged to leave it in the woods. Nothing further occurred till within a short distance of Trifoglc's, when a large wolf bounded close past me : he seemed, however, the more frightened of the two, which I was not at all sorry to perceive.

When I arrived at the tavern, I told Trifogle what I had seen. He said, it was very lucky I had not fallen in with the pack; for only the night before he had gone to a beaver-meadow, about two miles distant, to look for his working oxen which had strayed, when he was surrounded by the whole pack of wolves, and was obliged " to tree," to save his bacon. He was, it seems, kept for more than three hours in that uncomfortable fix before he durst venture down—" when he made tracks," as the Yankees say, " for hum pretty considerably smart, I guess."

My solitary journey was performed in the fall of 1830 : at the present time (1853) you may travel at your ease in a stage-coach and four horses, with taverns every few miles, and more villages on the road than formerly there were houses. Such are the changes that a few short years have produced in this fast-rising country !

CHAPTER XXII.

VISIT OF THE PASSENGER-PIGEON TO THE CANADAS. — CANADIAN
BLACKBIRDS. — BREEDING-PLACES OF THE PASSENGER-PIGEONS. —
SQUIRRELS.

THE passenger-pigeon* visits the Canadas in the early spring-months, and during August, in immense flocks, bringing with them an agreeable change in the diet of the settler.

Persons unacquainted with the country and the gregarious habits of this lovely bird, are apt to doubt the accounts they have heard or read respecting their vast numbers : since my return to England I have repeatedly been questioned upon the subject. In answer to these queries, I can only say that, in some parts of the province, early in the spring and directly after wheat-harvest, their numbers are incredible. Some days they commence flying as soon as it is light in

* The passenger-pigeon is not so large as the wild pigeon of Europe. It is slender in form, having a very long forked tail. Its plumage is a bluish-grey, and it has a lovely pink breast. It is, indeed, a very elegant bird.

the morning, and continue, flock after flock, till sun-down. To calculate the sum-total of birds passing even on one day, appears to be impossible. I think, the greatest masses fly near the shores of the great Canadian lakes, and sometimes so low, that they may be easily killed with a horse-pistol, or even knocked down with a long pole.

During the first spring in which I resided at Goderich, the store-keeper was out of shot, and the pigeons happened to be uncommonly numerous. I had a large fowling-piece with a wide bore; so I tried a charge of fine shingle off the beach at the first flock that came within close range, and had the satisfaction of bagging seven birds at the first shot—indeed, it was almost impossible to miss them, they flew in such thick clouds. I have frequently killed on the stubbles, from twenty to thirty at one shot.

Directly after the wheat is carted, the pigeons alight on the stubble in vast flocks. As they are chiefly the young broods, they are very easily approached : the sportsman should creep up behind them; for they are so intent on feeding, that they will seldom notice his approach till he is within fair range of them.

The hindmost ranks are continually rising from

the ground, and dropping in front of the others. This is the proper time to fire, just as the hind-rank are a couple or three feet from the ground ; firing the second barrel as the whole flock takes flight.

In the vicinity of the towns, sometimes a regular *battue* takes place, when all kind of fire-arms are in requisition, from the old Tower musket to the celebrated Joe Manton.

In July, the pigeons feed a great deal on wild berries, such as raspberries, huckle-berries, blue-berries, and a variety of other kinds. Many people would naturally think that such vast flocks of birds would alight on the standing grain, and destroy the crop : such, however, is not the case. Sometimes, during the seed-time in the spring, they are a little troublesome ; but I have never known them alight on the ripening grain. The Canadian blackbirds are far more destructive in that particular—especially that species with the orange-bar across the wings. These birds alight on the Indian corn crops and oats in such numbers, that they do a great deal of damage, particularly the oats, which they break down by their weight.

There is another kind of blackbird, smaller than the former, and speckled very much like a starling. Indeed, I believe it is a species of that bird ; for it frequents marshes, and lodges amongst the reeds at night. This bird is also destructive in the corn-fields.

There is yet a third species of blackbird, larger than either of the above, whose colour is of a glossy blue-black, very like our rooks. These birds are just as troublesome as the rest; but it must be admitted that they destroy an immense quantity of caterpillars and grubs. They are easily frightened away by firing a few shots. There is, however, no doubt but that they are a greater plague to the farmers than the pigeons : besides, the latter are excellent eating.

I once accompanied the Doctor on an exploring expedition through the tract. We encamped close to a breeding-place of these birds, when we were kept awake all night by the noise they made. Sometimes, too, a limb of a tree would break with the weight of the birds which had alighted on it, when there would be such a fluttering and flapping of wings, as made it impossible for us to sleep.

Towards morning, the sound of their departure to their feeding-grounds resembled thunder. For nearly two hours there was one incessant roar, as flock after flock took its departure eastward. The ground under the trees was whitened with their excrement, and strewn with broken branches of trees.

The Americans have a plan of capturing these birds, by means of a decoy, or stool-pigeon, and nets. Thousands are often taken in this way during seed-time in the spring. When I first resided in the township of Douro, the pigeons used to be very plentiful at that time, their chief breeding-place being in the township of Fenelon, in a direct line west from my residence, some forty or fifty miles. And yet, soon after day-light, they would be passing eastward over my clearing, so vast is their swiftness and strength on the wing.

It is a curious fact that, although thousands passed daily for many days in succession, yet not one of them returned by the same route they went. I have been informed that this breeding-place has been deserted for several years, owing to the settlements having approached too near to please the winged possessors.

This satisfactorily accounts for the decrease I have noticed amongst these feathered denizens of the forest, during the last seven or eight years. In consequence of their having been disturbed, they have sought a more remote breeding-place. I am not at all certain whether this decrease is

general through the province; but I feel quite
convinced that, as civilization increases, all kinds
of birds and wild animals will become less numerous, with the exception of crows and mice,
which are greatly on the increase. Rats also have
been imported, and appear to thrive well in the
towns; though, I am happy to say, they have not
found their way into my township yet—and long
may they be ignorant of my location.

There is also another animal, which I think
is more numerous than formerly—I mean the
black squirrel. These pretty little creatures are
very destructive amongst the Indian-corn crops.
I have seen them carrying off a whole cob of
corn at once, which I will be bound to say was
quite as heavy as themselves.

The form of this animal is very elegant; the
colour jet black—with a large bushy tail : the
fur, however, is too open to be of any value. The
flesh is excellent eating, far superior to that of
the rabbit. In a good nut-season, in the western
part of the province, the quantity of these animals is almost incredible.

I have heard old hunters say that, if the squirrels are numerous in the summer, the bears will
be plenty in the fall, and also that their numbers
give a sure indication of a severe winter. This

saying, I believe to be true; because neither the squirrels nor bears are plentiful, unless there is an abundant supply of beech-mast, butter-nuts, hickory-nuts, &c., which Providence has kindly provided in more superabundant quantity on the approach of a longer and severer winter than usual.

Besides the *Niger*, or black squirrel, there are three other species in Canada West; first, the *Cinereus*, or grey squirrel, which is larger than the black squirrel. Its fur is something better, but the animal is not near so numerous. Secondly, the *Ruber*, or red squirrel, smaller than the last, but equally destructive.

The chitmunck, or *Siriatus*, or ground squirrel, is much smaller and more mischievous than any of the former species. The ridge of the back is marked with a black stripe; the sides are of a reddish yellow, spotted with white; the feet and legs pale red; the eyes black and projecting. These pretty little creatures never run up trees, unless they are pursued. They burrow and form their habitations under ground with two entrances. During the maize-harvest, they fill their mouths so full of corn that their cheeks distend to the size of a hen's egg. The chitmunck sometimes inhabits hollow trees and logs.

I have frequently cut down trees in which they had deposited their winter-store, to the amount of half-a-bushel of beech-mast, Indian corn, and grain of different descriptions. It is a very curious circumstance that, before storing away for the winter, they carefully skin every beech-nut.

Towards the spring, when the days begin to be a little warm, they leave their winter-holes and enter the barns—compelled, most probably, by the failure of their winter-store. Great numbers are then destroyed by the cats. Their fur is of little value, and their flesh uneatable.

CHAPTER XXIII.

THE REBEL, VON-EGMOND, THE FIRST AGRICULTURAL SETTLER ON
THE HURON.——CUTTING THE FIRST SHEAF.

THE celebrated Anthony J. W. G. Von Egmond, who commanded the rebels at Gallows Hill during Mackenzie's rebellion, was the first agricultural settler on the Huron tract. He had formerly been a Colonel in the old Imperial Army ; and after Buonaparte's abdication and retirement to Elba, he joined the Allies, and held the rank of an officer in one of the Belgian regiments at Waterloo.

He was a pushing, clever sort of man ; and had he but been contented, and stuck to his last, instead of troubling his head about politics, he would, in all probability, have become one of the richest and most independent farmers in the Huron tract.

Within the short period of twenty months, Von Egmond had chopped and cleared, fit for a crop, nearly a hundred acres of land, fifty of which were sown wheat. As this was the first field ripe in the tract, the old man determined to celebrate the event by asking some of the gentlemen connected with the Canada Company to dinner, and to witness the cutting of the first sheaf.

Thomas Mercer Jones, Esq., one of the Company's Commissioners, Dr. Dunlop, Mr. Prior, the Professor, and myself, composed the party on this important occasion. As the distance was little short of eighteen miles through the Bush, and we had no way of getting there — except by walking — it was arranged that we should start the day previous, and sleep all night at Von Egmond's.

Accordingly, we left Goderich about eleven o'clock, A.M., by the newly cut-out road, through the forest. I wonder what our English friends would think of walking in their shirt-sleeves, with their coats and neckcloths thrown over their arms, eighteen miles to a dinner-party, with the thermometer ranging something like 90° in the shade.

The day was hot, though not unpleasantly so ; for the leafy screen above our heads effectually protected us from the scorching rays of a July sun, which would otherwise have been very oppressive.

The musquitoes were particularly civil—indeed the reign of these gentlemen was nearly over for the season. They begin to be troublesome in the middle of May. From the 1st of June to the middle of July, they are in the very height of their impertinence ; and, although they have not sufficient strength in their proboscis to penetrate a top-boot, yet they easily pierce through a summer coat and shirt, and a wee bit into the skin beneath. From the middle of July to the middle of August, they become much less venomous ; and are then only annoying for an hour or so in the evening, in the woods or marshes. By the 1st of September, they finally disappear for the season.

Our long road was considerably shortened by the amusing stories and anecdotes of the Doctor, who kept us in good humour during the whole journey. Nearly mid-way between Goderich and Von Egmond's, a small rill crosses the road : here we stopped for an hour, and refreshed ourselves with beef-sandwiches and brandy and water—no bad things in the Bush.

Close by the side of this little stream was a

small log-shanty, which had been erected by the people who had been employed by the men cutting out the new road, which, from this to the southern boundary of the Huron tract, was already cleared out, the full width of sixty-six feet, preparatory to its being turnpiked.*

We reached our destination about five o'clock, where we were received with every mark of respect and hospitality. We were shown up-stairs into a newly-finished room—the only apartment as yet completed in the tavern old Von Egmond was building. Here we found an excellent supper ready for us, to which, after a walk of eighteen miles, you may be sure we did ample justice.

In the morning, we walked over the farm with the old Colonel, and were much gratified by seeing the prosperous condition of the crops, which argued well for the goodness of the land. I think I never saw a finer crop of oats, or better promise for turnips, in my life. The wheat also looked extremely well. It was certainly an interesting sight, after walking for miles through

---

* This is merely an American term for a road which has been ploughed on each side, and the earth, so raised, thrown up in the centre by the means of a road-scraper, or turnpike shovel, worked either with horses or oxen. A road engineer or surveyor would call this grading, preparatory to gravelling or planking.

a dense forest, suddenly to emerge from the wooded solitude upon a sea of waving grain, white for the harvest.

> " The Harvest ! the Harvest ! how fair on each plain
>   It waves in its golden luxuriance of grain !
>   The wealth of a nation is spread on the ground,
>   And the year with its joyful abundance is crowned.
>   The barley is whitening on upland and lea,
>   And the oat-locks are drooping, all graceful to see ;
>   Like the long yellow hair of a beautiful maid,
>   When it flows on the breezes, unloosed from the braid.
>
> " The Harvest ! the Harvest ! how brightly the sun
>   Looks down on the prospect ! its toils are begun ;
>   And the wheat-sheaves so thick on the valleys are piled,
>   That the land in its glorious profusion has smiled.
>   The reaper has shouted the furrows among ;
>   In the midst of his labour he breaks into song ;
>   And the light-hearted gleaners, forgetful of care,
>   Laugh loud, and exult as they gather their share.*

About noonday, we all proceeded to the harvest-field, headed by our host and his lady, and her fair daughters. As soon as we arrived at the scene of action, a sickle was placed in the hands of Madame Von Egmond ; and she was requested to cut and bind the first sheaf of wheat ever harvested in the Huron tract—an honour of which any person might be justly proud.

> " Lord ! thou hast blessed the people,
>   And made the plant of bread

---

* Agnes Strickland.

To spring, where'er beneath thine eye
  Fair Nature's carpet spread.
Earth's thirst drank in thy freshening rain,
  Earth's bosom wooed thy sun,
Beautiful grew the golden grain,
  Like prize of labour won ! "

What were the red battle-fields of Napoleon, in comparison to this bloodless victory, won over the forests of the Huron ! The sight of that first sheaf, cut by the gentle hand of woman, was one that angels rejoiced to see ; while the fruits of his conquests were such as might well make "the seraphs weep."

Madame Von Egmond handled her sickle something better than a mere amateur, which make us conjecture it was not the first sheaf she had ever cut and bound. As soon as this interesting ceremony was over, we gave three hearty cheers for the Canada Company. A horn of whiskey was served round, in which we pledged our host and hostess, and drank success to the settlement.

On our return to the house, we found a capital dinner awaiting us. Indeed, the old soldier had spared neither pains nor expense in providing handsomely on the occasion. After the cloth was removed, a nice dessert was laid out, consisting of almonds and raisins, oranges, and red and black raspberries. The two latter dishes are easily procured, for they grow more plentifully in the angles of the snake-fences in Canada than blackberries do in England. They are a delicious fruit, and particularly grateful in a hot day to the weary traveller.

I need hardly describe our evening's entertainment, save that " we ate, drank, and were merry." Indeed, it would have been difficult to be otherwise with Doctor Dunlop as one of our companions.

END OF THE FIRST VOLUME.

TWENTY-SEVEN YEARS
IN
CANADA WEST

OR

THE EXPERIENCE OF AN EARLY SETTLER

BY SAMUEL STRICKLAND, C.M.

EDITED BY AGNES STRICKLAND

And when those toils rewarding,
  Broad lands at length they'll claim,
They'll call the new possession
  By some familiar name.
              AGNES STRICKLAND.—*Historic Scenes.*

VOLUME 2

TABLE OF CONTENTS

OF THE SECOND VOLUME.

CHAPTER I.

PAGE

Bravery and Humanity of Dr. Dunlop.—His Danger.— Popularity with the Irish.—His Speech on the proposed Tax on Whiskey.—Tosses a Copper to lose a Wife.—His Voyage in the "Dismal."— His Character.— Literary Merit. — His Personal Description 1

CHAPTER II.

Utility of the Lakes.— Internal Navigation superior to Russia.—Peter the Great and Captain Perry.—Theory of Evaporation.—Comparative Mean Depths, Number of Miles, and Elevation of the Lakes.—Fish.—Effects of the Lakes on the Temperature.—Warming Influence of Lake Huron over the whole Western Peninsula 10

CHAPTER III.

Healthiness of Canada West.—Its Dryness.—Its Heat and Cold. — Superiority of its Climate to that of England. — Beauty of the Canadian Forests in Autumn.—Felling Forests beneficial to the Climate.—Mean Temperature in Summer and Winter.—Decrease of Swamps.—Climate favourable to Agriculture.—Temperature of the Canadian Months.—Climatial Advantages over many Parts of the United States.— Annual Produce of Wheat. — Possibility of acclimatizing many Herbs and Trees.—Black Cherry, its Uses in Medicine. —Valuable as an ornamental Wood.—Native Grape.—Future Vineyards.—Hind's Tables of Temperature . . 19

CHAPTER IV.

PAGE

Old Indian Haunts.—Their Encampment near Goderich
Harbour. — Indian Wigwams. — Indian Missionary, Peter
Jones.—Indian Offerings to Manitou.—Personal Description
of the Indians.—Improvement in Indian Morals since their
Conversion to Christianity.—History of an Indian Family.—
Their miserable Condition.—My Remedy.—Indian Manufac-
tures.—Canoes.—Log-Canoe.—Elm-bark Canoe used by the
Chippewas.—Many Uses of the White Birch   32

CHAPTER V.

Aquatic Propensities of the Indians. — Indian Burying-
places.—Fragments of Pottery.—Pit discovered at Manvers.
—Indian Hunters.—Curious Oration of an Indian Chief interpreted by John Got. —Native Indian Preacher, Peter
Jones.—His Success.—Progress of the Indians in Reading
and Writing. — Indian Oratory. —Names given by them to
the English Settlers.—Peter Nogun makes a bad Bargain for
Jowler.—Good at Deer.—Indian Dance.—Captain George
Kishcow.—Indian Duel.—Indians at Evening Service.—Indian Hospitality and Generosity to my Daughter.—Population and Places of Resort.—Burial-place of the Chippewas
and Mississaugas. — Grave rifled by a Phrenologist. — Obsolete Indian Festival.—Belief in Immortality of the Soul
and the Flood   54

CHAPTER VI.

Ancient Indian Customs.—Religion.— Jugglers.—Resem-
blance of the Customs of the Six Nations to the Jews.—Land
of Souls.—Indian Proserpine.—Feast of Dreams.—Indian
Quacks —Courtship.—Naming the Child.—Dislike of the
Indian Nations to punishing their Children.—Inexpiable
War.—Its Cause.—The Huron Nation almost destroyed.—
The Wampum.—The Calumet.—Indian Oratory.—Method
of declaring War. — Treatment of their Prisoners. — The
Death-song.—Mischievous Effects of Raw Spirits   .   .   90

CHAPTER VII.

PAGE

My Voyage on the Huron to the Thames in the " Pioneer."
—Take in my Cargo.—Warm Welcome given to Mr. Campbell by a Highland Woman.—Irish Sonnet.—A new Acquaintance.—Specimen of Bachelor-housekeeping not recommen-
datory to Celibacy.—Mine Host sets Fire to his house *par
accident*.—Curious Dialogue between Him and his Cook.—
Excellent Supper.—Proceed on our Voyage   .   . 109

CHAPTER VIII.

We pass Goderich Harbour in the Gale.—Want of a Chart.
— Lake-sickness. — Dangerous Position. — Find Ourselves
among the Islands.—Dash through our Difficulties.—Harbour
of Refuge.—Camp on Shore.—My Walk on this *terra incog-
nita.*—Find five Steel Traps.—Miss shooting a black Fox.
—Beauty of the Scenery.—Our Hilarity.—Transparency of
the Waters of the Bay.—Visit of the Chippewa Indians.—
Noble Salmon-trout.—In Sight of Port.—Fresh Difficulties.
—Greetings from Shore.—Ship a Sea.—Cross the Bar.—Let
our Anchor go.—Accident to our Cable.—Man the Boat.—
Towing-line too short.—Jeopardy.—Resolve to swim ashore.
— Dangerous Predicament. — Providential Preservation. —
Home.—A solitary Fireside.—Return of my Wife.—Her
Anxiety during my Absence.—Her Terror on seeing the
Schooner stranded.—Recover my Health and Spirits under
her tender Care   124

CHAPTER IX.

I quit the Service of the Canada Company.—Leave Gode-
rich.—Homeward Journey.—Want of Accommodation at
Sebach's House.—My Landlady and her Brood.—Midnight
Adventures. —Disorderly Behaviour of the young Dutch
Boors.—Mine Hostess gives them a Thrashing.—Yankee
Guest.—Old Hickory Jackson.—Loyal Lawyer and Yankee
Fool.—The utility of Impudence.—Return Home.—Warm
Welcome.—Happy Party   139

CHAPTER X.

PAGE

Exchange my Land for a Lot in Douro and some Hard
Cash.—Advantages of Industry.—Canadian Orchards.—Bay
of Quinte. — Root-grafting. — American Graftsmen, and
Method of Grafting. — History of a Poor Emigrant.—He
sees a Ghost.—Cruelty of Caroline Grimshawe's Family.—
Generous Behaviour of Copping's Mother. — Dialogue be-
tween the Master Blacksmith and his Foreman.—Cheap Way
of being Good.—Distress and Poverty.—My Sister advises
Copping to go to Canada.—He reaches me in Penury.—
Change in his Circumstances.—His Settlement.—Our Search
for his Lot.—His Weariness and pathetic Exclamation.—
His Location.—Comfortable Circumstances and Decease after
some happy Years spent in Upper Canada.—The Bush.—
Our exploring Party.—Poor Copping's Lamentations.—We
give Names to our Locations.—Unpromising View of the
Blacksmith's Land.—His Lot turns out well.—His Success
as a Settler.—Conclusion of his History   .   .   . 149

CHAPTER XI.

My House. — Method of building and flooring. — My
Chimney.—Underbrushing.—My Hermit Life in the Woods.
—Nocturnal Visitation.—An Exit in Flames.—I meet the
poor Fiend by Daylight   177

CHAPTER XII.

The Wolverine.—Move into my new House.—Filial Piety
of the Irish.—Unlucky Journey to Peterborough.—Hospitality.—Accident.—Improvement in the Road. — My new
Location.—Arrival of my Family.—Ravages of the Cholera.
—A rough Cure.—I am appointed a Commissioner of the
Court of Requests.—The poor Scotchwoman and her Spinning-wheel   188

CHAPTER XIII.

PAGE

Falling Stars.—Aurora Borealis.—Damage to my House
by Lightning.—The Mistake of a Yankee Carpenter.—A
Beast saved and a Joke spoilt　　.　　.　　.　　. 208

CHAPTER XIV.

Rapid Increase of the Back-settlements.—Division of the
District.—Destruction of the Bridge.—Colonel B— and his
refractory human Steed.—Strike for Whiskey in the Middle
of the River.—The poor Temperance Colonel compelled to
come to Terms.—Peterborough.—The Otonabee River. —
Description of the Western or Back Lakes.—Sad Fate of a
Clergyman.—Beauty of the Scenery.—Love-sick Lake. —
Indian Lover. — Katharine O'Donohue's Disdain. — Stony
Lake and its Environs.—Clear Lake.—Progress of Peter-
borough　　.　　.　　.　　.　　.　　.　　. 216

CHAPTER XV.

Visit to the Falls of Niagara.—Tragical Recollections of
the Locality.—Battle of Lundy's Lane.—Gallant Conduct
of young Burnham and his Companions　　.　　.　　. 247

CHAPTER XVI.

The Rebellion of 1837. — March to Peterborough. — The
Relief of Toronto. — Return of the Volunteers to their
Homes.—Incorporated Battalions.—Militia Training.—Bad
Consequences of the Rebellion. — Good Effects of County
Councils.—Township Councils.—Municipalities.—Necessity
of Railroads.—Lumber Trade.—Lumber-shanties and Lum-
ber-men. — Timber-jambs.—Tom Burke's remarkable Es-
cape　　.　　.　　.　　.　　.　　.　　. 259

CHAPTER XVII.

PAGE

Domestic Manufactures.—The Colonist a Man of many Trades. — Shoe-Making. — Home-manufactured Soap and Candles.—Yarn-Dyeing.—Weaving.—Knitting.—Carpets . 287

CHAPTER XVIII.

Sugar-Maple. — Canadian Sugar. — Method of boiling Maple-sap into Sugar. — A Series of sweet Disasters led on by Prince.—Non-Vigilance of a Sugar-Sentinel.—Cow-Pilferers.—Dangerous Consequences to the Thieves, who are saved by an Operation.—Sugar-eating Bee.—Maple Vinegar. —Birch Vinegar and Beer 298

CHAPTER XIX.

The three great Wants of Canada.—Hints for the Education of Emigrants.—Bachelor Wants . . . 312

CHAPTER XX.

Need of Churches and Pastors in Canada.—Kind Assistance of my Friends in England towards this good Work.— Zeal of the Primitive Church.—Want of Schools and School-masters 321

CHAPTER XXI.

Death invades my Home-Circle. — Loss of my youngest Son, my Son-in-Law, my Grand-Daughter, my Wife, and my youngest Daughter.—Projected Return Home.—Embarkation.—Navigation of the Genesee River.—Rochester. — Syracuse.—Mohawk River.—American Steamers.—Rail-Carriages.—New York.—Voyage to England.—Return to Reydon.—Kindness and Hospitality of my English Friends . 332

TWENTY-SEVEN YEARS
IN CANADA WEST.

CHAPTER I.

BRAVERY AND HUMANITY OF DR. DUNLOP. — HIS DANGER.—POPU-
LARITY WITH THE IRISH.—HIS SPEECH ON THE PROPOSED TAX
ON WHISKEY.—TOSSES A COPPER TO LOSE A WIFE.—HIS VOY-
AGE IN THE "DISMAL."—HIS CHARACTER.—LITERARY MERIT.—
HIS PERSONAL DESCRIPTION.

As I may not have another opportunity of mentioning the name of my kind and eccentric friend
Dr. Dunlop, in connexion with my own, I shall
here devote a few pages to his memory, relating
some racy anecdotes which exhibit his character
in a new and interesting light.

For the following characteristic traits I am indebted to my friend Colonel Fitzgibbon. " Doctor
Dunlop, in his youth, was assistant-surgeon in the
89th Regiment, on the Niagara frontier, during the
campaign of 1814. He was at that time a young

man who appeared to have outgrown his clothes; at least the sleeves of his coat reached but a short way below his elbows, and his trowsers did not nearly reach his ancles. He was careless if not slovenly in his dress, and he seldom applied a razor to his chin. His proportions were almost Herculean, and his movements and gait were awkward and ungainly.

"When our army attacked Fort Erie by assault, we were beaten back with much slaughter ; great numbers of our men falling killed or wounded under the fire of the enemy. As daylight appeared, Dunlop, whose vocation, be it remembered, was that of man-curer not of man-killer, ran through the firing to witness the scene, when seeing that some of the wounded could not get to the rear beyond the range of the enemy's fire, he gallantly caught up a poor fellow and carried him to a place of safety, immediately returning to take up another, and so on until he had thus taken bodily possession of ten or twelve of his patients.

"One man, wounded in the knee, he heaved upon his back and bore to the rear, but on laying down his burden the Doctor found that the soldier had received, *in transitu*, a mortal wound in the back, and so intercepted the shot, which otherwise would have taken effect on Dunlop himself. It should be stated that he brought with him, slung over his shoulders, six of the soldiers' wooden canteens filled with wine intended for the wounded, with which he refreshed them, and attended professionally to their hurts under a noble tree, out of the reach of the shot he had so bravely encountered for their benefit.

" Those who enjoyed the friendship of this warmhearted man had frequent opportunities of knowing his kind and feeling disposition, for there never was a finer jewel, though roughly set, than poor Dunlop. His cheerful and undaunted spirit formed him for an efficient leader of British emigration.

" The 89th was chiefly composed of Irishmen, and among them he learned the management of those refractory subjects* better than any one of their own officers. His influence over them was very great, and during his long residence in Canada, after he left the army, he exerted his influence over the Irish emigrants and settlers, to the great benefit of the poor people themselves and to the advantage of the public. In a violent party-riot in the city of Toronto, about the year 1830, he did more than any other justice of the peace then present, in quelling the disturbance."

* Colonel Fitzgibbon being an Irishman seems perfectly aware that poor Paddy can be governed better by love than fear.

He was a humorous, witty man, and never regarded time or place when any opportunity occurred for displaying his facetious propensities. Upon one particular occasion, I remember, he amused the House of Assembly by his comical questions and witty rejoinders. I think it was seven or eight years ago when Montreal was the seat of government, that a bill was brought before the House to tax dogs and whiskey. The Doctor, who spoke on this occasion, asked—

"If any member present could inform him how many quarts of whiskey was usually made from a bushel of wheat, Indian corn, or rye?"

When the member for the Second Riding of Northumberland replied,—"He believed sixteen quarts."

"I believe," rejoined the Doctor, "the young gentleman is right, but heaven defend me from your sixteen quart-whiskey! I like a stiff horn.* I have read of the beast with two horns, and of the beast with ten horns, but I am a beast of many horns."

The whole House were convulsed with laughter at this sally of the Doctor's, the concluding assertion of which, I am sorry to say, was too true. In every other relation of life the Doctor's

* In allusion to a drinking-horn.

character might have safely borne the strictest scrutiny.

The following anecdote has been related of the Doctor. Its authenticity I do not doubt, for it is highly characteristic of the man.

The Doctor, and his brother the Captain, both old bachelors, lived together on their estate of Galbraith, near Goderich, with a respectable Scotch-body, as the Doctor called her, for their housekeeper. Now, whether any scandal had been raised, or whether the Doctor thought it would conduce to their greater comfort, if he or his brother were to marry the housekeeper, or whether he meant it only for a joke to teaze his brother, does not appear. Be that as it may, the Doctor proposed, in consequence, he said, of some unpleasant remarks, and their lonely situation, for one of them to marry her.

"Now, Sandy, you know I would almost as soon hang myself as put my head into the matrimonial noose, yet I think it only fair to stand my chance. So, what I propose is, that each of us shall toss up a copper* three times, and he who has the most heads shall be free."

As this appeared a very fair proposition the Captain at once consented to the arrangement,

* Canadian term for a halfpenny.

and they immediately proceeded to bring this friendly contest for a wife to an issue.

The Doctor would not have consented to run the risk of losing his liberty, if he had not been perfectly sure of winning, for by some chance he had become the possessor of a halfpenny with a head on either side.   So when they came to toss up, as might be expected, the poor unconscious Captain was duly elected for matrimonial honours, to the great glee of the roguish Doctor, who, I make no doubt, chuckled over his successful stratagem.

Strange as it may appear, the Captain honourably fulfilled this singular agreement.   I have understood that the lady filled her new station with great credit and propriety, and I have heard, at the death of the two brothers, inherited all their property.

Although the winner of Mrs. Dunlop had some reason to rejoice in getting a good wife so easily, yet I would advise all gentlemen before trying their chance in such a lottery, to examine whether their opponent is the fortunate possessor of a coin with two heads.

Dr. Dunlop was the first representative for the Huron District in the Provincial Parliament, and retained his seat as long as he lived.   While

employed in the Canada Company's service, he
encountered many perils, and on one of his
voyages met with the following adventure. During the early settlement of the Huron District, and before any saw-mill had been built, it
was necessary to purchase a quantity of boards
and other lumber for the Company's use. For
this purpose the Doctor went in a canoe from
Goderich, seventy-four miles down the lake, to a
Yankee village, at the mouth of the Black-water
river, near Fort Gratiot. Here he purchased what
he required, and hired a small schooner, which he
freighted with the lumber, and took passage in
her himself. It appears that, with the exception
of the owner of the vessel, there was only one person on board besides the Doctor, not one of whom
knew anything about the navigation of the
lake.

The Doctor, however, undertook the pilotage ;
he knew that there was a rocky shoal stretching
out some distance into the lake directly opposite
Kettle Point, but he was not aware that it extended
for miles. Consequently they were startled by
finding themselves amongst the rocks several miles
from the shore. Luckily there was little wind,
and the lake so smooth that every stone could be
seen distinctly in the water. In this emergency

the Doctor seated himself astride on the bowsprit, with his hat off and his red hair streaming in the wind, forming altogether not a bad representation of old Neptune.

From this nautical throne his majesty issued his commands of *starboard* and *larboard, port* or *steady,* as the rocks on either side appeared in view.   All his skill, however, proved unavailing— the vessel at last grounded, and as they had not sufficient help on board to heave her off, they were obliged to make a raft and abandon her to her fate.   However, they had the good fortune to land with their raft in safety near the mouth of the river Aux-Sables, yet distant many miles from any settlement.   The vessel became a wreck, and I believe the Company ultimately paid the owner for his crazy vessel, which the Doctor in speaking of always called the " Dismal."

The Doctor's character may be summed up in a few words.   He was a kind-hearted generous man ; scientific, enterprising, and possessing considerable literary attainments, as his articles published in "Blackwood's Magazine," and his "Back-woodsman," sufficiently prove.

In person he was well made, stout, broad-shouldered, and above six feet in height, with red hair and whiskers, blue eyes, high forehead, nose slightly aquiline, broad face, and a remarkably facetious and good-humoured expression of countenance.

I am happy to say that he overcame his only failing, but not in time to save his valuable life. However,

> " Take him for all in all,
> We ne'er shall look upon his like again."

Therefore farewell, kind, amiable, witty, Dunlop, but not for ever !

CHAPTER II.

UTILITY OF THE LAKES.—INTERNAL NAVIGATION SUPERIOR TO RUSSIA.—PETER THE GREAT AND CAPTAIN PERRY.—THEORY OF EVAPORATION—COMPARATIVE MEAN DEPTHS, NUMBER OF MILES, AND ELEVATION OF THE LAKES.—FISH.—EFFECTS OF THE LAKES ON THE TEMPERATURE.—WARMING INFLUENCE OF LAKE HURON OVER THE WHOLE WESTERN PENINSULA.

CANADA is yet in her colonial dawn ; but the dawn is one of cheering promise. She possesses a virgin soil, finely timbered forests, rich mineral ores, as yet little worked, and lands on the Huron tract of almost unrivalled fertility, with an immense water-power, which, when once put in use by a thriving and increasing population, will render her one of the greatest commercial countries in the world. Providence, by the gift of lakes, which from their vast extent may be fairly denominated inland seas, has marked her for a land of commerce. She enjoys the double advantage of an inland water communication, and an outward maritime one with Europe, the United States, South America, and the world in general. Her commercial relations are as yet only in their infancy. But what will they not be when the vast tract north-west of Lake Superior shall be opened for the reception of the produce of the West. Twelve thousand mariners are employed at present in the navigation of the lakes. Russia is the only commercial country that possesses the same natural advantages, though in an inferior degree, for the Russian lakes did not communicate with each other till the wisdom of her wise regenerator, Peter the Great, established a communication between them by the aid of Captain Perry, an English engineer, to whose genius Russia is indebted for her inland water communication by means of the canals he cut and the rivers he made navigable to facilitate her internal commerce. Poor Perry was an ill-used man, for the Czar would not pay him his salary for fear of losing his vast services—a common but shameful abuse of despotic power. He finally returned to England under the protection of our ambassador, poor in purse and injured in health. He had been, in fact, working for the benefit of unborn millions, for fame, for commerce, but not for his own profit.*

Nature, however, bountifully placed the Canadian lakes in a chain, and thus provided Canada with an internal navigation, which the science of our gifted but ill-used countryman first opened for

* " Memoirs of Captain John Perry," by himself.

Russia. But much as we must admire the wisdom of Peter the Great in conceiving the mighty design, we cannot but feel indignant at his injustice in robbing his agent of his hard-earned reward. He deprived himself of Perry's services at an important time, and probably had reason to regret the wrong he did to our injured and high-spirited countryman.

" The comparative depths of the lakes form an interesting subject of inquiry, and the vast area covered by their waters. The bottom of Lake Ontario is as low as most parts of the Gulf of St. Lawrence, while the bottoms of Lake Huron, Michigan, and Superior, are all, from their vast depths (although their surface is so much higher), on a level with the bottoms of Lake Ontario and the Gulf of St. Lawrence. Can there be," (asks our author, M'Gregor) " a subterranean river running from Lake Superior to Huron, and from Huron to Lake Ontario? " He considers " the discharge of water through the river Detroit, and that carried off by means of evaporation unequal to the quantity which the three upper great lakes may be considered to receive." *

In Dr. Arnott's admirable scientific work on the " Elements of Physics," we find the theory of evaporation with its vast effects perfectly ex-

* M'Gregor's " British America," vol. ii. p. 557.

plained ; and that too in a lucid manner, calculated to convey information even to the common-
est mind, although the matter relates to one of
the most mysterious agencies of nature. " There
are some lakes," he says, " on the face of the
earth, which have no outlet towards the sea—
all the water which falls into them being again
carried off by evaporation alone ; and such lakes
are never of fresh water alone, because every
substance, which from the beginning of time rain
could dissolve in the regions around them, has
necessarily been carried towards them by their
feeding streams, and there has remained.

" The great majority of lakes, however, being
basins with the water constantly running over at
one part towards the sea, although all originally
salt, have in the course of time become fresh, because their only supply being direct from the
clouds, or from rivers and springs fed by the
clouds, is fresh, while what runs away from them
must be always carrying with it a proportion of
any substance that remains dissolved in them." *

Thus the evaporation produced by frost in
winter, and heat in summer, and the natural
outlets of these lakes sufficiently account for the
uniformity of their level without the agency of a
subterraneous channel. The fact that these lakes

* Arnott's " Elements of Physics," vol. i. p. 277—8.

have a communication by the St. Lawrence to the sea sufficiently accounts for the freshness and purity of these vast bodies of water.

" A curious instance of a lake in the process of losing its saltness exists in that of Mexico, from which a drain was cut to relieve the inhabitants of the city from the consequences of an inundation. This drain, extending sixty miles from Mexico to the lower external country, has not only in the course of a hundred and fifty years freed the city from the water, but by the continual force of the stream is still lowering the surface of the lake, and is daily rendering the water less salt, and converting the extensive salt marshes around Mexico into fresh and fertile fields." *
In fact, a traveller this present year (1852) travelled some miles from the city before he could find the celebrated lake which once inundated the city.

That the immense body of water in the Upper Lakes of Canada do not find a lower level, as in the course of ages they probably will do, arises from the nature of the ground through which they are working their channel, which is hard, rocky, and irregular; for "where the soil or bed of a country through which a water-track passes is not of a soft consistence, so as to allow readily the

* Arnott's " Elements of Physics," vol. i. p. 279.

wearing down of higher parts and the filling up of hollows by depositing sand, lakes, rapids, and great irregularities of current remain. We have, for instance, the line of lakes in North America, the rapids of the St. Lawrence, and the stupendous falls of Niagara, where at one leap the river gains a level lower by a hundred and sixty feet. A softer barrier than the rock over which the river pours would soon be cut through, and the line of lakes would be emptied."* Such a change would not however benefit the province, and provident Nature, by the rocky shores that enclose these mighty waters, has insured the internal navigation of this highly favoured country for ages to come. The following table, from the pen of a scientific Canadian writer, will give the reader every information respecting the area, elevation, and mean depth of the lakes of Canada.

Names of Lakes.	Area in Square Miles.	Elevation above the Sea.	Mean Depth.
Lake Superior . . .	32,000	596	900
Green Bay . . .	2,000	578	500
Lake Michigan . .	22,400	578	1,000
Lake Huron . . .	19,200	578	1,000
Lake St. Clair . .	360	570	20
Lake Erie . . .	9,600	565	84
Lake Ontario . . .	6,300	232	500
Total Area .	91,860		

* Arnott's " Elements of Physics," vol. i. p. 279.

The greatest known depth of Lake Ontario is seven hundred and eighty feet; in Lake Superior, however, a line one thousand two hundred feet long has in some parts failed to reach the bottom.*

" These lakes contain an immense quantity of fish of considerable size. Fine sturgeon, salmon, some of which weigh sixty pounds, herrings, black bass, and various other kinds of fish are caught in the lakes, but it is remarkable that neither salmon nor herring have been caught in any of the lakes that do not communicate with the St. Lawrence. How either one or the other have got into the great lakes of Upper Canada must ever puzzle naturalists to account for."†

The lakes of Canada contribute to raise the temperature of the country by warming the winds that pass over their ample bosoms. In fact, the influence of this species of natural agency is remarkable, as the following extract will show :—

" The effect of winds on climate, by their prevalence, is considerable, but particularly on that of Upper Canada. Thus, whenever westerly winds sweep over the surface-waters of Lakes Huron, Erie, and Ontario, they will not only receive accessions of heat, but be also in some

* Hind's " Comparative View of Canada West."
† M'Gregor's " British America."

measure diverted from their courses. The mean temperature of the air at Toronto during the three winter months, December, January, and February, is 25·51°; while that of the surface water of the open lakes is never less than 32°, and generally about 33·5°, in other words 7° or 8° above the mean at Toronto. The effect of this difference is occasionally manifest in the high temperatures of the southern shores of Lakes Erie and Ontario, and especially on the Niagara river, where the mean winter temperature does not fall two degrees below the freezing point of water. A similar effect is produced upon the northern shores of Lakes Erie and Ontario, although in a less degree, while the warming influence of Lake Huron is felt over the whole western peninsula during the winter months. At Detroit, in latitude 42·24°, the mean of three years' observations gives 27° for the winter temperature, whereas the corresponding temperature at Laviston, in latitude 43·09°, or nearly three-quarters of a degree farther north, is 30°. The influence of the State of Michigan (frozen during the winter season) on the temperature at Detroit is sufficient to reduce it to that of Rochester, a degree further to the north. The duration of snow upon the ground, the average fall of rain, the serenity of the sky, and the humidity of the atmosphere are all affected on the shores of the Lakes by the great depth and expanse of their waters."*

"The peculiar temperature of Canada West originates from two causes. Its elevation may be referred to the mighty mass of water contained in Lakes Michigan, Huron, Erie, Ontario, and more remotely Lake Superior, water being an element in which much latent heat is found. The second cause may be traced to the serenity of the sky during the summer months, a serenity of long continuance." †

"The causes which tend to lower the temperature, we find the uniform extension of land north and north-west of the lakes, towards the polar regions, in the direction of the winter winds (north-west) ; extensive forests which, besides the shade they afford the soil, expose a great evaporating and radiating surface during the summer months ; the frequency of extensive swamps, and the clear winter sky." ‡

* Hind's "Comparative View of the Climate of Western Canada."
† Hind's Pamphlet.   ‡ Ibid.

CHAPTER III.

HEALTHINESS OF CANADA-WEST. — ITS DRYNESS. — ITS HEAT AND COLD.—SUPERIORITY OF ITS CLIMATE TO THAT OF ENGLAND.— BEAUTY OF THE CANADIAN FORESTS IN AUTUMN —FELLING FORESTS BENEFICIAL TO THE CLIMATE.—MEAN TEMPERATURE IN SUMMER AND WINTER.—DECREASE OF SWAMPS.— CLIMATE FAVOURABLE TO AGRICULTURE.—TEMPERATURE OF THE CANADIAN MONTHS.—CLIMATIAL ADVANTAGES OVER MANY PARTS OF THE UNITED STATES.—ANNUAL PRODUCE OF WHEAT.—POSSIBILITY OF ACCLIMATIZING MANY HERBS AND TREES.—BLACK CHERRY, ITS USES IN MEDICINE. — VALUABLE AS AN ORNAMENTAL WOOD.— NATIVE GRAPE. — FUTURE VINEYARDS. — HIND'S TABLES OF TEMPERATURE.

THE climate of Canada West is both healthful and pleasant ; and few persons long resident in the western province find themselves benefited by their exchange to the damper one of their native country.

I confess that I have suffered more with cold during this unusually mild winter of 1851-2 than in the land in which I have sojourned so long. The dry air of Canada, though so low in temperature, has not such chilling effects on my frame, as that of England. Besides the sharp piercing cold of the Canadian winter is really invigorating, and warm thick clothing protects the person from the effects of the climate, while nothing can guard the frame from damp which we continually breathe in England, and which no precaution can really exclude. Then the extreme variability of the temperature, and the chance of having no summer as a counterbalance for having no winter, is an unpleasant contingent : I therefore, prefer the certainty of having a long bright summer in return for a sharp winter, and a mild autumn clad in the gorgeous hues with which Nature chooses to decorate our Canadian forests. " It is, indeed, impossible to exaggerate the autumnal beauty of these forests. Nothing under heaven can be compared to its effulgent grandeur."

" Two or three frosty nights in the decline of autumn, transform the boundless verdure of a whole empire into every possible tint of brilliant scarlet, rich violet, every shade of blue and brown, vivid crimson, and glittering yellow. The stern inexorable fir-tribes alone maintain their eternal sombre green. All others, on mountains or in valleys, burst into the most glorious vegetable beauty, and exhibit the most splendid and enchanting panorama on earth."

The author from whom I have taken this

glowing descriptive passage, imputes the change in the hues of the forest, to the action of the frost on the acids contained in the leaves.*

The felling of these fine forests contributes to the amelioration of the climate, and it is conjectured that in some districts the absence of snow at some future time will form a subject of complaint when the farmer misses his former winter roads, which he found useful for the transfer of his produce to the market and flour-mill, or his timber to the saw-mill." †

" The lands in the Huron tract have only a winter of three months, and it is for nine months much warmer than England."‡   I do not wholly rely upon my own long experience of Canada West; I have carefully collected those of other men,— men of science and judgment, which I shall present in illustration of my assertion that the Canadian westward province is superior to our own island, in climate, at least.

" Great misconception exists in respect to the soil and temperature of Western Canada, for notwithstanding the eminent fertility of the soil, and the salubrity of the climate, and its superiority for agricultural purposes over the State of New York;

---

* M'Gregor's " British America."
† Mac Taggart's " Three Years in Canada."   ‡ Ibid.

the northern part of Ohio and Illinois, the States of Michigan, Iowa, Wisconsin, the Far West, and the whole of New England; in a word, over the wheat-growing states generally ; yet among multitudes of British and Irish desirous of emigrating a far different idea is commonly entertained.

" The impression in their minds being that the climate of Canada West is distinguished by intense winter, cold, and a brief, scorching summer, in which the cultivator can scarcely find time to secure his harvest." *

" The European emigrant in preferring these parts of the United States to which allusion has been made, chooses far greater extremes of heat and cold, and fixes his location not only in a more unhealthy climate, but in a soil far less fruitful, and more exposed to vicissitude."†

" Canada West possesses a greater immunity from spring frosts, and summer droughts, in comparison to many parts of the United States, and it has a more favourable distribution of clear and cloudy days, and in the distribution of rain over many days.   Canada West is also more salubrious.

* " Climate and Soil of Canada West."
† " Comparative View of Canada West," by H. Y. Hind.

" The climate of Canada, in many respects, is more favourable than that of Great Britain and Ireland, for it has a higher summer temperature, greater dryness, and enjoys a serener sky." *

" The clearing away of the immense forests which at present cover the fertile soil of Upper Canada, will produce a considerable change in the temperature. At present, during the nights of the summer season — which these forests by their nocturnal radiation lower—Humboldt has clearly shown, by the reason of the vast multiplicity of leaves, a tree, the crown of which does not present a horizontal section of more than one hundred and twenty or one hundred and thirty feet, actually influences the cooling of the atmosphere by an extent of surface several thousand times more extensive than this section. The upper surface of the leaves first become cool by nocturnal radiation ; these again receive heat from the lower stratum of leaves, which is in turn given off into space. The cooling is thus propagated from above, downwards, until the temperature of the whole tree is lowered, and, as a necessary result, the air enveloping it. As the forests of Western Canada disappear before the

* Hind's Pamphlet.

rapid encroachments of the settler, we may look for a rise in the minimum temperature of the spring, summer, and autumnal nights. Late spring and early autumn frosts will probably become rarer, as the country becomes more cleared. Notwithstanding the cold produced by the radiation of heat from the leaves of forest-trees during summer nights, there is no reason to suppose that the destruction of forests elevates the mean temperature of the year. The clearing them, however, exhibits the following results :—

" The elevation of the mean temperature during the summer months, the lowering of the mean temperature of the winter months, whose duration is, nevertheless, shortened.

" The acceleration of the coming of spring, the drying up of swamps, shallow springs, and the diminution of the water in creeks ; the disappearance of snow from exposed districts will also be accelerated." *

" Indeed, the destruction of forests seems to have a marked effect upon swamps, springs, and running streams. In all parts of the country neglected saw-mills may be seen, having been abandoned by their proprietors, owing to the want of

* Hind's " Comparative View."

water. This decrease may reasonably be ascribed to the felling of the forests, whereby extensive swamps are exposed to solar radiation and that supply of moisture which they received in the summer months from the condensation of the aqueous vapour of the atmosphere, by the leaves of the trees overshadowing them being altogether cut off." *

" The climate of Canada is favourable for agriculture, since a moderately humid atmosphere, in relation to cultivation, can scarcely be estimated too highly. The most interesting, and perhaps the most advantageous, form in which atmospheric influence exhibits itself, is that of dew. The quantity of this revivifying agent condensed on the leaves of vegetables in the Canadian Peninsula is very great, and furnishes one important reason why Western Canada is less liable to suffer from those destructive droughts which are common to the west of the Lakes, and not unfrequent towards the east and south. The terms rainy season and dry season are unknown in Canadian climatology; the distribution of rain over the months of the year is, in general, remarkably uniform." †

* Hind's " Comparative View of Western Canada."
† Ibid.

The able author of the Pamphlet from which these quotations are made, has proved a fact not usually well understood, that the climate of Upper Canada is healthier and more equal in temperature than a great many provinces of the United States. Indeed the severer temperature of the Lower Province, or Canada East, as it is now called, does not apply to that of Canada West, which the causes just quoted render milder even than many parts of the States.

Hind has made an ingenious classification of the mean temperature of the Canadian year, which is subjoined for the use of the reader.

"The hottest month in the Canadian year is July, the coldest, February. There are four months in the year during which the average temperature is less than the freezing point of water ; these months are January, February, March, December. These constitute the winter months.

"There are three months, April, October, and November, during which the temperature is above the freezing point of water, and below the mean temperature of the year. There are five months in the year during which the mean temperature is above the annual mean ; these are May, June, July, August, and September. These months, with October, constitute the agricultural or growing months of Western Canada. The mean highest temperature of the hottest month (July), is double of the mean annual temperature. The mean minimum temperature of the hottest month is the same as the mean annual temperature. The temperature is most uniform in August, and most fluctuating in April." *

"It is well known in America," remarks an intelligent government officer, " that the climate always improves, or rather increases in warmth, with the destruction of the forest and cultivation of the soil." †

"We are as yet imperfectly acquainted with the natural agricultural advantages of Canada West, but from what we do know from its peculiar situation among the great Lakes, we may positively assert its general superiority over any other portion of North America, with very few exceptions.

"The most important points in which the climate of Canada West differs from those of the United States which lie north of the forty-first parallel of latitude, may be thus enumerated:

* Hind's "Comparative View of the Climate of Western Canada."
† Mac Taggart's " Three Years in Canada."

" In mildness, the extremes of winter cold and summer heat being, comparatively speaking, much less, in being better suited to the growth of grain and green crops, on account of the more equable distribution of rain over the agricultural months ; and, also, in the humidity of the atmosphere, which, though less than that of an insular climate, is greater than that of localities situated at a distance from the Lakes." *

" Wheat of a fine quality, to the amount of two millions of bushels, is the annual 'average rate, at present, of growth in Canada West ; but, as emigration and population increase, the quantity, as a matter of course, must also multiply. Fine samples from the old country must be acclimated, just as many plants of our own produce have been, before they reach their maximum. Thus the new seed will not equal your expectations ; but if you sow from it again, you will find them realized." †
In respect to vegetable assimilation to climate, we all know that the hardy lauristinus and the scarlet-bean were confined in the early part of the last century to the green-house. There is little doubt that many herbs and useful vegetables may gradually be acclimated.

* Hind's Pamphlet.   † Ibid.

Canada has an indigenous growth of plums and grapes, which will improve by cultivation. The black cherry is, in its wild state, crude and astringent ; it is used medicinally in the United States for consumptive complaints ; the value of the tree in Canada arises from the beauty of the wood, which makes it prized for furniture. No attempt has been made to improve the native grape, which is small and crude ; but the fact that it ripens at all, exhibits a point favourable to the climate, since this fruit mainly owes its fine qualities to cultivation. The Canadian settler, who at present leaves the forest-vine to the birds of the air and beasts of the field, will, probably, some years hence, have vineyards as well as corn-tracts. Indeed vines from Germany might be tried for this purpose in the more westward tracts with, perhaps, a fair chance of success.

The tables exhibited in the following pages will give some important information on the subject of temperature to emigrants, which I have extracted from the scarce and valuable pamphlet,* for the sight of which I am indebted to the Canada Company, and of which I have already availed myself so largely.

* Hind's Pamphlet.

Table of the Mean Temperature of the Summer Months (June, July, and August) at Toronto, during the years 1840 to 1850, both inclusive ; also Table of the Mean Maximum Temperature during the same periods :—

Year.	Mean Summer Temperature.	Mean Maximum Summer Temperature.
1840 . .	63·90	81·5
1841 . .	65·3	88·9
1842 . .	62·33	82·9
1843 . .	63·33	83·7
1844 . .	62·55	85·6
1845 . .	65·30	88·1
1846 . .	66·16	88·4
1847 . .	63·26	82·5
1848 . .	65·41	87·1
1849 . .	65·30	84·0
1850 . .	66·81	85·3
Mean	64·51	85·26

To the east and west of the Lakes (especially in the latter direction) high summer means of temperature are invariably associated with low winter means ; in other words, great and often injurious extremes of temperature occur, particularly in the Western States. Compare the subjoined temperatures of the seasons at the stations named :—

Places.	Latitude	Winter Mean.	Spring Mean.	Summer Mean.	Autumn Mean.
Toronto . .	43·39	25·33	41·60	64·51	47·41
Hudson . .	41·15	25·70	48·20	69·20	46·40
Muscatine Iowa .	41·26	25·80	49·90	69·00	49·30
Council Bluffs .	41·28	24·28	51·60	75·81	52·46
Fort Crawford .	43·03	20·69	48·25	72·38	48·09
Fort Winebago .	43·31	20·81	44·67	67·97	46·10
Fort Dearborn .	41·50	24·31	45·39	67·80	47·09
Detroit . . .	42·62	27·62	45·16	67·33	47·75

TABLE OF THE MEAN SUMMER TEMPERATURES at various localities in Europe, compared with those at Toronto.

	Mean Summer Temperature.
Toronto	. 64·51
Berlin, Europe . . .	. 63·2
Cherbourg	. 61·9
Penzance	. 61·8
Greenwich	. 60·88
Cheltenham . . .	. 60·04

	Mean Temperature of the Hottest Months.
Toronto	· 66·54
Paris	. 66·02
Frankfort-on-the-Maine .	. 66·00
Berlin	. 64·4
London	. 64·1
Cherbourg	. 63·2

CHAPTER IV.

OLD INDIAN HAUNTS.—THEIR ENCAMPMENT NEAR GODERICH HAR-
BOUR.—INDIAN WIGWAMS.—INDIAN MISSIONARY, PETER JONES.
—INDIAN OFFERINGS TO MANITON.—PERSONAL DESCRIPTION OF
THE INDIANS.—IMPROVEMENT IN INDIAN MORALS SINCE THEIR
CONVERSION TO CHRISTIANITY.—HISTORY OF AN INDIAN FAMILY
—THEIR MISERABLE CONDITION.—MY REMEDY.—INDIAN MANU-
FACTURES.— CANOES,—LOG-CANOE. — ELM-BARK CANOE USED BY
THE CHIPPEWAS.—MANY USES OF THE WHITE BIRCH.

It is interesting to mark the rise of the towns
of Canada West; to compare them with what
they were, and to reflect upon what they will
become.

Some of these locations, reclaimed by civilized
man from the wild-forest tract, were once the
haunts of the red man, who still loves to linger
near the site of his old encampments. The Chippewas still repair at certain seasons of the year
to the environs of Goderich.

The bottom of Goderich harbour is formed by
a long strip of sand and gravel, which separates
the waters of the harbour from the lake. This

little peninsula is only a few yards in width, and dotted here and there with clumps of bushes. During the summer months it used to be the favourite camping-ground of the Chippewas. I have seen more than a hundred of them, men, women, and children, at one time occupying rude wigwams on this point. In hot weather they are not very particular how they construct their tents. A couple of slight poles crossing one another about six feet from the ground, fastened with bass-wood bark, are fixed in the ground at either end. A pole is then laid on where the end-sticks cross one another, and are securely tied, this forms the ridge-pole against which a few more poles are leant in a sloping direction covered with cedar bark.

If the weather looks settled they do not en-camp at all unless they intend to stay some time.

In winter, however, they take pains to make a warm camp, which is either circular or oblong. In either case the poles are planted from a foot to eighteen inches apart at the bottom, and closing together at the top. Birch-bark is generally used for the winter covering. The common size of a circular wigwam is about twelve feet in diameter. This will accommodate two large families. The fire is made in the centre, and a door-way is left opposite each end of the fire for the better convenience of bringing in wood, a blanket being fastened across these apertures in lieu of a door, which is merely put on one side by the person who wishes to enter.

During the sugar season the Indians construct much larger wigwams. I remember when I purchased the land I now reside upon, I found the remains of a very large sugar-boiling camp upwards of thirty feet in length by sixteen wide, furnished with bed-berths made with poles covered with bark, raised about fifteen inches from the ground, serving for seats as well as beds. The fire had evidently occupied nearly the whole length of this building, for the hooked sticks which had supported their pots and sugar-kettles still hung suspended from a pole above the hearth.

The Indian wigwams are very warm. I have slept in them in the coldest weather with only one blanket wrapped about me, without experiencing the least inconvenience arising from either draught or cold.

On my first acquaintance with the Indians I found them—particularly those who were in the habit of visiting Goderich—a poor, drunken, dissipated set, destitute both of morality and religion, which was entirely owing to that abominable custom practised by the fur-traders, of keeping their wretched victims in a state of drunkenness whilst bargaining for their peltry. I have seen forty or fifty Indians and squaws drunk in an encampment at the same time, rolling about on the grass, nearly naked, and while in that state pillaged by those white fiends, the traders, who dare to *call themselves Christians*. I am, however, happy to say, that a great reform has taken place among them—owing partly to the preaching of the Gospel to them, and partly parliamentary enactments inflicting heavy fines on any one selling spirits of any kind to the Indians.

Foremost in the good work of Gospel-diffusion may be mentioned Peter Jones, an Indian by birth, I believe, of the Mississauga tribe, for he speaks their language as though it were his own. I have understood he was the first person who translated the Gospels into this Indian dialect, and also rendered a book of Wesleyan hymns into his own tongue.

It is quite surprising to see what a change for the better has taken place amongst these poor creatures, once so benighted, within the last fifteen years. I was down at their encampment one day, before the conversion of the tribe, when I noticed an old Indian take his canoe and paddle off into the middle of the harbour. He then laid in his paddle and knelt down in the centre of his little bark, and commenced a long oration, during the delivery of which he from time to time threw into the river small pieces of tobacco, and concluded the ceremony by emptying some kind of liquor from a bottle, which I afterwards learned was whiskey. On making inquiry of one of the traders, " What the Indian meant by this extraordinary proceeding," he informed me " that the man was praying to the Great Maniton to make the waters yield them an abundance of fish and game, and the pieces of tobacco and the whiskey were intended as offerings to propitiate him. The word Maniton meaning presiding spirit."

It has been asserted that many of their traditions and religious ceremonies are undoubtedly of Jewish origin, and some think that the North American Indians are descendants of the lost tribes of Israel. I have, however, not the slightest doubt that this portion of the continent has been peopled from Northern Asia. I have come to this conclusion from two causes—first, from the proximity of the two countries, which, at Behring's Straits, is only thirty-nine miles across from the

Old World to the New. In the mid-channel there are two islands, called by the Russians the St. Diomedes, which are from two to three leagues in circumference—thus leaving either of the passages not more than twenty miles from land to land, which distance could be easily traversed in fine weather and a smooth sea by canoes. Secondly, the black hair, dark eye, slightly pointed at the corners, the high cheek bones and want of hair on the face, sufficiently prove, I think, their Asiatic origin.

It has been said, and is generally believed, that the Indians are in the habit of pulling out the hair of their beards on its first making its appearance. This I believe to be altogether a fiction, not only from my own personal observation, but also from the report of those who have lived for years amongst them. The half-breeds have more hair on the chin, which clearly proves that they inherit that troublesome appendage from their European fathers. The Indian complexion is not darker than the English gipsy, but has a redder cast ; the profile regular, the nose being thin and straight, and the eyes close together. They are naturally grave in their deportment, and silent on common occasions, but are eloquent public speakers.

Since their conversion they have become sober, religious, and, generally speaking, more moral and virtuous than their white brethren ; for, upon the first preaching of the Gospel, its effects are always more strikingly apparent than afterwards, as if upon the new converts the Spirit of God was more plentifully poured forth. In this I allude more particularly to those Indians who inhabit the villages of Rice Lake, Alnwick, and Chemong Lake, and who are more particularly under the superintendance of the Rev. J. Gilmour, the Baptist Minister at Peterborough, who has done much to better their condition both in a temporal and spiritual sense. However, these converts to Christianity are not Baptists, but belong to the Wesleyan Methodist Connexion, having local preachers amongst their own people.

I am sorry to say, the introduction of European diseases and vices have tended greatly to diminish the number of this very interesting people. I was told by a very clever medical gentleman, that consumption carried more of them off than any other disorder, and that this insidious malady had been entailed upon the present generation by the dissipation of their fathers. Happily for them, they have forsaken these intemperate habits. In fact, it is now as rare to see a drunken Indian as, twenty years ago, it was to see a sober one ; so great a blessing has the Gospel been to these tribes.

I have heard it said, that it was impossible for an Indian to lose his way in the bush ; and I was for some time of that opinion myself, until the following circumstance considerably shook my belief.

It appeared that an Indian, his squaw, and two children, one of whom was a lad of thirteen or fourteen years of age, left Owen's Sound, on the Georgian bay, Lake Huron, with the intention of travelling through the woods to Goderich, where a party of his friends were encamped for the winter.

The snow was deep, and the distance, in a straight line, nearly eighty miles. It seems that, after crossing the river Saugeen, the weather became cloudy, attended with frequent snow-storms; so that they had nothing to guide them but the moss on the trees, for it appears they had never traversed that part of the country before. However, from some cause or another they lost their way ; and their provisions also failed them. In this emergency they pitched their wigwam near a small stream, where they waited several days, hoping the sun would make its appearance. To add to the difficulties of the miserable couple, their youngest papouse, a girl, died from want and the hardships to which she had been exposed.

Although the Indian had some ammunition, he was unable to find any game ; not even a partridge. And the snow was so deep that it was quite impossible, in their exhausted state, to travel without snow-shoes, especially.

When they left Owen's Sound there was not more than eight inches of snow, but in consequence of the continued fall it had increased to a depth of upwards of two feet. So when, at last, the weather cleared up they were totally unable to proceed.

How long they remained in this dreadful situation is not easily known, but they were at last accidentally discovered by a party of French Canadians, who were out trapping, about twenty miles up the Maitland, and who told me they were perfectly horrified at the scene that presented itself to their view. The old Indian and his squaw, wasted to perfect skeletons, were lying in the wigwam, unable to rise. Near these anatomies lay the remains of some human flesh that had evidently been used for food, and which the trappers positively declared to be part of the Indian's own son, who had been shot through the back by his wretched father, as he left the wigwam to go to the creek for water. Be this as it may, both the Indian and his squaw, when I questioned them on the subject, after their recovery, denied it in the strongest terms.

As soon as their situation was known in Goderich, a party of Indians and trappers went to the wigwam and brought them to the town in litters. When I heard of the arrival of these poor creatures I went down to see them, taking with me some broth and other necessaries that I thought might be good for them. I think I never beheld two such miserable objects with a spark of life in them. They were groaning piteously, and appeared to be suffering excruciating agony. I found out at once the cause of this. They had been allowed to satisfy their ravenous appetite without restraint, and had gorged themselves till they were nearly mad with pain.

I gave them each a dose of laudanum, which had such a good effect that in a few days they were able to sit up and speak. Their miserable state excited such general compassion that almost every one sent them something to eat ; so that in a month's time they were as fat and strong as before their days of starvation.   Indeed, I could hardly have believed it possible for human beings to make flesh so quickly as they did.

Whether the Indian killed his son to sustain his own life and that of his squaw, rests entirely on the assertion of the Canadians who found them, though I believe there is little doubt that in their extremity they made use of his flesh.   This is the only case of cannibalism I ever heard of among the Indians, and even this terrible fact, if the victim had not been their own son, would have been no more than a case of stern necessity.   I am glad to be able to state that these unhappy parents were not Christians.

Before the conversion of these Indian tribes they were in the habit of painting their faces and eye-brows, upon every remarkable occasion, which certainly did anything but improve their appearance.   Some of the squaws are pretty, but as they advance in years, they grow fat and ugly. The men, on the contrary, are of a spare make, and very seldom become fleshy.   Their mode of life, as hunters, requires the greatest activity ;

while that of the squaws is of a more sedentary nature, being chiefly confined to the wigwam, their principal occupation being the making of baskets, brooms, and deer-skin mocassins, which they ornament very prettily with porcupine quills or beads. They have a curious method of dyeing the quills, which is effected by extracting the colour from pieces of English broad-cloth, from which process they obtain the most vivid dyes.

Some of these Indian designs are pretty, and even ingenious, and may be obtained at a reasonable rate.

The price of a pair of plain mocassins is 2s. 6d. Halifax currency ; handsome ones, worked with a pattern on the instep, wrought either with quills or beads, a dollar or 5s.

Their brooms are manufactured principally from the birch, iron-wood, black-ash, and blue-beech, the latter wood is considered the best and toughest for the purpose. The manner of making them is quite different from any I ever saw made in the old country. As all settlers far back in the bush are obliged to use these articles, I may as well describe the method of their construction. A clean growing young tree, about two inches in diameter, should be chosen, straight in the grain and free from knots. After removing the bark, small stripes of wood are drawn from one end of the stick with the grain, and as fine as possible, about eighteen inches in length, which is done by inserting a knife at the end of the stick and raising as much wood as will run with the grain the length required. When a sufficient thickness of fibres has been obtained for half the thickness of the broom, the same process is gone through from the other end; one set of fibres being turned back over the first, making the thickness required, which is securely tied with bass-wood bark. The handle is then reduced to the proper size and the sweeping part cut off even at the bottom. This kind of broom is considered the best sort for stables, barns, or to clean the yards about the back doors of houses.

The Indian baskets are made from the wood of the black-ash, beaten with a wooden maul till the wood readily separates in rings of one year's growth from the other, and is as it were stripped off in ribbons from one to two inches in width the whole length of the piece. These ribbons, or stripes, are again subdivided to any thickness required, dyed of various colours, and put by for use.

They use the bark of the hemlock pine to dye red, indigo for blue, and the inner bark of the root of the white-ash for yellow, which, when mixed with indigo, forms a good green. The baskets made of the wood of the black-ash are very light and pretty ; the settlers' wives purchase them for cap-baskets, and the larger ones to keep their linen in : a coarser sort is used by the farmers for a variety of purposes ; I have made many a one myself, and found them very serviceable.

The squaws manufacture the birch bark into a variety of articles, such as baskets, dishes, hat and work-boxes, and cradles, some of which are curiously ornamented with porcupine quills. The making of these things and tanning deer skins, together with their household or wigwam duties, constitute their chief employment when in camp or in their villages.

In their hunting and trapping excursions it is the squaw's duty to steer the canoe, build the wigwam, and assist in skinning the various animals taken in the chase : they are very industrious—indeed it is difficult to find them unemployed.

The men employ themselves in hunting, fishing, and in making a variety of hollow ware out of the wood of the butternut and black ash-knots, such as troughs, butter-dishes, bowls, and barn shovels. They make but a poor hand at carving, though I have seen some stone pipes tolerably well done; but of all their manufactures I consider their canoes to be the most ingenious.

As many of my readers, probably, may never have had an opportunity of seeing one of these canoes, I shall endeavour to describe the method of constructing them by the Chippewa and Mississauga tribes.

The bark used for this purpose is taken from the white birch (*Betula alba*). It strips readily from the tree at the proper season : the thicker the bark, and paler in the colour, the better it is for the purpose. The bottom of the canoe should, if possible, be of one entire piece, each end of which is turned up from the sides until they are contracted to a sharp point. This sudden contraction of the bark, to form the ends of the canoe, gives the centre part too much beam. To obviate this difficulty, incisions of a foot or more in length are made from the outside edge towards the centre on both sides of the canoe, and about two feet apart. At these incisions, wedge-shaped pieces are cut out, the widest part of the wedge being towards the upper edge of the bark. The edges of the incisions are then brought together and sewed firmly ; by this means the proper shape of the bottom, and at least half way up the sides, is obtained. Pieces of bark are then sewn to the upper edges of the bottom, to complete the height of the canoe. A strong knife is employed to trim the upper edge of the bark ready for the false gunnel, which is composed of two thin laths of cedar bent round the inside and outside of the upper edge of the canoe, from stem to stern, and fastened securely at both ends. These under or false gunnels thus firmly secure, between them, the upper edge of the bark. The canoe is now placed on its bottom in a level place, the sides are contracted to the proper width, and stakes driven into the ground on each side to secure it in its position. Thin laths of white cedar, not more than an eighth of an inch thick, and from three to four inches wide, shaved very smoothly, are placed length-wise, inside the canoe, of which it forms the lining. Ribs of cedar, half an inch thick by two inches in width, and from two to three inches apart, are then bent into the canoe, the upper ends of the ribs being secured between the false gunnels. The pressure by the elasticity of these ribs forces the bark into the proper form, and prevents the sides from collapsing. The upper gunnel is now firmly placed on the outward edges of the false ones, either with nails, screws, or wooden pins. Four pieces of hard-wood timber, three inches wide and an inch thick, called thwarts, are secured firmly, at equal distances, across the canoe from gunnel to gunnel, thereby strengthening and effectually preventing the canoe from spreading.

The roots of the tamarac, or cedar, are used by the Indians for sewing the seams and fixing the thwarts of their canoes, which they split and scrape, soaking them for some time in water before using them. A preparation of cedar or pine-gum, mixed with pitch or resin, is run neatly over the seams, which process completes the canoe.

The dug-out, or log-canoe, in general use by the settlers, is derived from the Indians, who still continue to construct them. These canoes are of various sizes and make, and some of them exhibit rude attempts at carving on the bow and stern. The largest I ever saw of this kind was made out of a pine-tree, and was twenty-six feet long, and three feet nine inches beam. I assisted to

unload a schooner with her on Lake Huron. She
would easily carry nine barrels of pork and four
or five men to paddle her. Pine, black walnut,
butternut, and basswood, are used for this canoe,
the two latter are the best for lightness, and the
wood is not easily split by exposure to the sun.
My boys and I have made canoes of this sort so
light, that one person could easily carry one of
them on his head over short portages. A canoe
of this kind is the best for hunting ducks, because the wild rice and rushes make no noise
against its side, which is a defect in the bark
canoe. Besides, the birch-bark canoe, they construct for temporary purposes, a ruder-built one
made out of an entire roll of the bark of the
swamp-elm, which is merely sewn up at both
ends, and the seams gummed. Two thwarts are
then fastened across the upper edges of the canoe,
to keep the bark expanded to the proper width,
which should be about three feet and a half at
least in the centre. These canoes are only used
to descend from the head-waters of rapid streams
which would be apt to injure the more elegant
one formed of the fragile birch bark.

The Chippewas, near Goderich, are the only
Indians I ever saw use the elm-canoe. The Mait-

land is too rapid to ascend, and as the Indians extend their hunting excursions to the head-waters, and even beyond, they find the distance is too great to carry their canoes, consequently, as soon as their spring hunt is finished, and their sugar season is over, they construct the temporary canoes above-mentioned, which they load with the product of the chase, baskets of sugar, traps, &c., and boldly descend the most rapid streams which flow into Lake Huron with their freight.

These canoes are very ably managed both by the male and female Indian, though the squaw generally fills an office rather opposed to our nautical notions, for she is almost invariably the steersman ; and, it must be acknowledged, performs her duty admirably well. In running down a rapid where there is much swell, they turn the bow of the canoe a little sideways, which causes it to ride over the waves without shipping so much water as it would if it ran straight through the swell.

The Indian canoe is admirably adapted for the purposes for which it is designed, being so light that a man or squaw can carry it for miles over the roughest portages. Great care, however, is necessary in descending rapids, for the least grate on the rock is apt to rend the birch-bark; therefore the Indians always provide themselves with a pan of gum and a roll of bark in order to repair such accidents, should they occur.

The bark canoe is elegant in its structure, and sits lightly on the water. Some people think them unsafe ; and so they are to those unaccustomed to them, but to those who understand their management, there is no safer craft, especially when laden.

Some of the bark canoes used by the Hudson Bay Company are very large, and capable of holding a good many men and a considerable weight of merchandise. The largest I ever saw-crossed Lake Huron from Saginaw Bay with a party of twenty-five Indians and some bales of fur. The morning was foggy when they entered the harbour, and from her carrying topsails I mistook her at first for a small schooner ; I was therefore greatly surprised when, on their approaching the wharf, I found out my mistake. They had an ingenious contrivance, which enabled them to hoist both main and topsails at the same time, and lower them instantaneously; a good precaution in squally weather.

It is very seldom you hear of accidents occurring by the upsetting of these canoes. Their crews, too, are expert in the river for this navigation. Besides this, they seldom venture out of sight of land on the great lakes, unless there is every prospect of a continuance of fine weather, of which they are excellent judges.

The birch-bark is almost invaluable to the Indian. It furnishes him material not only for his canoes, but also for a variety of domestic and ornamental articles. It affords him shelter from the fury of the thunderstorm as well as the winter snows, and forms his protection from the scorching summer sun and the night-dews of heaven, while by the brilliant light of the birch-bark torch, fixed in a cleft stick in the bow of his canoe, he is enabled to spear with unerring aim the swift maskinongi.

The bark of the birch-tree is about the eighth of an inch in thickness, but it has the property of being easily separated into leaves not thicker than paper, for which it is sometimes used as a substitute, answering the purpose tolerably well if a black-lead pencil be used instead of pen and ink. Indeed, I have often received letters written to me by the Indians upon this material.

The squaws have a curious method of forming patterns upon this bark with their teeth, producing very elegant and elaborate designs. They double a strip of bark many times into angles, which they bite at the sharp corners in various forms. Upon the piece being unfolded, the pattern appears, which is generally filled in very ingeniously with beads and coloured porcupine quills. The squaws perform this work in the dark quite as well as in the daylight.

CHAPTER V.

AQUATIC PROPENSITIES OF THE INDIANS. — INDIAN BURYING-PLACES.
— FRAGMENTS OF POTTERY. — PIT DISCOVERED AT MANVERS.
— INDIAN HUNTERS. — CURIOUS ORATION OF AN INDIAN CHIEF
INTERPRETED BY JOHN GOT.—NATIVE INDIAN PREACHER, PETER
JONES—HIS SUCCESS. — PROGRESS OF THE INDIANS IN READING
AND WRITING.—INDIAN ORATORY.—NAMES GIVEN BY THEM TO
THE ENGLISH SETTLERS.—PETER NOGUN MAKES A BAD BARGAIN
FOR JOWLER. — GOOD AT DEER. — INDIAN DANCE. — CAPTAIN
GEORGE KISHCOW.— INDIAN DUEL.— INDIANS AT EVENING SER-
VICE. — INDIAN HOSPITALITY AND GENEROSITY TO MY DAUGH-
TER.—POPULATION AND PLACES OF RESORT. — BURIAL-PLACE OF
THE CHIPPEWAS AND MISSISSAUGAS. — GRAVE RIFLED BY A
PHRENOLOGIST. — OBSOLETE INDIAN FESTIVAL. — BELIEF IN IM-
MORTALITY OF THE SOUL AND THE FLOOD.

THE Indians, men, women, and children, are
excellent swimmers and divers. Indeed, during
the hot months the children are continually in
the water, splashing and swimming about like a
flock of wild ducks. I remember once seeing an
Indian, named Bill Crane, dive across a mill-pond,
which I am sure was full sixty yards in width;
and from the ease with which he accomplished this
feat, I am sure he could have gone some yards
farther. I do not know if the squaws are equally

expert, as I have never had the pleasure of seeing them make the experiment, though I have
no doubt they can swim well.

In this part of the country there are few remains of Indian antiquities; but I have sometimes
found pieces of a coarse kind of pottery in the
bottom of springs near which it is most probable
the Indians had been in the habit of camping for
the sake of good water.

A few years ago a settler in the township of
Manvers, discovered a circular hollow, ten or
twelve feet deep, and twenty-five or thirty in
circumference. Nearly at the bottom of this
place a fine basswood-tree was growing, which,
from the number of rings, must have been more
than one hundred and fifty years old. Upon
opening the pit no less than one hundred and
thirty-eight human skulls were found. As this
spot is not very far from the Scugog Lake, it is
more than propable that some great battle had
been fought on this spot between some hostile
Indian tribes.

On the late Major Anderson's farm on Rice
Lake, near the *debouche* of the Otonabee river,
there are several large mounds, or tumuli, which
are said to be the burial-places of those Indians,
who fell in a great battle between the Mohawks

and Mississaugas, in which the former were defeated with great slaughter.

I was down at the store-house near the harbour one afternoon, when a party of Chippewa Indians landed with no less than five large bears they had killed within the week. As soon as the news spread, nearly all the population of Goderich came down to see the "critters," as the Yankees call every beast larger than a cat.

For the last month the inhabitants had been living principally upon salt pork, so that the sight of so much fresh meat made us look forward to a rich treat, consequently the poor Indians were beset on every side, begging for a piece in such Indian words as could be mustered for the occasion.

"I say, Nitchie,* cannot you spare me a ham?" exclaims one of the most modest of our townsmen. He might as well have asked for a whole bruin at once.

"Tiya!"† exclaims in answer the Indian chief, a fine weather-beaten old warrior, who wore a large silver medal, bearing the effigy of our late good sovereign, George the Third, which had been bestowed upon him for his gallant conduct, and

* This word signifies an Indian. Nitchienorbie means my friend.
† An exclamation of surprise or wonder.

the honourable wounds received in the last war with the United States of America.

"I say, old fellow, won't you give me a piece? I am very buckata,"* remarked a second.

"Pah mah cavahbetch,"† said the old chief. But at length quite wearied by their importunities, he stepped upon the carcase of the largest bear, and waving his hand in the most graceful manner to command the attention of his greedy audience, he commenced, in his own soft flowing language, a most animated oration. First, pointing to the bears lying at his feet, then to us, and then again suddenly turning round, he extended his arm in the direction of some cows and oxen belonging to the settlers, which were quietly grazing in the distance.

As soon as he had concluded his harangue, his place was immediately supplied by John Got, a French Canadian, who evidently could claim a sprinkling of Indian blood in his own veins.

"John, what did he say?" exclaimed twenty voices at once.

"He said," answered John, "that Indian very great hunter, kill plenty bear and deer—white man kill beef. Sometimes Indian very hungry, h ee his white brother kill an ox, he asks him for a piece, he says, 'No, go away; by and by give you

* The Indian word for hungry.   † By and by, perhaps.

the paunch, plenty good enough for blackguard Indian.' If Indian kill a bear, white man say ' you very good man, you my friend, give me piece.' Indian great hunter he no tell his brothers to wait for the paunch, but gives them a leg, or some good piece."

Accordingly, one of the huge beasts was immediately flayed and divided amongst the applicants for bear-meat, who in the end payed double the value of it, in one shape or another.

If an Indian makes a present, it is always expected that one equally valuable should be given in return, no matter what you give them, or how valuable or rich the present, they seldom betray the least emotion or appearance of gratitude, it being considered beneath the dignity of a red man to betray his feelings. For all this seeming indifference, they are in reality as grateful, and, I believe, even more so than our own peasantry. Indeed, I could cite many instances of their kindness to prove this assertion.

To the best of my recollection, it was in the autumn of 1830, that the Indian missionary, Peter Jones, visited the Chippewas (who were at that time encamped on their old and favourite ground, between Goderich harbour and Lake Huron), with the intention of preaching the gospel amongst them. He stayed all night at my house, and the next morning, being the Sabbath, he preached to a large congregation of his red and white brethren.

His sermon was delivered extempore, and, in my opinion, was both eloquent and instructive. He addressed the assembly first in English, and then in his native tongue.

The Indians listened to him with the deepest attention, while he set forth, in the most forcible manner, the sin of drunkenness. He told them "that Jesus Christ came to save the red man as well as the white, and earnestly entreated them to repent of their sins, and be saved through Him." His similes were beautiful and well chosen ; his language powerful and impressive. At the conclusion of his discourse he gave out a hymn in the Chippewa tongue, in which he was joined by the Indians present, who all have excellent ears for music ; indeed it would be difficult to find one who has not. The squaws sing very sweetly, and much more naturally than the over-strained voices of many of our fair cantatrices in Old England and the colonies.

Much praise is due to Peter Jones for his untiring energy and perseverance in this good work. To him and the Methodist missionaries is the merit of having converted these poor benighted creatures

justly due, a noble monument of Christian benevolence and love.   The Rev. J. Gilmour, the Baptist minister at Peterborough, has also done much
to ameliorate both the temporal and spiritual
welfare of the Mississaugas in that neighbourhood.

Since my long residence in Canada West, I have
only heard of one case of murder amongst the Indians, and this occurred long before their conversion.   I knew the man well.   His name was Bed-
ford.   He was jealous of his wife, and under the
excitement of drink shot her dead in the camp.
Some years after this tragical event I spoke to him
on the subject, when he expressed much contri-
tion, and said, "Indian very bad man then—drink
too much fire-water; Indian hear gospel preach,
now better man."   Indeed there can be no doubt
that the preaching of the gospel has wrought
mightily among them for their moral regeneration.

I consider the intellect of the Indian above
mediocrity—that is, if you compare him with the
uneducated peasantry of other lands.   They learn
to read and write well, and quickly ; and they
have decided talents for music and drawing.   I
have often seen an Indian construct a very correct map, with the rivers and lakes delineated
with great exactness.

It is a remarkable fact, that the Indians, who

are naturally taciturn, excel in oratory. They speak well on any public occasion, without embarrassment, and without previous study. Their language is beautiful and appropriate, and often sparkles with the richest imagery. Their general deportment is grave, dignified, and reserved. But when once you win their confidence they open themselves out to you, and the coldness of their manner disappears.

During the winter of 1834, three families of the Mississaugas built a large wigwam on my farm on a point at the foot of Kaw-che-wah-noonk Lake, and took up their winter residence in it. I often used to go down to their camp on an evening, accompanied by some of the members of my family and a young gentleman named Bird, who was staying at my house. When paying these visits I seldom went empty-handed : a few potatoes or broken victuals of any sort were always thankfully received.

As soon as we entered the wigwam they immediately made room for us on the blanket beside them. During these visits I often talked to them of their brethren, the Chippewas, whom they acknowledged to be the head of their tribe. This seemed to please them greatly and, I suppose by way of compliment, they gave me the name of

Chippewa, by which I am as well known in the section of the country in which I reside as by my legitimate name, time-honoured though it be.

They are very fond of giving names to their friends and acquaintances. Generally speaking, it is only the Indian rendering of the name you bear, or of some particular employment you follow. For instance, my friend, Mr. Bird, they called Penashie, which signifies a *bird*. My brother-in-law, Capt. Moodie, they named Tewagan, meaning a drummer. He, too, played beautifully on the flute, an instrument for which they had no Indian name, I believe their only one being a curious kind of drum, which they beat with one stick, producing a most monotonous sound. My brother-in-law's name being Reid, they called him Ekindermink, which means *to read*. My father-in-law's name, which was Robert Reid, it puzzled them to translate. They had no Indian word for Robert. But one day, after talking for some time to one another in their own language, they suddenly burst into an uncontrollable fit of laughter, a very unusual thing for such grave people. On my requesting an explanation of their mirth, one of them replied apologetically, " That they were only laughing at the name they had just invented for Robert Reid."

" Well, what is it ?" I demanded; "let me hear it."

" Wah-pous Ekindermink," replied one of my red brethren.

" Pray what is the meaning of Wah-pous Ekindermink ? " was my rejoinder.

" It means Rabbit Reid. Rabbit is as near Robert as we can find," and then they again laughed, in which I heartily joined.

My eldest daughter, who was an especial favourite, they named Openegeesacook, signifying in their dialect, a " fine day, every day for ever." No doubt this was intended as a great compliment, which was duly acknowledged in the shape of cocosh* and nappanee.†

The only game I ever observed them play in their camp is very similar to our well-known game of cup and ball. Instead, however, of catching a single ball on a point as we do, they have ten little bone cups, about the size of thimbles without bottoms. These cups are fastened to one another with a string, sufficiently loose to allow one cup fitting easily into the next, and so on throughout the whole set. A piece of string about a foot long is fastened from the cups to the centre of a sharp-pointed piece of wood eight or ten inches long. This stick is held with the

* Pork.   † Flour.

string over the finger exactly in the same manner as the cup and ball. The cups are jerked up and as many as possible caught on the pointed stick ; a smart hand will often catch the whole ten at once. I have seen some Indians so expert as to catch them so three or four times running. During some of our evening visits to their camp they used to ask us to join them in this amusement.

The two oldest Indians in the wigwam selected the parties who were to form the opposing sides, whichever side marked a hundred first being the winner of the game. The players sit round the fire in a circle, each person throwing the cups in turn. Every cup caught on the stick counts one ; but if the whole ten are secured they count twenty. We used to enjoy the amusement greatly, and the Indians especially delighted in the failures we made. Every time one of our party missed the cups they laughed immoderately at our want of skill.

They enjoy a joke amazingly, even though it should raise a laugh against themselves. Young Rowlandson, a neighbour of mine, offering old Peter Nogan a hound called Jowler for sale, the Indian asked him " If he were good for deer," meaning of course would he hunt them. Rowlandson replied, " Oh, yes, he is a first-rate fellow for deer." Upon which recommendation Peter was induced to purchase the dog; the price agreed on between them being two pair of mocassins and a haunch of the first deer killed by Jowler's aid.

The next day being fixed upon to try this paragon of deer-hounds, a fine buck was started and ran to the water where it was ultimately shot by young John Nogan, Peter's son. Jowler, however, was quite guiltless of his death, for after running a few hundred yards on the track he gave up and let Music, Peter's other hound, have all the glory of the chase to himself, to the no small mortification of my friend, who found he had made a bad bargain with Rowlandson.

When he saw Rowlandson at the camp in the evening he upbraided him with selling him such a useless animal, and one that was evidently "no good for deer." Just as Peter was making this complaint, Rowlandson chanced to cast his eyes in the direction of the slaughtered buck, which was hanging up at the farther end of the wigwam, where he espied master Jowler quietly making his supper off the shoulder of the beast.

"There, Peter, did I not tell you he was first-rate for deer; only see how he is tucking the venison into him; are you satisfied now?"

This sally was too much, even for the gravity of poor Peter, who laughed as loud and as long as any one in the wigwam, especially when I told him he was perfectly safe from being called upon to pay the haunch. I also induced Rowlandson to return to the poor fellow one pair of the mocassins.

Many of the old Indian customs have become obsolete, those tribes who have embraced Christianity having given them up from motives of conscience, while even those who are still heathen, gradually approximate nearer to the manners of the white man, either from motives of policy or pride. I once, and only once, had an opportunity of witnessing the national dance, which probably was the ancient war-dance once peculiar to the native Indian tribes throughout North America. Some years ago, during the first settlement of Peterborough, I witnessed this curious dance performed by the Indians, who had assembled opposite one of the government store-houses, for the purpose of receiving their annual presents.

It was on a lonely evening early in September, the most beautiful month of the Canadian year. The place chosen by these children of the forest for their night bivouac was then one of the sweetest spots to be found for miles, and had been for years their most favourite camping-ground. Several hundred acres of open plain were dotted here and there with clumps of oak and pine. In the spring of the year these openings were gay with wild flowers. Amongst the first to show their varied beauties might be seen the red, white and blue hepaticas, or liverwort, the white and yellow violet, and many others indigenous to the country. Later in the season, the cardinal-plant, lobelia,* lupin, and tiger-lily, and a profusion of flowery gems lent their aid to adorn the charming scenery of this sylvan spot.

This natural park lies on the west bank of the Otonabee river, and at the head of the navigation, surrounded on the north and west by gently sloping hills of moderate height. Through a narrow valley between these hills rushes a fine mill-stream, which, after meandering through the plain, falls into the Otonabee, opposite an expansion of the river called the Little Lake. Between this stream and the Otonabee the flourishing town of Peterborough is now built, this once charming spot being nearly covered over with the abodes of those who left their native land beyond the broad Atlantic, to found a name and a new home in this

* This plant grows wild in the woods, especially in damp places. It is used extensively among the settlers an an emetic.

highly-favoured country, and, I might add, to help to fulfil the great destinies of the Anglo-Saxon race.

Upon a green bank, twenty feet above the level of the bright waters of the Otanabee the camp-fires of the Indians blazed, cheerily throwing long lines of silvery light through the arched vistas of oak and pine, and casting a redder glare on the swarthy countenances of the sons and daughters of the soil.

It is sad to think that thousands of these interesting people have fallen victims to intemperance. On whom, I ask, will the punishment fall ? on the ignorant red savage or on the tutored white one, who, for the sake of gain, has caused thousands to perish, and entailed upon the rising generation diseases originating in the drunken habits of their fathers ?

I have said that consumption, before almost unknown amongst the Indians, is silently but surely doing its work, so that in a few years these original possessors of the soil will only be as a people that were.

But to return to my story. Upwards of a hundred Indians with their papouses were assembled on this occasion. Their presents had been distributed during the day, and already had the traders, like a hungry set of sharks, possessed themselves of many a good blanket, for which they paid their victims, by way of barter, a villanous compound, yclept New England rum, or, as the Indians call it, skitawahbo.* No wonder, then, that I found them in a state fast verging on intoxication. Both men and squaws were frightfully painted. The squaws had decorated their persons with the finery they had just received; necklaces of many-coloured beads, armlets, bracelets, and large silver brooches were the most conspicuous of these ornaments. I dare say the poor creatures fancied themselves as handsomely and fashionably dressed as the belles of our London drawing-rooms.

Mr. R——, one of the traders who appeared to have considerable authority amongst them, requested them to perform their war-dance for the amusement of the bystanders. Had they been sober, they would have treated the request with scorn, for they dislike to be made a public spectacle of. But all native pride gave way before the promise of more spirits.

A number of the Indians then formed themselves into a circle, each person facing the back

* I write this word as pronounced by the Indians, but cannot answer for the orthography.

of the man before him. Every one was furnished with either sword, tomahawk or club. Thus equipped, they began to dance round in a circle, following one another, brandishing from time to time their weapons, and uttering every now and then a guttural exclamation, resembling the word " how-ey," prolonging the sound on the last syllable. The tewagan, or drummer, stood in the centre of the circle, and beat time manfully upon that odd-looking kind of instrument with only one head, yclept an Indian drum.

The motion of the dancers was at first slow, but gradually grew more animated, until at length the dancers became greatly excited, whooping and yelling at a furious rate. This violent exercise continued for some time, when the slow march recommenced, which terminated the singular performance. Happily, this barbarous custom has become obsolete. Peace and Christianity have driven it from the land.

When the first attempts were made to induce the Indians to give up their intemperate habits, some of the oldest and most habitual drinkers were long before they could be prevailed upon to do so. I remember particularly two Credit*

---

* Part of the Mississauga tribe ; called Credit Indians, from their village at the mouth of the river Credit, twenty miles west of Toronto.

Indians, who were notorious drunkards, and long resisted any attempts made for their temporal or spiritual regeneration. Old George Kishcow, or Captain George, as he was generally called, and old Johnson, were the two who made such a stand against sobriety and religion. The favourite camping ground was Darlington and Whitby.

One day there was a meeting held at a school-house in the latter township, at which an itinerant minister was preaching. In the immediate neighbourhood several families of the Credit Indians were encamped, amongst whom was our friend Captain George, who was persuaded to attend the meeting, in company with his red brethren. He took his station close to the minister, who thought it was an excellent opportunity "to convert him from the error of his ways." In the midst of a powerful appeal to his uncivilized audience, upon whom he hoped he had made a suitable impression, the preacher laid his hand on old George, and said, "Brother, have you religion?"

"Oh yes," replied the Captain, "me got him here, won't you have some?" at the same time producing a flask of whiskey from the pocket of his blanket-coat, which he handed, with the utmost gravity, to the astonished minister. This was too ludicrous even for the most serious to suppress a smile.

Captain George fought on the side of the British during the last American War, and received a bayonet-wound just below the chest, but, luckily for him, in a slanting direction. He showed me the scar, and when I asked him the particulars, he told me that he and some other Indians were surrounded by a party of Americans, and that whilst endeavouring to break his way through them he received the wound before-mentioned.

" But," said he, and his eyes flashed as he spoke, " I throw my tomahawk, Yankee do this ;" then he threw up both his hands above his head, rolled his eyes furiously, and staggered backwards, imitating the fall of a dying man, and exclaiming at the same time, with much excitement, " I kill him."

It is considered rather an unusual occurrence for an Indian woman to produce two children at one birth. Unfortunately, Captain George's squaw proved an exception to the general rule, to his great annoyance. In this difficulty, he came to the house of my father-in-law, and very generously offered to make him a present of a fine male papouse.

" Me got one too many this morning—no nappanee—my squaw very buckata."

Colonel Reid thanked the Captain for his po-
lite offer, but at the same time " assured him
that he was quite over-stocked, for he had ten of
his own, which sometimes he thought nine too
many." He, however, kindly gave him the required flour and some other necessaries for the
lying-in lady. It appears from Charlevoix, that
it was considered among the Indians very disgrace-
ful to be the parents of twins, one of which was
invariably destroyed. Our Indian, it must be
confessed, was more mercifully disposed towards
his infant in wishing to present it to the Colonel.

The Mississauga Indians are about the middle
height, spare made, and active. Probably for a
day or a week's march in the woods the Indians
would tire the Europeans, but for constant fatigue
they can not compete with their white brethren.
They wrestle well, but know nothing about box-
ing.

I once saw two Indian acquaintances of mine
fight. They had been to Peterborough to sell
furs, and I suspect were a little the worse for
drink. However this might be, they quarrelled
on their way back to their wigwams, and fought
it out in true Indian style, wrestling, kicking,

biting, and scratching. Luckily they had neither knives nor tomahawks with them, or the consequences might have been serious. After twenty minutes of "rough and tumble," as this kind of fighting is called in Yankee parlance, the younger Indian (Tom Nogun) gave in, to the no small exultation of the old man his antagonist (Snow Storm), who, as soon as the fight was over, marched up to his discomfited foe, grinned in his face, clapped his hands, and crowed like a cock three times loudly and clearly. Tom's eyes flashed at this pointed insult, and for a minute I thought it would have caused a renewal of the fight; but no, he was fairly beaten, and prudently pocketed the affront. This is the only instance I ever saw of two Indians falling out with each other. Generally speaking they appear to live among themselves in great friendship and harmony one with another. I shall conclude this short sketch of my red neighbours by giving the following interesting anecdote :—

A few months before my return to England (1851), a party of Indians from the Chemong and Rice Lake villages encamped with their squaws and papouses on my point. The next day, being the Sabbath, they asked permission to attend at my house in the afternoon to hear me read the evening service and portions of the Scripture to my family, which, of course, I readily granted. They conducted themselves with extreme propriety during the domestic service, and afterwards sang some of the hymns which had been translated by the missionary, Peter Jones. They gave them in beautiful style and with great feeling. One little girl, a daughter of John Nogun's, sung a hymn by herself so prettily, that my daughter, Mrs. Beresford, was very anxious to get a copy of it in the Indian tongue. As soon as she made her wishes known, John Nogun promised to write out the hymn in question, and send it to her by the first opportunity. Very soon after this, I determined to go to England, in order to behold once more my venerable mother and dear sisters, and revisit my native land, from which I had been a stranger nearly twenty-seven years. Upon this occasion my eldest daughter, Mrs. Beresford, was my companion.

Our first day's journey lay through the Indian village of Rice Lake. Whilst we were waiting for a boat to cross the water, my daughter expressed a wish to call at Nogun's house and ask for the promised hymn. Unfortunately, John was away on a fishing excursion, but his mother, wife, and sister Eliza, were overjoyed to see us.

They made up a fire immediately, and fried some venison with slices of bacon, which they set before us with a hot shanty-cake and a good cup of tea, having previously put a clean cloth on the table and made everything look nice and clean. We had often given them flour and pork, and many a dinner and tea, which the grateful creatures remembered on this the first opportunity they had of showing their hospitality and gratitude.

They expressed the greatest surprise when they heard my daughter was going to cross the great salt lake, and that she would not be back for a year. When she rose to depart they hung about her and shed tears. That these tears proceeded from the genuine feelings of the heart I could not suffer myself to doubt.

We crossed the lake and stopped all night at the pretty village of Gore's Landing, when, early in the morning, a canoe arrived at the village containing the squaws of the Nogun family, who each brought for my daughter's acceptance a pretty bark-basket worked with coloured quills, and among the rest a tiny specimen of the art, made and presented by the little girl who had sung so sweetly at our Sabbath service.

A few months after our arrival in England, my

daughter was surprised to receive a letter from John Nogun, which I have copied verbatim from the original.

ORTONVILLE. C. M.

O for a thousand tongues to sing
  My great Redeemer's praise,
The glories of my God and King,
  The triumphs of his grace.

Oh ah pa kish ke che ingo dwok
  Ne gah ne she nah baig
Che nah nah kah moo tah
  Wah wod ne ke sha mun ne toom.

My gracious Master and my God   Ne gee che no sa we ge e shin
   Assist me to proclaim, to spread   Che win duh mah ga you omah
Through all the earth abroad   Awe gook kuk me gog
   The honours of thy name.   Azhewa be se you.

MRS. MORIAH BERESFORD,

   Excuse me for I am in Pour hand

   to print thise few notes

   you d find two verses Each lines

   English and Indian words

         Yours most Obedient friend

            JOHN NAUGON.

Rice Lake Village,
   July 9th 1851.

This specimen of Indian composition is not only curious but highly interesting as a Christian document, for it is the praises of the living God rendered from the English into the native tongue, by the Indian Missionary, Peter Jones, and adapted to the music of a Wesleyan hymn. Both music and words are fairly copied, and the epistle brief and amusing. John Naugun, in saying " I am in pour hand," means that he writes a poor or indifferent one. The writing, however, was an easier task than the English composition, such being always difficult to a foreigner. I trust my readers will not despise the first epistolary effort of the poor untutored Indian, who, before the gospel dawned upon him, only "saw God in clouds and heard him in the winds," but who now rejoices in the everlasting hope of salvation given to him in His blessed Son.

The following statement, taken from Preston's "Three Years' Residence in Canada," compiled by him from official returns of the Indian Department, shows the number of Indians dwelling within the limits of Canada West in the year 1840.

Chippewas	Michipicoton, Lake Superior . .	57
„	Sault Ste Marie, Lake Huron .	99
„	St. Joseph's	90
„	Manitoulin Island . ' . .	188
„	the country between Manitoulin and Penetauguishine . . .	202
„	Lake Nepissingue . .	59
„	La Cloche and Mississaugeeng .	225
„	the Upper St. Clair . .	312
„	the St. Clair Rapids . . .	401
„	Chenal Ecarté . . .	194
„	Rivière aux Sables . . .	217
Pottawotamies and Chippewas of Saugeen, Lake Huron		370
Hurons, Chippewas, Shawnies and Munsees of Amherstburgh and Malden . . .		214
Delawares, Chippewas and Munsees of the river Thames (Western District) . . .		762
Ottawas of Manitoulin Island . .		80
Upper Moravian Delawares . . .		300
Six Nations of the Grand River . .		2210
Mississaugas of the river Credit . . .		240
Yellow Heads of Cold Water and the Narrows		426
Indians of Rice Lake, Mud Lake, and Alnwick, &c.		508
Mohawks of the Bay of Quinte . . .		336
	Total . .	7490

The visiting Indians, or those who come to receive presents, are computed to be from three to four thousand in number ; but at the last distribution in 1839, it was intimated to them that such presents would thenceforward be discontinued. It appears by this statement that none of the Indian Tribes north and north-west of Lake Superior, or east of the Ottawa River, are included in this list.

No nations in the world are more particular respecting the interment of their dead than the North American Indians. Their belief in a future state of rewards and punishments induces them, perhaps, to take this care respecting the remains of their deceased friends. Indeed, such tenderness generally denotes in savage nations the idea of the soul existing in another land, and being conscious of any injury or neglect done to its earthly tenement.

The Chippewas and Mississauga Indians bury their dead on islands or near their favourite camping grounds. In the township of Colborne on the north side of the river Maitland, on the top of a high cliff overhanging Lake Huron, there still exists an ancient burial ground of the Chippewas.

A considerable part of this cemetery has evidently been undermined by the waves and fallen into the lake ; for when I visited the spot I saw the ends of several rude cedar coffins projecting from the face of the cliff. The use of coffins appears to be a modern practice. I have seen several interred with only cedar bark laid above and below the corpse, and sometimes even that is omitted. I have often found old Indian graves in the woods near the lake, a row of stones laid round the grave generally marking the spot where the red man reposes.

I was at a logging Bee at my brother-in-laws', Captain Moodie, one day, when some of the loggers found an Indian grave. On digging up with their handspikes about a foot below the surface they found the skeleton of a full-grown man. It was quite evident from the decayed state of the bones, that the body had been buried many years before. A broken stone-pipe and two flint arrowheads were all that could be found in the grave, although I heard several persons assert that they have seen tomahawks, pipes, silver and brass ornaments, and even copper sugar-kettles taken from Indian graves. As soon as we ascertained that there were no relics of this kind we collected the bones and buried them near a large rock, where there was little chance of their being disturbed.

Twenty-five years ago a young squaw, named Polly Cow, was buried on a small island near the head of Kaw-che-wah-noonk Lake at the time when the science of phrenology was all the rage. Unfortunately for the repose of poor Polly Cow, a young gentleman of my acquaintance exhumed the Indian girl for the sake of her skull, which, I believe, now graces the cabinet of some learned phrenologist in the old country. The island on which Miss Cow was buried has ever since been called Polly's Island.

The Indians of the present day express the greatest displeasure at the violation of their graves. A short time since, Isaac Iron and his family were encamped on a point of land in Deer Bay. During their sojourn there one of his papouses died, and was buried a short distance from the wigwam. A few years after this event he and his squaw landed at the point with the intention of encamping there for the night, when the first object which met their astonished gaze was the skull of a child stuck on the top of a stick close to the landing place.

Poor Isaac and his family were stupified with grief and horror, when, upon examining the burial place of their little papouse they found it had been recently violated, and the skull, as if in mockery, placed purposely to catch the eye of the poor unoffending Indian. A few days after the occurrence of this painful circumstance Isaac came to me and related, in simple but affecting language, the revolting incident.

"Chippewa," he said, "you one magistrate and good to Indian. Some bad man dig up my papouse, stick up head by our landing-place at Deer Bay; me very sorry for my little child."

During this recital the tears streamed down the brown cheeks of poor Isaac, who was one of the meekest creatures in the world. I asked him if he could swear to the person who had committed this outrage.

He said, "he thought he could, but he would not like to swear."

As there was no certain proof, I could of course do nothing in the matter; but I was heartily sorry for the poor fellow and his family, and secretly execrated the author of the outrage. If the person who disturbed the remains of Isaac's child had, out of mere curiosity, opened the grave, not knowing but that it was an ancient tomb, some excuse might be offered; but in this case there could be no mistake, its comparatively recent formation involving no possibility of doubt, and therefore it was a heartless and cruel act, with nothing to palliate or excuse it.

The native Indian, notwithstanding his apparent stoical apathy in respect to many things which affect the feelings of other men, entertains a veneration for the remains of the dead, surpassing that of more polished nations. His conversion to Christianity has in a great measure lessened this almost idolatrous affection to the mouldering relics of his ancestors.

Nor is this attachment peculiar to the Aborigines of Canada ; it may be traced to the shores of the Pacific, where caves are filled with a species of human mummies dried by art, and neatly sewn up in baskets of plaited rushes, the baskets being carefully replaced when they become worn or shabby.* The half-starved savage of Chili, notwithstanding his wandering and degraded state, taking long journeys to pay these melancholy duties to his deceased relatives. In Canada, where the art of embalming is unknown, an affecting custom, long since obsolete, though once prevalent among the Hurons and Iroquois, has been minutely described by Lafitan, the historian of the Indian nations :—" It should appear, that the highly curious and remarkable religious festival

* Commodore Byron's " Loss of the Wager."

held in honour of the dead, was not confined to the two tribes just mentioned, but was prevalent as an old pious custom throughout the Continent."

It is thus described by our author :—·" The Feast of Death, or Feast of Souls, is celebrated every eight years among the savages of America, or every ten years in some tribes, as the Huron and Iroquois.

" The day of the ceremony is appointed by public order, and nothing is omitted that can render it imposing. The neighbouring tribes are invited to the solemnity, when all who have died since the last celebration are taken out of their graves, and even those who have died at a distance are brought to the general meeting of the dead. Without question," remarks Lafitan, " the opening of these tombs displays one of the most striking scenes that can be imagined—this humbling portrait of human misery in so many images of death, wherein she seems to take a pleasure to paint herself in a thousand shapes of horror in many corpses, according to the degree in which they have become subject to corruption. I know not which ought to strike us most horror at a spectacle so revolting, or the tender piety and devoted affection of these poor people for their departed friends, which justly demand our admiration. They gather up the smallest bones, handling objects still so dear with melancholy affection, cleansing them from the preying worm, and regardless of noisome smell, bear them on their shoulders, without yielding to any emotions but regret for having lost friends so dear to them while in life, and so lamented by them in death.

"They bring them into their huts, where they prepare a feast in honour of the dead, during which their great actions are celebrated, and all the tender intercourses which took place between them and their friends are piously recalled by the survivors to mind — the strangers, who have come many hundred miles to be present at the commemoration, joining in the condolence, while the women, by their dreadful shrieks, demonstrate that they are pierced to the heart with the sharpest sorrow. Then the dead bodies are carried to the place of general reinterment. A great pit is dug in the ground, and thither, at a certain time, each individual who has experienced the loss of a person dear to him, attended by his family and friends, bears to the grave the corpse of a father, son, or brother. When thus met round the pit, the dust bones, or complete remains of the dead, are in solemn silence deposited therein, whereupon a fresh burst of sorrow once more takes place, and whatever they consider the most valuable is interred with the dead. The invited guests are not wanting in generosity, bringing with them presents suitable to the solemn occasion. Then all go down into the pit, each one taking a little of the earth, to be preserved by them with religious care. The bodies, ranged in due order, are then covered with new furs, and next with bark, upon which is thrown wood, stones, and earth, after which they take their last farewell, and return to their own wigwams.

" We have mentioned, that in this ceremony the savages offer as presents to the dead whatever they themselves value most highly. This custom, which is universal among them, arises from a rude notion of the immortality of the soul. They believe this doctrine most firmly, and it is the principal tenet of their religion : when the soul is separated from the body, they conceive that it still continues to hover round it, and to need and take delight in the same things with which it was formerly pleased. After a time, however, they believe that it forsakes its dreary mansion, and departs far westward to the land of spirits. They even assert that a distinction exists in the condition of the inhabitants of the unseen world, imagining that those who have been fortunate in war, enjoy a higher degree of happiness, having hunting-grounds and fisheries which are never exhausted, and other terrestrial delights for which they never labour. The souls of those, on the contrary, who have either been conquered, or slain in battle, will be extremely miserable after death."*

This singular festival resembles, in some of its details, the old Scythian custom of carrying the deceased about in his war-chariot if a chief, or more humbly if in a private station, to the houses of all his friends for forty days, during which period he was placed at the head of the board, to preside over the feast made in his honour. The gifts, too, cast into his grave, resemble those formerly presented to the dead in Canada. Nor is this the only parallel to be found between the ancient Scythian and Canadian Indian, for scalping was a custom peculiar to both. The use of birch-bark in the construction of huts, utensils, and canoes, is also found still in that part of Tartary which is supposed to be the ancient Scythia. It is only by tracing the analogy between the customs and manners of one unlettered nation to another, that we can form a just conclusion respecting their identity to each other. The resemblance between the Scythian and Canadian savage

* Lafitans' "Feast of Souls."

has very often excited the attention of learned men.

The custom of holding this strange religious festival is now certainly extinct, since the tribes who have been converted, of course, no longer practise it ; and the heathen ones have gradually dropped many of their ancient forms since their intercourse with the whites. It was in full force when Lafitan gave the description of the Feast of Death, which I have just quoted.

The North American Indian worships one God, of whose person he makes no image, and of whose attributes he has a sublime conception. Whether this faith has been derived from the ancient patriarchal one, that must have once been prevalent all over the earth, is uncertain ; but the Indian is familiar with the history of the deluge. Indeed, the general idea of the flood all over the earth seems fixed in the mind of the human family from Pole to Pole, as if to give the lie to the foolish quibbles of infidelity.

CHAPTER VI.

ANCIENT INDIAN CUSTOMS.—RELIGION.—JUGGLERS.—RESEMBLANCE
OF THE CUSTOMS OF THE SIX NATIONS TO THE JEWS.— LAND
OF SOULS.—INDIAN PROSERPINE.—FEAST OF DREAMS.—INDIAN
QUACKS.—COURTSHIP.—NAMING THE CHILD.—DISLIKE OF THE
INDIAN NATIONS TO PUNISHING THEIR CHILDREN.—INEXPIABLE
WAR.—ITS CAUSE.—THE HURON NATION ALMOST DESTROYED.—
THE WAMPUM.—THE CALUMET.—INDIAN ORATORY.—METHOD OF
DECLARING WAR. — TREATMENT OF THEIR PRISONERS. — THE
DEATH-SONG.—MISCHIEVOUS EFFECTS OF RAW SPIRITS.

WE have been considering the Mississauga
tribes in their converted and half-civilized state,
for those who are not yet brought into the Christian fold have adopted insensibly many of the
customs of the whites, and have forgotten, or at
least forsaken, those warlike habits which rendered them, like all the Aboriginal natives of the
Canadas and United States, a peculiar people, dif-
fering widely from all other nations on the face
of the earth, so that in describing the manners
and customs of one tribe we shall find a general
assimilation to all.

Let us then consider " the stoic of the woods,

the man without a tear," in his former state, before the Gospel dawned upon him, or civilization had subdued his ferocity. For the possibility of doing this we are indebted to the Jesuit Missionaries,* who sought in their native wilds these fierce races of men, with the benevolent design of converting them, and exposed themselves to death in the most frightful form under which it could appear.

These devoted missionaries (for widely as their religion differs from the purer tenets of our own, candour compels us to admire their fervent piety and unremitting zeal in pursuing the object they had in view) have left in the records of their Mission in Canada the earliest account we can cite of a people who, with the exception of those which regard their religion, have no historical records and no ancient traditions. It appears that they have a vague confused notion of the origin of man : and we find that the first woman, who, by-the-by, appears to have been an Eve without an Adam, had two sons, one of whom murdered the other.† The Deluge overflowed the whole earth, and, according to the Iroquois, destroyed the whole posterity of Youskeka, the Indian Cain, in the third generation, which compelled the

* See the Jesuit Missions.   † Charlevoix.

Supreme being to change beasts into men. However, it is certain that a general belief in the flood existed among the Indian nations prior to any Christian missionary coming among them; likewise a general belief in the existence of one Supreme God, to whom they give different names and attributes, but to whom every tribe assigned the creation of the world, are positive facts. The missionaries, also, in the expulsion of the Indian Eve, Atahensic, from heaven, seem to recognise the history of the fall of man.*

The immortality of the soul also forms a distinct feature in the Indian creed. But to the beasts serviceable to man this immortality is also assigned. The souls of children are supposed to enter other bodies and return to the world. Those who are drowned, or die by accident, are considered unfortunate, and their souls are deprived of happiness, in which we find those who fall in battle are included, probably until they have been fully revenged. None of those who come to such ends are interred in the general burying-ground. A very dreary superstition.† The festival formerly held for the reinterment of the dead has already been cited in a former chapter.

Besides the Supreme Being every Indian has a

* Charlevoix.   † Ibid.

genius, who attends him as soon as he has acquired
a certain degree of skill in the use of the bow.
The genii of the Canadian Aborigines are called
Okkis by the Huron nations, and Manitous by the
Algonquin. Manitou, or spirit, appears to be
the word in general use among the Mississauga
tribes, who, with the Chippewas, were formerly
included in the general name of Algonquin.

As the genius of the adult Indian is supposed
to be his guardian and protecting spirit, he has to
undergo a singular ordeal to discover him from
among that crowd of imaginary beings with which
the fancy of the Indian nations have peopled earth
and air. When the child was sufficiently skilled
in the use of the bow, it was the custom to blacken
his face and compel him to a rigorous fast for
eight days, during which he must repeat all his
dreams, which is the only means he has for discovering his invisible guardian under some sym-
bolical representation. Now, whether he determines
to end his fast speedily, or that the imagination
of an Indian child has little range, or that he
really trusts to his dreams for the recognition of
his guardian spirit, it is certain that the symbol
of the genius was soon discovered under the com-
monest forms, such as pieces of wood, birds' feet
or head, a pebble, or anything the child is accus-

tomed to see. These emblems are ever after
sacred to the Indian, they being to him what the
Dii penates, or household gods, were to the an-
cients.* Formerly every object in nature was
supposed to have its genius, although some of these
invisible beings were superior in rank and power
to the rest.

As soon as the child has been taught to discover
his genius, he is instructed in what manner he is
to reverence him and follow his counsel, which he
is led to believe will be given him in his sleep.
He is warned of the consequences of displeasing
him by disregarding his suggestions. A feast is
then made, and the figure of his Manitou is pricked
upon the body of the child.† The female Indian
has her Manitou, but she does not so supersti-
tiously venerate her guardian spirit as the male.

In order to render their genii propitious, the
Indians throw into the rivers and lakes tobacco,
or birds that have been strangled to render them
so. Every power in nature has its supposed
genius. The sun, the waters, the elements, have
also their sacrifices. They also paid the same compliment to the malignant genii to prevent them
from doing them injury. Occasionally they offered
victims, of which the dog was unfortunately that

* Charlevoix. † Ibid.

animal the most in use. It was their cruel custom to hang the poor beast up alive by his heels till he died mad.

The missionaries could not trace any affection to the Supreme Being in the devotion of the Canadian savage, and in fact the tutelar genius, or his emblem, seemed to have absorbed that veneration, "as indeed," remarks Charlevoix, "is common with every people who have deviated from the primitive religion—they lose sight of the reality in the supposed type."*

The jugglers exercised an immense influence over their countrymen. Their tutelar genius was, according to them, so powerful, that when they fell into trances or ecstacies, he made them acquainted with future events, however distant, and the worthy missionary is compelled to acknowledge that the oracles delivered by these impostors often came to pass, which he ascribes at once to the agency of the devil.

Some of the customs of the Indian nations resemble those of the Jews, and it is certain that the first missionaries seemed to identify the six nations with the Hebrews,† but Father Charlevoix, while he allows that in some respects there is a likeness, does not believe them to have been

* Charlevoix.   † Pere Prevoste, "Jewish Expositor."

Jews. He does not notice a remarkable fact that some of these Jewish tribes, who refused to return to their own country after the captivity, wandered to the borders of Scythia, and that if these Indians be of Scythian descent, they might have adopted many of the Jewish customs without being Jews by actual descent. The hunting-feast has been considered to be the Passover, and it is possible may have been an imitation of it.

The land of souls, according to the Indian nations, lies westward, and the spirits of the departed have to pass a river, in which they are in danger of shipwreck, guarded by a dog, from whom they have to defend themselves. They speak of a place of torment, where they must expiate their sins; and also of another place of punishment where the souls of those prisoners of war, who have been tormented, are to be found.*

There is much in these fables which will remind the reader of the Greek mythology. The fallen woman, or Indian Eve, Atahensic, being the queen of the Indian Tartarus, among the Iroquois or six nations: the seduction of human souls forming her sole employment; the Indian Cain, Rouskeka, however, taking infinite pains to secure them from the wicked designs of his mother, They

* Charlevoix.

have a legend so closely resembling the fable of Orpheus and Eurydice, that the circumstances being the same, nothing is wanting but the change of names to identify them together.*

" The idea that he who is the happiest in this world will also enjoy the most felicity in the next, pervades their prayers, in which they never refer to another world. Their songs were," Charlevoix believes, "originally prayers. They rely much upon their dreams, and the missionary relates the extraordinary effect these visions sometimes have upon individuals, who appear for the time to have gone out of their senses.† A festival, called the " Feast of Dreams," lasts fifteen days, and is held towards the end of winter, the 22nd of February. This solemnity the Iroquois call "The Turning of the Head," which in its bacchanalian character it seems to deserve. It was a sort of masquerade in which the inhabitants of the villages assumed all kinds of disguises, running from cabin to cabin, demanding the interpretation of dreams, which they do not choose to communicate, and destroying the property of those who cannot guess the dream, and who can only save their goods by giving the dreamer what he dreamt of, —an expensive mode of escape.

* Pere Charlevoix.   † Ibid. vol. ii. p. 157.

Sometimes one of these Indians dreams of murder, and immediately slays the person whose throat he pretended he cut in his sleep. Woe, however, to him if another person chooses to dream that he revenged the dead, for his fate is sealed immediately. The missionaries, who had more than once run the risk of their lives during this festival, believed that many of the Indians made their dreams subservient to their private resentment, in order to give a good drubbing to those who had offended them, waiting patiently for this public occasion till the feast came round, well knowing that everything they did then must be forgiven, when once the festival of dreams was over.*

The Autmans, or quack-doctors, are skilful in medicine, and expert in setting broken bones. In Acadia, in the Lower Province, the chief of the tribe was also autman. Expelling the devil was among the accomplishments of this influential person. When called upon to decide a doubtful case the autman would affirm, " that the devil would neither permit the poor patient to live or die, and ended by advising his friends out of

* Pere Charlevoix. This festival seems to resemble the Lupercalia of the Romans, and their Saturnalia also. It is now obsolete.

charity to end his days," which accordingly was done by pouring a quantity of cold water upon his face till he died. It is evident from this that in all dubious cases the sick person was destroyed.*

Courtships are very brief episodes in savage Canadian life, and the matches are made by the parents. When consent has been given, the young man enters the cabin of the young woman and seats himself by her side. Her permitting him to do so is her tacit consent to the marriage. The bridegroom treats his beloved with great respect, yet in the presents of the collar and straps for burdens, and the kettle and faggot, clearly implies his intention of becoming her master.†

Although the women are possessed of some authority in the tribe, they are only slaves in respect to their own husbands. Upon them fall the maintenance of their parents and their own children ; the last are considered their peculiar property, being wholly educated by them. The practice of nursing them for three years, and their severe toils, render these women very unfruitful, for they seldom have large families.

The child's nurture terminates in a festival, on which occasion, when seated on the knees of one

* Charlevoix.   † Ibid.

or other of its parents, its name is given, while the father and mother are praying to the genii, and to the babe's genius in particular, that he may be fortunate.* The Indians never chastise their children, considering that corporeal punishment only degrades them without improving their judgment. A handful of water flung in the face of the offender is the only affront offered by these mothers to their little ones.† This custom is still extant : I have myself often seen it practised.

The Indian considers man a free agent, and that no power on earth has a right to deprive him of that blessing. There is no constraint among them, and the French Missionaries found this freedom of action and will a great bar to the conversion of these nations. Crimes are seldom punished, and they consider that insane or intoxicated persons are irresponsible agents, coolly remarking upon any murderous mischief committed by them, " that it was unfortunate, but that the persons knew not what they did.‡ They always burn witches, but rarely put one of their own people to death for murder. They are extremely afraid of ghosts, and believe that the soul has many shapes or likenesses to its own body ;§ a idea which is to be found in Lucretius.

* Charlevoix.   † Ibid.   ‡ Ibid.   § Ibid.

The Aborigines of North America have no written records, consequently they have no historic annals. The inexpiable war between the Algonquins and their allies, the Hurons and Iroquois, constitutes the only oral tradition of their combats; it commenced before Monsieur Champlain arrived in Canada in 1603, and furnishes them with their sole historical data.* The warlike Algonquins and Iroquois were once friendly, having made an alliance offensive and defensive with each other, in which the Hurons were included. The Algonquins, who were celebrated hunters, and scorned agriculture, engaged by the terms of this treaty to furnish the Iroquois with game if they would give them corn in return. The Iroquois also agreeing to skin the beasts taken in the chase, and dress the skins. The pride of the Algonquin nation caused the treaty to be broken, and changed the union of the two nations into a fearful and inexpiable war.†

The occasion was this. Some Iroquois wishing to join the Algonquins in the chase, were reminded that they would be wanted to skin the elks. However, during three days they furnished their allies with no employment of the kind, whereupon the young Iroquois went out privately

* Charlevoix.   † Ibid.

to hunt, and returned in the evening loaded with game. The Algonquins were so much mortified by the success of their allies, that they rose up in the night and murdered all the hunters. The Hurons espoused the side of the Algonquins, which led to their being nearly exterminated.

If the Algonquins in the commencement of the quarrel, would have given up the murderers to their allies, there would have been no war ; but upon their refusal to deliver them, the Iroquois swore they would perish to a man rather than not be revenged on their enemies. Very dearly did the Algonquins pay, and still more dearly their allies, for having exasperated a brave people to despair.*

The wampum, or collars, adorned with shells, besides their ornamental uses, were used to signify, by their arrangement, certain characters or signs by which the public affairs of the tribe were distinguished. Red collars were sent to their allies when a war was in contemplation. These curious hieroglyphics were treasured up in the cabin of the chief, forming, in fact, the archives of the nation, being considered sacred.† The calumet, or pipe, was the symbol of peace, and held in universal veneration. The Indians be-

* Charlevoix.   † Ibid.

lieved that the Great Spirit never forgave any infraction of a treaty in which the calumet had been smoked as a pledge of inviolability.* The manner in which the pipe was adorned always denoted whether the treaty regarded war or traffic. From the disposition of the feathers the contracting nations could be known; and when war was in agitation, the feathers were red. †

The Indian is by nature an orator, and the eloquence of the chief is chiefly exerted in exciting his tribe to take up the hatchet; but he first observes a severe fast, paints his face black, and continually invokes his genius: then holding the collar, or wampum, in his hand, he tells the tribe "that the Great Spirit inspires him with the intention of revenging the blood of one of his brethren by marching to such a place to take scalps and captives—if he perishes, the collar will serve to receive him and the person he seeks to revenge, lest they should be hid in the dust; that is, perhaps it will be his recompense who buries the dead." ‡

After this obscure intimation, he lays upon the ground the wampum, which is taken up by the person wishing to become his lieutenant, who washes the blackness from the face of the chief,

* Charlevoix.　　† Ibid.　　‡ Ibid.

paints his face and hair, and greases his person. The chief then sings the death-song in a hollow voice, while the volunteers (for no one is compelled to follow him unless they choose to do so), sing their war-songs, but not in chorus, for each warrior has his own peculiar one. Then the council sits in deliberation, excluding, however, their chief ; if they approve his design he makes a feast, which consists only of a dog.

Then among the Iroquois a kettle is put on, and the volunteers throw into it little bits of wood with a mark upon each, by which the parties are distinguished. To draw back after this pledge has been given, would for ever disgrace the party, whose person also would not be safe.*

In a burst of eloquence the chief then once more explains his reasons for making war ; he reminds the warriors of their lost brethren, appeals to their affections and their revenge, and concludes by bidding the young men to prepare for the expedition by painting their faces, anointing their hair, filling their quivers, and singing. † He then takes his hatchet in his hand and sings. The warriors sing in their turn, and many dances are performed. That of the discovery is performed by a single warrior ; but in fact the whole method

* Charlevoix.   † Ibid.

of Indian warfare, it is said, is represented by these dances. Hanging the kettle over the fire is only practised when many nations are at war, and certainly agrees with the declaration of war in which they say, " they are going to eat their enemies." It is not, however, very clear that these Indians are really cannibals : Charlevoix thinks the expression and action may be merely allegorical.

The veteran warriors among the Six Nations, before marching against the enemy, always molest, revile, and even beat the young men who have never been in battle. They used bows, javelins, and wooden hatchets in war ; and before firearms rendered their armour useless, wore a curious sort of coat-of-mail which they afterwards abandoned.* Their warfare is always one of ambush ; but their method of dealing with their unhappy prisoners, and the conduct of these unfortunate persons during the tragedy of which they are the victims, seem peculiar to North America.

As the particular marks made and painted on the face of the victorious chief, or on the hatchet he leaves on the scene of his triumph, tells intelligibly enough his feats in war to the vanquished nations, so the cries of his deputy relate to his nation,

* Charlevoix.

or its allies, the number of the slain, and that of the prisoners, before he enters their villages.*

Before condemning a prisoner to death he is offered to supply to any woman, the husband, son, or brother she has lost. If she accept him, his wounds are washed, and he is unbound and carried to his future home. If he is rejected, the woman addresses the soul of the deceased, calling upon him to rejoice in the torments preparing for the prisoner. A herald informs the captive of his rejection, and leads him out of his cabin. He is followed by a second, who condemns him in these words,—"Thou art going to be burnt, my brother, be of good courage."

The victim usually replies, "It is well, I thank thee." He is then painted and adorned, and comes forth singing his own death-song. "I am brave and undaunted, and fear neither death nor torture. Those who fear them are less than women. Life is nothing to a courageous man. May rage and despair choke my enemies. Why cannot I devour them, and drink up their blood to the last drop?" He then recounts his own brave actions to the sound of his enemy's music, and does not fail to say everything cutting to their national pride during the whole tragedy. His forti-

* Charlevoix.

tude depends upon his strength of mind or power of enduring pain, but he is generally a hero.* The dreadful tortures to which these captives are subjected are too well known and authenticated to need repetition : like the other customs of the Indian nations, the abhorrent practice has passed away before civilization and Christianity.

The use of spirits broke the brotherly bond of affection among the Indians of the same tribe, for, according to the accounts given by Charlevoix, "the fire-water given by the English fur-traders converted a whole village into devils incarnate." This charge, I am afraid, is only too true, since I have already described the ill-consequences of selling spirits to the red men, whom intoxication fearfully excites.

I have collated the preceding narrative from Père Charlevoix, in order to show what the Canadian Indians formerly were. The Mississauga tribes are Chippewas, and once formed a part of the great Algonquin nation, whose eloquent language is considered by our author as the finest of the Canadian mother-tongues. I have found them a grateful and attachable people, and their conversion to Christianity has made them sober, indus-

* Charlevoix.

trious, and peaceable. They were formerly very warlike, and were celebrated for their skill in the chase, and their dexterity in performing the war-dances of their tribe. That of the fire-dance has been very graphically described by Père Charle-voix, but I have never seen it performed. There is an old grudge still subsisting between the Mississaugas and the Mohawks, the latter never failing to beat the former if they can do it slyly.

Consumption appears, from Charlevoix, to have been an hereditary disease among the Indian tribes of Canada, and they are very subject to it at this period.

The Mississauga, who have become Christians, are becoming perfectly civilized ; many of them have not only adopted the religion but the customs of the whites.

CHAPTER VII.

MY VOYAGE ON THE HURON TO THE THAMES IN THE "PIONEER."—
TAKE IN MY CARGO.—WARM WELCOME GIVEN TO MR. CAMPBELL
BY A HIGHLAND WOMAN.— IRISH SONNET.— A NEW ACQUAINT-
ANCE.—SPECIMEN OF BACHELOR-HOUSEKEEPING NOT RECOMMEN-
DATORY TO CELIBACY.—MINE HOST SETS FIRE TO HIS HOUSE PAR-
ACCIDENT.—CURIOUS DIALOGUE BETWEEN HIM AND HIS COOK.—
EXCELLENT SUPPER.—PROCEED ON OUR VOYAGE.

EARLY in October of this year, 1831, Mr. Prior hired a small schooner, called the "Pioneer," which was despatched to our transatlantic "river Thames" for the purpose of loading her with wheat, potatoes, and other stores for the use of the new settlement. It was, therefore, necessary to send thither some person to make the purchases, and transact the Company's business. This, of course, by right devolved on me; but at that time I was confined to the house by an attack of ague, and, consequently, had a fair excuse for stopping at home. I knew, however, there would be some difficulty in supplying my place, so I volunteered to go, thinking perhaps that change of air and scene might effect a cure.

To the best of my recollection, I went on board on the 5th of October, and we sailed the same evening, with a fair wind blowing fresh; and at daylight next morning, found ourselves in sight of Fort Gratiot, on the American side of the lake. This fort belongs to the United States, and is so situated as to command the entrance of the river St. Clair,* which river or strait connects the waters of Lake Huron with those of Lake St. Clair, from thence to Lake Erie it is called the Detroit.†

* " Lake St. Clair is about thirty miles long, and nearly the same breadth, and its shores, as yet, not well settled. It receives several rivers, the principal of which, named the Thames, winds for more than a hundred miles from the north-east, and on its banks settlements and embryo towns are growing. It has its Chatham, London and Oxford; and certainly the situation of the Canadian London is much better adapted for the metropolis of the province than York (Toronto). General Simcoe, the first Governor of Upper Canada, was exceedingly anxious that the seat of government should be established somewhere nearly equidistant to Lakes Ontario, Erie, and Huron.

" There is a large Delta at the upper end of Lake St. Clair, which appears to be increasing, and through which by several channels the river issues. On the east or American bank stands Old Fort St. Clair, and a few miles further up, where Lake Huron opens, Fort Gratiot was erected to command the river."—" British America," by John Mac Gregor, Esq.

† The river Detroit runs from Lake St. Clair into Lake Erie. Its navigation is not interrupted, and its fertile banks are thickly peopled. But different characteristics present themselves to these we meet elsewhere in Upper-Canada. The inhabitants are French Canadians, and on the banks of the Detroit they tenaciously retain all the habits and observances common to their country-men, the *habitans* of Lower Canada. Here for twenty or thirty

At the entrance of the river the current runs very swiftly for about the distance of a thousand yards, at the rate of seven miles an hour, so that it requires a strong leading wind to stem the current. This would, consequently, preclude the possibility of any hostile vessel attempting the passage.

Since my visit to this place, a town has been founded on the British side, nearly opposite, called Port Sarnia, which, from its situation, must become a place of importance ; and I understand it has been contemplated to make this port the terminus of the Great Western Railway.

The river St. Clair is, without exception, one of the finest in the country. The shore on the American side is low, but the land, however, appeared good, and well and thickly settled with thriving villages, churches, pretty villas with green venetian blinds and neat verandahs, with flourishing orchards and gardens, sloping to the water's edge. The Canadian side at this time presented

miles we again observe the village form of settlements, the pious priest, the decent church, and the kind, civil *habitan.* This is a rich, beautiful country, and if once the ague and lake fever were banished, the climate would be truly delightful. All kinds of grain, and the finest apples, pears, peaches, nectarines, and grapes grow in perfection. Near Detroit there is a settlement of simple, harmless Moravians." —" British America," by John Mac Gregor, Esq.

a strange contrast to the other. It was chiefly covered with a dense forest, to the river's brink ; varied here and there with patches of clearing. I should think the average width of the St. Clair varies from five hundred to six hundred yards, presenting a clear deep stream, crowded with steamers and schooners bound to the Far West. The only difficult part of the navigation is where the St. Clair empties its waters into the lake of the same name, forming a bar by the deposits it leaves at its embouchure, over which, during the dry season, there is scarcely nine feet of water. But I make no doubt, from the large class-steamers which now navigate the lakes, that the navigation over this bar has been greatly improved. The shores round Lake St. Clair are very flat and uninteresting, being almost. on a level with the water. From their appearance I should be inclined to think that, not many years since, this lake must have been double its present size, since, during the spring floods, many acres of these marshes are still flooded. The depth of the water seldom exceeds thirty feet, the extent being about twenty-six miles each way.

We had some difficulty in finding the mouth of the Thames, which empties its waters on the south side of the lake. At length we espied a

large tree of the swamp-elm species, and the only
one we could descry for miles, which our skipper
declared was the sole land-mark by which to
shape our course. In which he proved correct,
for an hour after we were sailing up the river
with a fair wind. The waters of the Thames,
which are nearly the colour of coffee, offer a
strange contrast to the bright green and pellucid
waters of the St. Clair. This dismal hue, however, is not at all surprising when we consider
the fine rich country it drains in its lengthened
course.

By a reference to the map of the province, it
will be seen that the head waters of the Thames
have their rise in the Huron tract, the principal
branches of which are the Avon and Black Creek,
besides several other inconsiderable streams,
which contribute to swell its current. After
leaving the Company's lands it flows through the
fertile and well-settled London district, to the
town of New London, where it becomes a handsome river, receiving several tributaries throughout its course of sixty-three miles, to Chatham,
from whence, to its embouchure, it extends about
sixteen more. The channel of this stream is very
tortuous, and for the first ten miles meanders
through extensive meadows, which are, for the

most part, flooded in the spring. A great many horses and droves of cattle are pastured here during the summer months. A few miles farther on the land rises, and the low meadows give place to fine old cleared farms, extensive orchards, with, here and there, groves of black walnut.

We anchored for the night opposite Goss's Tavern, and it was my intention to proceed the next day to M'Gregor's Mills, a short distance up the stream. Luckily, however, for me, I fell in with a Mr. M'Crea, who promised to furnish me with wheat and other necessary articles ; at the same time giving me a courteous invitation to reside in his house whilst we took in the cargo. Amongst other stores, I purchased for my own use a quantity of excellent apples, which I obtained for the trifling sum of six pence sterling per bushel. I was allowed to choose my own fruit from a ten acre orchard, gathering off any trees that suited me best into a corn-basket which held at least six pecks for my bushel measure. I bought potatoes from the same person for one shilling, being double the price of my apples, which were exceedingly plentiful in this section of the country.

Most of the substantial farmers in the vicinity of the river have ice-houses, the Thames water being warm and bad to drink in the summer season.   The tavern-keepers here put cherries in their whiskey, which give it a good colour and very pleasant flavour ; and mixed with ice-water this beverage makes an excellent drink in hot weather, being far more wholesome than malt liquor.

We were delayed a week while taking in our cargo, and afterwards by contrary winds; but at length we got under weigh, and dropping down the stream with a

> " Wet sheet and a flowing sea,
> And a wind that followed fast,"

crossed Lake St. Clair, and anchored for the night amongst some low islands at the mouth of the river, where we were detained three days for want of wind to stem the current of the St. Clair, which runs at the rate of three miles per hour.

As we had nothing else to do we manned the boat and went off duck-shooting ; and although we had only the schooner's boat, which was quite unfit for the business by reason of the noise it made in being propelled through the rushes, yet we had very good sport, having by three o'clock, P. M. bagged eleven brace of wild ducks and blue-winged teal,—the last I consider the most delicious of all the numerous species of American wild fowl, not even excepting the far-famed wood-duck, of which I have made honourable mention in a former chapter.

On our return home we passed a small log-house on one of the islands, where we saw two men busy building a boat ; so we went ashore and asked for a drink, the river-water being rather unpalatable.

On entering the house we perceived a decent old lady sitting at a spinning-wheel, who asked us in a very strong Highland accent, " What we wanted ?"   One of our party, who was of Highland parentage, though a Nova-Scotian by birth, answered her inquiry in her native tongue, which so overjoyed the good creature, that in her ecstasy she jumped up from her seat, knocking down the spinning-wheel and two or three chairs in her excitement, and throwing her arms round poor Campbell's neck, bestowed several hearty kisses on either cheek before he could recover from his astonishment.   I think he would rather she had directed her daughter, a fine comely girl who sat by the fire sewing, and regarded her mother and the victimised Highlander with an arch smile, to stand proxy for her on this occasion.

The old lady told us she had not heard the sound of her own native Gaelic since she lost her husband, more than eight years since, having left her native land when quite a girl, after her mar-

riage to one of her own countrymen, who had settled on this spot more than forty years ago ; she
pronounced herself happy and contented, informing us, " that her eldest son was married and was
a boat-builder." After these communications she
went to the door, and calling him in told him
how rejoiced she was to see one of her own countrymen, hospitably inviting us to stop and have
some refreshment, which she ordered her daughter
to prepare immediately.

Going to a cupboard, the good woman produced
a bottle, and insisted that we should take a good
stiff horn, as she called it, to which most of our
party seemed nothing loath, particularly her new
friend, Mr. Campbell. Our pretty cook soon placed
before us a dish of excellent black-bass nicely
fried, and a bowl of smoking hot potatoes in ragged
jackets, a sure sign they were well cooked and of
a good quality. I never see a dish of murphies,
as the Irish call them, without recalling a clever
repartee made by an Irish labourer in Peterborough, of the name of Murphy, who, when his
master remarked upon the tattered condition of
his coat, in a tone of reproof answered his lecturer
thus :—" And sure, sir, and did yees ever know a
good Murphy without a ragged jacket ?"

We offered our hostess a dollar at parting,

which she refused, and it was not without difficulty we induced her even to accept some of our
game.   So brightly burned in her aged bosom the
pure *amor patriæ* for her wild Highland glens—so
dear was the sound of her unforgotten Celtic to
her ears—poor Campbell, I am afraid, heard more
frequently, however, of the loving greeting given
him by his countrywoman than he thought at all
necessary or pleasant.

Our passage up the St. Clair was very tedious,
the wind being light and baffling.   To avoid the
strong current, we crept up close to the shore, the
water being sufficiently deep except where sand-
bars were formed by the embouchures of small
rivers and creeks into the main channel.   As we
were not always aware of these obstructions, we
were constantly running aground ; then the anchor had to be taken aft by the boat, and all
hands at the windlass, much to my annoyance.

One evening, as we lay at anchor, a gentleman
of the name of M‘Donald came on board the
schooner—a pleasant intelligent person, whom I
asked to take a glass of punch with us, which he
accepted ; and we soon became very sociable.
Our visitor discovered by my appearance that I
was an invalid, my attack of ague having degene-
rated into a low intermittent or dumb ague, as the

backwoodsmen call it. He therefore very kindly invited me to go ashore with him, and stay all night at his house, remarking "that he could give me a good supper, a good bed, and a hot glass of brandy and water," which he declared "was better than all the doctors' stuff in the world for ague." An assertion which, from experience, I believe to be perfectly true.

M'Donald was an old bachelor, and kept no female servant; but he prided himself upon having an excellent man-cook, who, he informed me, "had only one fault in the world, namely, that of sometimes getting drunk, which was generally the case on particularly inconvenient occasions. When I send him across the river to the store, or have company, the fellow is sure to be intoxicated," said he. "And you know it is very inconvenient for us both to be drunk at the same time. I tell you this, that you may not be surprised if you see him in that state this evening, for he went to the store for groceries just after dinner, and he has not returned yet." Having made me acquainted with the bacchanalian tastes of his cook, he ushered me into his parlour—a large room plainly furnished, but commanding a pleasant and extensive view of the river and the opposite shore, adorned with a number of pretty villas.

The evening was cold, so he proposed making a fire in a large double Canadian stove, which stood in the middle of the room. Now it happened that this was the first time a fire had been lighted this season ; and his cook, who thought the upper part of the stove or oven was a nice cool place in which to store the butter, had, during the summer, been in the habit of keeping a few pounds there for every-day use. At this time there happened to be a fresh supply of five pounds in a china dish, when M'Donald, not knowing or having forgotten all about this most original buttery, made up a good fire, which quickly heated the oven, and of course melted the butter, which, running down into the lower part of the stove, was instantly in a blaze, roaring like a furnace, and heating the stove-pipes red-hot, causing flames to ascend from the chimney at least ten feet into the air.

For some time the house was in great danger, but by wetting some blankets, which we laid on the roof in the vicinity of the chimney, and throwing, at the same instant, a quantity of salt into the stove, we soon succeeded in damping the fire without further damage, excepting the loss of the aforesaid butter and the china dish, which was broken by the heat.

We had scarcely got over this trouble when the old cook made his appearance, half drunk and in a terrible passion. To hear him, a stranger would have supposed, indeed, that he was the master of the whole establishment, upon whom all the loss would of necessity fall.

"So," said he, "you are a nice fellow, ain't you, to go and put fire into that stove, and destroy so much good butter and break our best dish. I can't go out of the house for an hour but what you do some mischief or other."

"Come, John," replied M'Donald, "cut short this impertinence, which I will not bear much longer. How should I know you chose such an odd place for the butter? If you would not stay away and get drunk as you do, when you are sent of an errand, there would be no occasion for me to do your work and light the stove."

"I wonder who was drunk last," retorted John, "and who carried you to bed last Thursday night. However, I shall leave you in the morning, and then I should like to know how you will get on." So saying, he slammed the door to, and took himself off, grumbling as he went.

"There," remarked my host to me, "this is the way in which I am constantly used by that fellow. I almost wish he would make himself scarce. But there is no fear of that : and he is such a good cook, having lived so many years with me ; and is, besides, perfectly honest; so that, after all, I suppose I must continue to put up with his impertinence, for I cannot do well without him."

Notwithstanding this little *fracas,* our irascible *artiste* prepared us a capital supper of venison steaks fried with slices of bacon—a real backwoodsman's dish ; and famous fare it was, with hot potatoes and the accompaniment of a good cup of tea. We did ample justice to this bachelor fare, after our labours in putting out the fire.

In the morning mine host showed me round his farm, which was a very good one. He had some fine alluvial flats near the river, that he had cropped the last summer with tobacco, assuring me "that it had succeeded very well." I have understood that the lowlands in the western district are better adapted for the growth of this plant, the climate being more suitable than any other part of Canada West.

Nearly the whole of this farm was fenced with black walnut rails, this species of timber attaining a large size in this district. I have seen canoes that would hold ten or twelve persons made from a single tree : the wood is finely clouded, and makes beautiful furniture. It really seems a pity that precious material like this should be used for such purposes as fencing. Some fine specimens of this wood, made up into furniture, were exhibited in the Canadian department at the Crystal Palace, likewise some noble planks in the rough, all which, being much admired, will most likely be the means of introducing it into general use in England.

At Port Sarnia we were again detained for want of a leading wind to carry us up the rapids into Lake Huron. During our detention (two days) I again amused myself with duck-shooting, this place being then famous for that sport. I went on shore, and walked over the ground where the flourishing village of Port Sarnia now stands, but which at this time consisted of one solitary log-house.

In the evening the long-looked for change of wind took place, it blew freshly from the south-west, which enabled us, by the help of a tow-rope, to ascend the current, and we found ourselves once more on the broad bosom of the mighty Huron.

CHAPTER VIII.

WE PASS GODERICH HARBOUR IN THE GALE.—WANT OF A CHART.—
LAKE-SICKNESS.—DANGEROUS POSITION.—FIND OURSELVES AMONG
THE ISLANDS.—DASH THROUGH OUR DIFFICULTIES.—HARBOUR OF
REFUGE.—CAMP ON SHORE.—MY WALK ON THIS TERRA INCOGNITA.
—FIND FIVE STEEL TRAPS.—MISS SHOOTING A BLACK FOX.—BEAUTY
OF THE SCENERY. — OUR HILARITY. — TRANSPARENCY OF THE
WATERS OF THE BAY.—VISIT OF THE CHIPPEWA INDIANS.—NOBLE
SALMON-TROUT.— IN SIGHT OF PORT.— FRESH DIFFICULTIES.—
GREETINGS FROM SHORE.—SHIP A SEA.—CROSS THE BAR.—LET
OUR ANCHOR GO.—ACCIDENT TO OUR CABLE.— MAN THE BOAT.—
TOWING-LINE TOO SHORT. — JEOPARDY. — RESOLVE TO SWIM
ASHORE.—DANGEROUS PREDICAMENT.—PROVIDENTIAL PRESERVA-
TION.—HOME.—A SOLITARY FIRESIDE.—RETURN OF MY WIFE.—
HER ANXIETY DURING MY ABSENCE. — HER TERROR ON SEEING
THE SCHOONER STRANDED.— RECOVER MY HEALTH AND SPIRITS
UNDER HER TENDER CARE.

THE increasing wind and sea warned us to prepare for a rough night. We, however, felt no alarm, for the gale was aft, and we calculated we should be able to make Goderich harbour at daylight, though distant from Port Gratiot seventy-two miles. As the darkness increased so did the gale, which, towards midnight, blew a perfect hurricane. Being well aware I

could be of little service, especially in my weak
state from the continuance of the dumb ague, I
turned in and slept, in spite of the noise and
howling of the storm, until I was awakened at
daylight by our skipper, who gave me the unwelcome intelligence that Goderich was in sight, which
it seems we had passed by during the darkness,
and were now some six or seven miles from the
harbour, so that we had no alternative but to run
for the Manitoulins, near the head of the lake,
where we might shelter ourselves till the storm
was over.

I dressed immediately and went on deck to see
how things looked, which, indeed, had anything
but a pleasant aspect. We were running parallel
with the shore from which we were about six
miles, Goderich being still in view. We were
scudding before the gale under a close-reefed
foresail and gib, the sea running in dark, heavy
masses, which threatened to poop us every minute.

We now retired to the cabin and held a council
of what was best to be done. Our crew and
passengers amounted, including myself, to eleven
souls, several of whom were Indian traders and
Frenchmen. Our captain opened the proceedings
by informing us that he had no chart of the
Lake or coast on board, that he had never been

higher up the Huron than Goderich ; upon which one of the Indian traders told us "that there was a good harbour at the mouth of the Saugeen, a fine river seventy or eighty miles above Goderich." But as none of us on board knew the land-marks at its mouth, we deemed it madness to attempt running in towards the land, as we knew not what dangers we might have to encounter.

At last it was agreed by a majority that we should hold the course we were then steering. The only one who opposed this plan was myself. I argued that if the gale continued we should be amongst the rocky islands before daylight, in which case our destruction was almost inevitable ; for I knew well from the study of the Canada Company's Maps that the iron-bound coast of the Manitoulins * stretched across the Lake for miles in a north-west direction, and that in the darkness our vessel ran the greatest risk of being dashed to pieces on the rocks. I therefore strongly recommended a more north-westerly

* These islands are three in number, stretching across the lake in a north-westerly direction from Cabot's Head to the Detour and the island of St. Joseph's, a distance of more than one hundred and thirty miles ; the most northerly of these is called Drummond's Island, the second Cockburn, and the third, the Great Manitoulin ; they almost divide the lake into two parts. There are several good harbours on these islands, and it is said both copper and lead are to be found in considerable quantity.

course, which would give us plenty of sea-room. My objections, however, were overruled by the general voice, so I had nothing left but to trust in Providence for the result.

At four o'clock in the afternoon we supposed ourselves off the Saugeen. The storm was now at its height, and blew with terrific violence. We shipped some heavy seas, which so frightened our skipper that he insisted on having some of the cargo thrown overboard. I was not aware of this proceeding till six or seven barrels of Indian-meal and other stores had been heaved overboard, I immediately put a stop to this proceeding, though not without considerable opposition.

There was no moon and the night came on as dark as pitch, and to add to our misfortune, every person on board was dreadfully sea-sick excepting myself. Indeed the rough lake passage having the same results, occasions the internal commotion to take the same form, and, of course, those who were suffering from its effects could scarcely keep the helm. I thought that long night would never end. Every moment I expected to feel the shock and hear the crash that would consign us to the deep.

Several times I went on deck, fancying I could hear breakers, and occasionally I thought the wind lulled, but it was too dark and the noise of the wind so great that it was impossible to be certain. Yet so sure did I feel that I heard the dash of the waves on shore that I did not think it prudent to leave the deck.

During those long hours of darkness and uncertainty many strange feelings crowded my mind and painful reminiscences. I thought I should never again see my beloved wife and young children. I remembered my mother, sisters, and brother, and dear familiar friends I had left at home in Old England at this dangerous crisis, for I had little hope we should escape shipwreck. I knew if we struck the rock-bound coast our chance was small indeed. A merciful Providence, however, had ordained otherwise, for the long-expected dawn at length revealed our position. We were surprised to find ourselves amongst the islands, for we had nearly run 200 miles since we were in sight of Goderich. Land was to be seen on all sides, or rather piles of rocks.

Directly in our course, and stretching for more than a mile into the Lake from a point of land, lay a reef of rocks upon which the sea broke with a thundering sound, throwing up the spray high into the air, and not five hundred yards from the schooner. To weather this reef was impossible, but luckily we noticed a narrow spot of smooth water about midway up the reef; so we determined to risk the passage. Indeed we had, to use an old saying, "Hobson's choice"—that or none. So we steered for the opening and passed gallantly through; but so near were we to the rocks on either side of us that we could easily have pitched a biscuit upon them from the vessel.

As soon as we were safely through we gave three hearty cheers, and on rounding the point we entered a beautiful and spacious harbour, completely land-locked with a smooth sandy beach at the upper end, in one corner of which a large creek of transparent looking water came rattling into the bay. As soon as our anchor was let go, we manned the boat and went on shore, taking with us the square sail to make a tent, and a stock of provisions and other necessaries; in fact we determined to recruit and make ourselves comfortable after the fatigue we had undergone. One party made up a large fire in front of the tent, and prepared for cooking the dinner, while the rest picked brush and wild grass for our beds, and erected the tent.

Whilst these preparations were going on, I took my gun and explored the shores of the bay, and walked up the side of the creek, which I followed

for a couple of miles.   The waters of this stream
were clear as crystal and of a greenish hue, and I
passed several very romantic falls : indeed as far
as I went the river presented a succession of cascades.   I saw a great many otter slides and beaver
cuttings.

On my return, near the mouth of the creek, I
found five large steel-traps, which, most likely,
some of the Hudson Bay Company's traders had left
by mistake, who probably had camped near this
spot ; but when loading their canoes to depart,
had overlooked them, since they appeared by the
rust to have lain there for upwards of a twelvemonth.   Our traders considered these traps quite
a prize, being at the least worth ten dollars.

I shot several rabbits and a brace of wood-ducks
to add to our larder.   While crossing a low sand-
ridge near the shore, a beautiful black fox passed
me, within twenty yards—a splendid shot, if I
could have hit him; but, unfortunately, my gun
missed fire, which was very unlucky for me, as the
skin of these animals is very valuable : I have
been informed a good one in season is worth from
10*l.* to 15*l.*   The pure black-skinned fox is extremely scarce ; in fact, during the whole of my
long residence in Canada, I have not seen more
than four or five of this rare species.

The scenery around our anchorage was very picturesque ; the rocks rose boldly, terrace above terrace, until a mile or so from the shore they had attained an altitude of at least a thousand feet. For five days we were wind-bound in this romantic little bay, and during that time " we ate, drank, and were merry." We amused ourselves with exploring the country, shooting, fishing, and telling our adventures, our recent peril making us enjoy our detention in this harbour of refuge.

Our merry sojourn ashore, on our pleasant terra incognita, at length terminated with the change of the wind, and we prepared to bid a long adieu to the harbour of refuge. What a change in its silent loveliness a few years will probably make! And where I awoke the slumbering echoes of the shore by the sound of my fowling-piece, the stirring hum of population will come and the voices of a numerous people will be heard.

Early on the morning of the 6th we weighed our anchor, and bade adieu to our harbour of refuge. The day was fine and clear, but about noon we were becalmed between two small rocky islands. The view from the schooner's deck at this time was exceedingly fine. Innumerable islands, as far as the eye could reach, dotted the north-east shore of the lake, while the main-land rose boldly; the scarp of the rock showing here and there, between their openings, the dwarf trees which clustered in thickets, wherever there was soil sufficient to nourish their growth.

What added greatly to the beauty of the scene was the extraordinary transparency of the water. Our vessel lay about half a mile from the land, in ten fathoms water, and yet the bottom of the lake was so plainly visible that we could see every seam in the rock and the smallest stones. If we looked over the side into the depth below, we at first experienced the same giddy sensation usually felt when beholding objects from a great height, as indeed we really were : the schooner seeming apparently suspended in the air. This purity of the water is only observable among the islands, for, from Cabot's Head downwards, the banks are of a clay formation, which, during a storm, discolour the waters some distance from the shore.

We made little progress the first day, and nothing occurred worth notice, with the exception of a visit from a number of Chippewa Indians in nine large bark-canoes, bound for Drummond's Island. These Indians came on board and bartered with us, giving us fresh salmon-trout for whiskey and apples. One of our passengers purchased the largest I ever saw for a quart of whiskey : it weighed no less than seventy-two pounds. I had seen one caught by a night-line, opposite Goderich, which weighed fifty-six pounds ; but I had no idea that fish so much larger, of the same species, could be obtained at the head of the Lake.

The next day we cleared the Manitoulins, flattering ourselves with the deceitful hope that we should make our port the next day ; but no ! the wind again headed us, and blew stiffly night after night, so that we were obliged to lay to. At last it shifted to the north-west, and freshened to a gale ; but, as it was in our favour, we did not care ; all we hoped was, to make Goderich before night-fall.

It was now three o'clock, P.M., and the white houses on the cliff were visible at the distance of about nine miles. We were all in high spirits till our skipper damped our ardour by informing us " that he thought it impossible for us to make the harbour ; for, though the wind was directly aft, yet, to make the desired haven, we should have to round a point where both wind and current would be dead against us." However, after much argument we finally determined to make the attempt.

As we neared the harbour, to our great satisfaction and joy, we saw that we were expected and recognized; for a large fire of brushwood was kindled on a high point of land at the harbour's mouth, and we could sea a crowd of persons on the beach waiting our approach. As we neared the bar, we found a heavy sea breaking on the shoal; and, in crossing, a tremendous one struck us, deluging our deck and causing our little vessel to quiver from stem to stern. We, however, succeeded in crossing the bar in safety, but were immediately met by the wind and current of the river. We let our anchor go as soon as possible, but unfortunately, the cable parting, left us exposed to great peril. The boat was instantly lowered, and manned with six of our best hands, including the captain, who, with a tow-rope, hoped to reach the shore. But, as misfortunes seldom come singly, as bad luck would have it, the rope proved too short, consequently the boat upset in the surf; though, luckily, all the crew succeeded in making good their landing.

There remained on board the schooner four persons besides myself, not one of whom knew anything about the management of a vessel. I saw at a glance that we could expect no help from the shore; and I was so heartily sick of this protracted voyage, that I determined to attempt swimming ashore, at all risks.   I knew there was considerable danger in the effort, but I thought if the schooner struck on the bar or was driven out to sea, that the risk would be still greater.   I therefore jumped on the taffrail, and, as the next heavy swell passed the stern, sprang into the water; at the same time calling upon my neighbour, Mr. Eberts, to follow me, which he had previously agreed to do.

I was a good swimmer, but had not calculated on the debility arising from nearly five weeks of ague.   I however buffeted the waves manfully till I struck the current of the river which set strongly along the shore of the Lake to the southward; consequently I was driven in the direction of the light-house point. *   The cliff at this point was more than a hundred feet in height, the first twenty from the Lake being a perpendicular bank of stiff clay, against which the waves dashed with great violence.   I found with all my exertion I could not weather this spot.   Luckily for me, however, I espied the head of a birch-tree which hung down from the cliff above.   This tree had been thrown down by the wind, but was still

* A high point of land on the south side of Goderich Harbour, reserved by the Superintendant of the Canada Company to build a light-house upon.

firmly secured to the bank above by a large mass
of roots and earth which it had turned up in its
fall, a fortunate circumstance to which I owed my
preservation, for I was carried directly into the
branches by the force of the waves, being left by
them at least ten feet from the water. I lost no
time in scrambling up the tree till I got firm
footing on the sloping bank, where, by the help of
young twigs and brushwood, I found myself,
after some difficult struggles, safe on the top of
the cliff, and within two hundred yards of my
own door. Feeling my preservation to be almost
miraculous, I did not forget to thank the Almighty for his mercy in restoring me in safety to
my family through so many dangers.

On reaching my house I was surprised to find
no one within, although a cheerful fire blazed on
the ample hearth. I was conjecturing what could
be the reason of this, when my dear Mary made
her appearance with my little Maria in her arms
to welcome and embrace her Wanderer, whom she
had mourned as though he had been lost to
her for ever. Ours was a blessed and joyful
meeting, full of the purest conjugal tenderness
and love. My poor girl then told me how she
had sat on the lighthouse point day after day,
watching till her eyes ached for the long-delayed

vessel, which few had ever expected to see again. She had continued to hope, even against hope, still clinging to the cherished idea that we were safe, till the day previous, which was the thirty-fourth of our absence, when upon being informed that a barrel, marked with the name of one of our party, had been picked up near the Saugeen by the Indians, she lost the confidence which had hitherto kept her up, and the same fear entered her mind that all the town's-people had long entertained, that the vessel had been dashed to pieces in the awful storm, and that consequently we had all perished. My dear wife could therefore hardly realise the joyful truth when Mr. Fullarton ran into the house and told her to cheer up, for the schooner was in sight and making for the harbour. Upon receiving this unexpected intelligence she ran down, filled with joy, to welcome my arrival; but what was her consternation upon seeing the schooner drift back over the bar, and finally strand on the beach, a few hundred yards from where I had, unknown to any one, effected my landing. After this sad scene she heard, in reply to her agonized inquiry, that I had jumped overboard with the intention of swimming ashore, and that I had been seen close to the point. The darkness prevented those in the schooner from ascertaining whether I had succeeded in making good my landing or not. Dreadfully alarmed she had hurried home from the harbour, knowing that if safe I should most probably be there, "And, thank God, my dear husband," she said, her beautiful eyes swimming in tears, "that you have been spared by a merciful Providence to me and your little ones." Warm dry clothing, a cheerful fire, and the tender cares of an affectionate wife soon restored me to my wonted health and usual spirits.

Thus ended my first and last voyage on the mighty Huron, that vast lake, or small fresh-water sea. The schooner, on examination, was not the least injured. By good luck she had missed the point and stranded herself on a sandy beach, opposite Read's tavern, and in a few days she was got off and brought safely into the harbour.

CHAPTER IX.

I QUIT THE SERVICE OF THE CANADA COMPANY.—LEAVE GODERICH.
—HOMEWARD JOURNEY.—WANT OF ACCOMMODATION AT SEBACH'S
HOUSE.—MY LANDLADY AND HER BROOD.—MIDNIGHT ADVEN-
TURES.—DISORDERLY BEHAVIOUR OF THE YOUNG DUTCH BOORS.—
MINE HOSTESS GIVES THEM A THRASHING.— YANKEE GUEST. —
OLD JACKSON HICKORY.—LOYAL LAWYER AND YANKEE FOOL.—
THE UTILITY OF IMPUDENCE.—RETURN HOME.—WARM WELCOME.
—HAPPY PARTY.

I HEARD such flattering accounts from my Douro
friends of the fast increasing prosperity of Peterborough and the neighbourhood, that at length I
made up my mind to give up my situation with
the Canada Company, and return to the farm I
had left in Otonabee. Several reasons prompted
me to this determination. One was the reduction
of my salary, which took place immediately after
Mr. Galt's retirement. The Company's affairs, indeed, after that event were conducted on a much
more economical plan by the new commissioners.
The diminution of my income did not suit a young
man with a fast increasing family, and I thought
I could better provide for them on a farm of my

own.   I however found out my mistake, after I
had left the Company, when it was too late to
remedy the evil, and I committed a second blun-
der in being tempted by a good offer to sell my
farm in Otonabee, close to the fast-rising town of
Peterborough, and purchase land ten miles farther
back in the Bush.

As soon as my wife and I had made up our
minds to leave Goderich, I sold my two town-
lots and the improvements upon them for five
hundred dollars, which paid me very well for the
speculation, for the lots cost originally twenty-five
dollars each, and the improvements about two
hundred, thus in little more than two years I
doubled my capital.

There can be no doubt that land speculation
is one of the surest and best means of making money in Canada, provided the speculator
can afford to sink his capital for a few years.
He must also be a person well acquainted with
the country and its capabilities, the quality of
the land and timber, number of mill privileges,
and the best and most eligible situations for
towns and villages, in which case there is no
danger of his being a loser.   Indeed, if the
land is well selected, there is almost a certainty of the speculator doubling his purchase-

money in the short space of from three to seven years.

On the 13th of February, 1831, I bade adieu to Goderich, where I had spent many happy days. I hired a Dutchman from the settlement with his lumber-sleigh and span of horses to move my family, consisting of my wife, her sister, and my two children. We commenced our journey in the midst of a heavy snow-storm, which had been falling without intermission since the previous evening ; this rendered the road almost impassable for our team, which had to break the road the whole way to the settlements. The snow was so deep that the beams of our sleigh were constantly imbedded, so that we were unable to accomplish more than eighteen miles the first day.

We found excellent accommodation at Von Egmond's tavern, which had just been completed. Not so, however, at my old acquaintance Sebach's, where we were doomed to stop the following night. Anticipating what we might expect by former experience, we took care to carry provisions and tea for our own use, which proved a necessary precaution.

The extent of our host's accommodations were very limited. They consisted of a public room, about sixteen feet by twelve, at the farther end of which a door opened into a narrow sort of closet, which served for a bed-room, where our hostess and four or five of her younger children slept. I think she had at least a dozen. The eldest of this numerous brood, whom she called Fater (his name, however, was Peter), could not be more than fourteen or fifteen years of age at the most. A Mrs. R——, and her little daughter Susan, who were moving into the neighbourhood of Peterborough, formed a part of our company, which almost filled the little room. Bad, however, as the inn was, we were glad to avail ourselves of its shelter. Besides, one thing at least we found comfortable, the large fire blazing cheerily on the ample hearth.

In regard to our sleeping we had some difficulty to arrange that important matter, since they had only two beds for our numerous party, and they were both in the same room. Under these circumstances undressing was out of the question. Luckily we had several horse-blankets and buffalo-robes, so that I was enabled to separate our dormitory by these fancy hangings. The teamster and myself contented ourselves with a shake-down before the fire, where five of our hostess's boys had already ensconced themselves for the night on a number of deer-skins.

About the middle of the night we were awakened by one of the Dutch boys tumbling into the fire in his sleep. He made as much outcry as if he had been half-roasted, though on examination we found he had escaped with only a slight burn on one of his hands.

This little incident having thoroughly roused his brothers, they seemed determined to let no one sleep for the remainder of the night. It was in vain that I threatened them with a suitable caning, if they were not quiet, for they either did not or would not understand English, and appeared to regard me and my cane with absolute unconcern. At length they became silent, and I had just fallen asleep when I was again awakened by a shriek from Mrs. R——, who seemed to be in an agony of terror ; and no wonder, poor woman ! for these impish Dutch boys had slily crept under the old lady's bed, and almost frightened her out of her wits by placing their shoulders under the mattress and, all lifting together, nearly succeeded in rolling her out of bed.

I could not help laughing at the trick, but the old lady, to whom it was no joke, was in a great rage, and shook her fist at the boys and scolded them soundly. Her irate eloquence was only received with shouts of laughter by her tormentors, in the midst of which our old Dutch hostess made her appearance, stick in hand, which she laid about her with great dexterity, to the no small discomfiture of her young rebel boors. This well-merited chastisement had the desired effect of quieting Master Peter and his brother imps, who let us sleep soundly during the remainder of the night.

Upon the evening of the fourth day we reached Farewell's Inn, in Whitby, where we put up for the night. After supper I sauntered into the barroom to speak with the landlord, whom I had formerly known. While I was conversing with Mr. F——, a stranger entered the room. The new-comer was a fine looking handsome man, considerably above six feet in height, and well put together; still I knew he was a Yankee the moment I looked at him, by his long neck, want of whiskers, and his free-and-easy manners.

"Come, landlord, let us have some bitters,—I guess it is my treat,—I am no slouch. I can tell you my names—I am called Tom Temple, and I am from the Green Mountains, State of Varmont. I am just taking a look at this country of your'n; come, boys, won't you liquor?"

So saying he filled a tumbler half full of raw

whiskey, and proposed the health of old Hickory Jackson.

"Pray," said I, "why do you call your President Old Hickory?"

"Wal, now, stranger, I will just tell you how that was. One time when our old gineral was going to 'tack the British, he made us a bit of a stump speech on the occasion.—' Now, boys,' said he, ' don't you see them are tarnation British, just step into the woods, and every one of you cut a good hickory gad,* and if you don't whip them fellows out of that I'll whip you.' Wal, we just done as Old Hickory told us, and if we din't take a most unrighteous snarl of them I'm sucked, that's all. And so you see, stranger, that's how he got the name of Old Hickory Jackson, and a tough un he is, you may depend."

Such was the extraordinary account given me of General Jackson's *nomme de guerre* by Mr. Thomas Temple, Green Mountains, State of Vermont.

It is certainly ridiculous to hear some of these gentlemen's constant bragadocio. This very man, before the evening was over, actually persuaded our landlord to hire him for the summer at twenty dollars a month to attend his saw-mill, only by

* Yankee for an ox-goad or rod.

dint of his own sheer impudence in praising himself.   I have no doubt that the man was capable
enough, but to hear him talk you would suppose
he had worked in every mill in the Union.   Indeed, his answer to the landlord, who asked him
" If he understood working in a saw-mill, and re-
pairing it when out of order ? " was characteristic
of the man, and in a few words conveyed all that
could be said on the subject.

"Wal, I guess I'm a clear saw-mill myself ? "
Meaning in Yankee parlance, that he understood
everything connected with saw-mills, and the
working of their machinery.

While on this subject I may as well relate a
laughable circumstance which took place in the
public stage-coach.   Mr. H. I. V——, a rising
lawyer in the county of Peterborough, was
travelling between Cobourg and Toronto, having
for one of his companions a thin, sallow-looking
importation from the United States.   Among
other topics the conversation turned upon the
marriage of our young Queen, when the names of
several royal and noble personages were mentioned by the different passengers.   The Yankee
listened with great attention to the various opinions expressed, when, addressing himself to the
lawyer, he said,—

" I guess now, Mister, you all make a mighty fuss about that Miss Kent, why our Mat's* son John went over the herring-pond the hul way to see her ; but I guess he din't like her well enough to take her."

" Why, you impudent scoundrel, is that the way you speak of our lovely young queen ! I will teach you to use more becoming language towards the Sovereign Lady of the realms."

So saying the loyal young lawyer seized the fool by the collar, and ejected him from the coach in the most summary manner possible, and at the greatest risk of breaking the long neck of the ill-behaved Yankee, who would scarcely venture to lampoon her Majesty in the presence of English gentlemen again. I guess he had had enough of it. My readers must not imagine that such men as I have described, however, are fair specimens of American manners ; perhaps these are extreme cases, for I have met many gentlemanly and some elegant persons both in Canada and America who ought not to be classed with people like him.

Upon the evening of the sixth day we arrived without farther adventure at my father-in-law's house. I need hardly say what a joyful meeting

* Matthew Van Buren, then President of the United States.

we all had after nearly four years' separation, during which period many eventful circumstances had occurred. I had buried my eldest child, a fine boy of three years old, to my great regret, but God had replaced him with a lovely boy and a girl, which I now presented with some paternal pride to receive their grandfather's and grandmother's blessing.

We were a very happy party that night assembled round the cheerful fire, talking over the past, and anticipating a fortunate future. Nor did I forget my mother, sisters, and brother, or dear old Reydon, while rejoicing in my reunion with the valued relatives I had gained by my second marriage to a lovely, amiable, and worthy young lady.

CHAPTER X.

EXCHANGE MY LAND FOR A LOT IN DOURO AND SOME HARD CASH.
— ADVANTAGES OF INDUSTRY. — CANADIAN ORCHARDS. — BAY
OF QUINTE. — ROOT-GRAFTING. — AMERICAN GRAFTSMEN, AND
METHOD OF GRAFTING.—HISTORY OF A POOR BLACKSMITH.—
HE SEES A GHOST. — CRUELTY OF CAROLINE GRIMSHAWE'S
FAMILY. — GENEROUS BEHAVIOUR OF COPPING'S MOTHER. —
DIALOGUE BETWEEN THE MASTER BLACKSMITH AND HIS FORE-
MAN.—CHEAP WAY OF BEING GOOD.—DISTRESS AND POVERTY.
— MY SISTER ADVISES COPPING TO GO TO CANADA. — HE
REACHES ME IN PENURY. — CHANGE IN HIS CIRCUMSTANCES.
—HIS SETTLEMENT.—OUR SEARCH FOR HIS LOT.—HIS WEARI-
NESS AND PATHETIC EXCLAMATION.—HIS LOCATION.—COMFORT-
ABLE CIRCUMSTANCES AND DECEASE AFTER SOME HAPPY YEARS
SPENT IN UPPER CANADA.—THE BUSH.—OUR EXPLORING PARTY.
POOR CAPPING'S LAMENTATIONS. — WE GIVE NAMES TO OUR
LOCATIONS.—UNPROMISING VIEW OF THE BLACKSMITH'S LAND.—
HIS LOT TURNS OUT WELL.—HIS SUCCESS AS A SETTLER.—CON-
CLUSION OF HIS HISTORY.

Soon after my return from the Huron tract, I
made a trade, as the Americans call it ; that is, I
exchanged my two hundred acre lot of land in
the township of Otonabee, for the same number
of acres in the township of Douro, and six hundred dollars in cash. I was induced to take this
step for several reasons, the principal of which

was, that I could increase the quantity of my acres, by purchasing wild lands in the neighbourhood, at a low price, which I could not do in the part where I was living. Then the situation of my new purchase was more beautiful, the land better, and the fishing and shooting second to none in the province—a great temptation to a young man, and especially to one fond of wild sports.

Though I was well aware that it would be years before my new location could possess the comforts I was leaving, still I looked forward, hopefully, to the time when, by my own exertions, I should have overcome all the difficulties of my new position, and established a pleasant home for my family.

I do not know a greater charm than, after years of toil and privation, to see what perseverance and industry have accomplished. To know that your pretty cottage, your orchards, your fruitful fields, and ornamental improvements are the work of your own hands ; and that a few short years ago, the solitary forest reigned undisturbed where now you behold all the comforts of civilization.

Many persons, on leaving England for Canada, fancy they shall see nothing but interminable woods and lakes. This was, no doubt, the case in regard to the Upper Province fifty years ago ; but they forget what the hardy bands of pioneer emigrants have effected in that short period, and that a belt of land, following the course of the great St. Lawrence, and the lakes from the embouchure of the Ottawa to the Saugeen river on Lake Huron, a distance of seven hundred and fifty miles, by an average depth of forty, have been reclaimed from the forest and thickly settled by a thriving and industrious population.

The farm-houses along the great leading roads are, for the most part, superior in appearance to those in the old country; though, in point of taste and ornamental arrangement, they fall short of them. This is principally owing to the want of shrubberies. The holly and ivy which impart such a charm to the English cottage will not grow, it is said, in Canada. This is the more surprising, as these ornamental trees are said to thrive best in a cold country; at least, so sings the poet :—

> " For the ivy, the ash, and the bonny holly tree,
>   Oh ! they grow best in the North country."

However, in some respect, to make up for this defect, Canada can boast of as fine orchards as can be found in any part of the world. From the river Trent to Belleville, on the Bay of Quinte, for twelve miles the road runs between almost a continuous line of them. In the month of May, when the trees are in full blossom, nothing can exceed the beauty of the country. That lovely sheet of water, the bay of Quinte, runs parallel to this pretty chain of orchards, the ground sloping gently towards the shore, fringed here and there with groves of hickory and butternut, which tend greatly to increase the natural beauty of the scene.

The best climate for fruit of all sorts, and where it most abounds, is undoubtedly round the head of Lake Ontario, and the peninsula lying between Hamilton and Long Point, on Lake Erie. The standard peach comes to perfection in this part of the country. Indeed, in some years the fruit is so plentiful that bushels may be seen lying rotting under the trees, their only consumers apparently being the pigs. The Western Canadians pay much greater attention to their orchards now than they formerly did ; the best kind of fruit being introduced from England and the United States.

The American nursery-men have a method of raising trees by root-grafting, which is by far a surer and more expeditious plan than that in common use.*   Instead of clay they prefer a

---

* In the spring of the year American graftsmen travel through the Canadian settlements provided with the best description of scions from American orchards. These men charge so much per

composition made of yellow wax and resin, which is found to be much the best for the purpose. The proper way to apply this mixture is by heating the composition and smearing over the place with a brush, where the graft is inserted and the cleft made by splitting the stock, which excludes the air much better, is quicker, and also less unpleasant than the old practice of kneading the clay over the graft with your hands, and which often falls off after the first heavy shower.

As soon as I had completed the bargain for my land, I commenced making preparations for my removal. Just at this time I received a packet of letters and a valuable parcel, by the hands of Samuel Copping, a Suffolk blacksmith, who was a near neighbour of mine when I resided in England. The history of his adventures and settlement will, perhaps, interest the reader.

During the spring of 1831, a poor working blacksmith, his wife and family, found their way down to my clearing; I had formerly known the man in England for a good natured, industrious creature; but he and his wife were better acquainted with my sister Jane, to whom their long and distressing illness had made them more inti-

hundred for grafting old trees. One year's credit is given, no charge being made for trees that have missed. A great many of the old orchards were originally planted from seedlings.

mately known : she thought them interesting people, anxious for spiritual instruction, and remembered that they had formerly been kind and helpful to their neighbours, by whom they were much beloved.   During a period of agricultural distress in Suffolk this family had previously been reduced to the utmost distress.   In the sore sickness of Copping it was some time before they could procure a nurse, but the people near one day gave them their gratuitous services ; until my sister was pleased to find there a handsome intelligent young woman who had come, to use a Suffolk phrase, "to do for the family."   Now, doing for a family in slang parlance, would stand for taking them in ; however, in Anglo-Saxon it signifies able assistance in the general management of a household ; and this the pretty Caroline Grimshawe was come to do ; "and all for love and nothing for reward," in grateful return for a home afforded her in childhood by the poor man, Copping's mother.

Caroline had a curious romantic story attached to her birth and bringing up, which I will relate just as her foster-brother told it to my sister :

"Ma'am," said he to my sister, "I was a native of Halesworth, in Suffolk; my parents were honest poor people, quite unlettered ; but clean and quite (quiet), burdened with a large family, yet just able, with God's help, to get along.

"It happened that a woman from Lincolnshire and her husband used to come to Halesworth with a huckster's cart; 'licensed hawker' was the word put on the cart; but huckster was what we called the man; nevertheless, my mother bought my father's shirts of them; and, as our house was out of the town, near it, yet standing by itself, these people used to lodge with us when they came our way, their cart being locked up in the farmer's barn, for whom my father worked. Grimshawe had several sons and daughters grown up; some were in trade, others in farms in his own county, and he was a wealthy man. My mother wondered he did not leave off travelling the country and set up himself for a gentleman, and his wife for a lady; but he had been a huckster all his life, and, I suppose, he liked it better than being a gentleman. It happened that late in life Mrs. Grimshawe was likely to have a baby, and worse than that, the child would come into the world at an inconvenient period, just in the time of the Suffolk journey. Both parents were rather sorry at the prospect of another child, for the woman hoped she should have had no more, and her family were grumbling about the expected addition to their number, and were inclined to give the poor little stranger an unkind welcome to this world of sorrow. Things were not mended by the death of the man, whose eldest sons were the executors of a will made many years before, and in which no mention of course was made of an unborn child.

" Well, the long and the short of it all is, that the poor widow Grimshawe took her Suffolk journey in the cart, and stopping at my mother's house, gave birth in her fiftieth year to a fine lovely girl, whom she named Caroline. My mother's month was just up from her confinement with me, for I was her seventh child, a slip of a thing not half so fine and thriving as Caroline. But my mother had a superabundance of nourishment for me while the widow had none for her hungry baby. So it was agreed between the friends that my good mother should share her milk between us.

" By this arrangement Caroline was left behind, in Suffolk, and the widow returned to Lincolnshire. Very fond was I of my foster-sister, whom my mother took to, just as if she had been her own ; and when the course of the year brought back the widow Grimshawe, she was *so* proud of her baby and so thankful to my mother, whom she paid handsomely for her trouble, and thanked too. Caroline was left with us, year after year, in this manner, and very dear she was to us all. I called her sister, but no sister I ever had was ever half so much to me. We slept in the same crib, and her fair face and golden curls must have made her look like a little angel, so close to my dark cheek and black straight hair : but no matter, she loved me just the same as if I had been prettier.

" The arrival of Caroline's mother was quite a gay time for us : she brought sweets and nice frocks for the children, and we lived so well while she stayed with us. She promised a Lincolnshire cow for mother, and agreed to hire a rich piece of meadow-land to pasture her on. This was to be done the next summer, when she came again. In this, her last visit to Halesworth, for so it proved to be, she often lamented to my mother the un-kind feeling manifested towards her fatherless babe by her grown-up family. 'She had borne her,' she said, 'at an unusual period of life, and this had made the child unwelcome.' She added 'that she herself feared little Cary would have none of her father's savings ; but she was working hard to save for her.'

"Time passed on, little Caroline was not well. It was midsummer, and the day had been hot, and my mother had put us both to bed in the afternoon, meaning to take us up at supper time. However, Cary was so sound asleep that she would not awaken her. So I had my supper and sat on my mother's knee just opposite the ladder leading to the two little chambers above. Now what I am going to relate may seem as strange to you, ma'am, as it does to me; therefore, I am only about to tell you what was told to me, for I do not remember it, being only five years' old at the time.

"Our house, as I before said, was close to the town, standing quite by itself. It had only one door and no regular staircase, but a ladder leading up to two small chambers, and these chambers had no doors, so that if any one were entering the first room they would be seen on the highest step of the ladder. The only door of the house was shut, because my mother was beginning to take off my clothes while I was on her lap. We were not alone. Two neighbours were with us, when looking up from my mother's knees I suddenly cried out at the top of my voice, 'Caroline's mother is come! Caroline's mother is come!'

"My mother and her neighbours naturally looked to the window which they supposed she had passed, and one opened the door; but no Mrs. Grimshawe was there.

"'Child you must have seen some woman like her pass the window, for you see nobody is here.'

"'Yes, yes, Caroline's mammy is here, for there she stands on the top of the ladder; and now she has gone into the chamber to see Cary,' was my answer.

"My mother and her friends looked up, but no one was there. It was still light, and my positive assertion troubled her. She ran up into the chamber and found the child in a troubled and unquiet sleep. She took her up in her arms and entered the other chamber, looked under the beds and in both the closets, thinking some strange woman had got into the house; but no one was there. She had been at home all day on account of Caroline's indisposition. No one could have entered the house without her knowledge. 'However, there was no accounting,' she said, 'for children;' so after she and the good women had wondered a little the matter was forgotten.

"A few days after this adventure she met an acquaintance who asked her 'what she meant to do with her nurse-child now her mother was dead.'

"She naturally required an explanation; upon which he told her 'he had seen the death of the widow in the newspaper,' who it seems had died of a fever on the road while on her way to Suffolk, the same day on which I had seen her enter the chamber where her child was sleeping.

"You see, Miss Jane," continued the poor blacksmith, "though I have seen a spirit, I do not remember it, nor can I guess why I alone saw that poor widow; but I can fancy that in passing away from the world on her journey to another, the soul of the poor mother might come to visit her orphan little one, to mourn over her who was to be robbed of everything but her undying love. Well she knew too that I was mortal fond of my pretty playfellow, which, perhaps, was the cause why she showed herself alone to me. But the child looked strange when my mother took her up, and her eyes stared as if she had seen a spirit, and she was kinder dull and heavy for some days after her mother's ghost had come to her bedside."

"Well, Copping," asked my sister, "did Caroline's brothers and sisters do justice to the little orphan?"

"No, Miss Jane, they disowned her altogether, as you shall hear; for first the farmer for whom father worked, and then the clergyman, wrote to ask them what they intended to do with the child. They answered by post from Lincolnshire, impudent-like, denying that their mother ever had had such a daughter, declaring that her age rendered the statement incredible.

"My mother was advised to send Caroline to the workhouse; but that she vowed she never would do, since the child whom she had nourished at her own bosom and who had been to her as a daughter, should not be reared in such a place as that.   Besides, her son Sam,' she added, ' was so fond of Caroline that it would break his little heart to part with her.'

"She kept her word, and being too poor to put her nurse-child to school, sent her with me to that free school at Halesworth, where so many poor children have had a good education given them.

"I learned a trade, or rather two, that of a tallow-chandler first, afterwards that of a blacksmith; and Caroline went to service.   She has just lost her kind old mistress, and has come to nurse us both, bringing with her the legacy of ten pounds left her by that good friend, to help us at a pinch."

My sister expressed her wonder that he had not married Caroline; but he replied, " No, Miss Jane, I always thought that she was my sister, and my brotherly feelings never changed towards her, and, indeed, never could.   My mistress * has often been surprised too; but I should have thought it just as bad as marrying my own sister."

* In Suffolk husbands always style their wives Mistress, and good wives call their partners Master.

There is something very beautiful in the kindness of the poor for one another when it is found under circumstances so trying. What could be more generous than the conduct of the impoverished mother of seven children in thus maintaining, educating, and clothing another child not at all related to herself! What a contrast between this tender foster-mother's treatment of the deserted orphan and the sordid, unnatural conduct of her own family! Yet Caroline was a handsome, clever, well-mannered girl, who might have done honour to a higher station than that from which they had excluded her! No doubt the law could have forced them to give up her portion; but her only friend being a poor, unlettered woman she was unjustly robbed of her rights. Poor Caroline had the misfortune, I am told, to get a bad husband, in a Norwich weaver—a sad conclusion to her singular story.

Copping was a good hand at his business, but the removal of a nobleman's racing stud from the village where he lived affected his humble fortunes: several good hands were thrown out of employ, and amongst them our poor blacksmith. He jobbed about from place to place, and, reluctantly enough, worked for Boniface B., a confirmed infidel, who did all he could to turn away from the truth his poor, working hand.   One day the following curious dialogue took place between them.

"As for religious people, I hate them," commenced Boniface.   "Now, Sam, there cannot be a better man than myself," remarked the reprobate master to his wiser foreman.   "Do you know a better, pray ?"

"Why yes, sir, I think I do know some a little better."

"Why, Bor, * I always pays you your wages."

"True, sir ; but then you know I should not work for you unless you did," was Copping's shrewd rejoinder.

"If I am not a good man I do not know what a good man is—Sam, can you say I am a bad man ?"

"Sir, I dare not call you a good one.   You get drunk very often, beat your poor wife, swear, and never go to a place of worship, and drink, smoke, and fight the live-long Sabbath day."

Bonny B. sneered as he made this taunting answer.   "I am not an old Methodist, for that is worse than anything else : besides, if I choose to go to the devil my own way I have a right to do so if I like.   However, Sam, as I said before,

* Bor is used universally in common Suffolk parlance by the working classes, and I believe is the diminutive of neighbor.

I always pays you your wages, and so I think I am a good man."

Well, Copping's very virtuous master, in his own opinion, was soon ruined, and he found employment with a worthy man some miles from home; but times were hard, and he was discharged when work was slack, and was forced to follow agricultural employments, and finally was set to labour on the roads. He came to my sister, and could not help weeping when he told her of his degradation. She advised him "to go to Canada," where his two trades, and some knowledge of rural employments, would soon make him a rich man. She finally overcame the reluctance of his wife, gave him a letter of recommendation to me, and traced out his route by the help of my correspondence with my family. He sold off his furniture, took leave of my sister, with many tears, and found his way up the country to me. He had only one halfpenny in his pocket and a dying child in his arms when he reached me. His wife and little Sarah were, however, in good health, and I soon found a shelter for them, and was only too happy to assist a virtuous Suffolk man from my own neighbourhood : and I shall now be able to show the change effected by coming out to Canada, in the circumstances of an honest, worthy creature, who would have worked industriously at his trade in the old country if, poor fellow, he could have found work to do. I will, therefore, describe the manner in which I settled my sister Jane's *protégé*, when I found a good-hearted, industrious man, always remembering in his prosperity with deep gratitude the painful poverty from which it was my good fortune to rescue him.

Fortunately for Copping, a friend of mine wanted a man and his wife for the remainder of the summer ; so that, at once, I was able to get both of them employment and the use of a small log-house, until such time as they could procure land and build one of their own.

A few days after Copping was settled in his new abode, his youngest child and only boy sickened and died. He had been ailing all the voyage, having been weakly from his birth. The poor father came to me in great distress on the morning of the child's death, and with tears in his eyes told me he had no money to buy a coffin or provide for the funeral expenses.

I told him not to be down-hearted ; for, as the child had been sickly so long, it was a merciful dispensation that the infant sufferer was taken from him. As for the interment, I assured him he need not trouble himself about that, as little

funeral expense was required in the bush. We
soon made a coffin. On the following day our preparations being completed, we carried the child to the
Peterborough grave-yard, followed by the sorrow-
ing emigrant and his surviving family; and I
buried him beside the grave of my own first-born
son, whom I had lost the year before—a circumstance that greatly consoled poor Copping.

Soon after this event I applied for and obtained a lot of land of one hundred and twenty
acres for him, on the same terms as the new
colony of emigrants located in the township of
Dummer : that is, to pay to Government five
shillings an acre, to be paid in five years and
actual settlement. His land was about two miles
above mine, in the township of Douro, where our
travels over our lots furnished us with a series of
adventures; more amusing to me and a friend,
than to our poor Suffolk blacksmith, who had
more good-nature than pluck, and who was ignorant of the toils and hardships of exploring for
land in the bush.

Nothing can really be more bewildering than a
lot of wild land covered with unfelled forests, so
inaptly but usually termed, in Colonial language,
the Bush. To examine and penetrate a lot of
two hundred or more acres, in its original state,

is always an herculean labour, attended with some difficulties, loss of time, and bewilderment. My lately purchased lot and Copping's grant were as yet terra incognitas to us both.

However, I was an experienced backwoodsman, while he, poor fellow, was quite out of his element, being fresh from Suffolk—that garden of East Anglia, with its rich corn tracts and lovely pastures.

Neither Copping nor myself, as I have said, had yet been upon our land ; so it was agreed that we should go up in September and commence a settlement, assisting one another in building shanties, &c. The distance from Peterborough to Copping's location being eleven miles, of which only the first four were cut out, the remaining seven following the upward course of the river, at that time was composed of a dense thicket of pine and cedar, in some places almost impassable.

Upon the 20th day of September, 1831, Copping, a young Englishman of the name of Rowlandson, and myself started on our expedition, each carrying an axe and eighty pounds' weight in blankets, provisions, and other necessaries.

Although the distance, in a straight line, was not so very great, yet, owing to the want of a road, or indeed any track, we were obliged to deviate so often from our course, and had so many times to climb over fallen timber or wade through wet cedar-swamps, that the distance was nearly doubled. Had we only known that good hard wood-land, easy to travel through, lay not more than forty rods from the river, we should have got on much better. But we were afraid of leaving the river, as we had no other guide.

I knew by the diagram of the township that my land came down to the shore of the first lake above the rapids ; but, when within a mile of our desired haven, poor Copping sat himself down on a log and declared he could go no further. Persuasion was useless ; " I am wholly done, sir ! I can't carry that pack another step." He then burst into tears, crying and lamenting his hard fate in this odd way :—" Oh, Master Samewell,* I wish I were home again at Wangfor; † you would not catch me here again, I know." For he was not a strong-minded man, and had a poor constitution by nature.

" Well," said I, " Copping, it is of no use being down-hearted ; that won't get us out of our diffi-

* His Suffolk way of pronouncing Samuel.

† The village of Wangford, in Suffolk, where the poor blacksmith used to live before he came to Canada West.

culties.   You will laugh yourself, by and by, at
these little troubles.   Come, pick up your pack,
and let us proceed.   I know we cannot be very
far from my land.   Besides, the sun will soon be
down, and we have our camp to make, fire-wood to
chop, and a number of other things to do before
dark."

All our arguments, however, proved in vain ;
for, to use Copping's own words, " He was done
—wholly done ;" so at last Rowlandson and I
took compassion on him, and divided his pack
between us, leaving him only his axe to carry,
with which he managed to get along.

Thus doubly weighted, we toiled on till the
bright waters of Kaw-che-wah-noonk Lake glit-
tered before us, in the rosy hues of the setting
sun.   A few rods farther on, a pretty little
stream contributed its scanty tribute to the swift
flowing Otonabee.   Upon a rising knoll of hard
wood, beside this rill, and in full view of the lake
and river, we pitched our camp for the night.

A good supper and a glass of whiskey punch,
in which we drank success to our new location,
put us all into good humour.   Even poor Copping
cheered up ; and, having a good voice, sang us
two or three real old Suffolk ditties, with a suitable drawl at the end of each line.   (By the by,

the blacksmith was a musical genius, and had played the tambourine for years in the Wangford band.)

As this was our first night, and the commencement of a new era in our lives, I served out another glass round ; and now it was proposed that we should name the new possession by some familiar name.

" And soon their native England,
    And Suffolk's verdant vales,
Will seem like dreamy memories,
    Or scenes in fairy tales.

" But brighter hopes shall greet them
    Amidst the pathless wild,
Than e'er on Britain's cultured soil
    For British peasants smiled.

" The hands that wove the useless flowers
    Are called the sheaves to bind,
While golden harvests of their own
    The sons of labour find.

" The children's faces brighten
    Around the evening blaze,
While industry forgets the toils
    Of busy, well-spent days.

" And when, those toils rewarding,
    Broad lands at length they 'll claim,
They 'll call the new possession
    By some familiar name.

" The name beyond all others
    Endeared in grief or mirth,
Of that far distant village
    Which gave *the* exiles birth." *

* Agnes Strickland's " Historic Scenes."

Accordingly, my place was named after the home of my childhood, *Reydon*, the Saxon meaning of which signifies red-hill. This name was equally appropriate for my new settlement, which, half a mile from the river, attains an elevation of seventy or eighty feet above the level of the lake. When the land was first disturbed by the plough, it presented the appearance of a reddish loam, which tint, however, cultivation and exposure to heat and frost have considerably darkened.

Copping's place we called Wangford—the name of the adjoining parish to Reydon.

As soon as it was day-light, we commenced operations in earnest. The work of three axes soon made a clearing in the forest; and, before the end of the week, we had cleared at least a quarter of an acre; chopped and piled the logs for a small house, and had laid the foundation of it. This latter business was attended with considerable difficulty, as we had no road to bring up oxen to draw the logs; but, luckily, we found a sufficient quantity of straight cedars close to where I intended to build my house, which, being only designed for a temporary residence for a year or two, till I could find a better situation, and clear up sufficient land to prevent the danger of fire, was not of very imposing dimensions.

With great labour, and the help of five or six additional hands, who kindly volunteered their services from the settlements, on the last day of the week I was enabled to raise the rough walls of my house.

According to my agreement, the following Monday was fixed upon to find out Copping's lot, and build his shanty. A house was then quite above his means.

His land was back from the lake, so we determined to run a blazed line, as straight as possible, through the woods—only deviating where the nature of the ground made it imperative. Though only two miles and a half, this job took half a day. I had nothing better than a pocket-compass; yet so well did I lay the course, that the road now travelled does not deviate, in any place, its own breadth from the line I ran.

As soon as we found the corner-post of his lot, we followed the concession line across the western boundary of his land, which looked very unpromising; for it was a cedar swamp throughout nearly the entire distance. Poor fellow! he looked ready to cry, and would certainly have turned back in disgust, and given up his land without further inspection, if I had not cheered him by addressing him thus :—

"Come, old fellow, do not be down-hearted : we have only examined one end of the lot, and these cedars are so thick, we cannot see fifty yards in any direction. Let us now strike out an easterly course, which will take us up the length of the lot ; and if we find the swamp continue, we must give it up as a bad bargain, and look out for another location."

However, as I suspected, on changing our route the land continued to rise, and in a few minutes we emerged from the swamp, and had the satisfaction of finding that the remainder of the lot was good. The swamp proved to be only a narrow belt, through which the concession line happened to run the entire length. I mention this little circumstance to show how an inexperienced person may be deceived.

The emigrant should not only examine both concession lines, but also go through the entire lot from east to west ; because it often happens that both lines may be swampy, and all the centre good ; while a few acres of cedar swamp are really desirable, for furnishing rail-timber and building-logs. I therefore consider eighty acres of hard wood timber, out of one hundred, to be a good lot ; that is, provided the soil be equal in quality to the appearance of the timber, which is not

invariably the case.   But only a residence in the
country and sound judgment can detect a de-
viation from the general rule.

We pitched upon a very pretty hill for the site
of the blacksmith's shanty.   A nice little spring-
brook ran round the base of this hill and across
a small alluvial flat—a little meadow of nature's
own making—containing only one tree—a beautiful Butternut—the prettiest, to my mind, of all
Canadian forest-trees.

As soon as the walls of the shanty were up,
we put on the rafters, and split cedar laths to
nail the shingles, which we also completed before
Rowlandson and I left him.

I may as well finish this chapter by concluding
the history of this Suffolk emigrant and his family.

Being a hard-working industrious man, Copping
set up his business—that of a blacksmith—in the
neighbourhood, which enabled him, in a very
short time, to pay the Government the price of
his land.   Soon afterwards, a young Scotch gentleman settled on the adjoining lot, when he made
Copping an offer of £50, for as many acres of uncleared land adjoining his own ; which proposal
was joyfully accepted.   Thus, in the short space
of three years, did the lately-destitute emigrant
and his family find themselves in possession of a

comfortable home. For they had built themselves a good substantial log-house, barn, and suitable out-buildings, and, besides their farm, possessed £50 in hard cash, a horse, a yoke of oxen, and two milch cows, pigs, &c., whilst they still retained twenty-five acres of cleared land, and twenty-five of forest, all free from debt or encumbrance of any kind.

I wonder how long the poor blacksmith might have drudged on at his journeyman's work in England before he could have realized such a sum ?

Some years after his settlement at Douro, the poor man, who was naturally of a weak consti-tution, caught the ship-fever, which had been im-ported by some Irish emigrants, and died, leaving his wife and two little girls well provided for.

We had no clergyman near us then ; so the neighbours collected on the Sabbath afternoon, and we buried the poor Suffolk blacksmith in a secluded spot under the shade of the sugar maple on his own woodland. I read our beautiful church service over the remains of my humble friend. A rude fence of logs was placed round the grave, but they have long since decayed. Nothing now marks the spot but the more luxuriant growth of the wild flowers which wave above his tomb.

His widow married again, and survived him upwards of fifteen years. His eldest daughter married a farmer, " well to do " in the world. The youngest is still single ; but, if report speaks true, is likely soon to become a bride. The farm left by the Suffolk man is much increased in value, and has become the joint property of his two surviving daughters.

CHAPTER XI.

MY HOUSE.—METHOD OF BUILDING AND FLOORING.—MY CHIMNEY.
—UNDERBRUSHING.—MY HERMIT LIFE IN THE WOODS.—NOCTUR-
NAL VISITATION. — AN EXIT IN FLAMES. — I MEET THE POOR
FIEND BY DAYLIGHT.

On my return from locating my *protégé*, Copping, Rowlandson and I busied ourselves in making
our camp a little more comfortable ; for I did not
expect that I could get my log-house completed
before Christmas, if so soon. (I forgot to mention
that the lot of land I was clearing was a frontage
on the river and lake, which I purchased of Government. This was a good bargain, for the soil
is of fine quality, having besides the advantage of
joining that which I had received in exchange
for my Otonabee farm.)

I think it was on the 21st of September when I
commenced operations on my new purchase. I
could not, therefore, reckon on more than two
months' open weather, during which time a great
deal had to be done. The completion of my house,

and the underbrushing of twenty-five acres of land before the snow fell, were amongst some of the most important of these transactions.

I must tell my readers, that settling in the bush now, and twenty years ago, is quite a different affair : at the present time good roads and saw and grist-mills exist in almost every township, which was not the case when I located myself in Douro. There were then neither mills nor factories in my township, nor in the adjoining ones of Smith to the west, or in Dummer to the east, the nearest mill being in Peterborough, ten miles distant. But if it had been twice as near, there was no road or any possibility of drawing up boards or lumber of any sort : so I had nothing better for it than to do as better men had done before me, *viz.* to hew boards out of the solid timber, a work of much difficulty and labour. I shall, however, be minute in giving these particulars of my settlement, because it may prove useful to those emigrants who may, from circumstances, be placed in a similar position.

I remembered once having seen a very respectable partition in a log-house made of planks, split out of a black-ash tree : of course these boards were rough and uneven on the surface.

I thought, however, I could improve upon this

primitive method of manufacturing boards. I selected the cleanest and straightest grained pine-tree I could find, and which was about three feet in diameter. With the assistance of Rowlandson and a cross-cut saw, I cut the cleanest part of the trunk of this tree into logs eight feet in length. I then lined with a black mark one of the ends into planks four inches wide : these I split out of the log with wedges, commencing with the ouside-slab first. It must be borne in mind that all Canadian timber splits best through the centre of the log, with the exception of pine, which splits best the way I have described. The American term is "slabbing," because the timber is split off the log in broad slabs, or planks. A person who understands it will split thick planks in this way with great exactness.

My first attempt at this species of plank-making was very successful, my lumber tolerably straight, and level on the surface ; I however improved it very materially by the following process.

I cut a square notch on the top of two large logs, laid nearly the length of my plank, apart from each other ; I then placed one edge of the plank in the notches, which I wedged firmly. By this method, after lining the upper edge, I was enabled to hew the surface of the plank with my broad axe, and reduce it to the proper thickness. As soon as the surface was smoothed, I struck a straight line on each side of the plank, which I dressed with my axe, thereby forming a square straight edge, easily jointed with the plane.

In this manner did I prepare my flooring and partitions, which for a time answered a very good purpose ; as roof-battens for shingle on narrow cedar boards are easily split. Those I made were six feet long, and varied from four to eight inches in width, and an inch thick.   A board of this length reaches across three rafters.   (The white cedar splits very freely.)   I boarded both ends of my house with planks made in this manner.

The most difficult job I had to do was to build a stone-chimney.   This was a work of time; for I had first to make a large log-canoe to bring the flat building-stone from the shores of the lake and river ; and after they were landed at the nearest place to the house, we had to carry them on hand-barrows upwards of fifty yards.

I might have made what is called a stick-chimney much easier and in half the time ; but I had a serious objection to that plan : firstly, because these chimneys are very likely to catch fire ; and, secondly, in a general way, they do not draw so well, and look more unseemly.   Where good building-stone abounds, I would never advise stick and clay substitutes for the sake of saving a little expense and trouble.

There is another kind of chimney which, I think, answers very well for a shanty, if constructed with cats.* Four upright poles are placed in the corner of the shanty, where the fire-place is intended to be built : these poles are bored with an auger about a foot apart. Rings or steps, like those of a ladder, connect these poles together: a space is left open on the front side of this four-sided ladder from the floor, three feet upwards, leaving sufficient space for the fire-place. The clay-cats are then kneaded strongly round the rings, and all the interstices well filled up ; some well-tempered clay is plastered inside the chimney, which, as the work progresses, soon hardens and reddens inside by the heat of the fire. This kind of chimney draws well, and throws out a great heat.

My chimney was the first piece of stone-work I ever attempted : I took as much interest in the construction of it as a school-boy would have done in building a miniature house. I had a mason's stone-hammer, with which I managed to dress the

* Clay and straw, mixed and made into rolls or squares, and used a good deal by the *habitans*, are called cats.

arch-stones, which though roughly done, were be-viled on scientific principles. When the arch-stones were ready for putting in, I fixed a wooden centre-piece, slightly curved, to support the weight of the arch, which was a span of five feet. To set up the arch, I considered, was the most difficult part of the business; however, I succeeded very well, and had the satisfaction to find that, after the chimney was finished, and the centre-piece supporting the arch burnt-out, every part of the work stood firm: besides, I had the additional pleasure of finding that my chimney drew to per-fection.

It was the middle of November before this needful work was completed. I still had a great deal to do before the house would be habitable; and yet I was obliged to leave it and go with all dili-gence to my underbrushing; for it was necessary to complete this before the depth of the snow-fall should put a stop to further work. The snow is of little consequence, however, when felling the large trees, as they are generally cut three feet from the ground.

As soon as the underbrushing was finished, I hired another man and commenced cutting out a sleigh road to Peterborough. I got some assis-tance in this work from two families who had bought land fronting the river, a few miles nearer the town. I was, however, obliged to give an axe-man twenty-six dollars to finish cutting out the last two miles ; for it was necessary, in consequence of the winter setting in with unusual severity, to hasten the completion of my house, which was still unshingled.

I lived, hermit-like, in the woods, after the renowned example of Robinson Crusoe, passing my time, not unpleasantly, in healthy labour ; building my house and cheering my solitude with the agreeable idea of bringing home my wife and little ones—to a home of my own making.

I had always had a turn for carpentry, which now stood me in more stead than the classical education I had received in England. The cultivated mind, however, will find charms in the rudest wilderness ; and, though Nature was just now my book, I read her ample page with more pleasure for being conversant with the literature of my own and other lands.

Hopefully I worked on, singing with more cheerfulness than skill, and occasionally contemplating my house, as it progressed under my hands, with something like professional pride.

Then the cold weather came on. But, no matter ! A good fire and plenty of stirring work kept me warm, and I remained the denizen of the woods, undeterred by the keen air or the fear of bears and wolves.

Christmas was passed, and I was still an inhabitant of an open slab-hut. I had selected for the site a level spot close by the place where I was building my house. A large black oak, which I had felled, served to form the back of my camp. A pole lashed firmly across two trees, twelve feet apart, and as high as I could reach, formed the front. A row of split slabs, one end resting on the oak and the other supported by the front pole, formed the roof. The ends of my camp were stuffed with hemlock-brush to keep out the wind and rain. My bed was composed of the same material, picked fine and covered with a buffalo robe ; and so, with a roaring fire in front, I feared neither frost, nor snow, nor rain.

It was during my sojourn in this open hut that the following singular adventure befel me.

Reader, did you ever see a ghost ? A tall spectral-looking figure, with large saucer eyes, glides before you; and ere you summon courage to address it, vanishes from your astonished sight ? Well, Canada is no place for ghosts. The country is too new for such gentry. We have no fine, old, ruined castles, crumbling monastic walls, or ivy-clad churches—no shelter here but the wild, wild wood. However, it was no ghost I saw, as you shall hear.

I had occasion to send Rowlandson to Peterborough for a supply of provisions and other necessaries; but owing to the distance I did not expect him back till the next day.

As I had frequently slept in the woods alone, I thought nothing of it. I had been busy shingle-making all day, and continued my occupation until late in the evening. The night was cold and frosty; so I had built up a large fire in front of my camp, laid my shingle-tackle within reach, and I was soon fast asleep.

How long I had slept I know not, when I was suddenly awakened by a sensation of something heavy scraping my breast; and on looking up, what should I behold, but a hideous-looking creature standing over me, with his two fore-paws resting on my breast, a long-flowing white beard, eyes which shone like coals of fire, and a pair of horns which would not have disgraced Old Nick himself; and to tell the truth, my first impression was that the old gentleman had really paid me a visit.

I had, however, no time for reflection—a stamp on the breast soon roused me to action. Seizing hold of the shingle-beetle, I dealt his majesty such a blow on the head, that it sent him straight into the middle of the fire.   His rough, shaggy coat was instantly in a blaze, and uttering the most unearthly yells, he rushed into the woods, and literally vanished from my sight in a flame of fire.

All that I have related happened in less than a minute.   I had no time to be frightened ; but I was certainly much puzzled to know what the beast was, which had paid me such an untimely visit.   At first sight I thought it was the devil himself, but on consideration was satisfied my visitor could not be that terrific personage.

I have heard and read much of his satanic majesty being painted in all colours, but I never heard of his wearing a white beard; and, besides, he did not stand fire well enough for a person brought up in that element, though he certainly had the horns and the cloven foot, and his general appearance was not unlike the pictures I have seen of the gentleman.

Well, the next day cleared up the mystery.   On my road to Peterborough I had to pass the resi-dence of the C——ds, two young gentlemen who had recently settled in the township ; when to my surprise I saw, standing by the road-side, a large billy-goat, whose coat, burnt in large patches all over, explained at once the nature of my nocturnal visitant. It appears that the C——ds had only brought up the goat from the front a few days before. Master Billy had strayed up the road to my place, and although his reception was so warm, it proved to be his first and last visit.

This adventure was certainly a comical one; but I dare say, if all ghosts were as warmly received, they would often be found quite as terrestrial in their nature as my ugly but harmless nocturnal visitor.

CHAPTER XII.

THE WOLVERINE.—MOVE INTO MY NEW HOUSE.—FILIAL PIETY OF
THE IRISH. — UNLUCKY JOURNEY TO PETERBOROUGH. — HOSPI-
TALITY.— ACCIDENT. — IMPROVEMENT IN THE ROAD.— MY NEW
LOCATION.—ARRIVAL OF MY FAMILY.—RAVAGES OF THE CHOLERA.
—A ROUGH CURE. — I AM APPOINTED A COMMISSIONER OF THE
COURT OF REQUESTS.—THE POOR SCOTCHWOMAN AND HER SPIN-
NING-WHEEL.

AFTER the adventure related in the last chapter,
nothing material occurred during the winter,
except the occasional howling of wolves at night,
or the more startling cry of the wolverine.
This animal is very fierce, and often commits
nocturnal depredations in the sheepfolds of the
Canadian farmer. Their skins sell at a price
ranging from five shillings to seven and sixpence,
and are used chiefly in the province for making
ornamental sleigh robes. About four years ago
some settlers in the township of Asphodel chased
one of these animals up a tree, determined to
capture him alive, if possible : none of them had
ever seen a wolverine before, and they were not
aware of the danger they ran in attacking the
beast without fire-arms.

A piece of rope having been procured from the nearest house, one of the party actually undertook to mount the tree, and noose the beast single-handed. The party below cheered him on, but not one man offered to assist him. Nothing daunted, however, our bold adventurer climbed up within eight or nine feet of the animal, who lay crouched in the fork of the tree, only a few branches of which were below the place occupied by the wolverine. On one of these our hero took his stand, and fastening one end of the rope to a branch above his head, and having a slip noose at the other, he prepared to ascend the tree. It seemed to him no very difficult feat to throw the noose over the beast's head ; but in this he was greatly mistaken ; for as soon as he approached the wolverine, the animal appeared determined to resist the invasion of his sanctum. So unmistakable were the symptoms of the intended attack, that the man retreated to his old position. Some of his companions below now suggested the plan of dropping the noose over the creature's head, by means of a forked stick. This plan was immediately put in practice, and luckily succeeded on the first attempt. The moment, however, that the rope touched his neck, uttering a fearful cry, he sprang full at our hero's throat, and so sudden was the attack, that nothing could have saved him, had it not been for the precaution he had taken of tying the other end of the rope to the limb above : had the rope been only one foot longer, his fate would have been sealed to a certainty. As it was, the rope brought up the wolverine with a jerk, and left him hanging from the bough, a sad warning to all nocturnal sheep-stealing depredators.

I saw the skin of this animal, which was a very large one. He must have been a brave fellow who ventured to attack such a formidable beast unarmed, and at the greatest possible disadvantage. As it turned out, he might consider himself very fortunate in escaping uninjured. I much question whether our wolverine-hunter would venture a second attack under similar circumstances.

On new year's day, 1831, I moved into my new house, the dimensions of which were only twenty feet by fourteen : still, it was a paradise compared to the open camp I had just vacated. The walls of my new domicile were neatly hewn, and the interstices between the logs pointed with mortar. A good stone fire-place was placed at one end, capable of burning logs three feet in length, which warmed the house thoroughly, even in the most severe weather.

With the help of Rowlandson I pushed on with my chopping. I had underbrushed twenty-five acres before the snow fell; but owing to my house building I had not been able to chop so much as I could have wished. Under these circumstances I determined to let out some clearing by contract.

John C——, a decent Irishman, whom I had occasionally employed during my residence in Otonabee, was very anxious to raise the sum of ten pounds, to remit home to the old country, to assist his wife's father and family to emigrate to this land of promise. In this emergency I agreed to advance the sum he required, provided he contracted to chop, clear and fence seven acres, ready for sowing fall wheat by the first week in September, at twelve dollars per acre, the balance to be paid him on the completion of his job. To these terms he readily agreed. I must do the Irish emigrants the justice to say that they are more willing to send home pecuniary assistance to their poor relations in Ireland, and so to help them to emigrate, than any other class of settlers.*

* The tide of emigration which has lately taken place from the shores of Ireland, has been deplored by various journals; but I must say that in my opinion we have no cause for regret; as it is well known that the labouring population of Ireland do much better abroad than at home—are more peaceable, contented, and industrious—less bigoted; and not so easily duped by political agitators.

I have known them frequently borrow money, at a heavy rate of interest, for the purpose of remitting it home to their friends—a beautiful trait of national character. These debts of honour are invariably paid by the recipients as soon as they are in a position to do so. I only remember one case of a party being sued to recover an advance so made during the three years I had the honour to sit as a Commissioner of the Court of Requests.

On referring to a useful little pamphlet, by Frederick Widder, Esq., one of the Commissioners of the Canada Company, I find the following note :—

"As illustrative of the success which has attended settlement in Canada, it may be well to mention that in less than seven years from 1844, to the 31st of December, 1850 inclusive, upwards of 77,061*l*. 13*s*. 1*d*. were remitted through the Canada Company by emigrants from the British Isles and Germany, to their friends at home, to bring them out to this province. The largest proportion of this sum has been remitted by Irish emigrants."

Two acres more I let out to a brother-in-law of the aforesaid John C———. The remaining sixteen acres Rowlandson and I ourselves finished chopping by the middle of April.

A good chopper, after the land is underbrushed, will fell the trees and cut them up into fifteen or sixteen foot lengths, and pile the branches into heaps, of an acre of land, on an average, in eight days.   After the brush and tops of the trees are burnt, a yoke of oxen and four men will log or roll up into heaps an acre per day : this latter work in new settlements is mostly done by "bees."*

Early in the spring I built an addition to my house, preparatory to bringing home my wife from her father's, where she had been residing during the winter.

I shall never forget the trouble and time it took to bring up the first load of provisions and other necessaries, along the new cut-out river road.   The distance from Peterborough was barely ten miles ; yet it took my brother-in-law William, Rowland-son, and myself nearly two days to accomplish the journey.   I think, if any of our English friends could have seen us, it would have excited their astonishment in no small degree.

The road, as I before mentioned, was only just cut out, the width not exceeding ten feet, and in some places even less.   It followed the

---

* A Canadian "bee" is a practical example of duty to one's neighbours.   The whole community convene on an appointed day, in order to give help in time of need, which help is repaid in like manner, "*pour l'amour de Dieu.*"

windings of the river the whole way from Peterborough to my place. The creeks were unbridged, and the swamps uncross-wayed. To travel on this beautiful road we had a carriage of a most unique description — one of my own manufacture. Rough as it was, it was the only vehicle that had any chance of going through without breaking down. The wheels were made of two rings, six inches thick, cut off the round trunk of an oak-tree about thirty inches in diameter. Three inch holes were bored in the centre of these rings of oak for the axle-tree. A strong pole, twelve feet long, was morticed into the centre of the axle for the oxen to draw by, and a small box or rack built on the top of the axle-tree, to which it was fastened by some inch and a quarter oak-pins. The front of the rack was fastened with cord to the pole to hinder it tipping up. Our load consisted of a barrel of salt pork, a barrel of flour, a keg of whiskey, groceries, &c.

We left Peterborough about eleven o'clock, and for the first three miles we got on famously, for the road was tolerable, having been cut out and frequented for several years. But as soon as we got into the newly cut road, our troubles began. Every few minutes the axle would catch against the underbrush stumps which had been left insufficiently cleared down. Then we had to stop and cut handspikes, and prize the wheel up high enough for the axle to slip over the obstruction. This annoyance would occur every few minutes; and if we were so fortunate as to get along a few hundred yards without being brought up with a jerk by some stump or stone, we were sure to stick in a mudhole or swamp, instead. Then it was something to hear the shouting and roaring at the unfortunate oxen, and yeo-hoing with our handspikes. In this manner we proceeded at a snail's pace, Rowlandson driving the cattle, whilst William and I marched in the rear, each shouldering a handspike, ready for action.

With all our exertion we were benighted within two miles of my clearing, and directly opposite the shanty of a Scotch gentleman, who had just commenced operations in the bush. Of course we knew we should be welcome, for no one thinks of shutting his doors against benighted travellers in the Canadian bush.

Accordingly we beat up I——'s quarters. He made us extremely welcome, and gave us a hearty supper of pea-soup and shanty cake, and plenty of hot toddy to cheer us after our day's toil.

The little shanty was very much crowded with

the addition to its inmates made by our party.
Indeed, it was hard work for the little Scotch boy,
Watty, to make room for the bed we were to occupy. Amongst other things which he had moved
out of his way was a large iron pot of pea-soup
which he had left on the floor near I—'s bed, who
was then in the act of undressing. Now, whether
it was owing to the darkness of the shanty, or
the obfuscation of the whiskey-toddy, I will not
pretend to say, but somehow or other poor I—
popped his naked foot into the hot pea-soup.

He was naturally a good-natured man ; but the
best-natured fellow in the world under such circumstances would be very apt to fly into a passion and rattle out an oath or two, and our friend
on this occasion was no exception to the general
rule.   Consequently, such a storm fell upon the
head of the luckless Watty, as made me almost
tremble for the poor lad's safety.   What then was
my astonishment to hear Watty say to his master,
the moment he paused for want of breath, " Ae,
mon, but ye 'll ken where you set your fut
anither time."

Watty looked so droll, and said this so coolly,
that we all laughed heartily, in which I— himself joined ; for after all he was more scared than
hurt.   The soup had been some time off the fire,

and, although it made his foot smart, and reddened the skin, it did not raise a blister.

We started early in the morning, and succeeded after much difficulty, in bringing the load in safety to my house.

Such are some of the trials of a bush life. But, after all, what are they compared to bad health and a thousand other ills to which the flesh is heir? Besides, it gives me additional pleasure every time I drive my horses and buggy to Peterborough, to remember that twenty years ago I could scarcely get through on foot, where now I ride and drive with comfort and safety.

The spring of 1832 was an early one for Canada. The snow was all off the ground before the first day of April; and by the first of May the woods had put on "their summer livery of green." This was fortunate for me, because the dry fine weather enabled me to get a spring-burn of five acres, which I logged up in the usual way by a "bee." Part of the land so cleared, I planted with Indian corn and pumpkins, and the rest with potatoes, turnips, and garden stuff,—such as cabbages, carrots, onions, &c. As soon as my spring crops were in, I prepared to remove my family to their new abode. My wife had been recently confined with her third baby, so that I had been obliged to postpone her removal until she should be able to perform the journey on foot; for the road, as yet, was too dangerous and rough either for riding or driving.

My dear Mary had never yet seen my location. All she knew of it had been derived from my description, which I dare say I had drawn in very glowing colours, not sufficiently taking into consideration that the great charm of a new settlement to young men is the abundance of hunting, shooting, and fishing; the latter alone of which women can enjoy.

My location at this time had little attraction to offer to the ardent admirer of natural beauties; for as yet I had not opened my clearing to the lake. Therefore the woods still shut out the beauties of the river, islands, and lake-scenery. Upwards of twenty acres, too, were as yet uncleared, and lay piled in large masses, while the recently burnt fallow, with its blackened stumps and charred rampikes* did not contribute much

---

* It used formerly to be a custom in the new settlements to leave uncut all trees which had lost their heads by the wind or from other causes, because they were not considered to injure the crop more than any other stump, and because they were very apt to be burnt down, especially if dry, thereby saving a great amount of labour. The chopper who contracts to clear land has a right to leave all such headless trees as he can throw his axe over. This custom is much abused, or else the axe-men are stronger in the arm than other people, for a stump forty feet high is not an uncommon sight. Many of these unsightly ornaments are sharpened by the fire—hence the name of rampike.

to improve the landscape. I was, therefore, fearful my wife would be disappointed after the flourishing descriptions I had given of her new home.

Whatever might have been her thoughts, she wisely kept them to herself; she praised everything I had done, and prepared at once to assist me in making the inside of our house as comfortable as possible, which our joint exertions soon accomplished.

In the end of July, or the beginning of August of this year, my sister Catherine, then Mrs. Traill, now so well known as the author of that popular little work the "Backwoods of Canada," and her husband, Lieutenant Traill, emigrated to Canada West. My brother-in-law, William, came up late one evening from his father's house, a distance of eight miles, to tell me that she and her husband had just arrived in Peterborough.

This was the first intelligence I had received of her marriage or emigration. Of course I was delighted at the thought of again seeing my sister, from whom I had been separated so many years; and although I had never attempted the passage of the Otonabee in a bark canoe, so anxious was I to welcome her, that I determined to run the rapids a distance of ten miles by the river. My readers may judge of the rapidity of the current and the heavy swells I had to encounter, when I tell them that the fall in the river between my place and Peterborough, according to the Government survey,* amounted to one hundred and forty-seven feet. My brother-in-law having volunteered to go with me, I was not afraid to encounter the danger, although it was nearly dark when we started. We were both at that time totally unacquainted with the rapids and sunken rocks we had to encounter. The river was then very low, which made the undertaking doubly dangerous; yet, strange to say, we escaped without even injuring the bark of the canoe. Three times, however, we were obliged to go on shore and empty our canoe, which had half filled whilst running down some of the roughest chutes. I have often run the rapids since, both in canoes and upon rafts, and I have found it required a good knowledge of the river to escape the numerous rocks and shoals. However, we providentially escaped all dangers, and arrived safely at Peterborough.

My sister, who had only just recovered from a severe attack of Asiatic cholera, which had laid

---

* This survey was undertaken during the administration of Sir John Colborne, by Messrs. Baird and Rubidge.

her up at Montreal, had already retired for the night; but hearing my voice, she immediately dressed and came down to see me. I need hardly describe the joy of this meeting. Those only can fully comprehend the feeling who have been separated for years from those they love. It was agreed that as soon as possible they should come up to my house, and reside with me until their own house was ready. Fortunately, they were enabled to purchase the lot next to mine, which had a very pretty frontage on the lake. Their journey through the bush, and reception at my house have already been described by my sister in her " Backwoods of Canada."

That dreadful and mysterious disease the cholera, had already made fearful progress in the colony. At Montreal, three thousand of the inhabitants perished out of a population of thirty thousand souls; while in Quebec and Toronto, nearly the same proportion died of this fell disease. In the little town of Peterborough, at that time containing under five hundred inhabitants, twenty-three deaths occurred. But only one case happened in the township of Douro, which was cured, I believe, through my agency. Mr. Sandford, a merchant in Peterborough, had sent up a man to my farm to rake up ashes from the bottoms of log-heaps I had just burnt for the purpose of making potash. This man's name was Robinson. His wife had died a few days before of cholera, with which circumstance I was then unacquainted. He came to me in the afternoon, and said, "Sir, I am sorry to inform you, but I believe I have symptoms of cholera," complaining, at the same time, of cramps in his fingers and great internal relaxation.

I immediately gave him half a tumbler of raw brandy with forty drops of laudanum; put him across the river upon the Smith Town road, and bade him run for his life to Peterborough that he might get medical aid. I told him to persevere as long as he was able, for if he could promote a violent perspiration it would probably save him.

He took my advice, and after running about two miles, the perspiration broke out, and the symptoms immediately abated. He, however, continued to run the whole distance, which exertion, aided by the brandy and laudanum, he confidently believed saved his life.

It is a very curious fact that, although Douro escaped the cholera, a remote corner of the newly settled township of Dummer, immediately in the rear of the former township, was attacked, and eleven persons died from this fatal epidemic. The same circumstance occurred in the township of Otonabee, though not with quite such fatal results.

This fall I was enabled to sow twenty acres of fall wheat, which I had all in the ground by the tenth day of September. My next year's chopping opened my farm so much that I was enabled to select a much better situation for a house, my present one being placed on a ridge of land elevated from thirty to forty feet above the river, having a gentle slope towards the water's edge. I cleared the whole breadth of my land next the river and lake, which opened a pretty view from the house.

One of the first things I did after I moved into my new house was to sow a bed in the garden with apple-pips. This was in 1833, and as soon as the young stocks were large enough, I grafted them with the choicest fruit I could obtain—about one hundred—which I planted out the following year in an orchard to the south of my house. A year or two afterwards, I planted a hundred and fifty trees in a second orchard, north of the house, besides a great variety of plums and greengages. The last apple-trees I set out were seedlings: I waited until they bore fruit, and then selected those trees I disapproved of, for grafting. By these means I have now two capital orchards, which last year gave me upwards of a hundred bushels of as fine fruit as can be produced in the country, amongst which may be enumerated the Ribstone pippin, Newtown pippin, Pearmain, Pomme-de-gris, Pomme-de-neige and many other sorts equally good. As for plums, bushels of them rot upon the ground in an abundant year.

I should advise the emigrant, who becomes an agriculturist, to pay great attention to orchard planting, and, indeed, to devote a portion of his first-cleared fallow for that purpose. The trees should be planted in rows four square rods apart, so that, look at them whichever way you please, they will present a straight row. By this method you will be able to work the land well with the plough, which is essential to the well doing of your orchard.

The young trees should be washed with hot-lime wash, or scrubbed with strong wood-ashlye, or soft-soap, every two or three years, which will prevent canker, and keep the bark bright and clean. Instead of clay for grafting, it is better to use a composition made of bee's-wax, rosin, and grease, put on hot with a brush. The farmer must remember, that whilst he is sleeping his trees are growing, and that, by paying proper attention to his orchard, in a few years he will have an abundance of fruit and cider, which will not only pay him better than any other portion of his farm, but add greatly to its ornament. I do not know any thing that gives a greater air of comfort to a farm, than a well-loaded orchard.

The American settlers, who know the benefit to be derived from a well-stocked and cultivated orchard, invariably plant one the first or second year, taking care to put a good fence round the trees, to protect them from the sheep and cattle. A Yankee could not do well without his "apple-sarce " or pumpkin-pie.

The southern Irish would do well in this matter to take a lesson from brother Jonathan ; for they are, invariably, the last to plant orchards or gardens, or to erect comfortable dwellings, but content themselves for years in the rudest log-shanties, which a pig would almost disdain to live in. There can be no excuse for this : it shows a downright want of energy and proper pride, and I might add laziness. I do not, however, mean to say there are no exceptions, but a disregard to comfort and decency are the general character-istics of the lower orders of the southern Irish.

During the administration of Sir John Colborne, I was appointed one of the new commissioners for holding the Court of Requests for the township of Douro and Dummer, which I continued to hold until the court was abolished, and the Division Court instituted in its place. Under the old Court of Requests, a suit could not be instituted for any sum above ten pounds. The commissioners were generally appointed from the magistracy or from the most influential persons in the division.

The new Division Court is presided over by a district judge, who must be a lawyer; and a sum of fifty pounds can be sued and recovered in this court at the same cost as one of five shillings. This is a great boon to the inhabitants; but it has almost ruined the fraternity of lawyers.

Messrs. Traill, Thompson, and myself used to hold a court once a month for our division. The average number of cases did not exceed fifteen, and the amount sued for seldom exceeded two pounds upon each summons. The commissioners were entitled to one shilling each for every case decided by them. This court was in reality a Court of Equity : not being clogged by the technicalities of the law, we gave our judgment according to the weight of evidence laid before us, without prejudice or partiality.

If we had had a reporter, I dare say some of the cases heard in our court would have been to the full as entertaining as the far-famed Bow-street police reports.   I will give one example.

A poor old Scotchwoman was sued by a carpenter who had made her a spinning-wheel.   The machinery, wheel, &c., being found by the defendant, all the carpenter had to do was to make the stool, and put the parts together so that it would spin.   The plaintiff's bill was six shillings for making the defendant a spinning-wheel.

"What objection have you against paying this account, Mrs. C—— ?"

"Why you ken, your honours, it is no spinning-wheel—for it wunna spin:" here she produced the wheel, and challenged any of the women present to spin a thread if they could.   Several tried their hands without success, therefore it was clearly proved to be no spinning-wheel.   Whereupon, we gave our decision in favour of the defendant, to the great satisfaction of the court, and especially of our female spectators.

CHAPTER XIII.

FALLING STARS.—AURORA BOREALIS. — DAMAGE TO MY HOUSE BY
LIGHTNING.—THE MISTAKE OF A YANKEE CARPENTER.—A BEAST
SAVED AND A JOKE SPOILT.

I THINK it was on the 14th of November, 1833, that I witnessed one of the most splendid spectacles in the world. My wife awoke me between two and three o'clock in the morning to tell me that it lightened incessantly. I immediately arose and looked out of the window, when I was perfectly dazzled by a brilliant display of falling stars. As this extraordinary phenomenon did not disappear, we dressed ourselves and went to the door, where we continued to watch the beautiful shower of fire till after daylight.

These luminous bodies became visible in the zenith, taking the north-east in their descent. Few of them appeared to be less in size than a star of the first magnitude; very many of them seemed larger than Venus. Two of them, in particular, appeared half as large as the moon. I should think, without exaggeration, that several hundreds of these beautiful stars were visible at the same time, all falling in the same direction, and leaving in their wake a long stream of fire. This appearance continued without intermission from the time I got up until after sunrise. No description of mine can give an adequate idea of the magnificence of the scene, which I would not willingly have missed.

This remarkable phenomenon occurred on a clear and frosty night, when the ground was covered with about an inch of snow. Various accounts appeared in the newspapers at the time, as to the origin of this starry shower. It was, however, generally considered that it was not meteoric, since its elevation must have been far above our atmosphere; for these stars were visible on the same night all over the continents of North and South America. Besides, it is a well known fact that more or less of these luminous bodies have been seen on or about the 14th of November, likewise on the 12th of August, provided the weather be clear, than at any other time.

> " ' Oh ! for an angel's mighty wing,
>   To track thy radiant flight,
>   Thou unexplain'd, mysterious thing,
>   That glancest through the night.

" Traveller of paths to man unknown,
    Through boundless fields of air,
  Scarce marked by mortal eyes, ere gone,
    None knows, none guesseth where.

" Comet art thou ? or wandering star
    On thine appointed round ?
  Or seraph in his shining car,
    On some high mission bound ?

" Say, hast thou thine appointed place
    Amidst the starry train,
  Which thou dost through unbounded space,
    Press onward to obtain ?

" Or wilt thou that unwearied course
    Through countless ages run,
  With fresh and unabated force,
    As when 'twas first begun ?

" Meteor or star, whate'er thou art,
    Our purblind race below
  May muse, and dream, and guess in part,
    But ne'er will fully know !

" Weak reason's powers could never reach
    To thy meridian height ;
  Nor science her disciples teach
    To calculate thy flight."*

Among other celestial phenomena witnessed in
this country, I cannot pass over in silence the
splendid appearance of the Aurora Borealis, the
most beautiful displays of which generally take
place in the months of October and November. It

* Agnes Strickland's " Historic Scenes."

is seldom seen during the very severe months, or during very severe weather; but any Aurora I ever witnessed in England will give but a faint idea of the grandeur and gorgeous appearance of this most magnificent of all electric phenomena.

It generally makes its appearance about nine o'clock in the evening. The first indication is a dark cloud or vapour towards the north, a little above the horizon, which, rapidly increasing, forms a vast arch luminous on the upper edge. As soon as the arch has risen to a certain height, it appears to become stationary, and throws off the most splendid coruscations, which rise from the arch to the zenith, filling the northern half of the heavens with a glow of light. These golden streamers dance along with great rapidity, changing their form and colour instantaneously, at times flickering with a pale light, and anon assuming a golden hue, and the form of ranges of vast organ-pipes. I have seen some Auroras, where all the prismatic colours were most vividly and beautifully pourtrayed.

The finest Aurora I ever beheld, occurred a few days before the rebellion broke out. The arch rose nearly to the zenith, and then broke up into detached masses of beautiful colours, amongst which the most conspicuous were green, violet, and red. In a few minutes, streamers of a bright rose-colour radiated from the zenith in every direction, forming a most magnificent canopy. This gorgeous spectacle lasted for nearly three hours, and then gradually faded away.

While I was contemplating this magnificent appearance, my servant, an old Wiltshire man, came up and said,—" Zur, doant you think that be a zine of war? for, I do know, I ze'ed sumat lioke that when I war a boy, and the war did follow directly." I could not help langhing at Bill's belief that this was a supernatural sign of war and bloodshed. It was, however, curious enough that the rebellion in Upper Canada broke out a few days after this singular appearance in the heavens, to the great delight of old Bill, who had prophesied the event.

Thunder-storms in Canada West are of frequent occurrence during the summer season, and are sometimes very violent. Those of the summers of 1837 and 1838 were particularly so. In the July of the latter year my house was struck by the electric fluid, which shattered the whole gable end. I had left a cross-cut saw leaning against the chimney in the garret, which saved the lives of my wife and several members of my family, the lightning splitting the chimney till it came to the saw, which it took as a better conductor, knocking down part of the parlour ceiling in its passage to the earth. My little boy Arthur, who was then a baby in his mother's arms, was stunned by the explosion, and my eldest daughter, who was reading in the open verandah, had her arm burnt ; while her cousin, sitting near her, was burnt on the forehead. The house was filled with soot from the chimneys, and a great many stones were hurled down by the shock. The chains of a pair of scales hanging up in the store-room, were melted and broken into small pieces. Luckily, the saw caused the fluid to leave the chimney ; for, had it continued its course, my wife, her aunt, and several of my children, who were near the fire-place at the time, must have been killed by the descent of the electric fluid.

My house was so shaken by this disaster, that I found it was absolutely necessary either to be at the expense of a thorough repair, or to build a new one. After due consideration I preferred building my present house, which is of frame-work on a stone foundation, being lathed and plastered inside, and rough-cast without. The dimensions of my new house were then thirty-eight feet by twenty-six, to which I afterwards added a wing forty feet by twenty. A verandah, nine feet wide, running along the front and one end, made the house cool and pleasant in summer. In very hot weather we often dined and drank tea in the open verandah in order to enjoy the coolness of the air.

During the time I was building my new house, a lady came up from Peterborough on a visit to my wife, and on that occasion she rode on a small black donkey, which she had brought with her, a few months before, from Ireland.

I had, working with me at this time, a Yankee carpenter who had never seen a donkey before. Soon after the creature had been turned out into the pasturage, I happened to be looking towards the field, when I saw the carpenter creeping along very cautiously, rifle in hand. Supposing that he saw either a bear or deer in the field, I snatched up my gun and ran down towards him. What, however was my surprise, as I drew near, to see him raise his rifle and aim at the unfortunate donkey, when I called out to him,—"Hallo, what are you going to do? you will kill that donkey!"

Luckily the poor beast was partly hidden by an angle of the fence and a quantity of raspberry-bushes, which had caused the man to reserve his fire till he had got a better shot.

" Donkey ! " he ejaculated, slowly lowering his rifle ; " wal, if that don't beat all nature, I do declare.   I swar if I din't think 'twar a bear.   If you han't sung out, I should have let go, that's a fact.   Wal, if ever I saw such a critter ! "

He walked round the critter, as he called it, two or three times, examining the harmless beast with great admiration.   Our poor friend would not have liked losing her donkey, whose long ears ought to have saved him from the tragical consequences of being taken for a bear.   My interference saved her sable steed, and lost the Canadians a good joke, which they would have long enjoyed at brother Jonathan's expense.

CHAPTER XIV.

RAPID INCREASE OF THE BACK-SETTLEMENTS. — DIVISION OF THE
DISTRICT. — DESTRUCTION OF THE BRIDGE. — COLONEL B— AND
HIS REFRACTORY HUMAN STEED.—STRIKE FOR WHISKEY IN THE
MIDDLE OF THE RIVER.—THE POOR TEMPERANCE COLONEL COM-
PELLED TO COME TO TERMS.—PETERBOROUGH.—THE OTONABEE
RIVER.— DESCRIPTION OF THE WESTERN OR BACK LAKES.— SAD
FATE OF A CLERGYMAN.—BEAUTY OF THE SCENERY.— LOVE-SICK
LAKE. — INDIAN LOVER. — KATHARINE O'DONOHUE'S DISDAIN. —
STONY LAKE AND ITS ENVIRONS.—CLEAR LAKE.—PROGRESS OF
PETERBOROUGH.

OUR settlements in the back country, after the
Irish emigration under the Hon. Peter Robinson,
and the Wiltshire emigrants, located in the township of Dummer, under the superintendance of
Lieutenant Rubige, began to increase rapidly.
Peterborough soon doubled its population :
churches, mills, and taverns were erected, and
two small steamers, the Pemedash and Northumberland, plied daily on the waters of the Otonabee,
between Rice Lake and Peterborough. It was
soon found necessary, from the growing importance of the back country, to divide the district

which had hitherto been known as the Newcastle district. When this division took place, the new district was called after our late excellent governor, Sir John Colborne.

To meet the wants of the new district, a court-house and jail were built on a fine rising ground, overlooking the waters of the Otonabee and the town of Peterborough. Nothing can exceed the beauty of the situation, which commands an extensive prospect on all sides. This edifice is built of stone, and cost upwards of eight thousand pounds, which speaks well for the prosperity of the district.

Numbers of small villages have arisen in the different townships, the principal of which are Lindsay in the township of Ops Keane, in Otonabee, Metcalfe in Emily, Norwood in Asphodel, and Warsaw in Dummer.

A town-plot has lately been surveyed, within half-a-mile of my house, to which the name of Lakefield has been given. As it is situated on one of the finest mill-powers on the Otonabee river, at the head of the rapids, it may become a place of some importance, especially as a bridge must ultimately be thrown across the river at this place, to connect the townships of Smith and Douro. At present the town is only in its infancy, consisting of a saw-mill and a few scattered houses. Through the benevolence of my Christian friends in England, I have been able to collect as much money as I hope will build the walls of a church, sufficiently large to accommodate the Christian population of the settlement, which, I hope, will supply the spiritual wants of the village, and become a general blessing to the neighbourhood.

Formerly, there used to be a bridge over the river at this spot, which was raised by public subscription. This was, however, unfortunately destroyed, some years ago, by a large raft of square timber, striking the abutments during an unusually high spring-flood, which carried all before it.

Some years before this bridge was erected, Colonel B——, a gentleman with whom the reader is already acquainted, having heard a great deal of the beauty and capability of this part of the country, and being offered a quantity of land very cheap by an old U. E. Loyalist, was induced by the proprietor to go with him to examine the location. Colonel B——, who was an old man and had a large family to provide for, thinking he might find something to suit them here, immediately consented to accompany the owner to view this *terra incognita.*

Now, it happened that the proprietor, whose name was Bates, was a blacksmith by trade, and a great drinker by inclination : the colonel, on the contrary, was a strong advocate for temperance and temperance societies.

As they had a long bush-road before them, Bates proposed the expediency of carrying a pocket-pistol with them, to refresh them on the way. To this not unreasonable proposition the colonel would not listen, and the poor blacksmith, being out of funds, was compelled to submit to his enforced abstinence, vowing, however, in his own mind, that he would take the change out of the colonel before he had done with him.

They left Peterborough on horseback, and took the newly-cut out river-road, through the township of Smith, which they followed to its termination at John Nelson's clearing, within one mile of the falls at Lakefield, then known by the name of Nelson's Falls, where they left their horses, and proceeded on foot through the woods, by a path beaten by the settlers on their fishing excursions to the falls.

On their arrival at the river, they found that there was no boat or canoe to be obtained, and they had no axe to make a raft, or any means of crossing, unless they could find a ford. This they succeeded in discovering, half-a-mile further up the stream, at the commencement of the Nine Mile rapids. The river in this place is very wide, running swiftly over a bed of limestone, as level as a floor, being at low water not more than knee-deep. Here Bates proposed that they should cross by wading. The colonel, however, who had only just recovered from a violent attack of intermittent fever, durst not attempt the passage.

The blacksmith then volunteered to carry him over on his back. The colonel demurred for some time, being afraid his steed would fall, or get tired, for the distance across was nearly two hundred yards, and he feared it would be too much for his strength.

The blacksmith, however, overcame all the colonel's scruples, by declaring himself quite capable of conveying him over ; so he yielded, and Bates boldly commenced the passage with the colonel mounted on his back. All went on well till they reached the deepest part of the ford, when Bates began roguishly to complain of the colonel's weight, and the following dialogue ensued :—

" I am afraid, your honour, I shall never be able to carry you over ; the current is so strong, and the water deepening at every step."

"For heaven's sake, don't put me down," exclaimed the colonel; "if I get wet it will prove my death."

"It is quite impossible, sir, to go any further," coolly remarked Bates, purposely stumbling, to the great consternation of the colonel.

"Oh, my good fellow, pray mind your footing, or we shall both be down. Cannot you turn round, and go back?" coaxingly urged the rider to his refractory steed.

"I guess not, mister: if I attempt to turn, I shall be swept off my feet by the current, and you would get a taste of the drink to a certainty," rejoined the human horse, adding, "If you han't been so tarnal stiff about the grog, I should have felt as strong as a lion, and could have swum with ye like a duck."

"My good fellow, if you will only get me safe across, I will give you anything in reason."

"Well, colonel, if you will solemnly promise to treat to a gallon of whiskey on our return to Peterborough, I'll do my best to put you safe across and back again," quoth the steed, with a knowing grin, as he turned his head over his shoulder, to observe how his rider took his broad hint.

The colonel groaned.

"It's against my principles to give whiskey, you know."

"And it's equally against mine to go on without," replied the incorrigible toper. "Come, you had better be smart, for you are main heavy, and I am afraid I shall drop you:"——here he gave another lurch.

"Hold on," said the colonel. "I will agree to give you the whiskey;" for bad as a restiff steed might be on land, he considered such an animal far worse in the water.

"On your honour, colonel?"

"On my honour, Mr. Bates!"

The steed, who had thus struck for wages in the midst of the swift-flowing Otonabee, as soon as the necessary preliminaries were settled, became tractable, and bore his terrified rider safely to the shore.

On their return to Peterborough, the colonel honourably paid his debt, to the great satisfaction of Bates, who used often to tell the story as a good joke against my friend. Some time afterwards he sold the land for a very small sum, to the Hon. Zacheus Burnham, the present proprietor, who has laid out the town-plot of Lakefield on the adjoining lot, which property has now become very valuable.

The navigation of the upper lakes commences here, interrupted only by a few short portages. Since it may be interesting to my readers, I shall attempt a short description of this chain of lakes, and the resources of the country through which they flow.

Peterborough is situated at the foot of the first rapids which interrupt the navigation of the Otonabee river. Its future size and prosperity depend not so much on the immediate surrounding country, as upon the timber, mineral, and agricultural resources of the valley of the Otonabee, which is as yet only partially settled. The Otonabee takes its rise out of a small lake, the Indian name of which is Kaskquashibioh. This lake is on the dividing ridge between the waters flowing eastward into the Ottowa, westward into the Huron and Simcoe, and southward into Lake Ontario. For the first hundred miles from its source to Balsam Lake, it flows through an unsurveyed country. Little, therefore, is known of the quality of the land, or its mineral productions, except what can be gathered from the report of Indian traders, who seldom or ever leave the course of the river. From diligent inquiry among these people, and from the report of a friend of mine who had been many miles above Balsam Lake on a trapping expedition, I understand that fine groves of red and white pine are abundant, and that some tracts of good land are to be found near Gull and Lune Lakes. It is generally believed that mineral wealth abounds in this district. I have seen some fine specimens of silver and copper ore, said to have been found in this part of the country.

The river enters the surveyed lands between the townships of Sommerville and Bexley, lying on either side of Balsam Lake, a fine sheet of water abounding in fish. The lands of these townships are not generally good, though some portions of them might be settled : there is how- ever, a great deal of valuable timber which will be available in a few years. Bexley is the small- est and most remote township in the County of Peterborough. Following the course of the lake downwards, the next township on the western shore is Fenelon, the land of which, in the imme- diate vicinity of the lake, is of an indifferent quality, with the exception of South Bay. This township, however, is considered tolerably good, and these parts of it are well settled. Near the east shore of Balsam Lake there is a large island containing upwards of a thousand acres, which is the site of a small Indian village of the Mississauga tribe. The Indians do not, however, appear to like their location, for many have deserted it for the more prosperous villages of Chemong and Rice Lake.

From the head of Balsam Lake to the foot of Kawchewahnoonk Lake, a distance of upwards of eighty miles, the river spreads into a surface, form_ing a number of beautiful lakes, varying from one mile to six in breadth, connected together by narrow straits, called portages, the principal of which are Cameron or Fenelon Falls between Cameron and Sturgeon Lakes, Bobcadgeon between Sturgeon and Pigeon Lakes, Buckhorn and Deer Bay Rapids and the Burleigh Falls. These lakes, or expansions of the Otanabee, water the townships of Verulam, Harvey, Ennismore, Smith, Burleigh, Methuen, Dummer and Douro. The land of several of these townships is of excellent quality, and all are rich in timber and building-stone. Those townships lying on the granite range, viz., Methuen, Burleigh, Harvey, and Sommerville, are known to contain iron ore : fine specimens of copper, silver, and plumbago have also been found. Little of these latter townships is known ; for, with the exception of the settlement on Sandy Lake, in the township of Harvey, which I alluded to in a former chapter, no emigrant has as yet ventured to locate himself in these, comparatively speaking, unknown regions.

This, however, will soon cease to be the case; for already the lumbermen, the hardy pioneers of the more remote townships, are making preparations to commence the work of destruction upon the noble pine forests of Burleigh and Methuen, Messrs. Gilmour and Co. having purchased large tracts of these lands from government solely for the sake of the timber. In another year the sound of three hundred axes will waken the slumbering echoes of the rocky glen and wood-crowned height, where the foot of the white man never trod before.

The first portage, as I before mentioned, occurs between Cameron and Sturgeon Lakes. The river, which is here about eighty yards in width, is precipitated over a lime-stone rock, nearly in the form of a horse-shoe, twenty-six feet in height. Before the construction of the locks and dam at Bobcadgeon, it was said that a person could walk across the river behind the curtain of the falls. Raising the water has destroyed this curious and natural bridge, and taken some feet from the perpendicular height of the falls.

That enterprising and much esteemed gentleman, James Wallis, Esq., of Peterborough, laid out a village, and built grist and saw-mills at this beautiful and romantic spot, where a small church of the Establishment has also been erected, principally owing to the exertions of Messrs. Wallis, Langton, and Dansford, aided by a number of old country gentlemen, settled along the beautiful shores of Sturgeon Lake.

The sad fate of their first minister, the Rev.— Fiddler, threw a sad gloom over the settlement. It appears that the reverend gentleman with two other persons, were endeavouring to bring a large boat into the mill-race above the falls, when from bad management and the height of the river at the time, they missed the mouth of the race, and were precipitated over a dam six feet in height, and then over the main fall into the raging abyss below, where their boat was dashed to pieces, and all three perished.

Sturgeon Lake is a fine sheet of water twelve or thirteen miles in length. Its name is not derived from the quantity of fish of that species it contains—for it has none—but from a supposed resemblance in form to the sturgeon. The river Scugog empties its waters into this lake and several minor streams. The land is of an average quality : the shores are pretty, and rise gradually from the water's edge to a considerable elevation.   This section of the country is at present but thinly settled.

A narrow strait connects Sturgeon with Pigeon Lake.   On an island between these lakes, a dam and locks have been constructed at a considerable cost; but like several other government jobs of the same kind, they have been badly planned and worse executed.

As a proof of this, I need only mention that in excavating the canal and lock at Bobcadgeon Rapids, the best of building-stone was thrown on one side, and the lock built of timber; and it is so ill-constructed that the gates will neither open nor shut, consequently it is useless to the public. The best constructed lock and dam in the county is that at Whitlow's Rapids, a mile below Peterborough.   But though no fault can be found with the workmanship and material, yet the entrance to the lock is planned so badly, that during high water even steamers run the greatest risk of being swept over the dam by the force of the current, a misfortune that actually occurred twice to the Forester steamboat, which on the last occasion sustained considerable damage.

Pigeon Lake is a considerable expanse of water, though less picturesque than any other of the chain.   The small township of Ennismore, chiefly settled by southern Irish, located by the late Hon. Peter Robinson, lies to the south, and the uninhabited township of Harvey on the north. I say uninhabited township; for there are at present only two families residing in it, one at Buckhorn Mills, and the other near Sandy Lake, about five miles apart. This township abounds in valuable groves of pine timber, and, judging from the face of the country, is no doubt rich in mineral wealth.

The shores of Pigeon Lake are for the most part swampy, especially at the mouth of Pigeon Creek. The drowned land has been caused mostly by the construction of the Government dam at Buckhorn Rapids, which has flooded some thousand acres of the low lands, on the borders of the lake.

Buckhorn Lake is a mere continuation of Mud or Chemong Lake, being one of the prongs—as the Indians say of the horn—Deer Bay being the opposite one. The populous and excellent township of Smith forms a long peninsula between the waters of Chemong Lake and the river Otonabee. The Buckhorn saw mills and the Government dam are constructed nearly in the centre of the Buckhorn Lake, where the waters are suddenly contracted within rocky banks scarcely a hundred paces from shore to shore. Over this spot an excellent bridge has been built, connecting the townships of Harvey and Smith. The Government dam at this place raises the water of Upper Buckhorn, Chemong and Pigeon Lakes to the lock at Bobcadgeon sufficiently for the purposes of navigation.

Below the Buckhorn mills the real beauty of this chain of lakes begins. Rapids, waterfalls, islands, rocky promontories and many other fine features make them and Stony Lake the resort of the lovers of the picturesque, and picnic parties in these localities are very frequent.

Lower Buckhorn, Deer Bay, and Love-sick Lake resemble each other in scenery. In fact, for several miles the limestone and granite formations range side by side, as clearly defined as if a line were drawn to separate them.

To the right bold cliffs of limestone rise, having their summits crowned with hard-wood and pine, which lift their umbrageous heads, tree above tree, in almost endless succession. To the left, rough pinnacles of moss-covered granite are seen above the pine-covered heights. The surface of the lake is thickly dotted with islands of red granite, some of which are bare red rock mixed with veins of pure quartz, with here and there a red cedar growing in their deep fissures. Others again are richly clothed to their summits with oak, pine, and maple.

In the autumn the scene is varied by the prospect of fine fields of wild rice, over which clouds of wild fowl are continually hovering. The entrance of Deer Bay, a fine sheet of clear water, is about a mile in width, where it joins Buckhorn Lake, from which it is separated merely by a range of small rocky islands, some of which are well-wooded, whilst others are bare. On either side the entrance of Deer Bay, a bold promontory stands boldly out into the waters of the Buckhorn. These promontories are beautifully adorned with various descriptions of timber from the water's edge. Cliffs, nearly three hundred feet in almost perpendicular height, fairly encircle Deer Bay, excepting at the upper end, where a small stream enters the lake. This precipitous range of limestone continues on the right shore to a short portage called the Deer Bay Rapid, when the limestone formation ceases, and is superseded by granite.

The foot of the upper promontory at the entrance of Deer Bay is the favourite camping-ground of the various hunting and fishing parties who, every fall, resort to these beautiful lakes to enjoy a few days' good sport, or to roam at will

over the delightful islands which everywhere attract the lover of natural scenery. Directly across
the lake opposite to the camping-ground, a fine
stream of water debouches into the lake. This
little river is called Deer Bay creek. About half
a mile up this river there is a singular pool surrounded on every side by high granite rocks
covered with moss, and clothed with red pines
and cedars. On the north side of this basin the
river forces its way through a narrow chasm in
the rock, plunging its impetuous waters over a
ledge of black-looking granite into the pool below,
whose surface is continually agitated by the descending torrent. A corresponding fissure on the
opposite side releases the imprisoned waters which
for several hundred yards flow down the rocky
descent into the more placid waters of the Buckhorn.

One of my most favourite places of resort was
the rocky moss-covered height, directly above the
dark eddying pool I have just described, where,
hid from observation, I used to ensconce myself,
book in hand, with my trusty double-barrelled gun
by my side. Here I have watched for hours
flock after flock of the bright-plumed wood-ducks,
as they swam up and down the eddy, perfectly
unconscious of their danger. Waiting till a suffi-

cient number had collected, I then gave them the contents of both barrels, one while sitting, and the other as they rose from the pool : in this manner I used to kill great numbers. This spot is a favourite haunt of the wood-ducks, who love the solitudes of the quiet pool and wood-embowered stream.

The portage of the Deer Bay Rapids connects the foot of the Buckhorn with Love-sick Lake. I think I hear my female readers exclaim, " Oh ! what a strange name ! surely there must be some story connected with it." And so there is ; and the tale shall be related for the benefit of my fair readers, just as I have heard it.

Some few years ago (for the name is of modern origin) a handsome black-eyed Indian, Richard Fawn, fell desperately in love with a blue-eyed maiden from the Emerald Isle. But Katharine O'Donohue smiled not upon the passion of the red man, the true lord of the soil. It was in vain that he sought her love in the most approved form of Indian courtship. She had no mind to be the inmate of his wigwam, or the manufacturess of mocassins, baskets and brooms. Poor Richard was disconsolate, and retired from the presence of his hard-hearted love—his Irish Barbara Allen— in despair.

Nothing more was heard of our love-sick swain for several days, when at last he was discovered by some of his friends on an island in this lake, nearly dead from hunger and grief. Poor Richard, finding his Irish love remained insensible, gave up his resolution of dying for her, and allowed himself to be comforted by his friends, who, to commemorate his despairing sojourn on the island, called the lake on which it was situated, Love-sick Lake, which name it has ever since retained.

The portage at Deer Bay Rapid is very pretty, and one of the best places for duck-shooting on the lakes. In the fall of the year, and on a windy day, the ducks fly through this pass continually. The sportsman may load and fire as quickly as he pleases. In the evening, when the night-flight commences, it is astonishing to see the number of wild fowl passing this spot on their way from Stony Lake to the great rice-beds at the entrance of Deer Bay and the Buckhorn Lake.

Some sportsmen use mock decoy-ducks made of wood, hollowed out and painted to represent different kinds of wild fowl. The proper way to manage the decoys is to fasten a short piece of cord from one to the other, and a long string from the foremost decoy with a stone tied to the end by way of an anchor. The decoys should be

anchored in the stream either at the head or foot
of a rapid where flocks of ducks are in the habit
of alighting. When the decoys are moved, they
should swim about a foot apart from each other,
and the agitation of the water will make them
bob up and down as naturally as possible, so that
any person, unless previously told, would mistake
them for real ducks.

Flocks of wild fowl flying over these decoys
are deceived, and alight beside them when the
sportsman, who is hid opposite, is generally able
to get a double shot. This is a very good plan
where fowl are plentiful, particularly late in the
autumn, when the fall and winter ducks make
their appearance in immense flocks. The township of Harvey and part of Burleigh lie on the
north side of Buckhorn, and Love-sick Lake and
Smith Town on the south. Love-sick Lake is a
small sheet of water about two miles square; there
are probably from twenty to thirty small islands
scattered on its bosom. In Deer Bay and Buckhorn there must be upwards of a hundred, some
of which contain several acres of land on their
surface, whilst others are composed of masses of
granite in every imaginable shape and form. I
forgot to mention that a mile or so above our old
camping-ground on the south shore of Buckhorn

there is a curious petrifying spring, now called the Victoria spring. It is very copious, and rushes out of the limestone rock at least a hundred feet above the lake. Every substance it touches in its course is covered with a coat of lime: branches of trees, sticks and moss are speedily converted into stone, or rather thickly encased in lime. The water is the coldest I ever drank, even in the heat of summer. Under the cedars which border the stream, the air is quite chilling, and not a musquito or black fly is to be seen within some yards of the brook. Where the creek runs into the lake, and for some distance from the shore, the bottom is white with the lime deposits. As soon as Love-sick Lake is crossed, you enter a wide river-channel full of granite islands. Following the course of the stream, you come to the Upper Stony Lake portage, where a fall of five or six feet occurs across both channels of the river, which is here divided by a small island, over which the canoes must be carried for a distance of about thirty yards. Two hundred yards below this portage a second perpendicular fall and portage similar to the last occurs—with this difference, that the island is much higher and the portage much longer. The third and final portage is about the same distance as the last : here the canoes must be again carried over a high granite rock to the shores of Stony Lake to avoid the Burleigh Falls, twenty-six feet in height. From the summit of this portage-rock a delightful view is obtained of Stony Lake, with its thousand islands, wooded hills and rugged rocks. To the west are the rapids and cascades you have just passed. On the left you hear the roar of the Great Burleigh or Peninsula Falls ; to the right, the Little Burleigh plunges its broken waters into the deep lake beneath.

The Burleigh Falls are well worth seeing. The Otonabee here forces a passage by four narrow channels through a barrier of granite, which skirts the western shores of Stony or Salmon-Trout Lake. Two thirds of the waters of the Otonabee are forced through the narrow chasm of the Great Burleigh, by a descent of twenty-six feet into the deep blue waters of the bay, which, during the spring and fall floods, cause a heavy swell on the lake in the immediate vicinity of the falls. So many eddies and whirlpools are formed in the bay, by the descending torrent, as to make the navigation dangerous for the passing canoe without a skilful steersman.

Viewed from Stony Lake, the landscape is one of remarkable beauty. The four cascades foaming

and tumbling into the bay through the lofty walls
of granite, overarched by the rich foliage of the
dwarf oak, the more lofty pine, and the gnarled
branches of the red cedar, whose roots are seen
firmly fixed in the deep fissures of the overhanging rocks, present a picture whose varied features
are not easily described.

The best fishing in Stony Lake is to be found
at the foot of these water-falls, especially in the
month of October, when vast quantities of fine
salmon-trout are caught by the trolling-line, and
bass-bait, maskonongé, black-bass, and white-fish
also abound, besides many other varieties.

I encamped on an island near the Great Burleigh for a few days in October 1849, when, one
morning, between breakfast- and dinner-time, my
two eldest sons and myself caught, with our
trolling-lines, thirty-five salmon-trout, eight
maskinongé, and several large lake bass, the total
weight of which amounted to 473 pounds.

The black-bass, which is a very delicious fish,
not unlike the sole in flavour, can be taken
readily with the rod and line or by trolling.
The best kinds of ground-bait are worms, craw-
fish, gallinippers, a small green frog, or a minnow;
for trolling, a mouse made of musk rat-fur, a red
and white rag, or the skin of the head and neck

of the red-headed woodpecker. The black-bass bites freely, and weighs from one pound to four ; the lake bass from three to seven.

Stony Lake, including Clear Lake, which is only separated from it by a range of lofty granite islands, is, from east to west, twenty miles in length, by an average breadth of two miles and a half. Besides several deep bays, it indents the shores of Burleigh, and one of large extent on the Dummer side, called Gilchrist's Bay, from the upper end of which a short canal has been cut through a ridge of rocks, into White Lake, to increase the waters of the Indian River, for the benefit of mill-owners in Dummer, Douro, and Otonabee.

About a mile and a quarter from Burleigh Rapids, is a precipitous rock, upwards of two hundred feet above the lake. Nearly at the foot of this rock, and elevated between sixty and seventy feet above Stony Lake, is a small sheet of water, containing about fifty acres, called by the Indians Deer Lake. Three years ago a pic-nic party encamped on the borders of this lake, when the ladies, delighted with its lovely situation and singular beauty, gave it the name of Fairy Lake, which it has ever since retained.

From the circumstance of its level being so

much higher than the waters of Stony Lake, from which it is only separated by a granite cliff not more than one hundred and fifty paces broad, and from its being surrounded on every side by high rocks of the most fantastic shapes, I conclude it to be of plutonic origin. It resembles, indeed, the crater of some extinct volcano, only that I have not detected lava or scoriæ in its vicinity. Indeed, I am inclined to think that the whole granite formation of the shores and islands of Lower Buckhorn, Love-sick, and Stony Lakes, has been under the influence of subterranean fires, and has been torn and scattered by tremendous earthquakes. My reason for supposing this is, that I observed, when sailing through some of the narrow channels between the islands of these lakes, the formation was so exact, that had it been possible to have brought the opposite cliffs together, they would have fitted each other, which makes me conclude that they must, some time or another, have been rent asunder by the agency of some terrific convulsion of nature.

Stony Lake is seen to the best advantage from the top of Hurricane Point, and Eagle Mount :— it is difficult to say which is the more beautiful. Eagle Mount is the highest point of an island nearly in the centre of the lake, containing, probably, an area of thirty acres. The landing-place is on the north side, where the rock slopes gently to the water's edge. Some parts of this island are finely wooded, whilst others display bare rock, only covered in places with moss. The south side of the island is very precipitous, and, I should think, nearly four hundred feet above the lake. From the highest pinnacle, called Eagle Mount, the view is, beyond all comparison, the finest I ever saw. The whole expanse of Stony Lake, with its many hundred islands, the bold richly-wooded shores of Burleigh, Methuen, and Dummer, and the glittering waters of Clear Lake, are all spread, like a map, before you. In the fall of the year, when the woods have assumed their gorgeous livery, nothing can exceed the magnificence of the scenery.

I have now described the main western waters of the Otonabee. From the eastward, Stony Lake receives two considerable streams, Eel's Creek and Jack's Creek. The former rises in the unsurveyed lands, nearly ∗one hundred miles to the north of Stony Lake. It is an impetuous stream, full of rapids and waterfalls, and half a mile from its mouth the navigation is interrupted by a succession of cascades. A mile further up, Jack's Creek empties its waters into the lake by a splendid fall of at least twenty feet in descent. This creek takes its rise out of a large sheet of water, called Jack's Lake. The Indians have a portage ten miles long, from the waters of Stony Lake to Jack's. About midway between the two, there is a very high hill, supposed to be the loftiest land in the county, being little less than a thousand feet above the waters of the lake. From the summit of this mountain nine lakes can be seen, and a sea of woods, only bounded by the horizon. All this part of the country is still unsettled, and little is known of its capabilities for settlement.

Report speaks indifferently of the lands in this section of the county ; however, extensive groves of red and white pine, are known to exist, and vast quantities of iron ore, particularly in Marmora and Belmont. I have seen some fine specimens of copper from the latter township. My brother-in-law, Mr. John Reid, the county engineer, assured me, that when running lines in Belmont, he often was obliged to use pickets instead of his compass, on account of the local attraction of vast masses of subterranean iron, which he almost everywhere met with.

Gentlemen who are travelling through Canada, either for pleasure or information, should certainly visit this chain of lakes, and I will venture to say they will be highly gratified, particularly if they select the latter end of September for their excursion, for at that season of the year the weather is generally fine, the foliage of the trees being dressed in their brightest hues. Fish and game are plentiful, and the temperature is delightful.

Clear Lake, as I before observed, is only parted from Stony Lake by a line of granite islands, after passing which the limestone recommences, and with it the good land and the settlements. Smith bounds Clear Lake to the south-west, and Douro to the north-east, for a distance of five miles. This is a fine sheet of water, without an island or rice-bed on its surface. The shores are bold and thickly wooded, the only natural curiosity being the battery, a high limestone terrace, or indeed a succession of natural terraces, on the Douro side and near the foot of the lake. Viewed from the water, it presents the appearance of a well-laid wall of masonry, composed of layers of stone varying from ten inches to thirty, which are as straight as if they had been cut with the chisel. I should think this vast quarry of grey limestone exceeds eighty feet in perpendicular height, and better building-stone cannot be found.

A river, or strait, half a mile in length, connects Clear Lake with Kawchewahnoonk Lake. The first dam across the river since leaving Buckhorn Mills occurs here, which has raised the waters of Clear and Stony Lakes at least five feet above their ordinary level. A saw and grist mill has been built on this spot by Messrs. Patrick and Matthew Young.

Below the Mills the river again spreads its waters into a narrow lake, seldom exceeding three quarters of a mile in width, studded here and there with pretty islands richly wooded. The settlements become more frequent as you advance : rafts of timber destined for Quebec, sawn lumber for New York, the skiff and the canoe, enliven the scene, and prove that you are once more within the pale of civilization and the haunts of the white man. This lake, or expansion of the river, is called by the Indians Kawchewahnoonk. At the foot of this lake, and just where the Nine Mile rapids commence, my farm is situated.

Seven years ago, immediately below my farm, my brother-in-law and myself constructed a dam across the Otonabee river, opposite the village of Lakefield. We built it on a new principle, and were our own engineers. The work has stood the spring-floods well, although the river is subject to a perpendicular rise of six feet. A few yards below the dam, we erected a saw-mill, which is in full operation, and is calculated to cut logs from one foot to four in diameter, and up to twenty-six feet in length.

The river from Lakefield is only navigable for rafts and lumber, though sometimes a bark canoe, or skiff, ventures to run the rapids ; but no person should attempt it, unless he is acquainted with the river, and a good canoeman. The distance to Peterborough is about nine miles, and the fall in the river, according to Beard and Rubidge's survey, one hundred and forty-seven feet. There are dams across the Otonabee, within half a mile of one another above Peterborough, for mill-purposes. At Peterborough the rapids cease, and two steamers ply daily from thence to Gore's, landing on Rice Lake.

I have endeavoured to show, by tracing the waters of the Otonabee from their source to the Rice Lake, that the town of Peterborough from its situation must be the outlet of all the produce of this vast rear-country, and that the lumbering trade alone must add greatly to its prosperity. Last year, upwards of one million feet of square timber passed through Peterborough on its way to Quebec. The principal lumber men on these waters are Messrs. Gilmour and Co., Charles Perry and John Gilchrist, Esqs.

Peterborough already exports, yearly, a great quantity of picked boards and deals to the state of New York, and some thousand barrels of superfine flour to Montreal, and these branches of commerce are daily increasing. A railroad alone is wanting to ensure the prosperity of this thriving town, but which will doubtless follow the march of civilization in due order.

CHAPTER XV.

VISIT TO THE FALLS OF NIAGARA. — TRAGICAL RECOLLECTIONS OF THE LOCALITY. — BATTLE OF LUNDY'S LANE. — GALLANT CONDUCT OF YOUNG BURNHAM AND HIS COMPANIONS.

My active life, during the period of my engagements with the Canada Company, and the multiplicity of my avocations on my own farm, prevented me from beholding the grandest object not only in the Canadas, but on the whole earth.   In fact, I wanted to see what water could do in the exemplification of the finest cataract in the world, where it is certain that the hand of the Omnipotent has produced one of the noblest works of creative power.

Business having called me to Toronto, I determined, before returning home, to visit the celebrated Falls of Niagara.   Accordingly, I took my passage in the Magnet steamer, and landed at the town of Niagara in time for the stage.   The morning had been fine, but towards night a drizzling rain commenced, which continued without intermission till daylight the next morning.   Luckily,

the stage was a covered one, and my fellow-travellers were two clever intelligent persons, bound
on the same errand as myself. One of them was
an English gentleman, who had come the whole
distance from his native land purposely to see
the Falls : his companion was an officer on leave
from his regiment quartered at Halifax. Of course
we could talk of nothing else but the great Niagara,
whose mighty thunderings we could distinctly hear
in the distance.

The night was excessively dark : not a breath of
wind stirred the chestnut and hickory trees which
skirted the road ; not a sound broke the stillness
of the night, save the sullen roar of the cataract.
Owing to the darkness of the night we did not
expect to see the Falls before daylight the next
morning. Judge then of our surprise and pleasure
when the sudden turn of the road revealed to our
astonished gaze " The thunder of waters," as the
word " Niagara" signifies in the Indian tongue.

The first sight of the falling sheet of water I
shall never forget. The milky whiteness of the
cataract contrasted so strongly with the surrounding darkness, that it became distinctly visible, so
that the Falls did not appear a hundred yards
from us, when in reality we were then more than
half a mile distant from them.

We put up at the Pavilion Hotel, within a few yards of the table-rock—indeed, one of the garden-walks opened upon it.   This magnificent hotel, one of the largest in Canada, was burnt to the ground shortly after I quitted its roof. Being un-acquainted with the locality, I did not deem it prudent to venture near the edge of the precipice upon so dark a night ; accordingly, being rather fatigued, I retired early to rest, determining to rise early and make the most of my time during the following day, as I was unable to prolong my visit.

I therefore went to bed, but not to sleep, for the incessant thunder of the Falls, and the shak-ing of the windows and doors by the concus-sion of the air, made that impossible.   Long be-fore sunrise I had taken my station on the table-rock, lost in admiration of the grandeur and sublimity of the scene.   Looking up the river, sheets of foam, tumbling cascades, and white-crested breakers, hurrying onwards—ever onwards—to the vast cauldron below, meet the eye of the spectator, filling his mind with astonishment and awe.   But what is this to the scene beneath the great curtain of green waters, falling—ever falling—wave upon wave in endless succession, till time shall be no more !

Misty clouds rise from the boiling deep, while

bright rainbows span the river. The more we gaze the more grand and magnificent does the scene appear. Who can behold the mighty Niagara and say "there is no God," or forget Him " Who hath measured the waters in the hollow of His hand, and meted out heaven with a span, and comprehended the dust of the earth in a measure, and weighed the mountains in scales, and the hills in a balance ? "

The height of the Falls has been variously estimated : recent accounts make the perpendicular, Canadian, or Great Horse-shoe Fall, 157 feet; and that on the American side 161 feet. The width of the great Fall from Goat Island to the Canadian shore is 1,200 feet in a straight line. By following the curve made by the Falls the breadth is about a third more.

Goat Island divides the Horse-shoe from the American fall, which is 600 feet wide. Over this channel the Americans have constructed a bridge which connects Goat Island with the American shore. There is a third cataract, called the Scoloper Fall, which does not exceed 100 feet in width : it divides Goat Island, over which also a bridge has been erected. The total width of the cataracts, including Goat Island and following the edge of the precipice, will be little less than three quarters of a mile.

Close to the Canadian shore the rock over which the waters of the Great Fall are precipitated, considerably overhangs its base ; consequently, the curtain of the descending waters is thrown some distance from the foot of the rock, forming a sort of cavern, which has often been explored by the adventurous as far as Termination Rock, a distance, I was told, of 120 feet.   This cavity receives its only light through the mighty mass of water descending in front, which appears brilliantly green. The effect of this, I am assured, is very beautiful.

Crossing the ferry, near the Clifden Hotel, a steep flight of stairs conducts you to the upper edge of the American Fall.   Following the course of the river upwards for a short distance, you cross the bridge to Goat Island, a beautiful spot covered with fine trees, which have been judiciously thinned, and walks have been made to the best points from which the river and Falls may be viewed to the greatest advantage.

All the smooth-barked trees on this island are carved with the names of visitors to the Falls, as high from the ground as a person can reach, amounting to many thousands. The effect is very curious.

The views from many parts of Goat Island are excessively fine. I give the preference to that looking upwards from the head of the island. Some prefer the prospect from the tower, which is built on a rock some 50 or 60 feet from the north shore of the island, nearly on the edge of the great Fall. To gain the tower the adventurer must cross planks thrown from rock to rock, between which the water rushes with impetuous haste to take the final leap.

From the top of this tower you see the river for a mile above you, covered with white-crested breakers. At your very feet the heavy mass of waters descends into the abyss below with a mighty roar, which makes the very rocks tremble beneath your feet. Two or three years since a suspension-bridge was thrown across the river a short distance below the Falls. I have been informed that the view from this bridge is unequalled. When the wind is blowing in a right direction, the thunder of the cataract can be heard at a great distance. I have myself heard it at Niagara, a distance of twelve miles. The spray or vapour from this immense body of falling water, when the sun is shining and the atmosphere clear, can be seen at a vast distance. I have seen it distinctly from the highlands ten miles east of Toronto. The distance, in a straight line across the lake, could not be less than 60 miles. It appeared in the distance, from the reflection of the sun, like a pillar of fire.*

The Falls of Niagara, besides their natural interest, possess a remarkable political one, for they form a part of the barrier between the rival dominions of two vast nations, which the magnificent arm of Omnipotence has planted ; for the Niagara river forms the boundary line between Canada West and the United States, and the Americans claim their portion in this stupendous miracle of nature.

Niagara has its recollections, its records, its tragedies.   Twenty Indians† plunged into its raging vortex to escape the tortures of their

* " The accumulated waters flowing from four mighty lakes and all their tributaries, after being for two miles agitated like a sea by rapids, come to a precipitous rock, where they pour down their whole mass in one tremendous plunge of 160 feet high.   The noise, tumult, and rapidity of this falling sea, the rolling clouds of foam, the vast volumes of vapour which rise into the air, the brilliancy and variety of the tints, and the beautiful rainbows which span the abyss, the lofty banks and immense woods, which surround this wonderful scene, have been considered by experienced travellers as eclipsing every similar phenomenon.   The noise resembles that caused by the discharge of a thousand pieces of ordnance ; and is heard, and the clouds of vapours seen, at the distance or thirty or forty miles.   The Fall, called the Crescent or Horse-shoe, descends in a mighty sea-green wave; the other, broken by rocks into foam, resembles a sheet of molten silver."--The Encyclopædia of Geography.

† Ottawa Indians, pursued by the Iroquois.

enemies.   Hemmed in on every side, no other alternative remained but this act of desperation.
One survived the daring plunge, the remaining
nineteen escaped death in a more agonizing form.

In the last American War the environs of the
Falls were the scene of a sanguinary engagement,*
when the thunders of battle were mingled with
the thunders of the waters† in one vast magnificent
chorus.

The destruction of the Caroline was one of the
most magnificent spectacles ever witnessed, to
which the anticipated political results must have
given additional interest, though fortunately
they did not follow in the shape of war.   Those
who saw the flaming ship illuminating the country and lighting up the Falls, over which the
irresistible force of one of the greatest powers of
nature was impelling her, describe the scene as
one of unequalled sublimity.   The night was in-
tensely dark, yet every surrounding object was
distinctly visible in the wild glare caused by the
" Caroline," as she rushed into the thundering
abyss below.

* The Battle of Lundy's Lane.
† " The Indian name signifies the thunder of waters : it is not
pronounced in the manner we are accustomed to, but thus—
O-ni-au-gea-rah."—Sir F. Head.

Many accidents have occurred by canoes and boats having been carried past the mouth of the river Welland—or Chippewa Creek, as it is more commonly called. This river empties its waters into the Niagara river, at the village of Chippewa, about one mile and a half above the Great Horseshoe Fall. A few hundred yards below the entrance to the Chippewa Creek, the waters of the Niagara river attain a fearful velocity, which continually increases as it approaches the dreadful gulf. At first it runs smoothly but swiftly, till, gathering strength and meeting rocks and inequalities in the bottom, it breaks into cascades and foaming waves, leaping and contending together in wild and indescribable confusion. The descent between the first ruffle caused by the rapids and the Great Fall is upwards of 70 feet. From the upper point of Goat Island nothing can be grander than the scene, for from thence the spectator beholds the whole mass of the descending waters, rushing downwards in full career against the rocky island, upon which he is stationed, with seeming force enough to drive islands and rocks into the boiling gulf below. Small is the chance of escape for the crew of any bark unfortunate enough to pass the friendly harbour of the Welland, few ever escaping the certain death

awaiting them at the termination of their awful
voyage.   It was near this spot that an incident
of most exciting and overpowering interest took
place last year.

Just below the harbour of the Welland, a small
boat was lying moored in apparent security, when
two little boys, animated by the adventurous
spirit, not uncommon in creatures of their age
and sex, unmoored the skiff, and getting into her
launched away, awake only to the enjoyment of
their voyage, and utterly unconscious of their
peril.   An instant previously, these infants had
been seen by their mother sporting on the shore.
She looked for them again, but they were
gone — were hurrying to the rapids.   Her cry
thrilled every ear, but her wild impulse was
checked; stronger arms than hers retained her
firmly, and stopped the despairing effort of maternal love, which prompted her to save her children or perish with them.   Her screams vibrated
many a manly heart, but the endeavour seemed
too utterly hopeless even for pity to attempt or
courage to achieve.   One young gallant breast was
more compassionate, or more brave.   He believed
that the innocent, unconscious children could be
rescued.   His humanity nerved his will, but he
knew that, unless he could find minds noble and

generous as his own, the effort he meditated must
be made in vain. He asked for companions in his
daring voyage, and he found them in two youths,
like himself scarcely out of childhood, who ran
with him to the shore, and, unmooring another
boat, embarked together on the wild waters, and
rowed with desperate strength to overtake the
children before they reached the rapids. God,
who had inspired the noble impulse, was with the
generous three,—they gained the other boat, and
as it rushed forward to destruction caught the
infants and left the skiff to its fate. But though
their first object was attained, they had yet to
accomplish what no mortal hand had then achieved
—they had to turn the bow of the boat in an
oblique direction, and ascend the mighty current,
which they must effect, or lose their own lives as
well as those of the children whom they had just
rescued from destruction. We may imagine the
cool, energetic courage of Burnham and his gallant
mates, and how their efforts were watched by
numerous spectators from the shore, and by her
eyes who had seen with wild maternal hopes and
fears her children taken into the boat, and how,
while all despaired, the heart of a mother hoped
and prayed, and believed that God would yet save
the frail ark which contained her treasures and

their generous preservers. He did hear them.—He nerved the arms of the young rowers, and well and skilfully they stemmed the current, and made the shore, bringing back the infant fugitives to the sacred sanctuary of a mother's arms. What are the blood-stained laurels of the greatest conqueror the world ever saw,—what his achievements, to the holy victory won over the rushing waters by these noble young victors in the cause of humanity !

I am sorry that I cannot remember the names of Burnham's companions. His own was familiar to me from my having formerly known his father during my residence at Goderich, and I am happy to record this touching memorial of his brave and heroic son. Nature has her own order of nobility, and this gallant trio, of which young Burnham was the leader, hold a high place in her ranks.

Among the annals of the sublime frontier of British North America, many interesting facts may be quoted—many gallant actions recited ; but none of which a Briton may be so justly proud as the heroic enterprise I have just cited with genuine national pride.

CHAPTER XVI.

THE REBELLION OF 1837. — MARCH TO PETERBOROUGH. — THE
RELIEF OF TORONTO.—RETURN OF THE VOLUNTEERS TO THEIR
HOMES.—INCORPORATED BATTALIONS.—MILITIA TRAINING.—BAD
CONSEQUENCES OF THE REBELLION.—GOOD EFFECTS OF COUNTY
COUNCILS.—TOWNSHIP COUNCILS.—MUNICIPALITIES.—NECESSITY
OF RAILROADS.—LUMBER TRADE.—LUMBER SHANTIES AND LUM-
BER-MEN.—TIMBER-JAMBS.—TOM BURKE'S REMARKARLE ESCAPE.

I HAD been a resident in Douro about five years,
when an event of vast importance in the history
of Canada occurred, which threatened the dis-
memberment of the colony from the parent country, and involved the immersion of both Provinces
in anarchy and civil war.

For several years preceding the rebellion of
1837-8, the country had been agitated by the in-
flammatory speeches and writings of William Lyon
Mackenzie and his political coadjutors.   Little
danger, however, was apprehended either from
them or their writings, especially by the loyal
inhabitants of the counties of Northumberland
and Peterborough, who were completely taken
by surprise on hearing that a body of rebels,

headed by William Lyon Mackenzie, were actually in arms and on their march to invest Toronto. The fall of 1837 was the most open season I ever remember in Canada ; as a proof of which I may mention, that on the 4th of December of that year, I was working in my orchard, guiding a yoke of oxen, and holding the plough myself, for fear the young trees should be injured.

A snow-storm came on that evening about four o'clock, but I continued to work till dark in spite of the snow, for I was anxious to finish the job before the ground closed.   I was just unyoking my oxen, when a near neighbour of mine, Mr. James Caddy, the son of the late Colonel Caddy, of the Royal Artillery, came up to me with a printed paper, which he placed in my hands, informing me, at the same time, of the out-break of the rebellion, and that all the volunteers who could be mustered must march for Toronto as early as possible in the morning, under the command of Captain Cowel, formerly of the 1st Royals.   The paper, indeed, contained the proclamation of Sir Francis Bond Head, calling upon the loyal militia of Upper Canada to assist him in putting down the rebellion.

Having made an arrangement with young Caddy to meet me at ten o'clock the same evening, I commenced immediately my preparations for the campaign, by cleaning up my double-barrelled gun, and running a quantity of balls. I had little time for taking leave of my family before my young friend made his appearance, similarly equipped; and, in spite of the snow-storm and lateness of the hour, we instantly began our journey to Peterborough on foot, only halting at my father-in-law's house for a few hours' rest.

The next morning, accompanied by my brother-in-law and several other gentlemen who had joined us during the night, we attended the rendezvous and enrolled ourselves in the band of Peterborough Volunteers. At this very time I held the commission of a lieutenant in the 2d Regiment of Durham Militia; but as the distance prevented me from joining them at once, I thought it best in the meantime to march with the volunteers.

At eleven o'clock A.M., everything being in readiness, we got the order to march, which was received with the most enthusiastic cheering, both by the volunteers and the inhabitants, who escorted us out of town, bidding us "God speed in the good cause." Thus, within twenty-four hours from the reception of the Governor's proclamation did a fine body of nearly four hundred well-armed and well equipped volunteers, leave Peterborough to assist in putting down rebellion, and upholding the cause of legality and order.

The loyal Militia of Canada West, I fear, would have been less active, could they ever have imagined that the Rebels they were then called upon to put down, would, at the close of the Rebellion, have been compensated for the losses they had themselves occasioned. That the men who had disgraced themselves by the murder of the gallant Moodie, Hume, Wear, and Usher, were not only to be allowed to return to the country they had outraged and invaded, but to receive honour and emolument at the expense of the really loyal inhabitants,—the true bulwarks of the British Crown —was a turn of policy which it is not easy to appreciate.

Who, indeed, would have supposed, that the devoted loyalists of Upper Canada were to be trampled under foot for the sake of conciliating invaders and anarchists—men who have no real sympathy for anything truly British—who are only quiet as long as it suits their purpose ; and who will,most probably, upon the first opportunity agitate for annexation to the United States of America ?

At Port Hope we were joined by the 2d battalion of the Northumberland Militia, under the

command of Colonel M'Donnell, and the 4th Northumberland, under Colonel Brown : these two
battalions left Peterborough the day after the volunteers. We found several other bands of loyalists already assembled in Port Hope, which swelled
our little army to upwards of a thousand men.

Many and contradictory had been the reports
which reached us—every hour brought different
intelligence. The first news was, that Toronto was
burnt and the loyalists in full retreat ; that seven
thousand "patriots," as they styled themselves,
were assembled at the Rush Hill to intercept the
Militia marching to the relief of Toronto ; and
various reports of the same kind, which only served
to inflame the ardour of our little band, who were
anxious for the coming fray. Judge, then, of our
astonishment when our Colonel received a des-
patch, accompanied by a proclamation from Governor Head, informing us of the action at Montgomery's Tavern—Gallows-hill, as it is generally
called—and the dispersion of the rebels; thanking
us, at the same time, for our loyalty and devotion, and permitting us to return to our homes
and families.

Of course, the news of the dispersion of the
rebels was received with great cheering along the
whole line ; though the well-deserved epithet of

" cowardly rascals," was freely bestowed upon Mackenzie's rabble army by men who wished to fight, yet found their services were no longer required.

On our return to Peterborough the volunteers were again in request, and received orders to march to the rear townships of Ops and Mariposa, to intimidate the disaffected in those townships, and intercept some of the rebel leaders who, it was supposed, had escaped in that direction. The country was found perfectly quiet, and the volunteers once more returned to the comforts of their homes.

On Mackenzie's occupation of Navy Island, every colonel of a Militia regiment was ordered to send up to head-quarters a draft of men, in order to form a number of incorporated battalions for active service. The men required were to be drafted by ballot, unless sufficient volunteers offered their services.

The 4th Northumberland regiment, under the command of Colonel Brown, volunteered almost to a man. About three hundred and fifty of the youngest and most able-bodied were selected, a number considerably more than the quota required. I had just received my commission as a captain in this Militia regiment; consequently I had the command of forty-five fine fellows from my own

township of Douro.   The distance from Peterborough to Toronto by the road is something like
100 miles.   The roads were almost impassable,
owing to the openness of the weather ; indeed,
there was no sleighing till the beginning of February, a circumstance almost unprecedented in a
Canadian winter. Our march to Toronto occupied
six days, during which nothing material occurred,
with the exception of our taking charge of a few
prisoners, delivered us by the magistrates, all of
whom we safely lodged in Toronto jail.   In the
course of three weeks the greater part of our
men volunteered into the Queen's Own, one of the
incorporated battalions, under the command of
Colonel Kingsmill, when I again returned home,
but was soon after appointed to a commission in
the 7th Provisional battalion, which was stationed
at Peterborough, and in which I continued to
serve for six months, until the battalion was disbanded in May, 1839.

The chief grievances complained of by Mackenzie and his adherents were, the domination of
the family compact, the clergy reserves, and the bad
management in the land-granting department —
besides a long list of petty grievances. That reform
was much needed there can be little doubt ; but
there was nothing to warrant open rebellion.   Few

countries on the face of the earth had less to complain of than the Canadas—no tithes, no poorlaw, no game-licenses, and a mere nominal tax for a county-rate, half of which was expended on roads and bridges, to the great benefit of the country.

In the townships the inhabitants had the privilege of nominating their town-clerk, collectors, assessors, and road-surveyors, or path-masters. The reformers were not contented with this state of things. Nothing less would satisfy them than universal suffrage, vote by ballot, and a responsible Government.

Sir Francis Bond Head has been much blamed by some for his withdrawal of the troops from Toronto in the very face of rebellion. In answer to this charge, he says " he felt perfectly satisfied that he could depend on the loyalty and courage of the Militia," and in this, at least, he was not disappointed.

It must be owned, however, that had Mackenzie marched at once boldly against Toronto, before the arrival of the Militia, the consequence might have been much more serious. I must refer my readers to Sir Francis Bond Head's account of the rebellion for his opinion, and the reasons upon which it was grounded. It is not my intention to enter into any history of the rebellion, which has already been ably handled by the brave veteran Colonel Fitzgibbon, to whose courage and vigilance Toronto eventually owed her preservation from fire and sack. Lieutenant Colonel Sir Richard H. Bonnycastle, Royal Engineers, and Sir James Edward Alexander, have recently embodied much historical information on the war in a book entitled " Canada as it Was, Is, and May Be."

In 1847 a new Militia Bill was prepared, and passed the House of Assembly. It is very defective and will, most probably, be amended. According to the provisions of the bill, all able-bodied men, from sixteen to sixty, are compelled to enrol their names at least twenty days before general training, which all men from sixteen to forty must attend, on the twenty-eighth day of June, yearly.

The Militia regiments were then reorganized and all vacancies filled up. In the county of Peterborough, the 2nd and 4th Northumberland were united, and called the Peterborough regiment. It was composed of seven battalions, each battalion being commanded by a lieutenant-colonel.

The township of Douro and half the township of Dummer form the 2nd battalion of the Peterborough regiment, of which I have the honour to be major. The Militia officers receive no pay, unless called upon for actual service, when they are put on the same footing as officers of the line.

Under the present law the Militia training is apt to excite the ridicule of regular soldiers. After an hour or two of hard work, when you have at length succeeded in forming your men into line, the appearance they make would agonize a martinet. Let my military readers fancy seven or eight hundred men, of all heights and sizes from four feet six to six feet four, clad in white linen coats, black coats, blue coats, grey coats, and some, indeed, with no coats at all; while straw hats, black hats, cloth caps, Scotch caps, or the *bonnet rouge*, form their various head-coverings, and you have a slight picture of the figure and appearance of the men on a training day. However, Napoleon would have thought nothing of the dress and everything of the men, and as for our loyalty and activity they at least will pass muster.

Much good is, doubtless, effected by this general muster and enrolment. Every Militia-man knows his company and who are his officers, and his obligation to join his battalion in time of need.

It is well known with what alacrity these men turned out on the very first appearance of danger in 1837, and how nobly they performed their duty has now become a matter of history ; those who formed the provisional battalion, at the time they were disbanded, were little inferior, indeed, in discipline, to regiments of the Line.

For a long time the Upper Province suffered from the effects of the Rebellion ; money was everywhere scarce, and the value of land much depreciated.

The formation of county councils, though much condemned at the time, must now be admitted to have done more to promote the prosperity of the country and satisfy the people, than any other measure that could have been adopted. These councils have the entire management of all local affairs connected with the county. They have the power of taxing absentee lands to a certain extent, of laying on the county-rate school-tax, and every thing connected with education, and the appointment of all county officers, with the exception of the High Sheriff, Judge of the District, Court and County Registrar.

Three years ago a considerable alteration took place in Canadian affairs by the formation of township councils. Under the new Act each township, containing a certain number of rateable inhabitants (I believe three hundred), becomes a municipality.* The municipality consists of five councillors, who elect one of their number as chairman, and he becomes the reeve and chief magis-

* MUNICIPAL CORPORATIONS, UPPER CANADA.

Acts 12 Vic. cap. 81. " The Upper Canada Municipal Corporations Act of 1849, 13 and 14 Vic. cap. 64."

" The Upper Canada Municipal Corporations' Law Amendment Act of 1850," and 14 and 15 Vic. cap. 100, " The Upper Canada Municipal Corporation Law Amendment Act of 1851."

The Municipalities under these Acts have discretionary powers of taxation for promoting public improvement within their respective circuits.

There are — 1st. Township Municipalities ; 2nd. County Municipalities ; 3rd. Police Villages ; 4th. Incorporated Villages ; 5th. Incorporated Towns ; 6th. Incorporated Cities.

The qualifications of Electors and Candidates are fixed by the Acts, and ascertained from the collector's rolls of the previous year.

MUNICIPAL ELECTIONS.

The elections take place in each Municipality in the first Monday in January for the choice in—

Townships or union of townships, five councillors for each. When divided into rural wards, one councillor is chosen for each of the five wards in the township or union :

Incorporated villages, five councillors for each :

Towns, three councillors for each ward ;

Cities, two aldermen and two councillors for each ward.

In police villages the elections take place on the second Monday in January, for the choice of three police trustees.

QUALIFICATIONS OF MUNICIPAL VOTERS.

The qualification of voters are for—

Townships,—freeholders, and householders of the township or ward entered on the roll for rateable, real property, in their own right or that of their wives, as proprietors or tenants, and resident at the time in the township or ward :

trate for the year. If there are five hundred householders and freeholders in the township, the council may elect a deputy-reeve, who with the

Police villages,—same as for townships :

Incorporated villages,—freeholders, and householders of the village entered on the roll, for rateable real property, in their own names, or that of their wives, as proprietors or tenants to the amount of 3*l.* per annum or upwards, and resident at the time in the village.   The property-qualification of village-voters may be partly freehold and partly household :

Towns,—freeholders and householders of each ward entered on the roll for rateable real property, held in their own name, or that of their wives as proprietors or tenants, to the amount of 5*l.* per annum or upwards, and resident at the time in the ward.   The property qualification of town voters may consist partly of freehold and partly of leasehold :

Cities,—freeholders, and householders of the ward entered on the roll, for rateable real property, held in their own names or that of their wives as proprietors or tenants to the amount of 8*l.* per annum or upwards, and resident at the time in the ward or its liberties :

Counties,—the several township, village, and town councils in each county, choose their reeves, and deputy reeves where the population admits of it, and these form the county council.

Qualifications of Municipal Councillors.

The qualifications are as follow :—

A township councillor must be a freeholder or householder of the township or ward ; seised or possessed of real property, in his own right, or that of his wife, as proprietor or tenant rated on the roll in case of a freeholder, for 100*l.* or upwards ; and in case of a householder, for 200*l.* or upwards.

A police trustee must be entered on the village roll, for rateable property, in his own right or that of his wife as proprietor or tenant for 100*l.* :

Village councillor must be a freeholder or householder of the village, seised or possessed of real property, in his own right or

reeve has seats in the county council, where they represent the interests of the township municipalities.

The township councils have the appointment of all township officers for the year, the appropriation of all money-grants for roads and bridges belonging to the municipality, and they can levy rates for purposes of improvement, and can borrow money or lend, can sue and be sued, and have

that of his wife as proprietor or tenant rated on the roll, in case of a freeholder for 10l. per annum or upwards ; and in case of a householder for 20l. per annum or upwards. The property qualifications of village councillors may be partly freehold and partly leasehold :

A town councillor must be a freeholder or householder of the town, seised or possessed of real property, in his own right or that of his wife as proprietor or tenant rated on the rolls of the town : in the case of a freeholder, to the amount of 20l. per annum or upwards, or in the case of a householder to the amount of 40l. per annum or upwards. The property qualification of town councillors may be partly freehold and partly leasehold.

A city alderman must be a freeholder or householder of the city, seised or possessed of real property, in his own right or the right of his wife as proprietor or tenant rated on the roll of the city. In the case of a freeholder to the amount of 40l. per annum, and in the case of a householder to the amount of 80l. per annum and upwards.

City councillor must be a freeholder or householder of the city, seised or possessed of real property in his own right or that of his wife as proprietor or tenant rated on the rolls of the city : in the case of a freeholder to the amount of 20l. per annum or upwards, and in the case of a householder to the amount of 40l. per annum and upwards.

A special qualification is attached to aldermen and councillors

the jurisdiction over all property belonging to the township. Townships may be divided into five wards, each ward returning a councillor : this, however, rests on the will of the inhabitants as to the division into wards.

In well-settled townships, or towns, the new municipal act works well, but is certainly much more expensive to the inhabitants. In my opinion, it would have been much better to have in-

generally, that each must be seised or possessed to his own use or that of his wife, of the real property for which he shall be assessed either in fee or freehold, or for a term of one year or upwards, situate within the village, or town, or city, or the liberties thereof, for which they may be the candidates respectively.

FIRST MEETINGS OF MUNICIPALITIES.

Township councils are held on the second Monday after the elections, to choose from among the councillors a town reeve ; and where there are five hundred resident freeholders and householders on the collector's roll of the township a deputy town reeve for the year.

County councils are composed of reeves and deputy reeves of townships, towns, and villages in each county on the fourth Monday in January. They choose from among the reeves a county warden for the year.

A village council,—on the second Monday after the election, to choose from among the council a town reeve, and in certain cases a deputy town reeve, the same as in townships.

A town council,—on the second Monday next after the election, to choose from among the councillors a mayor for the year, also a town reeve, and where the numbers on the roll admit of it, a deputy town reeve, the same as in townships and villages. A city council,—on the second Monday after the election, to choose from among the aldermen a mayor for the year. — Scobie's " Almanack Canada West for 1852."

creased the township representation to the County-Council, instead of forming so many additional municipalities.

The lowness of the qualification (100*l.* on the assessment-roll), tempts many persons, who are totally unfit for office, to offer themselves as candidates for municipal honours. I really think a mental qualification is far more necessary ; in proof of which I need only state, that in a municipality not one hundred miles from Peterborough, two councillors were returned, one of whom could neither read nor write, whilst the other could write his name, but could not read it after it was written : surely such persons are not fit to represent the interests of a community. The sending of a few such persons to the county council, consisting of thirty or more members, would not matter much, for they would have little power to do mischief; but in a township-council, consisting of only five members, if two of them should prove to be so illiterate, it might become a serious matter. The county councils at present consist of a warden, clerk of the council, who in some county-councils is also the county-treasurer; and they also include the reeves and deputy-reeves from all the towns and townships in the county. In 1851 the Peterborough county council contained fifteen members, of whom I had the honour to make one, having been returned as reeve for the township of Douro.

Notwithstanding some defects, the municipal councils have worked well, and have been the means of greatly increasing the prosperity of the country, chiefly by causing good leading roads and bridges to be constructed through their respective counties. The people in general have no objection to be taxed for public works, provided they have the control of the expenditure through their representatives. The erection of towns and counties into municipal corporations has done much to satisfy the people; only give them rail-roads, so that they may be able to keep pace with the Americans, and I feel confident there will be little dread of separation from the mother-country, or annexation to the United States.

The time has now arrived for the construction of rail-roads in Canada. The only question is, in what direction they should be carried. Those who live on the frontier along the shores of the great Lakes, of course think the most desirable route would be in their locality, while they who reside in the rear township, advocate the formation of a line of road from some point on the Georgian Bay, in Lake Huron, through the back settlements to Prescot, on the St. Lawrence. The supporters of this road contend that the lumber-trade alone would support this line, besides opening a vast country for settlement; and that it would be much the shortest route for the great western trade of Huron, Michegan, and Superior. This is a vast country, and has immense resources, though hitherto our chief treasures have been locked up. For want of means of transportation, immense forests of pine and oak timber, not in the immediate vicinity of water, have been destroyed by fire, for the purpose of getting rid of what the settler considered a nuisance. Beautiful trees of the wild cherry, butternut, black walnut, and bird's-eye-maple, have shared the same fate, or have been split into rails for fencing purposes. If, however, by the construction of railroads, this valuable timber could be exported, either in log or sawn up into planks and boards, it would add greatly to the prosperity of the country, for the timber would become of more real value than the land; so that what before was nothing but a nuisance, and cost money and labour to get rid of, would become a real source of wealth.

Much might be said, with equal propriety, of the mineral wealth of the country, which at present cannot be made available on account of the difficulty of transport.

A friend of mine, engaged very extensively in the lumber-trade, called upon me a few days before I left Canada for my long-intended visit to England. In the course of conversation he said, "should you have any opportunity of conversing with persons connected with, or interested in, the lumber-trade, you, who know so well, ought to explain to them the great loss and very wasteful manner in which the white-pine timber is prepared for exportation under the present system." As I have had little opportunity of mentioning this subject, which I consider of some importance both to the lumber-merchant and the consumer, I shall devote a portion of this chapter to the purpose of explaining it ; hoping that it may meet the eye of those interested in the trade.

Under the present system, all white-pine timber intended for exportation, excepting masts and spars, is squared by gangs of lumbermen in the woods. Now, it is a well known fact, that to square a stick of pine timber, especially if it be at all tapering, a very large proportion of the clear stuff must of necessity be hewn off. For proof of this I need only adduce a fact which every saw-miller in Canada is well aware of ; namely, that in white

pine, the clearest stuff and freest from knots, is
that part of the timber which joins the sap-wood.
In a saw-mill, the best boards are those cut on
the outsides of the log, while reducing it to the
square.　On a saw-log, twelve feet long and three
feet in diameter, at least ten good clear boards,
averaging sixteen feet each, will be obtained,
which, by the present system, is blocked off and
left in the woods.　But this calculation is
under the mark ; because the square timber
got out for exportation is generally in very
long lengths, and as the pine-tree tapers considerably, the butt-end of the tree must nearly
double the diameter of the top ; so that it follows, as a matter of course, that to reduce the
tree to the same square, the whole length of
the stick, nearly one-fourth of the timber—and
that the most valuable part—is left in the forest.
To obviate this difficulty, I would propose to hew
the timber octagonally, instead of squaring it, as
heretofore, merely cutting off the sap-wood ; by
which means a great saving of both timber and
labour would be effected.

Nearly all the best pine has disappeared from
the settled parts of the country—at least, all
within a reasonable distance of water-communi-
cation.　Every year the lumbermen must pene-

trate further back to obtain the necessary supplies for exportation. As no other country but Oregon can ever compete with Canada in the article of white-pine timber, and as that country is so far distant from England, Canada as yet need fear no competition from that quarter. As there is an increasing demand for sawn lumber of this description in the United States' market, white-pine will most probably maintain a price sufficiently high to warrant the lumberman penetrating into the innermost recesses of the most distant Canadian forests.

It is very different, however, with the red or Norway pine of Canada, the alteration of the duties in England having almost destroyed our commerce in that article. I give in a note below[*] a comparative statement of the export of lumber

* EXPORTS OF TIMBER FROM CANADA, BY SEA, FROM 1845 TO 1851.

	1851.	1850.	1849.	1848.	1847.	1846.	1845.
White Pine, feet . .	15228120	13040520	11621920	10709680	9626640	14392320	15828880
Red Pine, do. . .	2774240	3586840	4076600	4865560	4460880	5206040	5182320
Oak, do. . .		1116240	1123320	879040	1806080	1742680	1307440
Elm, do. . .		1026640	1413600	1171760	1591520	1793320	1423920
Ash, do. . .		47280	66600	59680	91040	188960	207080
Birch, do. . .		180290	134120	92360	108560	147880	183360
Staves, Standard M.		1265	1324	1163	990	979	1407
Do. Puncheon M.		2792	2495	1721	1740	2203	3652
Do. Barrel . .		107	114	159	100	273	652
Deals, Pine, pieces .		2207086	2282390	2485010	} 3399520	{ 2081260	{ 3002015
Do. Spruce, do. .		614277	618881	361881		386807	527259
Tamarac, feet . .		36600	146000	125468	1372420	771489	
Lathwood, cords . .		4423	3432	3849	4218	5007	

Scobie's " Toronto Almanack," for 1852.

during the last seven seasons, by which it will plainly appear that there is a fall in the exportations of those articles in which Norway and other countries compete with us. However, the tables of export will, fortunately for us, display a large increase in the exportation of that article which no country now produces but Canada; namely, white-pine timber.

It is both curious and amusing to visit a lumber-shanty during the season of operation, especially at the time of drawing the timber to the nearest lake or river, when the different gangs of men are all at work.

The workmen are divided into gangs. A gang of men cut down the trees, taking care to throw small trees, called bedding timbers, across the path the tree will fall, for the purpose of keeping it from freezing to the ground or endangering the edge of the workmen's axes against stones or earth. This plan has another advantage, for in the deep snow it greatly facilitates the loading of the timber. As soon as the tree is felled, a person, called a liner, rosses * and lines the tree on each side, and the axe-men cut the top of the

* Taking off the bark a few inches in width along the entire length of the trunk on the space that is to be lined, so that the black mark may be more distinctly seen by the scorers.

tree off, at the length determined on by the liner: they also square the butt-end of the stick, leaving a sort of rough tenon with a mortice-hole through it at both ends of the timber, which are made on purpose to pass the withes through when rafting them. The tree is now ready for the hewer's gang, which generally consists of the hewer and three, or at most four, axe-men, all of whom stand on the prostrate trunk of the tree, except the hewer.

One man then cuts a row of notches as deep into the side of the tree as the line-mark will allow, or nearly so, between two and three feet apart ; a second splits the blocks off between the notches ; and the third scores the rough surface, taking care not to cut too deep. The hewer then follows with his broad axe, and cleans off all the inequalities left by the scorers.

A second gang, similar to the first, only one axeman less, now take possession of the tree, which has been already squared on its two sides by the first gang. The tree is now turned down upon one of its hewn faces, measured off, and lined on both outside edges ; and the same process is gone through, as before described, which finishes the operation of " making," as the lumber men term squaring the timber.

The very straightest and best trees, if large enough, are felled for masts, which must not be less than seventy feet in length when dressed; but the longer they are, the better and more valuable — eighty, ninety, and even one hundred feet being not at all uncommon. Great care must be taken in felling these trees by preparing plenty of bedding timbers for them to fall on; for any sudden irregularity on the surface of the ground might cause the top to break off too low down, and thus spoil a valuable stick of timber.

All the preparation requisite for making masts in the woods is to peel off the bark, carefully dressing off with the axe any inequalities or knots there may be on the trunk. In squaring the butt-end, a large mortice—or grub-hole as it is termed—must be left to pass the chain through to draw the mast. The great trouble, however, is to get such immense trees to the water, especially if the snow be very deep. In the first place, a road must be cut through the forest at least twenty feet wide, and as straight as possible; for it is impossible to make a short turn with a stick of timber from seventy to a hundred feet in length. High hills, however, must be avoided; but, generally speaking, the land descends towards the water, and masts are seldom brought from any great distance inland on account of their great weight.

A large-sized mast, after being loaded on a bob sleigh, * requires from twelve to sixteen span of horses or oxen to draw it, besides a number of men who follow with handspikes, and who assist in starting the timber in case of any stoppage occurring. It is really an amusing sight to see one of these huge trees in motion, drivers of all nations shouting to their teams in their respective dialects, the whipping, shouting, and scolding composing a complete Babel of sound. The great difficulty is to get the tree into motion, and this can only be done by starting all the teams to-together, not a very easy task with such a long string of cattle.

As soon as the waters are sufficiently high in the spring for floating the timber, it is rolled from the bank into the river. Then commence the most dangerous and arduous duties of the lumberman. Extensive jambs of timber are often formed on shallow bars, or at the heads of islands or sunken rocks. I have seen jambs of squared timber and masts piled twenty feet high by the force of the current, and many yards in length.

* A term given by lumbermen for a short strong-built sleigh, made purposely for drawing timber and masts.

The lumberman encounters no small danger in breaking these jambs, which can only be done by one party of men going upon the jamb with hand-spikes, while another party work a windlass on the shore, from which a rope is fastened to the timber on the jamb. Sometimes, when least expected, the whole body of timber will suddenly move off, tearing, and grinding, and driving everything before its irresistible force.

The lumbermen, on the first move of the jamb, make for the shore or their canoes, leaping from one stick of timber to another, and woe unto him who misses his footing and falls amongst the rolling timbers, the chance of his escape from being either crushed or drowned is small indeed. Scarcely a year passes without accidents of this kind occurring.

A few years ago a neighbour of mine, an Irishman, one Tom Burke, had a wonderful escape from this double peril. He was assisting, with a number of others, to break a jamb of square timber at the head of Hely's Falls, on the River Trent : he was on the jamb with his handspike, trying to loosen the timber, when the stick he was standing upon suddenly moved off, and by the jerk he was thrown into the rapids. He had only just time to seize hold of one of the floating timbers, when he was hurried down the raging falls. The chances against the poor fellow were a thousand to one ; yet, strange as it may appear, he escaped almost without injury : luckily for him the stick to which he clung, by drifting into an eddy at the foot of the falls, enabled him to swim ashore. To the astonishment of his companions, he had sustained no injuries beyond some bruises and slight abrasions of skin on his breast and one knee, caused by his touching the rocks in his passage down the falls.

The French *habitans* make the best shanty-men : they are more cheerful and less likely to fight and quarrel, notwithstanding their evil propensities of card-playing and cock-fighting. I had heard such very bad accounts of the lumbermen that I quite dreaded their coming into the township; however, I must do them the justice to say, that although large bodies of them have been lumbering close around me for the last four or five years, I have received nothing but civility at their hands; nor has a single application for a summons, or warrant, against them been made to me in my magisterial capacity.

The lumber-shanties are large, warm, and comfortable. Standing-bed berths are constructed on the two sides and one end of the building, similar to those on board ship : the door is at the unoccupied end : the raised hearth, or fire-place, ten or twelve feet long, occupies the centre of the shanty, and is kept burning night and day, which effectually keeps out all cold.

The food provided for the men consists of fat barrelled pork and beef pea-soup, and plenty of good bread, potatoes, and turnips. Tea, sugar, onions, or other luxuries, must be provided at their own expense.

The dress consists generally of Canadian grey cloth trowsers, a flannel shirt, or coarse Guernsey frock, and a blouse made of fustian, or a blanket coat fastened round the waist with a red or tri-coloured sash. Shoe-packs, a species of mocassin peculiar to the Lower Province, cow-hide boots, and a *bonnet rouge* for the head, complete the costume of the Canadian lumberman.

CHAPTER XVII.

DOMESTIC MANUFACTURES. — THE COLONIST A MAN OF MANY
TRADES. — SHOE-MAKING. — HOME-MANUFACTURED SOAP AND
CANDLES.—YARN-DYEING.—WEAVING.—KNITTING.—CARPETS.

In a great and populous country the division
of labour is the source of its wealth—a fact displayed by our first and greatest writer on political
economy, Adam Smith, whose original genius developed a secret hitherto hidden from general
observation. He also showed that colonies, before they attain a certain standard of civilization,
do not realize this wealth, because the labour of the
colonist of necessity embraces a variety of trades.
But, in course of time, a gradual increase of population makes it more profitable for him to fix upon
that one which his own skill, or the fact of its
being in greater demand, calls on him to practise
solely, the profit from which allows him to purchase, with his gains, the articles he had hitherto been compelled to manufacture himself, at
the cost of much labour, under very disadvanta-
geous circumstances.

Canada is at present in a sort of intermediate state. In the remote settlements where there are few towns, and those very distant, the backwoodsman must still practise a variety of trades which even money cannot procure, unless a store or general shop be at least within twenty or thirty miles. In the neighbourhood of towns some necessaries can, as in England, be purchased with the proceeds of the settler's industry.

Individual labour in the infant state of the colony was the usual order of things in Canada; for the towns of the western province were so remote, that a distant and dangerous journey had frequently to be accomplished before a man could have a pair of shoes made or mended for him. When we consider the roughness of the roads, or the necessity of traversing the trackless forest, we may be sure that if a man met with an accident to his shoes he must, in such a state of things, either mend them himself or go barefoot. Necessity is said to be the mother of invention; and the industrious officer who, having become a backwoodsman, determined to learn the art of cobbling, feeling sure he should be no worse for the acquirement, and that his shoes would be a great deal better, was not wanting in wisdom. He purchased the necessary tools and materials, and soon became so expert as a *mender*, that after a time he was inspired with the laudable ambition of *making* a pair of shoes. Now it is a certain fact, that if a gentleman or lady choose to learn any mechanical art, they become really more expert than less educated persons, because they exercise their reasoning powers upon that point, and bring them to bear upon it with a certain force, originating from the lofty principle of overcoming every difficulty lying in their way ; the subjection of their will to meet an existing necessity being, perhaps, the first and most laborious trial, to which the rest is trifling in comparison.

I have seen gentlemen who had served their country honourably in the army or navy, making their own and their children's shoes, of an evening, after the labours of the day were over, looking contented and even cheerful, while practising a trade seemingly so at variance with their birth and education. In many cases, the father of the family makes for himself and his boys, while the lady manufactures those worn by herself and her daughters ; or the women make the tops and do the binding. However, he is a poor backwoodsman who cannot make his own boots and shoes ; for in Canada an officer must do more than turn his sword into a pruning-hook—he must occasionally change it into an awl. Fortunately for him, he is considered not only none the worse for doing so, but a great deal the better ; and, it is a certain fact, that he is always better off.

As our population increases, a division of labour must take place ; for the exorbitant price of things must then be lowered, and it will be more for our interest to purchase necessaries, than to manufacture them for ourselves.

If my readers recall the celebrated reply of Dr. Franklin, when examined before the House of Commons, to this question,— " What will the Americans do for cloth for their coats if they separate themselves from the mother-country ? " they may form some idea of the manner in which young colonies ought to provide for their own wants, by their individual industry. " What must they do ?" was his reply : " wear their old coats, till they can learn how to make cloth for new ones." In that answer the future independence of his country might have been clearly seen. British North America had not then learned those arts in which Canada is by no means deficient.

Well, in Canada we do not wear our shoes in holes till we can learn to mend them, or obtain them at an extravagant price from the distant store, or from Old England : we prefer making new ones ourselves to that disagreeable alternative. We love the dear mother-country ; but we are not dependent upon her for the privilege of being shod.

The Canadian settler must, in fact, supply himself by his own productive industry with many comforts, and not a few actual necessaries. As the excise laws are unknown in the Canadas, such indispensable articles as soap, candles, and sugar are usually made at home.

Every farmer kills his own beef, pork, and mutton ; consequently the materials, both for soap and candles, are at hand, ready to be applied to their proper uses. The rough tallow is melted into cakes, and afterwards run into moulds of different sizes for candles : grease, lye, and resin produce good soap, at a cost of little labour and at no other expense. The ladies of the family generally relieve the gentlemen of this work, which usually falls to their share of the household duties. I really believe that many genteel families in England would supply themselves with these expensive and indispensable articles, if the exciseman did not restrain them from exercising such a branch of domestic economy.

It is quite essential that the wives and daughters of the Canadian agriculturist should rival the fair Penelope in spinning, and even exceed her—as indeed they ought——for the Grecian lady spun with a distaff, and had never known the superior aid of the modern spinning-wheel, much less the great-wheel, or big-wheel, as our American neighbours call the Irish importation, to which they have added the improvement of the patent head, which enables our fair Canadian spinsters to produce a finer thread, and make a greater quantity of yarn in any given time, than they could do previous to the introduction of Brother Jonathan's patent big-wheel.

So many home-comforts depend upon this ancient branch of feminine industry, which the use of the spinning-jenny has almost entirely super-seded in the mother-country, that in Canada, the single ladies are, literally speaking, all spinsters : in fact if they were not, their fathers and brothers would often display Shakspeare's " ravelled sleeve of care."

As this is an important part of domestic economy, it may be useful to describe the manage-ment of the wool before it is fit for the dear girls' industrious hands.   As soon as the sheep are sheared, the wool must be picked and greased : after this, it is sent to the carding mill to be carded——an operation which costs twopence per pound.

(This part of the business can be done at home; but it is very troublesome, and the expense is so trifling, that the saving is not really worth making.) When the wool is carded, it is ready for the wheel, and the ladies of the family, or if there are no ladies, their substitutes, hired spinning girls, convert it into yarn, which is then dyed, reeled, and hanked, which processes it undergoes at home. It is now ready for the weaver, who charges from fivepence to sixpence per yard for his work; many farmers, however, have hand-looms in their own houses.

For winter wear, both warp and weft of these native cloths are of wool; but for that destined for summer use, the warp is cotton. Flannels and Tweeds are also frequently made with a mixture of wool and cotton.

After the weaving is finished, the cloth must be sent to the fulling-mill, where it receives its completion, unless it is of a very fine quality, in which case it must be sheared and pressed.

The common Canadian grey cloth, generally worn by the settlers of the Western province, is a strong, warm, serviceable fabric, costing about four or five shillings per yard, Halifax currency.*

* Halifax currency is less than sterling : the bank value of the sovereign is twenty-four shillings and four-pence half-

The dye-stuffs in general use are indigo, log-wood, red-wood, and copperas, and the bark of the butter-nut tree.

The soil of Canada is capable of growing both hemp and flax of good quality ; but the produce has not been yet applied for the manufacture of fine linen cloths. Some settlers grow both these plants for furnishing them with bags, sacks, and ropes ; but, as the population of the colony in-creases, these neglected articles will, no doubt, not only be extensively cultivated, but form a valuable branch of commerce.

The manufacture of maple sugar contributes so largely to the comforts of the Canadian settler, that I shall devote a whole chapter to the descrip-tion of our sugar-tree, and the manner of convert-ing its sap into molasses or sugar.

Our wives, daughters, and sisters, besides spin-ning yarn for our garments, provide us with warm stockings, socks, gloves, Guernsey frocks, and com-forters, of their own knitting, and furnish us, in their leisure time, with many useful and ornamen-tal articles.

They provide us, too, with carpets of a strong, useful kind, the best of which are made of yarn of

penny. In payment of store-debts the merchant generally allows five dollars.

their own spinning and dyeing, whilst others are contrived by an ingenious economy, which collects odd pieces of rag or cloth, cuts them into long strips, joins and forms them into large balls for the weaver, who makes use of a warp made of strong twine : the material on the balls forms the weft in manufacturing the carpet. The ladies call this article a rag-carpet, and it serves the purpose very well till it can be replaced by a good yarn one.

Among the home productions of Canada, the counterpane, or quilt, holds a conspicuous place, not so much in regard to its actual usefulness, as to the species of frolic 'yclept a Quilting-bee, in which young gentlemen take their places with the Queen-bees, whose labours they aid by threading the needles, while cheering their spirits by talking nonsense.

The quilts are generally made of patchwork, and the quilting, with down or wool, is done in a frame. Some of the gentlemen are not mere drones on these occasions, but make very good assistants under the superintendence of the Queen-bees.

The quilting bee usually concludes with a regular evening party. The young people have a dance. The old ones look on. After supper, the youthful visitors sing or guess charades. Mirth, good humour, and pleasant company, generally abound at these quilting-bees, which are not liable to the serious objections which may be made against other bees in Canada.

If several gentlemen receive an invitation to tea, they may be assured that their services are required at a quilting-bee, which often is followed by courtship and matrimony : indeed it is one of the methods taken by the Canadian Cupid to ensnare hearts and provide work for Hymen.

The ladies sometimes call a bee for paring apples for tarts and sauce for winter use. This important business (at least *they* choose to consider it so) takes place soon after the fruit has been gathered in. The apples are peeled, cored, and strung up from the ceilings of the attics to dry. When they are wanted for pies, puddings and tarts, they are boiled with sugar, and prove very good for those purposes.

Some home-made preserves are prepared at small cost by the following process:—Plums, raspberries, and strawberries are boiled with a small quantity of sugar, and spread, about half an inch thick, on sheets of paper, to dry in the sun. This will be accomplished in a few days ; after which the papers are rolled up, tied, and hung up in a dry place for use. When wanted for tarts, these dried fruits are taken from the paper, and boiled with a little more sugar, which restores the fruit to its former size and shape.

Our ladies make jams and jellies after the orthodox European fashion, and, in short, contribute all they can to our comfort and enjoyment. They have some public encouragement, too, for their domestic manufactures, as prizes have been awarded at the annual provincial show for every species of home-production. Great competition ensues, and our ladies send yarn-cloth, quilts, carpets, preserves, soap, candles, sugar, knitted garments, hose, flannel, to Toronto, Kingston, or wherever the annual display of Canadian industry is to be held for the year. Very proud and happy are our industrious Queen-bees made by obtaining the honour of a prize on these occasions. Our advance in productive domestic industry has been greatly increased by these exhibitions; for the ladies—God bless them ! are naturally ambitious; at least, old Chaucer has declared—

" That woman most affecteth sovereignty."

and in Canada their aspiring minds are continually seeking to make us happier, wiser, and better. Good cause, indeed, has the colony to be proud of her admirable daughters !

CHAPTER XVIII.

SUGAR-MAPLE. — CANADIAN SUGAR. — METHOD OF BOILING MAPLE-
SAP INTO SUGAR. — A SERIES OF SWEET DISASTERS LED ON BY
PRINCE.— NON-VIGILANCE OF A SUGAR-SENTINEL.— COW-PILFER-
ERS.—DANGEROUS CONSEQUENCES TO THE THIEVES, WHO ARE
SAVED BY AN OPERATION.—SUGAR-EATING BEE.—MAPLE-VINEGAR.
—BIRCH VINEGAR AND BEER.

AMONG the domestic manufactures of Canada,
one of the most important to the settler is the
art of making sugar from the maple-tree, *Acer
saccharinum*. Almost every agriculturist annually manufactures more or less of this luxury
in the spring. Now, supposing each family to
make one hundred pounds of sugar on an average,
which I believe to be under the quantity manu-
factured, the number of pounds produced must be
immense. Besides the article of sugar, molasses,
of an excellent quality, is produced later in the
season, and vinegar in abundance.

The commencement of sugar-making depends
altogether on the season. I have known sugar
made in February, March, and April : as a general

rule, however, the twentieth of March may be considered about the average time for commencing operations. The best and purest sugar is made in the early part of the season. Later in the year it will not grain properly, and is then converted into molasses.

The sugar-maple is probably the most common tree amongst the hard-wood species in Canada West. It is to be found generally in groves of from five to twenty acres: these are called by the settlers sugar-bushes, and few farms are without them.

The settler having selected his sugar-bush, should under-brush and clean the surface of the ground, by removing all rotten logs and falling trees. It should also be surrounded with a fence, to hinder the cattle from drinking the sap and upsetting the sap-troughs, which they are very apt to do, to the great annoyance of the sugar-boiler.

The boiling place should be as near as possible in the centre of the bush, from which roads wide enough to admit a sleigh and yoke of oxen should be cut in every direction.

The common way in use by the settlers is, to suspend their sugar-boilers over the fire from a thick pole, by means of iron chains: this is a bad plan, and subject to many inconveniences. The best method is to build the sugar-kettles into an arch, either in the open air, or in a shanty built for the purpose. A store-trough should be made from the trunk of a white pine, capable of holding from fifty to one hundred pails of sap, which must be placed conveniently for the boilers, who must also be provided with as many empty barrels as can be mustered ; for during a copious run, it is often difficult to find a sufficiency of vessels to hold the sap.

In a good season, from eight to twelve hundred pounds of sugar and molasses can be made from a bush containing five hundred troughs. The troughs should be made of pine, black ash, cherry, or butter-nut, and capable of holding from three to four gallons each. No sap-wood should be left on the bottom of the trough, or it will soon rot; and care should be taken as soon as the sugar season is over, to set the troughs up on their ends, against the north side of the tree, which preserves them from being cracked by the sun in summer, or buried too deep in the snow in winter.

If (as of course) the farmer wishes to preserve his sugar bush, the best method is to tap with an inch and quarter auger, and use round spiles, hollow in the centre, which may be driven for about the depth of an inch into the auger hole. Care must be taken to set the trough directly under the drop, and as level as possible, if the sugar-bush is intended to be destroyed in a few years, which is often the case where maple is the prevailing timber, the settler tapping those nearest to the house first, and cutting them down as they interfere with his clearing—in which case the axe is preferred to the auger, as being the quicker operation, and producing a better flow of sap.

The sap runs best after a frosty night, followed by a warm sunny day and brisk westerly wind. The tap should be made on the south side of the tree, in the early part of the season, and on the north, when it requires renewing.

I received this hint from an old Wiltshire man, a neighbour of mine, who was in my sugar-bush one day, when I was busy spiling my trees. Seeing me tap one on the north side, he told me I was wrong.

" Why so?" I inquired.

" Why, you see, zur, the best way be to tap the tree on the zunny zide; becase you zee, zur, the zap do run best on the zunny side of the tree."

The sugar season generally lasts from three to four weeks; but as soon as a very minute black fly is seen gathering in clusters about the sap-troughs, you may be sure the season is nearly at an end.

The most expeditious way of collecting the sap, and bringing it to the boiling place, is to drive through the roads with an ox-sled, on which is securely fastened a large barrel or puncheon, in the bung-hole of which is inserted a wooden tun-dish, large enough to hold a pail of sap. A piece of sheet-iron, punched full of holes, is fixed in the centre of the tun-dish, to prevent leaves and coarse dirt, or sticks, from getting into the barrel. As soon as the vessel is full of sap, it is driven to the boiling place, and emptied into the store-trough.

The fires are now lighted, and the process of evaporation commences by keeping the kettles constantly boiling, night and day, until a quantity of sap is boiled down into a thin molasses, suffi-cient to make a batch of sugar. The molasses must be put into a deep wooden vessel, and allowed to cool and settle. The liquor is then carefully poured into a copper boiler, taking care not to disturb the sediment at the bottom of the vessel.

The next operation is to clear the molasses from the earthy particles and other impurities contained in the sap. Various clarifiers are made use of for this purpose. I consider eggs the best and if eggs cannot be obtained, milk will answer very well for a substitute : six eggs are sufficient to clarify fifty pounds of sugar.

The eggs should be beaten up with about a quart of the molasses, then poured into the sugar boiler and stirred well, while the liquor is cold, then hung upon a crane over a slow fire. As soon as the molasses begins to simmer, the feculence will gather and rise to the surface of the boiler, with the egg. The moment the liquor begins to boil, the crane must be swung off the fire, and the surface skimmed carefully. If properly managed, scarcely any impurity will be left, and the molasses will look bright and clear.

Great attention must now be paid by the sugar-boiler. He must not leave his station at the kettle for a moment; for the liquor is continually rising to the surface, and would boil over instantly, unless watched with the greatest care.

To the uninitiated, the greatest difficulty is to know when the liquor is boiled enough. The common way of ascertaining this is, to make a narrow hole, an inch long and an eighth of an inch wide, through a thin piece of wood, and if this is dipped into the molasses, a thin film will fill the hole in the stick, which, if blown, will throw out a long-shaped bubble, if the sugar is

sufficiently boiled. Some persons merely drop a
little of the hot molasses on a lump of snow. If
it hardens when cool, it is enough. It is then
made into cakes by pouring into tin pans or moulds,
which completes the operation.

My readers must not suppose from this description, that sugar making is a light and pleasur-
able employment. On the contrary, it is one of
the most laborious occupations, whilst it lasts,
that falls to the lot of the settler to perform. In
the first place, the troughs have all to be cleaned
and set, the trees tapped and spiled, wood cut and
split for the fires, the sap collected, strained, and
boiled down into syrup, and the syrup clarified
and boiled into sugar ; and when this is happily
accomplished, and you are congratulating yourself
on the possession of a fine batch of sugar, and are
about to take it off the fire, perhaps it suddenly
boils over, or is upset, or some other accident
happens, which deprives you of the fruits of your
last three or four days' labour.

The first time I attempted to make sugar was
during my residence at Darlington. I set bravely
to work, and made forty very nice sugar troughs,
tapped my trees and had the pleasure of seeing a
splendid flow of sap. My troughs were not long
in filling, and I was prepared to collect their

contents, when, I was very much astonished to find that the troughs I had seen running over a short time before, were now scarcely half full. I was wondering what could be the cause, when a neighbouring sugar-boiler came to see how I got on. On explaining my misfortune, he laughed and said—" No wonder, for I see you have made your troughs of bass-wood, and they always leak, because the grain of the wood is too open. Now, when we make troughs out of bass-wood, we always burn them inside which in a great measure remedies the evil; but I would advise you never to use bass-wood if you can conveniently get any other, for it will not last more than two or three years at most." I thanked my neighbour for his information, which experience has proved to be correct.

But to return to my first essay in the mysteries of sugar-making. My boilers were all nicely arranged, filled up with sap, and a raging fire under them: I did not, at this stage of the business, know what I could do to keep the kettles from boiling over, which I expected they would do every moment. At this critical juncture my kind neighbour again came to my assistance, and informed me that " the usual plan was to suspend a small piece of fat bacon by a string, from the bale of the kettle, an inch or two below the rim, this being supposed to hinder the liquor from boiling over." To a certain extent, it does certainly prevent this misfortune, but not altogether. I have since adopted a much cleaner and much surer method, which I can recommend to the notice of all Canadian sugar-boilers.

A barrel filled with sap should be placed in an upright position on a platform elevated above the boilers. A small brass cock (or rooster, as the Yankees call it) should be fixed into the lower part of the barrel under which a narrow slip of board hollowed out in the centre should be suspended, the lower end of this miniature trough resting on the rim of the boiler. The cock can then be turned to regulate the supply of cold sap, the smallest run being sufficient to check the liquor from boiling over, though not enough to put it off the boil. The great evaporation going on prevents the kettle from filling up by the continual supply of cold sap. In hopes of benefiting the rising generation of emigrant sugar-boilers, I have been tempted to digress from the story of my first attempt at sugar-making.

No schoolboy ever watched a pot of treacle during its transformation into *toffy*, with greater interest than I did the conversion of the bright amber-coloured molasses before me into sugar. My youngest brother-in-law, a lad of fourteen, came into the bush with my dinner, just at the critical period when it is difficult to know if the sugar is boiled enough to grain properly. He was as great a novice in the art as myself, but he was wise enough to suggest the propriety of tasting— the sweet stuff, as he called it—as the surest method of determining the question. It appeared to be a much more difficult thing to decide upon than we had at first imagined ; nor did we come to a final decision, until at least a pound of the precious liquid had evaporated, not by steam, but by the less scientific process of tasting. At length it was pronounced sufficiently boiled, and was duly transferred from the boiler into the moulds, when I had the satisfaction of finding it grain beautifully. I placed the two tin-dishes containing the first fruits of my ingenuity, on the snow to cool, and went with my brother-in-law to the farther end of the bush for sap to re-fill the boilers. While we were thus engaged, we were alarmed by a loud bellow, and, on looking in the direction of the boilers, were horrified at beholding our bull, Prince, running off, with his tail in the air, and followed, in his mad career, by several other head of cattle. I knew something was the matter, and, on hastening to the boilers, I found the rascally bull had popped his head into one of my tins of hot sugar, the heat of which had so astonished his weak nerves, that he made off with the best part of a pound of the liquid sticking round his muzzle, to his unlucky gain, and my infinite mortification and anger.

Misfortunes never come singly; and so it was with me in this instance; for I was, soon after Prince's tragical exit, busily engaged filling up the boilers, when I heard a sudden shout, but before I could turn round to see what was the matter, found myself knocked down by the top of a small tree, boilers and all. Luckily for me, the thick pole from which the kettles were suspended, took off the force of the blow. My brother-in-law had chopped down a small birch-tree for fire-wood, and it had fallen in a contrary direction to what he expected; and, although I was not much hurt—the top twigs alone having struck me—yet, at the same time it must be admitted, that I was most severely birched.

Although my initiation into the sweet mysteries of sugar-making and molasses was not unattended with misfortune, I rapidly acquired the art, and can now manufacture as good an article as any settler in the country.

Some years after my first essay, when my sugar-boiling establishment was on a much larger scale, I found it necessary to sit up all night and drive the kettles, in consequence of the large accumulation of sap from two good runs. We had worked hard all day, and had boiled down as much sap into syrup as would make upwards of fifty pounds of sugar. After supper, fatigued and drowsy by our day's work, we agreed, as there were three of us, to sleep by turns. We drew lots to see who should take the first watch of two hours, which, unluckily for me, as the proprietor of the establishment, fell upon J. B., a young English gentleman, one of my household, who was duly installed into his important office of sugar-sentinel. My companion and myself then stretched ourselves in the camp before the fire, and were soon lost in a pleasing forgetfulness. How long we had been in this comfortable state of somnolescence I know not, being awakened from my nap by a strong smell of burning, which, upon jumping up, I found to proceed from the three large sugar-kettles, which were literally red-hot, every particle of sugar being literally burnt to a cinder. And where was the guardian of the kettles? Why, fast asleep in the camp, and totally unconscious of the misfortune his mis-timed and faithless nap had occasioned.

At another time I lost nearly the same quan-tity by three of my own cows breaking into the bush while we were at home for dinner. I had poured a large quantity of molasses into some vessels to cool, preparatory to mixing the eggs for clarifying the sugar. The beasts drank up every drop, which caused them to swell so much that they would certainly have died from the effects of their intemperance if I had not performed a sur-gical operation upon each of the animals by making an incision through the skin into the stomach, and inserting a small tube into the ori-fice, which relieved the pressure, and saved the lives of my cows. These are some of the troubles connected with the manufacture of maple-sugar, many of which can, of course, be obviated by carefulness and experience.

Besides the trouble arising from four-footed depredators, you are apt to receive manifold visits from young ladies and children, who, of course, only come to see the process ; but who, somehow or another never make their appearance during the first part of the operation, but wait patiently until the sap is transformed into a more mellifluous substance, when spoons, tins, and ladles are in great requisition. I have even known my sugar-shanty made the rendezvous of a picnic party, to my no small discomfiture. Indeed, I might just as well have made a sugar-eating bee, so great was the consumption of that article.

Towards the close of the season a small quantity of fresh lime thrown into your store-trough will be found beneficial, by destroying the acidity. It is, however, better and more profitable to make the latter runs of sap into molasses or vinegar.

The usual way of making vinegar is to boil down three pails of sap into one, adding a little yeast when the liquid is milk-warm. Your barrel when full should be set in some sunny place with a piece of glass over the bung-hole: the addition of a gallon of whiskey to the barrel will much improve the strength of the vinegar.

Maple-sap also makes capital beer, which is both wholesome and pleasant to the taste. Some people add essence of spruce or ginger to the sap.

The sap extracted from the yellow birch makes both excellent vinegar and beer. The flow of sap from the birch is much more copious than from the maple. I have frequently known from twelve to fifteen gallons taken from a large tree in one day.

CHAPTER XIX.

THE THREE GREAT WANTS OF CANADA.—HINTS FOR THE EDUCA-
TION OF EMIGRANTS.—BACHELOR WANTS.

CANADA, in her present state, exhibits three great wants for the supply of which she must look to the mother-country. She requires population, pastors, and school-masters.

The first of these requirements would benefit Great Britain in a very extensive manner. We ask her for her superfluous thousands, to whom she offers the miserable home of the workhouse, while we proffer comfort, independence, and a cheerful old age.

We do not want the idle, the over-educated, the sickly. We want men, women, and children, of hardy and industrious habits, who finding work slack at home, resolve to emulate the ants and bees, by leaving the parent hill or hive, for a land where their united industry will furnish them abundantly with the necessaries of life, and enable them to sit by their own chimney-corner to enjoy, in their peaceful old age, the happy home their toils have founded in the wilderness.

The expense of passage-money, and the deep affection with which the Anglo-Saxon races regard their native haunts, deter many thousands who pine from want in England from coming out to Canada. But this rooted love of home was not the ancient characteristic of a migratory people, who swept the seas in their long yawls, and after pillaging the shores formed settlements in England. Attachment to home gradually fixed itself in succeeding generations, but new ideas and habits may be received. The peasantry are an unreflective body, and rely much upon the superior classes for guidance and advice. Let it be given them, then. Tell them that a few months' struggle in another land will ease them of the weight of care that now oppresses them. Remind them that the effort of going out is the only painful one they will have to make. Since toil is to them a habit, they have not, like the emigrant gentleman, or the wife of an officer of the Guards, to unlearn a life.

How does nature herself teach us the necessity of removal? The young ants are provided the first year of their wonderful existence with wings, in order to permit them to remove far

from the parent nest. These wings fall off after
the infant colony is founded,—a curious fact in
natural history, illustrative of that admirable economy by which animated nature is ruled and
governed. The ants, having once migrated,
have no more need of wings, the possession of
which would make them injurious to man and
beast ; for the stings of these insects in the winged
state cause an intensity of pain, which would render them worse neighbours than in their wingless
state they could possibly have become.

The bee throws off her annual swarms, and
sometimes—perhaps always—with a battle. It
is possible that the young insects do not like to
quit the hive or hollow tree where they have been
fed and nurtured. Yet parental foresight compels them to migrate to other trees and hives, not
only for want of room, but because they must seek
for honey in other fields. These unknown fields
to the bee, with her confined vision, are the
Canadas, Australias, and New Zealands of our
world.

The insect colonisers have all received from
God himself, if I may presume to say so, a fixed
educationary system in their admirable and unerring instinct. They know how to build, to collect
material for building, and to procure food. For

migrating they only obey another fixed and immutable law of Providence, which bids them fly off and put their tools and instinct to their proper uses.

Man, however, has fewer instincts. Religion and reason were to be his laws. Therefore, he must acquire those useful arts which are born with insect life. But the necessity of emigration is a lesson, stern enough, it is true, but yet as stringent to him as that which sways the ant and bee.

Since the necessity exists, the wisdom of our legislature should provide the youthful population with an education which would render them fit for emigration to a colony.

It is a good thing to make the children of the poor acquainted with reading, writing, and arithmetic ; but an exclusive attention to these objects is both unwise and injurious, for they were not designed for the whole business of their lives. Industrial schools are of more vital importance. A much larger portion of infant time should be passed in acquiring mechanical and agricultural skill on the part of the boys; while spinning, sewing, house-work, washing, baking, cooking, milking and every branch of dairy-work should form the chief portion of the educationary system for the girls.

In towns and cities educate the infant pauper

population for emigration. I grieve to use the word "pauper"; but I wish to fix the attention of the reader on the lowest state of poverty under which orphan infancy can dawn. We want carpenters, coopers, hand-loom weavers, shoemakers, masons, tailors, blacksmiths, in fact, artisans of every kind. Workhouses, and ragged-schools in cities ought to supply us with these instructed in the arts we need. Possessed of such a useful education, aided by the learning of which the benevolence of the present day is lavish of bestowing, each industrious honest lad would in a few years possess a little freehold farm of his own.

In the country, every house of industry should have a piece of land for spade husbandry, and a small farm for more extensive agricultural employment, in order to make her rising male population acquainted with every branch of cultivation, management of stock, &c.

The country girl, besides her spinning, knitting, and sewing, would learn the healthy and useful arts of milking, churning, and cheese-making, in addition to housework and plain cooking. With these acquirements she would be a treasure in a colony, and we would promise her, in a few years, cows and a dairy of her own.

The city girl would be of course more limited in her sphere of operations ; but hand-loom weaving, spinning, knitting, shoe-binding, sewing, cutting out, and making up clothes, housework and plain cooking, would find her employment in the colony. Then her superior intelligence—for the sight of many objects does quicken human intelligence—would lead her also to acquire a knowledge of those rural employments of which the want of opportunity alone has left her ignorant.

Having thus pointed out the colonial education which parish authorities ought to give their young inmates with a view to emigration, let us consider in what manner the young swarms should be conducted to their new hives.

Government should have ships and commissioners expressly for the purpose. Care should be taken of these children on the voyage, and on their way up the country. Good masters and mistresses should be sought for them, and inquiries and visits occasionally paid them by persons appointed for the purpose.

Regular depôts should be formed in such towns as Montreal, Quebec, Kingston, Toronto, and other places, under matrons and governors, for their transmission to families requiring their aid ; and little fear need be entertained of the kind treatment of these apprentices, in whose behalf, it should be enacted that they should not go away empty-handed from their three years' bondage, but should receive a certain sum in money, stock, or goods.

The emigrant-labourer and his family might, besides the help afforded by the parish, have a sermon preached for his benefit. Few neighbours, used to see him worshipping with them every Sabbath, would, I think, refuse to contribute their mite to help to smooth his rough path in a Bush life.

In manufacturing districts, the poor hand-loom weavers, stocking-weavers, and many other artisans, who are struggling for bread, notwithstanding their industrial skill, against " their gigantic monster enemy, steam-worked machinery," would find work plentiful and extremely remunerative in every Canadian town, where cheap food and 7s. 6d. a-day would afford wealth to the poor, half-starved, drooping manufacturer.

Shoemakers would find plenty to do in a country where gentlemen, if they do not learn to make their own, must, in the back settlements, go barefoot.

Well! though the clever and amusing M'Taggart does beseech people not to emigrate, I must entreat you to come out, if you like work. If you do not, poor fellows! you had better stay where you are, since idleness in Canada, as in England, will always cover a man with rags.

Industry in man, woman, or child, gentle or simple, is necessary in Canada. Therefore the idle, luxurious, and dissipated must not leave their homes, unless they resolve to work either with willing hands or clever heads—they will find employment for both in a colony.

The best plan, however, in regard to emigration, is for gentlemen to provide for their younger sons in this way. A premium for three years, paid to some respectable settler, to engage him to instruct the young emigrant, and a further sum to provide him with land and stock, would set a young gentleman forward in life at a small expense to his friends, and with the certainty of a comfortable independence for himself. Youth, with its buoyant spirits, readily overcomes hardships and difficulties ;—besides the example of the settlers' sons, his companions, who, of course all work, soon reconciles him to labour.

The amusements of shooting and fishing, riding and exploring excursions, quickly make newcomers much attached to the country. The privilege of wooing and winning some object of his affections, and easily providing for the wants of a family, is a stimulus ever before the eyes of the young man, whose hopes of domestic love are so often crushed by circumstances in England.

I really believe that if young ladies, not too much addicted to the "*far niente*," condescended to visit our settlements, we could find good husbands for them all, in a country where wives are lacking, and much valued and appreciated. However, if the brothers of large families come out, no doubt the sisters will visit them, and our bachelors will not remain long in their present uncomfortable state of forced celibacy.

CHAPTER XX.

NEED OF CHURCHES AND PASTORS IN CANADA. — KIND ASSISTANCE
OF MY FRIENDS IN ENGLAND TOWARDS THIS GOOD WORK.—
ZEAL OF THE PRIMITIVE CHURCH. — WANT OF SCHOOLS AND
SCHOOLMASTERS.

THE second great want of Canada West in-
volves more momentous matters than the settlement of the country, for it concerns the immortal
interests not only of the present, but of unborn
generations.   We need pastoral direction and
places of worship.

Without Christian instruction, all the promise
of the fine colony is like that of an unfruitful
tree, whose blossoms fall untimely to the ground.

We call upon the Church of England—that
Church, so pure in its doctrines, so perfect in its
beautiful liturgy, so sublime in its ordinances,
to help Canada, and not to leave our children un-
instructed, or compel them to derive their religious
code from other sources, or to remain in darkness
and heathenish apathy.   We want churches, too,
as well as teachers, that every Sabbath we may

meet together to pray, to praise—to adore the Lord our God—as a Christian people should do. We require the word to be preached to us — we are longing to receive in our own parish-church in sweet communion the Lord's Supper, and in that sublime ordinance to recognise " Our Divine Master's love in thus dying for us." We wish to bring our little children "to His holy baptism," and to have them confirmed and strengthened in their riper age, that we may see them partakers with us of the holy sacrament, and may behold them growing up in the fear and love of the Lord.

It is the blessing of pastoral instruction we demand of the dear mother-country. We ask her for devoted men—not men of extreme views, but men whose love to God will make them overlook the rough and toilsome pilgrimage in the wilderness—men whom the love of Christ will bring out to us in charitable answer to our call, " Come over and help us," even as St. Paul did to the visionary man of Macedonia, believing that God had called him there to preach the gospel.

" Behold what a great matter a little fire kindleth." Since my return to England, kind and pious friends and unknown brother Christians have aided my wish to provide a church for the hitherto churchless township of Douro in Canada, and a fund is already raised which will enable me to commence the building on my return. Lakefield is the spot to be so highly favoured; and when once the foundations of the little temple in the wilderness are laid, we hope a pastor will soon follow the church.

It is true—only too true—that the pastor should precede the church, for such was the custom of primitive times, when a converted heathen people, following the direction of apostolic teachers, laid with them the foundation of that outward and visible church, the type of that mystical and invisible one of which they had become members. We are about to reverse the picture—we in building a church invite a pastor. We, who have been grateful for a chance pastoral visit, take this method of securing a spiritual blessing for ourselves and our families.

I cannot resist, in this portion of my work, an expression of my deep sense of the generous manner in which friends in my own immediate neighbourhood, and also in Norfolk, Tunbridge Wells, and in other places, have contributed to the church about to be built at Lakefield. They have been so willing—so zealous—in this good work, that I trust their forwardness will bring down a blessing upon themselves and upon our church, which will be raised by the united efforts of Christian brotherly love, a meet offering to Him—the Chief Corner-stone upon whom our foundation is laid.

The good examples of these Christian friends may raise up friends for Canada, and scatter the blessings of the reformed religion over this vast country, that other townships may also have their pastors, till the whole rising population may grow up children of the Church of England.

Hitherto, the inhabitants have chiefly received their religious instruction through various branches of dissent, whose ministers have shown much zeal and attention in supplying instruction to an increasing and pastorless population.   In our peculiar situation, we must feel grateful for Christian instruction of any kind, living, as we do, in a land of spiritual dearth.

Why have we been hitherto so deserted and forgotten, while the " living waters" refreshed so abundantly our native land ?   It was not so in those glorious primitive times, when, during the grievous persecutions of the Church, the banishment of the teachers of Christianity only spread the Word on every side—when churches and schools rose in the deserts, whither the pastors had been exiled. Why, in receiving the apostolical doctrines of these devoted men, have we not followed their examples, as well as received their precepts ?

It is a certain fact, that few persons dissent from the pure apostolic doctrines of the Church of England, while many do from those of her ministers. Yet it is certain that a really good pastor of the Church is venerated and esteemed as the very perfection of the Christian character.   The affections of the English people still naturally cling to their clergy. It is only when chilled by neglect, or left unvisited in sickness or calamity, that the parishioner leaves his church, because his minister has first left him.   Yet the assertion still holds true, " that a house-going minister makes a church-going people ;" and we trust that the destined pastors of our wilderness will visit our people in their homes, as well as preach to them in their churches.

Much good would result from the clergymen of our establishment itinerating from place to place, taking up their abode in private houses, where they would always be honoured guests, and preaching and reading prayers during their sojourn.   A real necessity exists for their performing such charitable missions, till the scattered villages get churches and ministers of their own. To show the need of such itineration, I need only state that my own county of Peterborough, containing eighteen townships (of which Douro, in which I reside, is one) possessed only three churches, to supply the wants of a population, which, at the last census, numbered more than twenty-seven thousand souls, and which now would amount, from emigration and increase, to nearly thirty thousand.

In all these townships there are many dissenting chapels of various denominations—a fact honourable to dissenters, however painful it may be to the Canadian members of the Establishment to see themselves left behind in Christian effort by men who doubtless have done a good work by providing places of worship and a ministry for the poor, who but for them would have been left to spend the Sabbath in drunkenness and sin.

To give the preponderance to the Church of England establishment, that church in Canada, which at present is only that of a rising aristocracy, must become also the church of the poor, or else how can any congregation truly say, "The rich and the poor meet together. The Lord is the maker of them all?" Yet that any sect of dissent is the religion by choice of the people cannot be said with truth in the face of the following fact. In the year 1838, when the 7th Provincial battalion was formed, while taking down the names and religious professions of the volunteers, I observed that two-thirds, at least, were members of the Established Church, which surprised me, as I knew many of them attended dissenting chapels regularly every Sabbath-day.

I was induced, in consequence of this, to ask the question, " Why do you profess one form of religion, and follow another ?" The answer was a painful one to me. " We are in heart members of the Church of England, but we have no church in our township, and we do not see a clergyman of the Establishment once in three years ; so we are glad to attend any Christian minister who will come amongst us." It is thus that, for want of churches and missionaries, thousands are ultimately estranged from the Church. These persons were like children neglected by their mother, only waiting to be cared for to return to her bosom.

If, till a church could be raised, devout ministers, duly authorized by their bishops, would come among us to preach, pray, and administer the Sacraments, each of our houses, in turn, would become temples of the Lord ; and there would be no need for any member of the church to unite himself to a dissenting congregation for want of a minister of his own.

There is a fast rising sect in Canada, the members of which denominate themselves "Bible Christians." These people are a species of Methodists, and are moral and well-living; but in choosing their own preachers they are rather guided by their eloquence than learning, or perhaps sound doctrine. Many of their ministers can neither read nor write, and therefore are disqualified by their ignorance from teaching others. A regular and authorized ministry of devout men, learned, and yet condescending to the weak and ignorant, would bring into the fold of the Establishment many who are now estranged from the doctrines and liturgy of our venerable Church.

I remember, when a boy, how much the people in England were neglected by many among the clergy, and left to form their own religious opinions, for want of Christian educational instruction, and pastoral visits at their own houses and cottages. Such neglect was the main cause of dissent. The clergymen were above their flocks, and the sheep wandered from them to other folds, to ministers who entered into their joys and sorrows, and were not divided from them by the Anti-Christian barrier of pride, or the false one of diffidence; for, strange to say, the timidity of a young clergyman may be erroneously ascribed to pride, and may equally alienate from him the affections of his people.

I am happy to see a general change for the better has taken place during my long absence from my native land, for the worldly have passed into eternity, and have been replaced in their ministry by wiser and abler men. Many of those good pastors, too, who were shining lights in the Christian Church, when I was a boy, have passed to their rest, leaving their dear and honoured names as examples to the rising generation, upon which holier times have dawned, and over which a reformed ministry is now exercising a mild and spiritual dominion.

Since my return to England I have become acquainted with a number of excellent clergymen, who, like the Apostles and pastors of the glorious primitive Church, " visit the widow and fatherless in their affliction, and keep themselves unspotted from the world,"—and, if all were like them, the meeting-house would be deserted and the parish-church well-filled, while a pure morality, based upon Gospel principles, would replace the erratic and erroneous doctrines of an unlearned and un-ordained ministry.

Our last great want is that of schoolmasters and schoolhouses. But if we obtain pastoral instruction this need will also be supplied. Sabbath schools, under the immediate superintendence of the clergyman, will be formed, and our children of all ranks may be instructed together in a little building close to the church, for of course a school-house enters into our plans for Lakefield, as well as a church. Soon, very soon, a national-school, we hope, for day-scholars, will follow these establishments. Indeed, the settlement will grow round the church, which will form the nucleus of a town, in a few short years, about it, and with a rapidly increasing population our church will soon be filled, we trust, to overflowing, and we shall see Christianity, pure, vital Christianity, like a fertilizing stream, diffusing civilization and morality over the land,—putting down the orgies of drunkenness, and pointing to the reward of faith and perseverance in well doing, in the happiness of another and better world, of which " the Lamb is the glory and the light."

> " The churchless, soon, are godless too ;
>   The unbaptized grow base and blind ;
> And where no sacraments renew
>   The sin-worn heart and earth-toned mind,
> All virtues die, all vices bloom,
> The soul becomes a sensual tomb,
> And men the Saviour yearned to cherish,
> Eternalize their guilt—and perish !

"By Lake Ontario's rocky shore,
   Where creedless pagans once abounded,
And exiles heard the torrent roar,
   By wood and wilderness surrounded,—
Churches arise, and saintly bands
Have come from far and famous lands,
And Apostolic symbols reign
O'er rescued swamp and ransomed plain."*

---

* These beautiful lines, on the Canadian Church, are from
"Lyra Christiana," an interesting collection of poems from the
admired pen of that Christian poet, popular preacher, and amiable
man, the Rev. Robert Montgomery, Incumbent Minister of Percy
Chapel, London.

CHAPTER XXI.

DEATH INVADES MY HOME-CIRCLE. — LOSS OF MY YOUNGEST SON, MY SON-IN-LAW, MY GRAND-DAUGHTER, MY WIFE, AND MY YOUNGEST DAUGHTER. — PROJECTED RETURN HOME. — EMBARK-ATION. — NAVIGATION OF THE GENESEE RIVER.— ROCHESTER.— SYRACUSE.—MOHAWK RIVER.—AMERICAN STEAMERS.—RAIL CAR-RIAGES.— NEW YORK.— VOYAGE TO ENGLAND.— RETURN TO REYDON.—KINDNESS AND HOSPITALITY OF MY ENGLISH FRIENDS.

My life, for some years after the termination of the rebellion, presented too little variation to make it worthy of record. It had its pleasures and cares, its toils and repose ; but these were shared by the most amiable of women, whose sweet companionship in my worst periods of trial and privation, left me no cause to complain. A numerous and promising family grew up around us, adding year by year a new link to the chain of affection : indeed, no man was ever happier in the domestic relations, or possessed more home-blessings than myself.

The marriage of my eldest girl did not break up our cheerful circle, for she was located near us within a mile's walk, so that we had gained an affectionate son without losing a daughter—a fortunate circumstance for all parties, but especially for Maria's mother.

But while apparently at the height of domestic felicity, death made a sudden inroad into our happy home-circle. His first victim was a sweet promising little boy, just at that engaging age when infancy begins to lisp in pretty broken language its wants and wishes in the parental ear. My son-in-law died next, in a distant city, of cholera, leaving my poor young daughter a widow on the eve of her first confinement, scarcely in her twentieth year—an early age, indeed, for such a heavy bereavement.

The blow threatened to destroy her. She had been so happy, and her husband had been so full of health and manly beauty, that the news seemed almost incredible to us and most terrible to her. We broke it to her as gently as we could, and brought her, in her desolation, to that home which she had left a few months before a happy blooming bride. Our own loss, too, was heavy—poor Beresford was very dear to us; he was a remarkably fine and interesting young man. But what was our sorrow in comparison to hers, whose happiness had been crushed by this sudden and dreadful reverse. For some anxious weeks we watched our suffering child, over whose fading and emaciated form the shadow of death momentarily appeared to depend.   Her health seemed so entirely broken up that we never expected her to survive her approaching trial.

The mercy of God, youth, and the incessant care of her dear mother, enabled her to get over that period of maternal peril.   My poor girl gave birth to a daughter, and the sight of her orphan babe gave her a wish to live, though, for some weeks after her accouchement, her state was so precarious that she was unable to leave her bed, to which she was still confined, when it pleased the Lord to take away her child.

But the gift had not been made in vain—her spirits rallied from the moment she had seen her infant, and she meekly submitted to the Divine will, when the blessing was withdrawn from her again.

She suffered—but not alone.   Her admirable mother had shared all her feelings, forgetting in her long vigils by her sick-bed, her own delicate situation while soothing the pains and sharing the grief of her daughter.   Why should I dwell upon the event that once more shattered my domestic circle—taking from me my dear wife—my home-comforter—my sweet familiar friend!   Sufficient it

will be to say, that God was pleased to recal my
dear wife to himself half-an-hour after the birth
of our fourteenth child, a daughter, to whom I
gave the ancestral and now celebrated name of
Agnes Strickland, with the addition of *Mary*,
which was that of my lamented partner. My
Mary was taken away suddenly, but not unprepared for the Saviour whom she loved and trusted,
who was with his servant when she passed through
the valley and shadow of death. Never was any
woman more deeply and deservedly lamented.
Reader, you will find her character in Scripture,
under that of the virtuous woman, whose price is
beyond rubies. Her loss was a heavy blow to her
dear parents, as well as to her afflicted husband
and children.

Thus, by a similar calamity, I had the misfortune to lose two admirable wives : the first dying
in her first confinement, after the birth of my
eldest son ; the second in child-bed of my youngest
daughter. Heavy was the early bereavement ;
but those to whom the wife is dearer than the
bride, will easily suppose that the loss of her who
for nearly twenty-two years had formed my greatest
earthly blessing, was heavier still.

My widowed daughter received from her dying
mother the charge of the little infant, whose birth

had cost us all so much. This precious trust seemed to replace her own in her heart : never, indeed, was a motherless baby so loved and cherished. The sad event that had marked her entrance into the world, knit her so closely to us all, that she seemed the general point of attraction. Most lovely and precocious indeed was this child of many tears ; and we anticipated for her long years of life, when she was seized with a complaint indigenous to the country, and very fatal to infants, which cut off our little Agnes at the engaging age of five months, to the infinite grief of her sister-mother. Thus, in the space of one little year, I had lost my little son, my son-in-law, my grand-daughter, my beloved wife, and my youngest daughter. It seemed, indeed, that death had bent his bow against my family, and would not spare till he had pierced our hearts again and again within this brief but fatal period.

It was long before my daughter was comforted for the loss of her infant-sister. Religion and time brought balm ; but the trials of the young widow had been more than any feminine constitution could bear: she drooped, and her medical attendant prescribed change of air, scene, and climate. Canada, the land of her nativity, was too full of painful remembrances to afford her the chance of amendment. My own family and that of her husband wished much to receive her in England, and my own heart, too, yearned once more for my old home and its beloved inmates. It was necessary to consider the expediency of the voyage, and to arrange in what manner it could be best accomplished without exposing my child, in her delicate health, to unnecessary fatigue and peril.

Having made every arrangement for a twelvemonth's absence from home, I left Douro on the 8th July, 1851, accompanied by my eldest daughter, and a friend of mine, who was on his way to Jersey. We reached Gore's Landing, on the south side of Rice Lake, the same day, and halted there till the following noon, which enabled us to bid adieu to my sister, and a number of kind friends in the immediate neighbourhood.

An hour and a half's drive over an excellent plank and gravel road, through a charming country, brought us safely to the pretty and thriving town of Cobourg. Here we were detained until past eleven, waiting for the arrival of the steam-boat "Admiral," which was two hours behind time, owing to a heavy swell and head-wind on the Lake.

We were accompanied to the wharf by several kind friends, who saw us safely on board; and in a few minutes our noble steamer was proudly breasting the blue waters of the great Ontario.

For twenty-seven years I had been a sojourner in the wilds and woods of this fine, free, and independent country. I had learned to love it—to look upon it as my home, my adopted country, and the native land of my children. I felt I was leaving them and many dear friends, whom, perhaps, I might never more behold. No wonder, then, that I experienced some regret, as the fast-receding lights of Cobourg faded from my sight.

I was, however, cheered by the remembrance, that I had an aged mother still living, and kind sisters, who would welcome the return of their long absent brother to the home of his childhood, and that I should have the pleasure of presenting my Canadian daughter to them.

The Lake was rough, but my daughter proved an excellent sailor; and we made a capital run across, to the mouth of the Genesee river, which is almost opposite to Cobourg, and distant about sixty-five miles.

The Genesee river * is deep and narrow, seldom exceeding in width a hundred and fifty yards. Its banks are very high and precipitous. About four

* Charlevoix, in his curious work on the Canadas, gives the following description of the Genesee, which he calls the Casconchiagon, the Iroquois name for this river, as the following extract will show :—" This river is called Casconchiagon, and is very

miles from the mouth of the river is the landing-place, distant from the city of Rochester nearly three miles, where we found a number of omnibuses awaiting our arrival, and had the greatest difficulty in keeping our luggage from being divided and taken possession of by two or three different drivers. In fact, in the confusion I left one of my trunks behind in the steamer, and did not discover my mistake till I reached Rochester. Luckily, I got back in time to recover my property before the steamer left the wharf.

The navigation of the Genesee is interrupted immediately above the landing-place by a succession of stupendous falls. The road leading from the cataracts to the city of Rochester follows the right bank of the river, which, for the first mile, is wildly picturesque. It is excavated out of the rocky bank, which has a sharp ascent for about a mile. To the right, the precipitous rock towers from two to three hundred feet above

narrow at its discharge into the Lake. A little higher it is two hundred and forty feet in breadth, and it is affirmed that there is water to float the largest ships. A league from its mouth, you are stopped by a fall which seems to be about sixty feet high and two hundred and forty feet broad; a musket-shot above this you find a second, of the same breadth, but not so high, and half a league higher still a third, which is full a hundred feet high, and three hundred and sixty feet broad. You meet after this with several rapids, and after sailing fifty leagues up the stream, you discover a fourth fall, nothing inferior in height to the last mentioned : the course of this river is a hundred leagues."

the road-way, which, in some places, it overhangs.
To the left, fully as deep below, through a
rocky chasm, rush the foaming waters of the
Genesee. Two splendid cataracts, one a few rods
above the other, and more than a hundred feet
in height, complete the picture. A parapet of
large blocks of stone has been built on the edge
of the precipice, to prevent carriages from being
upset into the deep gorge below.

Rochester is a handsome, well-built town, and
owes its chief prosperity to its mighty water-
power. Here, indeed, are some of the finest
flour-mills in the world. The rail-road from
Buffalo to New York, runs through the town.
We breakfasted at the Waverley, one of the best
hotels in Rochester, and close to the railway
station, and left for New York by the half-past
nine train. Our route lay through a pretty and
fruitful country, beautifully diversified by hill and
dale. The wheat-harvest had just commenced, and
the weather was lovely, which added greatly to
our enjoyment. We passed through the populous
and thriving towns of Canandaigua, Geneva, Se-
neca, and Auburn, which latter place contains
the celebrated State Prison.

We changed trains at Syracuse, a large town,
midway between Rochester and Albany, where
we were allowed twenty minutes to dine. The

country from Syracuse to Senectady is very beautiful, the road following the course of the Mohawk the whole distance.

> " From early dawn to setting sun
> I 've seen the mighty Mohawk run."

The names of the towns we passed through became more classic as we approached Albany— such as Rome, Utica, Troy, &c. At the little falls on the Mohawk the scenery is highly picturesque. We arrived at the station in Albany about eight o'clock in the evening, and immediately went on board the " Hendric Hudson," one of the largest of those floating steam-palaces which ply upon the Hudson. These boats are splendidly fitted up, with every comfort and luxury.

The " Hendric Hudson " is said to be 321 feet in length; the "Isaac Newton" 333 feet. This is the largest boat on the north river, and their rate of steaming is equal to twenty miles an hour.

We left Albany about nine o'clock in the evening, and were safely moored at her wharf, in New York, between five and six in the morning, having made the run of one hundred and fifty miles, including all stoppages, in the short space of eight hours, and the whole distance from Rochester, five hundred miles, in twenty hours, for which we paid the reasonable charge of something like one pound five shillings sterling per head.

I must say that travelling is both cheaper and pleasanter in the United States than in England. So much attention and deference are shown to the fair sex, that I will venture to affirm, that a woman, gentle or simple, might travel from one end of the Union to the other without fear of insult. I like the manner the railroads are managed, which is much better than in England. The carriages are more commodious, better fitted up, and better ventilated. Venetian blinds are fitted to the windows, and brass hooks over each seat, for hanging up hats, umbrellas, and carpet-bags. The doors open at each end of the carriage, the passage being through the centre, with a row of sofa-chairs, capable of containing two persons on each side. The railroad runs generally through the centre of every town on the route, notice being always given by the conductors to the passengers of the number of minutes the train will stop at each station.

At all the stopping places abundance of refreshments of all sorts—creams, ices, jellies, &c.—are handed through every carriage, so that the passengers have seldom any occasion to leave their seats. The prices of the refreshments are remarkably low. A five-cent piece will procure either a glass of brandy and water, or an iced cream.

The passengers' baggage is equally well managed. Zinc tickets are numbered and strapped to each box or trunk, and counter-checks bearing the same numbers are handed to the passenger on the arrival of the train at its destination. The numbers are called over in a loud voice, and delivered to the owners by their producing the duplicate tickets.

We stayed five days in New York, during which time we visited the principal places of amusement. New York is already one of the largest cities in the world. The activity and bustle in every part are truly astonishing, while the amount of shipping in the north and east rivers struck me as being greater than in Liverpool. It is really a wonderful place, and many years will not elapse before it will vie with London in population and mercantile importance.

On the 16th of July, we sailed in the " Hungarian," 1300 tons burthen, Captain Patterson, and had a remarkably pleasant passage of twenty-two days. We left Liverpool on the 7th of August, and reached my mother's house on the 8th, just one month from leaving our Canadian home.

I received a warm welcome at Reydon from my dear mother and sisters, to whom my return was, indeed, a surprise. It would have been a still more delightful reunion, could the whole eight have once more met beneath the parental roof.

This, however, was impossible, as I had left two sisters in Canada, and my brother was on his way to Calcutta. But the links of family affection were still firm and unbroken. Death had not entered my mother's home-circle since we parted, to sever her branches from the parent-tree, and for that mercy we were deeply grateful.

Since my return to England, my daughter and myself have experienced the utmost kindness and attention, not only in my native Suffolk, but in Norfolk and Kent.

In my own immediate neighbourhood I have been indebted for much attention and hospitality from former friends and schoolfellows, having, in fact, revived the old friendships of my youth, and formed many new ones. I am now on the eve of returning to my distant home, and wish to express to you, dear friends and neighbours, in the last pages of my work, those grateful sentiments your kindness has awakened in my heart.

May God bless you all, and keep you in his holy protection! Be assured that I shall always remember your dear and honoured names with warm interest and affection.

THE END.